The Green Thumb Garden Handbook

BY GEORGE ABRAHAM

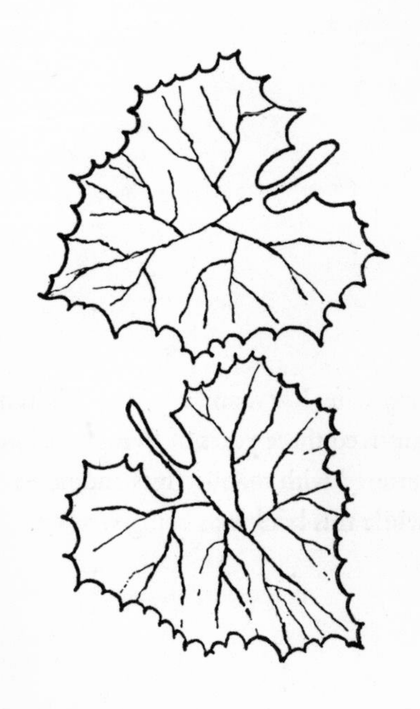

PRENTICE-HALL, INC. / *Englewood Cliffs, N.J.*

Library of Congress Catalogue Card Number: 61-15631
Printed in the United States of America
36517-T

To my wife, Katy, and our two children
who survived three years of living in a house
cluttered with manuscripts and notes
while this book was being written.

Foreword

Writing this book was like taking a long trip through exotic countries: We have touched much of lasting value, but some points of interest had to be omitted.

Home gardening with an estimated 40 million adherents, is America's number one hobby today, far too big a field to be covered exhaustively in any single volume.

Thousands of varieties of plants can be used in scores of combinations of different soils. They can be nurtured and treated with literally thousands of different plant foods, fertilizers, sprays and insecticides offered on the market under countless trade names in various kinds of packagings.

Meanwhile, more new products and techniques emerge in a never-ending stream at a faster rate than ever from government and commercial experiment stations and research laboratories as well as from the campuses of agricultural colleges. No man can keep track of them, much less check the validity of all of them. Add to this the ever-remaining fact of the wide variety of climate and other growing conditions in this 50-state country of ours.

Fortunately, the overwhelming number of home gardeners know little and care less about these things. Our long experience in assisting home gardeners has taught us that they have neither interest nor patience to hear of complicated biological jargons or concepts.

What the home gardener *does* want to know, our experience has convinced us, is how to plant an attractive green lawn on his premises and keep it as free from weeds, plant diseases and insects as possible. Likewise, he *does* want to know how to have and keep trees which offer shade, colorful blossoms or delicious fruit or, perhaps, all of these. And, he *does* want to know how to arrange and maintain shrubs and flowers which beautify the land surrounding his home. The home gardener, we have discovered, wants all of these things quickly and with a minimum of work, worry and expense.

The purpose of this book is to fulfill exactly these wants and needs of the home gardener and accomplish it in the same simple, conversational, easy-to-understand language which has endeared our "The Green Thumb" newspaper column to hundreds of thousands of readers over the last 15 years.

In these years we have received and answered more than half a million questions mailed to us on cards and letters by these readers. We have learned the kind of problems which beset most home gardeners and through our work under glass and in the field have found the practical ways these problems can be solved. We know that the time and effort—and money—even the most avid home gardener can or is willing to devote to his hobby is limited. We know that the great bulk of this huge body of hobbyists is made up of housewives, office and factory workers, executives on all levels and professional men. As the life-span increases and retirement age is lowered, more and more retired persons join this throng of home gardeners.

In writing this book we have kept these wants and requirements of our prospective readers in mind at all times. We have tried to do this on the basis of our own knowledge and background. We have grown up in the agriculturally rich, scenically beautiful Finger Lakes region of Central New York State; we have studied horticulture at Cornell University's State College of Agriculture; we have more than a score of years of experience in writing for the layman on agricultural subjects; we operate a greenhouse and a small-town florist business, and we till seven acres of land surrounding our home, including experimental orchards, vineyards and other test areas where we can try out any technique or product to our own satisfaction before recommending or writing about it for others.

Despite this heavy reliance on our own efforts and experience, the undertaking of this book has caused us to become deeply indebted to others whose help and encouragement contributed to the finished product.

These include personnel at agricultural experiment stations and extension horticulturists who have answered our questions and made available to us their notes and reports for use in this book. Space prevents mentioning their names and the specific use of each of their contributions.

Perhaps, the most profuse thanks of all must go to those hundreds of thousands of readers whose written questions to us over the years have not only sustained our "The Green Thumb" newspaper column with grist for our typewriters, but whose composite questions are the foundation and frame upon which this book is built. If it had not been for their unending flow of questions there would have been no columns and there would now be no book.

I am using the terms "we" and "us" advisedly in this foreword. Even though this book, like "The Green Thumb" newspaper column, carries my name in the by-line, both are really part of a joint family project in which my wife, Katherine, is a full partner and which also involves our two loving children, daughter Leanna, 14, and son Darryl, 12.

I would, therefore, be unforgivably remiss, indeed, if I failed to reserve a deservedly prominent place for them in this list of credits. Leanna's and Darryl's childhood has obviously been profoundly affected, not adversely I hope, by their parents' dual allegiance to "The Green Thumb" and them. Far from being discouraged in the face of that situation, Leanna and Darryl have put their shoulders to the wheel to help us.

They have done so in passive ways, such as fending for themselves when it was apparent their parents' presence was more urgently required at the typewriters or in the greenhouse, or florist shop or on our surrounding land. Leanna and Darryl have also assisted very actively with the column and this book by sorting mail, running errands, by doing chores in the greenhouse and florist shop and assisting with the housework.

Finally, my thanks must go to my wife who has worked side by side with me on this as well as all other Green Thumb endeavors. We have managed to keep our tempers through tiring and seemingly endless days and nights of researching and writing when a sense of frustration often seemed to overcome one or the other and the temptation to give up the whole project was strong. Somehow, when one weakened the most, the other became stronger and, thus, mutual encouragement at critical moments saw us through.

My special personal thanks go to the following for their direct assistance: Prof. Roger Way, Pomologist; Dr. Earl Stone, Soil Specialist, Agronomy Dept.; Dr. Robert E. Lee, Prof. Floriculture; Dr. Harold E. Moore, Jr., Bailey Hortorium; Dr. A. J. Pratt, Vegetable Crops Dept.; Russell Mott, in charge of Conservatories, all of Cornell University.

Ladislaus Cutak and R. J. Gillespie, Missouri Botanical Garden, St. Louis; Bernard Harkness, Taxonomist, Rochester (N.Y.) Parks Dept.; Dr. P. P. Pirone, Plant Pathologist, N.Y. Botanical Garden; Dr. Robert Schery, Director, the Lawn Institute, John Kelly, Kelly Brothers Nurseries, Inc., J. E. Miller Nurseries, Amchem Products.

Charles Wilson and Fred Statt and other members of the Joseph Harris

Seed Co.; Robert Wood, in charge of Conservatory, and Richard Hart of G. B. Hart Co.; Joseph Robson, Robson Seeds; Associated Bulb Growers of Holland; Dr. Raymond Allen, Director of Kingwood Center; Merry Gardens, Burpee Seed Co.; Robin Wyld, Helen Reinhard, Rhea Charles, Mrs. Louise Warren, Mrs. Hazel Potter, Mrs. Elta Mehlenbacher, Mrs. Doris Mehlenbacher, Ann Hunt, Walter Froelich, Mrs. Hollis Cornell, Larry Dorhman, Eleanor Fritz, Mary Lou Lindsey, Flossie Pruner, Peg Bacon, Mildred Schryver, Doris Teachout, Marian Sliker.

I'm gratefully indebted to Tom and Frances Reilly of Dansville, N.Y. for their magnificent help with our manuscript.

Now, our wish and hope is that our labors will indeed serve the home gardener in the United States. We trust we will see the results as we travel along the highways and byways by seeing ever more beautifully-kept lawns and gardens populated by ever happier home gardeners everywhere throughout the whole landscape of America.

GEORGE ABRAHAM

Naples Valley Greenhouse

Naples, N.Y., March 15, 1961.

Table of Contents

1

How to Grow a Lawn

You can say a friendly hello to the world with a well-kept lawn. Even the proverbial red carpet cannot be more inviting than the green carpet provided by a neat, healthy lawn around your front-door steps. It serves as a welcome mat for you, your family and your guests. It makes for a pleasant sight for passersby. It beautifies your grounds. It adds to the appeal—and to the value—of your home.

As a clean shave and a trim haircut improve the appearance of a man, so your lawn can make your home more pleasing to look at. And as tousled, unkempt hair and a stubby, uneven beard will make even a well-dressed person look sloppy, so will even the most luxurious home lose some of its charm if the lawn surrounding it is uneven and discolored, blemished by ugly weeds, tarnished by unsightly bare spots and otherwise untidy and neglected. A "beatnik" lawn can destroy the beauty of a whole neighborhood.

Yet, no part of the home landscape is easier and less expensive to care for than the lawn. The secrets of a beautiful lawn are simple and fundamental: use reasonably suitable soil, nourish it adequately with plant food, sow proper seeds in the right way, then keep the growing grass well mowed (and, if you prefer, well watered during prolonged dry periods). You are bound to have one of the best-looking, healthiest lawns in your community!

But it is important that you follow each of these steps in the *right* way.

Each step is explained in detail on the pages which follow. You will see the job is really not very difficult. But if troubles should arise—such as weeds or plant disease—there's a detailed section later in this chapter on how to deal with these problems. And if you still have questions, you may be able to find the answers in the Green Thumb Lawn Clinic at the end of this chapter.

PREPARING SOIL FOR A LAWN:

Grass seed is not very hard to please. It will grow in almost any soil. But growing grass and having an attractive lawn are not necessarily the same things. To grow a good lawn, meaning one with healthy, vigorous grass, you need reasonably good soil. Grass will grow at its best in soil which is neither too loose nor too tight, but just porous enough to absorb water readily.

In most cases you can use the existing soil a lot cheaper than you can import costly topsoil. In fact, tests show that the cost of building up the present soil is only one-third that of buying topsoil, assuming you can manage to find good topsoil for not over $5.00 a yard. Fertilizer, good seed and ample organic matter help a lawn to help itself. Grass started from an enriched subsoil will at the end of two or three years have enough humus from its own root growth and clippings to nurse itself along, with the help of annual feedings, for the duration of your home. The only time you have to buy extra soil is when you want to bring the lawn up to proper grade, or when the existing soil is nothing but pure gumbo, too poor to serve as a good seed bed for grass. (See section on "Soils" for detailed information.)

Spread 50 to 60 pounds of a balanced fertilizer evenly over each 1,000 square feet of lawn or, if you use manure or compost, spread two or three cubic feet over each 1,000 square feet of lawn and mix it with the soil. If you prefer, you can also use peat moss (about three bales for each 1,000 square feet of lawn).

This mixing will strengthen the sand or loosen the clay, whichever is necessary. You need make no chemical analysis of the soil because you can hardly overdo this procedure. (Never add sand to clay because this will pack the clay even tighter.)

If you use peat moss, or if you already have suitable soil, be sure to add plant food or a complete fertilizer. Every soil should be fed before planting. "Complete" fertilizer or plant food means it contains all three of the chemical substances your lawn will need:

Nitrogen (which gives your lawn its rich dark-green color and also promotes leaf and stem growth).

Phosphorus (which stimulates root growth and helps plants make a fast start).

Potassium (which helps plants resist diseases and encourages a luxuriant condition).

Now you have soil geared to play host to a fine, healthy turf. It's neither heavy nor sandy, nor so hard that it will crack when it dries, leaving open spaces. If you have special problems, such as planting a lawn on a slope or in shady, virtually sunless areas, you will find answers later in this chapter. Otherwise, you are ready to rake the soil evenly and loosely.

In raking, don't attempt to find every little stone. Some gardeners finish with a large pile of stones and pebbles to be hauled away. Leave them on the lawn. A light rolling will take care of them. Grass roots grow under them and find protection there from the hot sun. However, if you have purchased topsoil, it should be free from stones because you paid for soil, not stones.

You are now ready to begin seeding.

SELECTING GRASS SEED:

What kind of grass seed will give you the kind of lawn you like best? By and large, a mixture of a few different types of grass seeds makes a better lawn than does seed of a single variety. All varieties have advantages and disadvantages. Some are more drought-resistant and remain green long after other varieties have dried and turned brown in summer. Others are likely to die if mowed too short and, therefore, should never be used by those who like a "crew-cut" lawn. Still other varieties of seeds produce wiry grass which is hard to mow. Some varieties are very susceptible to plant diseases and one variety must be planted either alone or only with members of its own family of grasses or it gets crowded out.

Read the label on the package before you buy any grass seed mixture. And don't let the names of grasses on the label confuse you. Here is what the terms on the labels mean and what each of the varieties of grasses are like.

Most grass seed mixtures are classified as having seeds of:

1) persistent, fine-textured grasses
2) coarse or temporary grasses
3) white clover

The coarse or temporary or "hay" grasses will not give the kind of lawn most people want. As the word "temporary" indicates, these seeds serve best when a lawn is wanted quickly to cover the soil for one season until proper preparations can be made for seeding a permanent lawn. These coarse and temporary grasses include Tall Fescue, Meadow Fescue, Timothy and Redtop and the rye grasses including Italian Rye, Perennial Rye, Domestic Rye and Common Rye.

Persistent, fine-textured grasses will, as their name implies, give the kind of permanent, fine-textured lawn home gardeners like to have. The main varieties are Kentucky Bluegrass, Red Fescue (including Chewings and other varieties), Colonial Bentgrass and Rough Bluegrass (also known as *Poa Trivialis*).

The labels on the grass seed mixture package sometimes list these varieties under their particular names. For example: "Common Kentucky Bluegrass" and "Merion Kentucky Bluegrass". Or, in the case of the fescues, "Creeping Red Fescue," "Illahee Red Fescue" and "Pennlawn Red Fescue." Or, in the case of the Bentgrasses, "Highland Bentgrass" and "Astoria Bentgrass."

Any mixture for seeding a permanent lawn should be made up of at least 80 per cent of these persistent, fine-textured grass seeds.

The most rugged of them is Kentucky Bluegrass which needs the least care and is probably the best suited for most amateur gardeners who want a good lawn without spending too much effort and money. But Kentucky Bluegrass has two disadvantages: it can be permanently injured if it is clipped or mowed very short; and, like most grasses, it turns brown in dry weather. But, fortunately, it recovers its rich green color quickly when the dry season is over. A seed mixture containing at least 40 per cent Kentucky Bluegrass (plus another 40 per cent of other persistent, fine-textured grasses) will usually produce a good lawn under average conditions. Lawns which are exposed to more than an average amount of sun should preferably be seeded with mixtures containing at least 55 per cent Kentucky Bluegrass.

An improved form of Kentucky Bluegrass, known as "Merion Bluegrass," has been called a wonder grass by some, but experience has shown that its likable characteristics are partly outweighed by certain serious shortcomings. It came into use after a small patch of grass on a golf course remained green after all other grasses around it had turned brown under exposure to the summer sun. Merion was selected from this patch and the seed supplies were built up and offered for sale. It is supposed to be more drought-resistant though it eventually dries too, and turns brown in the summer. The Merion produces a dense, dark green, broader-bladed turf, is less prone to be injured by close mowing, is very resistant to leaf-spot diseases, but susceptible to cereal rusts and curvularia (fading-out disease). Other disadvantages are: slow to sprout, needs intensive care, builds mat more than other Bluegrass, is a heavy feeder and does not do well at Southern extremes of Bluegrass belt.

Merion, unlike other grasses, does *not* grow well in a mixture with other varieties except other Bluegrasses. It usually gets crowded out by other grasses within a year or two after planting.

For very dry soils, Red Fescue is the best-suited variety. Rainier, Creeping Red Fescue, Pennlawn, Illahee Fescue, and Chewings Fescue are popular because they are more drought-resistant as well as shade-tolerant than most other varieties and can withstand considerable neglect. They usually take longer to attain their healthy green in early spring, but retain their color longer into the summer than other grasses, which by that time have usually become brown.

A moderate amount of fescue is desirable in a mixture for a home lawn. Its rather quick sprouting makes it useful as a nurse grass. Disadvantages of the fescues are that they die easily if clipped or mowed very short or if they are overwatered. It takes more power to mow them if they are used alone than it does most other varieties. This toughness has earned the fescues the nickname "wire grasses." Fescues do better when used with Bluegrass in the mixture.

Bentgrasses are not very popular with experts even though this variety may produce good lawns which withstand close clipping exceptionally well. Some Colonial Bentgrass in the mixture with Kentucky Bluegrass thickens the turf in midsummer when the Bluegrass is semi-dormant. This thickening, aside from its improved appearance of the lawn, also helps keep weeds out. But Bentgrasses are very susceptible to diseases, require intensive care, more feeding, watering and mowing to look well.

Redtop and rye grasses are of the temporary varieties. Any mixture containing more than 10 per cent of them is likely to produce an inferior lawn. Their use is practical, however, on slopes. The fast sprouting of the seed helps prevent the washing away of the soil by rains as well as the washing away of the seeds of slower-growing grasses in the mixture. (See section on "Lawns on Slopes" later in this chapter.)

A pound of the seed of the fine-textured grasses costs about three times as much as a pound of seed of coarse grasses, but this doesn't mean that it is more expensive to plant a lawn with the fine-textured seeds. If that sounds confusing, here's the solution to the apparent inconsistency: seeds of fine-textured grasses are much smaller and lighter so that a pound of them contains about eight times as many seeds as a pound of the coarse seeds.

For example, a pound of Kentucky Bluegrass contains about 2 million seeds, but a pound of rye grass contains only about 250,000 seeds. A pound of coarse seeds makes a cheaper and bigger package, but contains fewer seeds than a pound of fine-textured seeds.

Some grass seed mixtures contain White Clover seed which many gardeners consider to be a weed. It is a broadleaved plant which draws nitrogen from the air and nourishes the soil with it and, thus, in turn, supplies that important substance to the grass. Clover is deep-rooted and drought-resistant and, thus, adds a green touch to the lawn in summer when the grass has turned brown. Mowing clover will not harm it. Its disadvantage is that it becomes slippery when the lawn is wet and it stains badly. To many folks it is objectionable because it has white flower heads and grows in patches.

Some seed mixtures include the intermediate or giant forage varieties of clover rather than the dwarf type (labeled "Wild White Clover" or "Kentish Wild White Clover") preferable for lawns.

WARM-SEASON GRASSES

ZOYSIAS: The much-publicized Zoysias (*Zoysia japonica* and *Z. matrella*) form a good sod in midsummer, being more durable to summer traffic, tolerant to low fertility, heat and drought-resistant and requiring less mowing. Disadvantages of Zoysias are that they turn to an unsightly brown from autumn until mid-spring, are not resistant to traffic and weed invasion when dormant, and they must for all practical purposes be started from plugs or sprigs of sod. Not all Zoysias are consistently hardy in northern winters.

U-3 Bermuda grass, a southern grass, has the same advantages and disadvantages of Zoysia, with lack of winter hardiness a special hazard. If you like either grass, plant them on a trial basis on a small area, and if they perform to your satisfaction, enlarge the plantings.

SEEDING RATES FOR LAWNGRASS

SEED MIXTURES PREDOMINANTLY:	LBS. PER 1,000 SQ. FT.*	MILLIONS OF SEEDS PER LB.
I. "Northerners", normally planted autumn or early spring:		
Kentucky Bluegrass	2–4	2
Fescues	5–7	⅓
Bentgrass	1–2	7
Poa trivialis ("Rough Bluegrass")	2–3	2½
Redtop	1–2	5
Wheat grass	2–4	⅕
Clover (5–10% in mixtures)	1/10–1	¾
II. "Southerners," normally planted spring or summer:		
Bermuda (hulls removed 50% lighter rate than unhulled)	1–4	2
Bahia	2–5	⅕
Carpet	2–4	1¼
Centipede	¼–1	½
Zoysia (mostly vegetative, untreated seed slow)	1–2	5
Buffalo ("burs")	1–2	1/15
Gramas	2–4	1
Lespedeza, Korean	1–3	¼

* Accurate, uniform distribution is seldom possible at rates less than 2 lbs. per 1,000 sq. ft., unless the seed is "extended" or mixed with cornmeal, sand, sifted soil, fertilizer or vermiculite. (Courtesy, American Potash Institute and The Lawn Institute.)

WHEN TO SOW GRASS SEED:

The soil is loose and mellow, the seed bed is well prepared. The seed has been carefully chosen. The next step is to scatter the seed evenly. But what time of year should this be done for best results?

Fall is by far the best time to seed a lawn although probably four of every five home gardeners do the job in spring. In most climates the ideal time for sowing seed and for the early growth of the seedling grass is between the last part of August and the early part of October. This is the time which nature itself selects for seeding. Wild grasses bloom in summer, but nature delays dropping of seeds and their after-ripening until

August or September. At that time, the seed falls on soil which is yet warm, but the season of droughts is over, the hot days are getting shorter and the cool nights are getting longer. Dews are heavier. Soil moisture conditions are more favorable. Unlike spring thundershowers, the fall rains tend to be more gentle, soaking into the soil for the benefit of the grass. Fall grass seedlings will be vigorous yearlings the following spring and will be better able to withstand the heat and weeds which come in summer.

But there are other advantages to fall seeding:

The great hordes of weeds and insects which flourish during hot weather die with the first frost, making available more space, nutrients, sunlight and freedom for the grass. It can then grow during its favorite cooler season unhampered by competition. Also, there is less exposure to plant diseases in fall. And there is economy in fall seeding too. Fewer seeds will produce equal or even better turf. Tests have shown that four pounds of seed scattered evenly over 1,000 square feet of soil in fall will produce grass of equal or better quality than an abnormally high seeding rate of six to eight pounds of the same seed mixture sown in the spring!

If seeding can't be done earlier, it is probably better to do it even as late as December than to wait until spring because December seedlings will still have more months of good growing weather before summer than spring seedlings.

Finally, fall is preferred by gardeners for grass seeding because garden chores are less demanding than in spring, thus giving more time for devotion to the lawn work.

But, if you can't do the job sooner, it can be done in spring too. Owners of new homes, for example, may not want to leave the soil bare from spring to fall, especially if children track the dirt into the house. The first rule for spring sowing is: The earlier you do it, the better. The earlier the seed is in the soil, the greater the opportunity for the grass to grow strong enough to withstand the summer heat.

But, early doesn't mean you should throw your grass seed on the snow as some gardeners have been known to do. Seed makes expensive bird food. Birds will pick up seed far more readily from snow than from soil.

Seed cannot germinate until it reaches the warm earth. There is no advantage in scattering it on the snow. You better wait until all snow has cleared, rubbish has been removed and the soil has been properly prepared and "built up" as was explained earlier in this chapter, before seeding.

If at all possible, seeding should be done before May 15 or after August 15. If you must do it during the three intervening months, it will be to your advantage if you protect the seed by covering the soil with straw or some other material. This will protect the seed from the summer sun as well as conserve moisture in the soil from evaporation. Instructions on how to cover lawns (a gardening technique known as "mulching") are in the section on "Lawns on Slopes" later in this chapter. Or, you might prefer to plant a temporary lawn with any of the fast-growing temporary coarse grasses to be replaced during the more favorable planting season.

THE SEED GOES INTO THE SOIL:

You have now arrived at that happy moment when you are scattering the seed evenly over the soil. And you are already looking forward to the even happier moments when the first green will be seen and, eventually, when the soil is densely covered with a rich, green carpet of grass.

Saying the seed goes "into" the soil means exactly that: grass seed usually needs to be pushed down a bit into the soil unless the surface is loose and lumpy.

If this is done, the seed will not be blown away by winds, the grass roots can obtain a stronger hold faster on the soil, and the warm earth enveloping the seed will hasten its germination.

To push the seed firmly into the soil you can use a light roller or else you can pull the backside of a broom-type rake over the seeded soil. If you use a roller of the water-ballast type, don't fill it to more than about one-quarter. More about this is in the section on "Rolling Your Lawn" following this discussion. But don't push the seed too deep into the soil or the grass may never come up.

A common error in seeding is to use far more seed than is necessary. This is not only wasteful—often it is *harmful.* Some amateur gardeners throw twice or three times as much seed as is necessary for a good lawn. The grass then comes up too thick and the result is about the same as if you were crowding 100 persons into a house built for ten. Life would be uncomfortable and unhealthy for all and possibly none would thrive for long.

Some gardeners say the reason why they oversow is to make up for the poor soil. But poor soil cannot support large numbers of plants as well as a few. If the soil is poor it can be helped by "building it up" as was explained earlier in this chapter, not by extra-heavy seeding. For the proper quantity of seed, consult the chart at the end of the section on "Selecting Grass Seed" earlier in this chapter or check the label on your seed package.

Lawn seed germinates normally in seven days to two weeks or longer. But germination and the rate of growth of your lawn may be quite uneven. That's nothing to worry about. It happens because seeds are bound to rest in the soil at different depths and because some varieties in the seed mixture grow faster than the rest.

Rolling Your Lawn:

It has been said with much truth that a roller is the most misunderstood, overused lawn tool. Excessive or wrong use of a roller can do as much damage as proper use can be of benefit. There are only four important uses for a roller:

1. To press grass seed into the soil. Use a light roller for this purpose. That means one weighing 75 to 100 pounds. Go over the newly seeded soil just once because if you push the seeds too deep, the grass may never come up. And if you press the soil too firmly, it will not remain porous enough for best growth conditions.
2. In early spring, following a fall seeding, a roller is useful to press the young grass seedlings back into the soil after they have been heaved up by the action of winter frosts. Use a light roller for this.
3. To press small stones back into the soil so that they will not be hit by the lawn mower blades.
4. If the soil has become unusually loose, light rolling will make it firm again and also push back the roots of possibly loosened grass. But don't overdo that job. Grass thrives best in porous soil.

Wrong use or overuse of a roller can do much damage. An overly heavy roller will compact the soil, especially if the soil is wet. Compacted soils prevent penetration of water, air and nutrients. The grass roots need all of these. Lack of them will cause roots to grow thin and shallow. Wet soil will stick to the roller. Therefore, delay rolling until the soil is dry and, of course if you plan to roll newly seeded soil, don't water it until the rolling is done.

Finally, a roller is not the proper tool to smooth uneven lawns. It can't be expected to do that job properly even if the roller weighs 40 tons. To straighten bumps and depressed areas in your lawn, add topsoil to smooth the surfaces. Or, you can lift the present topsoil off with a spade, fill in the depressed areas with other soil, then replace the topsoil. Weeds frequently take over where grass growth has been impeded by the use of a very heavy roller.

WATERING YOUR LAWN:

Maybe this will surprise you, but few gardening topics are as controversial as how to water a lawn. And all the prevailing opinions on the subject, if you'll forgive the pun, hold a lot of water. That even goes for the extreme school of thought which says that you can have a healthy lawn without watering it at all.

The major opinions—and you can see they run pretty much the gamut of possibilities—fall under three headings on what to do about watering a lawn:

1. Don't.
2. Do it lightly, but often.
3. Do it rarely, but plentifully each time.

The one thing on which there *is* general agreement is that a newly planted lawn should be watered generously and often from the time of the seeding through the sprouting and growing of the new grass. Frequent watering of newly seeded grass will encourage fast growth. The faster and the more densely the grass grows, the less opportunity will there be for weeds to get started.

Watering the soil generously once a week after the seedlings are up will encourage them to grow deep roots which, in turn, will enable them to better withstand later droughts. Deep roots also help prevent heaving of the soil by alternating winter freezes and thaws.

But now let us turn to these three differing and mutually exclusive opinions about watering well-established lawns:

The "Don't" Theory—Those who say don't water your lawn at all, point out quite accurately that most "perennial" (persistent fine-textured) grasses normally enter a semi-dormant state during the hot summer season. You need have no worry if these grasses turn brown and at times seem to be dead during prolonged dry periods. They bounch back from their straw-like appearance to rich greenness after the first good rain. What's more, tests have shown that grass which has been allowed to remain dormant in summer will be more vigorous in autumn than grass which has been kept green by watering during the summer. And, unwatered lawns frequently have fewer weeds than watered lawns.

Your choice of the "don't" theory becomes easy for you to make if your community enforces a ban on lawn sprinkling, if you are forced to declare your own ban because of the expense of sprinkling, if your own spring or well water supply is running low, or if you lack the time to do the lawn chores. If any of these fit your situation, you're likely to be a "don't" exponent by necessity and convenience, if not by choice.

But many a home gardener wonders, with obvious justification, why, after spending the effort to beautify his home with a lawn, he should allow it to turn brown at the one time of the year when he can appreciate it most. In the summer, the lawn is free from snow and rain and more time is spent outside the home on the adjacent grounds. These thoughts will lead many a home gardener to examine with care the two theories which follow.

The "Lightly-and-Often" Theory—Watering lightly and often can keep your lawn cool, lush, rich and sparkling with greenness even at the height of a severe drought. Golf-course keepers prove that the theory works. But, remember, they keep watering their turfs with unfailing regularity, usually daily, and never allow the soil to dry. That's the crux of the lightly-and-often theory. It works well as long as you keep the soil uniformly moist all of the time. Anyone will agree that's easier said than done by most home gardeners. Built-in sprinklers with automatic timers are the ideal solution, but the average home lawn grower isn't likely to install such complicated apparatus.

Once the soil has been allowed to dry to a depth of much more than an inch, the lightly-and-often theory runs into serious trouble. And a hot sun and brisk wind dry soil quickly. Then, watering merely the surface, when the soil has been allowed to dry to a considerable depth, will only "tease" the grass. It will be encouraged to develop shallow roots which weaken it and make it less resistant to drought. Besides, this kind of "surface watering" is more encouraging to weeds than grass. That's why many home lawn growers prefer to turn to the less burdensome "rarely-and-plentifully" theory which follows.

The "Rarely-and-Plentifully" Theory—Because surface watering of a very dry soil encourages shallow grass roots and weeds, many gardeners make it their rule to water "deeply or not at all." Once the soil has been allowed to dry to a depth of two or three inches, a lot of water is needed to bring the moisture level up again. Average soil under drought conditions loses about 50 gallons of water daily for each 1,000 square feet, or 350 gallons a week. Under "average" conditions, about three hours of steady sprinkling are required once a week to replace that amount. Once that has been accomplished, no watering will be needed according to this theory for about a week. Then, the complete job needs to be done again. If you want to measure how many inches of water your sprinkling is depositing, place several tin cans on your lawn near the sprinkler.

HOW TO MOW A LAWN:

Delilah shore off Samson's locks, the Bible tells us, and he lost his strength. The opposite is likely to be true for grass. Clipping it, if done the right way, will strengthen it and help make your lawn handsome, healthy and, if such is possible for a lawn, happy. The key phrase here, however, is "the right way." Doing it wrong can damage your lawn. And so these questions naturally arise:

How often should I mow my lawn?

How short should I clip the grass?

Should I rake the clippings or leave them where they fall?

If you live in a northern climate, you will also ask: should grass be left long or clipped short, and should fallen leaves be allowed to remain on the lawn when snow is about to cover the landscape for the winter?

Mow High and Often! Remember these four words! They're the best answer to the first two questions. Mowing "high" means never cut your grass shorter than an inch (except in late fall, as explained below, when three-quarters of an inch is ideal).

In hot weather, especially when droughts are about to come, grass should never be cut shorter than 1½ to 2½ inches. "Scalping" or shaving your lawn closer than that invites troubles. Many fine lawns have been ruined by cutting so close that the soil showed. Such close mowing exposes the bottoms of the plants to the hot sun, weakens the roots and also encourages the growth of crabgrass. Moreover, during the warm season, short grass allows the sun and wind to dry the soil quickly so that the sun may heat the soil so much as to possibly injure the grass roots.

In contrast, high, thick grass protects soil from the sun and wind and discourages the growth of weeds. But don't carry this idea too far. There is no advantage in allowing grass to reach a height of much more than three inches, if that much. Grass taller than that may be injured by "shock" from the sudden loss of leaf surface if you mow it very low from that height in a single cutting. That's why you should mow often, cutting a little each time before the grass grows too tall.

Keep the cutting blades of your lawn mower sharp at all times. Dull blades can "bruise" the tips of the grass resulting in a yellowish or brownish appearance of the lawn. If yours is a newly planted lawn, begin mowing as soon as the grass has grown to about two inches. Keep it well mowed because this will encourage "stooling" or filling in at the base.

An average lawn needs about 20 to 23 cuttings each year and each of these cuttings should ideally remove from one to two inches of grass leaves. Mowing with such regularity will also result in cutting away the seed heads of weeds and, thereby, will keep them from multiplying. An often-used lawn mower is the strongest weapon against weeds at a lawn grower's command.

In the course of an average year, the home lawn grower will mow a total growth of about 36 inches of grass and all of this clipped grass contains valuable soil nutrients. These grass clippings contain nitrogen, phosphorus and potassium, the same three important substances mentioned earlier in this chapter as requirements for building the soil up to make it an ideal host for a lawn. If these clippings are raked and removed, the soil must eventually be "fed" or fertilized to replace the loss of these vital substances. A more practical way is simply to leave the clippings as they fall. They will decompose and turn into a perfect soil conditioner, resupplying the soil with valuable chemicals. It has been said quite accurately that these decayed clippings together with rotting subsoil grass and decomposing root growth will in a few years gradually convert themselves into a kind of topsoil which is nothing less than "tailored to your own grass."

But one word of warning. If you have allowed your grass to grow to a height where clippings measure more than four inches, it's better to rake them and remove them from the lawn. Otherwise, clippings of that length might bunch together and cover the lawn like a mat, causing plant diseases common in grass. Diseases germinate easily and quickly under matted clippings.

Even when removed, these clippings need not be wasted. Pile them in a corner of your garden and leave them, until they rot, for later use as compost. In this way, the nutrients they contain will be saved for repeated use.

Just as grass clippings are valuable food for your lawn, so are all kinds of leaves which fall from trees and shrubbery onto your lawn each fall.

Like grass clippings, leaves contain soil nutrients. It is, therefore, wasteful to rake and burn leaves when they can be of such good use right on the lawn where they fall. But leaves, because of their size, are even more apt to become matted than long grass clippings. To avoid that danger, it is best to grind the leaves. Some rotary lawn mowers have attachments which do such grinding as they mow. These attachments even grind tall weeds and return the pulverized residue to the soil where it acts as a soil conditioner.

In fall, once the hot days of drought are past, it becomes advisable to cut your grass progressively shorter until it stops its annual growth and becomes dormant in late autumn. At that time, grass should preferably measure about 1½ inches. Tests have shown that grass at that length survives winter with far less susceptibility to diseases, winter killing and smothering, than grass which enters and passes the winter season at 3 inches or taller. Tall grass is likely to become matted from being pressed down either by its own weight or by the pressure of rain or snow. And matting, as was explained a few paragraphs ago, leaves grass susceptible to diseases and other harm.

The kind of mower you use—reel, or the newer rotary type—is a matter of personal preference. The important thing for the sake of your lawn is that the machine is in good condition. Follow the manufacturer's instructions carefully as to oiling and other care. With most mowers, oil should be added every five operating hours and replaced every 25 hours. Crankcase oil should be changed every year at the start of the mowing season in early spring.

Rotary mowers cut by impact, the whirling blade hitting the grass. Good reel mowers are probably preferred by those who want to do an especially exacting job, but rotary mowers are liked for their incomparable ability to cut tall and wiry weeds. Dull blades leave a light grayish cast to a new-mown lawn. Keep blades sharp! All mowers can become dangerous machines in careless hands—and in the vicinity of careless toes. As a safety precaution, a mower's motor should never be allowed to run even for a second without an adult's hand on the handle, and special care must be used when running such a mower on slopes.

Feeding Your Lawn:

Why feed a lawn? Growing a lawn has one big disadvantage as compared to cultivating a field: you cannot rotate the crop to rebuild nutrients in the soil. Your only crop is grass. But nutrients are lost from the lawn's soil and must be replaced if the grass is to thrive year after year.

Heavy showers leach nutrients from the soil. If you are in the habit of removing grass clippings and throwing them away after you have mowed your lawn, you are taking away the nutrients contained in these clippings. Also, various natural soil processes tie up nutrients so that grass roots cannot utilize them.

To replace the looses caused by all these various factors, every lawn should be fed one good "meal" of plant food at least once a year.

Most lawns probably suffer more from starvation than from any other single factor. Watering a lawn is not a substitute for furnishing it with lawn food or fertilizer. Grass growing on an impoverished soil needs longer to retrieve its greenness after a drought than grass on a well-fed soil. Starved soils also pose an open invitation for weeds which can thrive on fewer nutrients than grass. Starved grass tends to grow in bunches or in "tufts" rather than forming a tight, carpet-like soil cover. This spreading into tufts opens space for invasion by weeds. A good meal for such lawns pays off in a better-looking, healthier cover of grass.

What to Feed—The kind of plant food you give your lawn isn't as important as the fact that you apply it. All lawns respond favorably to plant food which contains the three chemical substances discussed earlier in this chapter in the section on "Preparing the Soil for a Lawn." These substances are nitrogen, phosphorous and potassium. They are contained in many kinds of "organic" as well as "inorganic" plant foods in varying quantities. Organic foods are those made up of once-live matter such as rotting lawn clippings or leaf mold or rotting manure. Inorganic foods are those produced through chemical processes in a laboratory.

You can buy inorganic plant food at stores that sell seed. One such plant food is "5–10–5," meaning it contains 5 per cent nitrogen, 10 per cent phosphorous and 5 per cent potassium in a 100-pound bag. Or you can use a liquid plant food such as "23–21–17", applied at time of watering.

"10–20–10" plant food contains the same proportion of each of these ingredients, but twice as concentrated and should, therefore, be used at half the rate. These plant foods are in the form of powders or liquids. The chart below shows the correct amounts to use for various types of plant foods.

How to Feed—The amounts shown need not be followed exactly, but using much more than suggested can result in "burning" of the grass

Plant Food	Amount to be used for 1,000 sq. ft. on Established Lawns	New Lawns
4–6–0 (sewage sludge)	25 lbs.	50 lbs.
5–10–5	25 to 40 lbs.	40 to 50 lbs.
10–6–4	10 to 15 lbs.	20 lbs.
10–10–10 or 10–20–10	10 lbs.	20 lbs.
Liquid Plant Food (23–21–17)	1 pound to 22 gals. of water for each 2,000 sq. feet	

leaves. It is important that the plant food be spread evenly. Otherwise, as the food affects the color of the grass, there will be light and dark streaks on the lawn. A mechanical spreader will do the job as perfectly as possible. If you apply inorganic plant food, be sure the grass is dry when applying to avoid burning. Then, at once after the application, water the lawn to wash the plant food from the grass blades into the ground. An advantage of liquid foods is that they do not cause burning. If slight burning occurs, the grass will usually recover quickly without any treatment by you. If you have clover on your lawn, you may want to nourish that plant by spreading 35 to 50 pounds of ground limestone on each 1,000 square feet every three or four years. This limestone can be mixed with the plant food. But limestone should not be applied more often than suggested, especially if the soil is alkaline. See the chapter on "Soils" for more information on lime.

When to Feed—The ideal times for feeding your lawn are fall and early spring—or both! The chances of leaf burning are slimmest then. Rains (and after fall, the melting snows) take the food down into the soil next to the root system. A lawn fed in fall will resist next summer's drought more ably. A lawn fed in early spring is encouraged to grow new shoots for a tighter, better turf. You can feed your lawn as often as three times each year, especially if its pale green color and slow summer growth indicate the need. After one or more good meals, grasses will begin growing beneath the surface as well as above. You'll notice the increase in yield and, to your delight, the improvement in your lawn's quality.

LAWNS WITH PROBLEMS

Shady Lawns—The sun, which causes many lawns to become dry and brown, is nevertheless a friend of grass. And too much shade, meaning lack of sun exposure, is an enemy of grass. Shaded lawns need far more plant food than lawns blessed with adequate exposure to the sun's rays.

If the shaded part of your lawn happens to be under a shallow-rooted tree, such as a maple, your problem may be doubled by the fact that the tree's shallow roots rob the soil of nutrients needed by the grass. Additional amounts of plant food are even more needed for grass growing in shaded areas under shallow-rooted trees.

Aside from giving added feedings, you can improve growth of grass in shaded areas by selecting for such spots those varieties of grasses best suited to shade.

Red Fescue is a grass which can flourish in shaded areas where other grasses fail. A seed mixture containing about 70 per cent of it is likely to do well in shaded areas. If the soil is moist, rough-stalked meadow grass (*Poa trivialis*) will be ideal for planting in a shady spot. After you have seeded your entire lawn with your selected seed mixture, you can re-seed the shady spots, where the general mixture has failed to sprout, with Red Fescue or meadow grass seeds.

There's one great compensation once you have managed to produce a lawn on shady spots: because of its protected position from the sun, the grass is likely to stay green longer during droughts unless tree roots compete. But in some shady areas almost any grass will simply refuse to grow. In such a case, you'll probably save time and effort by constructing a flagstone or concrete terrace or a rock garden. Or, if you prefer, you can plant a grass "substitute" as is explained later in this chapter.

LAWNS ON SLOPES

Trying to grow a lawn on steeply sloping terrain may bring two baffling problems: mowing on steep slopes can be very difficult. But what may prove even more difficult is to get grass growing in the first place. Rains tend to wash the seed and even the topsoil away before any growth can get under way. Sometimes it is possible to start a lawn on slopes by using a seed mixture containing some of the very fast-growing temporary grasses such as Redtop and rye grasses. Their fast growth helps prevent the washing away of topsoil and of the seeds of the slower-growing permanent grasses.

If this is unsuccessful, the best method for growing a lawn on a slope is to mulch the seed, which means protecting it from wash-out with a temporary cover. Mulching also helps prevent quick drying of the soil and in that way hastens germination of the seed. Materials used for mulching are straw, hay, burlap, cloth netting and plastic sheeting.

Straw is the cheapest and probably the most satisfactory mulching material. It is clean and it is easy to put on and take off. Its disadvantage is that it is easily blown off by the wind and, therefore, should be anchored. A two or three-inch layer of straw, just enough so that the ground can barely be seen, is sufficient. Oat straw is most suitable for the purpose, but hay and wheat straw can also be used. The mulch should be removed as soon as grass begins to sprout. Otherwise, the mulch might smother the seedlings.

Hay as mulch is more difficult to spread and, also, it contains weeds which may get hold in the soil. Mushroom manure has been used as a mulch, but is difficult to remove. Burlap bags, cut into strips, serve as a satisfactory mulch if tacked to the soil with pegs. Cotton netting, also tacked down, has the advantage that it need not be removed because it gradually rots. The newest method of mulching, however, is the use of plastic "polyethylene" sheeting which can be fastened with wooden stakes, wire staples, spikes or clothespins driven into the ground. Since this plastic tends to magnify the sun's heat and then keeps that heat from escaping from the soil during the night, germination is likely to be rapid. The plastic also helps prevent evaporation of the soil's moisture.

But there is a danger that the magnified sunbeams will cause the seedlings to burn if the plastic cover is left on during very hot days. It should be removed in any event once the grass has reached a height of about one inch.

If the slope is unusually steep so that the growing and mowing problem is very severe, you might consider the same advice given at the end of the preceding section for lawns so shady that grass is difficult to grow, namely, you may prefer to plant a grass substitute. This is discussed in the following section.

GROWING GRASS SUBSTITUTES

When grass refuses to grow because an area is too shady, or when mowing is extremely difficult because of a steep slope, you can cover the soil with greenery other than grass by planting a "grass substitute."

Ivy (English or Baltic type) and Ground Myrtle give a good carpet of green in areas too shady for grass. So do Japanese Spurge and Trailing Myrtle. Vines and dwarf shrubs make good ground covers for steep banks.

Or, you might want to try *Euonymous,* Hall's Honeysuckle or Memorial Rose. Plant them in staggered rows about six feet apart. Dwarf shrubs suitable for steep banks are coralberry, Japanese barberry and weeping forsythia. Honeysuckle grows fast and must be cut twice a year to keep it from spreading to parts of the ground where you don't want it. Other suitable ground covers to substitute for grass are St. John's Wort (*Hypericum*), Canby *Pachistima,* Periwinkle (*vinca minor*), Bearberry, Cotoneaster, Wintercreeper (*Euonymous forteunei*) and Purple-leaf Wintercreeper and *Andorra* Juniper, a ground-hugging, small evergreen.

Also in use as a ground cover for areas too shady for grass to grow, especially under trees, is "Mondo Grass," also called "Snake's Beard," which was originally known as *Ophiopogon Japonicus.* It is not a grass, but an Oriental plant with grass-like leaves, belonging to the lily family. It is a tough, wiry plant which develops small flowers followed by pale blue berries. But it is not generally recommended for large-scale use in cold regions.

BARE SPOTS

When your lawn, or any part of it, has less than one-third good, healthy grass, it's probably best to plow the area, turn the topsoil over and start a new lawn as explained at the start of this chapter. But if there exists at least one-third good grass, the simpler and less expensive way probably is to repair the poor portions.

Bare spots in lawns can come about for several reasons:

Perhaps the seed was planted too deeply or not deep enough. Or, it was washed or blown away. Young seedlings may have died from the lack of water or drowned from too much of it. Diseases may have killed the sprouts. Or, the soil is starved and needs plant food. The best time for re-seeding bare spots is early fall, but it can be done successfully at any time of the year if the lawn is kept properly watered. With proper care (as explained for new lawns earlier in this chapter) new grass will grow within about a month after seeding.

"BURNED" LAWNS

Unsightly, brown "burned" spots on grass can result from an overdose of chemical fertilizers, infestation of insects, spilled gasoline and several other causes.

To avoid spilling of gasoline or oil on grass, don't tip your power lawn mower and don't fill your car's gasoline tank to the top, so as to avoid possible spilling as you enter or leave the driveway.

Fertilizer burns when applying chemical fertilizer can be prevented by using them in moderate amounts at each feeding, but never during very hot weather or when the grass is moist from rains, dew or watering. Instead, water the grass thoroughly *after* applying the fertilizer so as to wash it off the grass blades into the soil where it can do no harm. If you use a fertilizer spreader, be sure to shut the machine off when you stop it on the lawn.

Even the sun can "scald" the lawn if a rubber mat or a piece of metal or, sometimes, an item of clothing is left on the lawn while the sun is at its height on a hot day. Sometimes, insects are the cause of the brown "burned" spots as is explained in a section on insects later in this chapter.

Still another frequent cause of brownish spots on grass, which proves puzzling to unsuspecting home gardeners, is dogs voiding on the lawn. And another source of brownish lawns is shallow soil above cesspools, septic tanks or just above a large hidden stone. An easy remedy for brown spots caused by shallow soil is frequent watering to replace the evaporated moisture.

None of these "burned" discolorations is to be confused with the over-all browning of lawns during droughts. Grass recovers from these dry periods without damage as was explained in the section on "Watering Your Lawn."

WEEDS—AND HOW TO KEEP THEM AWAY

It's been said that weeds do not make a poor lawn—poor lawns make weeds.

A well-nourished soil thickly covered with healthy, vigorous, frequently-mowed grass offers little hospitality to weed seeds. They cannot thrive in the shade of flourishing grass which gives them more competition than they can survive. What's more, growing weeds find it most repugnant to have a lawn mower clip them and snip off their seed heads with annoying regularity. A lawn mower is a formidable enemy of weeds.

Weeds flourish at their best:

—in soil which has become too impoverished to play host to healthy grass.

—in soil which has bare spots.

—when grass has become sparse enough for weed seeds to gain a foothold without competition from grass.

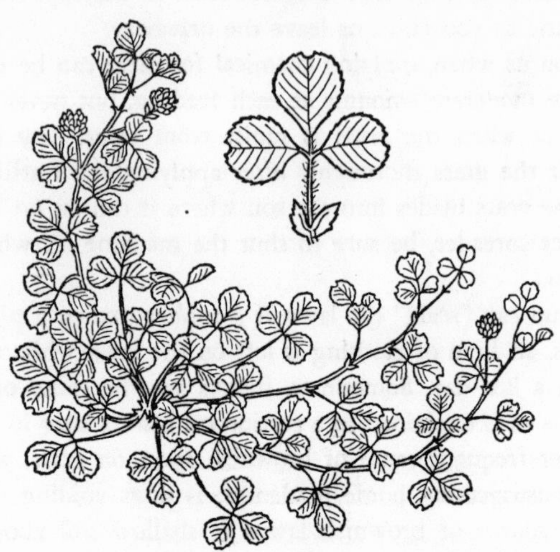

All lawn weed illustrations *Courtesy* Amchem Products

Black medic (*Medicago lupulina*).

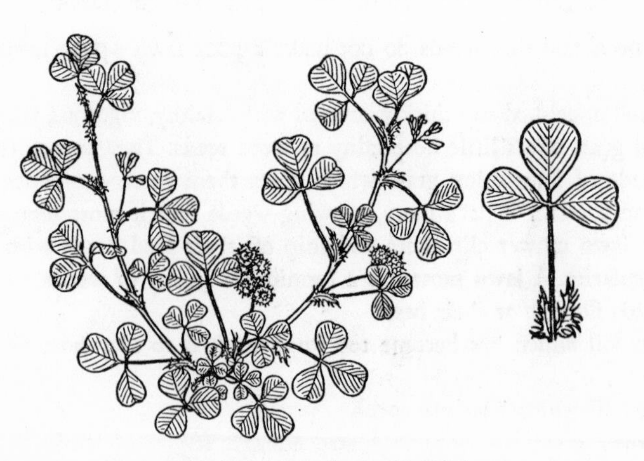

Bur clover (*Medicago hispida*).

Narrow-leaved Plantain (*Plantago lanceolata*).

Sandspur (*Cenchrus pauciflorus*).

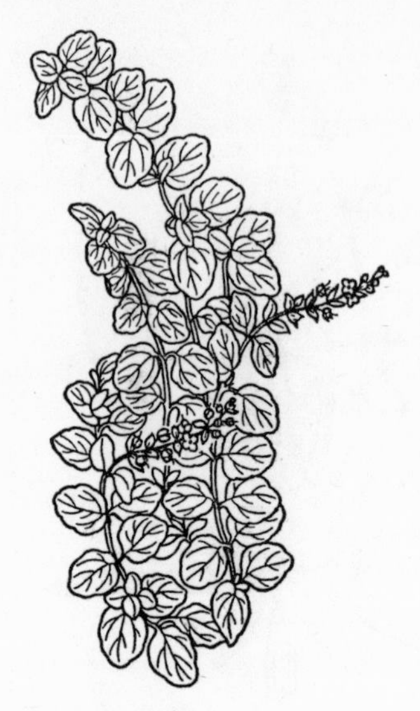

Thyme-leaved Speedwell (*Veronica serpyllifolia*).

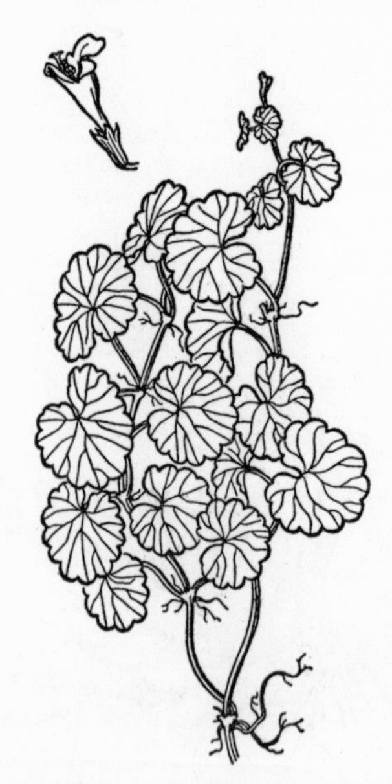

Ground Ivy or Gill-over-the-Ground (*Nepeta hederacea*).

Quack Grass (*Agropyron repens*).

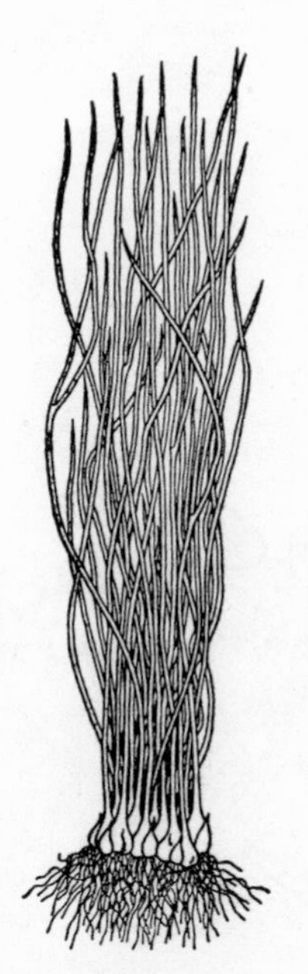

Wild Garlic (*Allium vineale*).

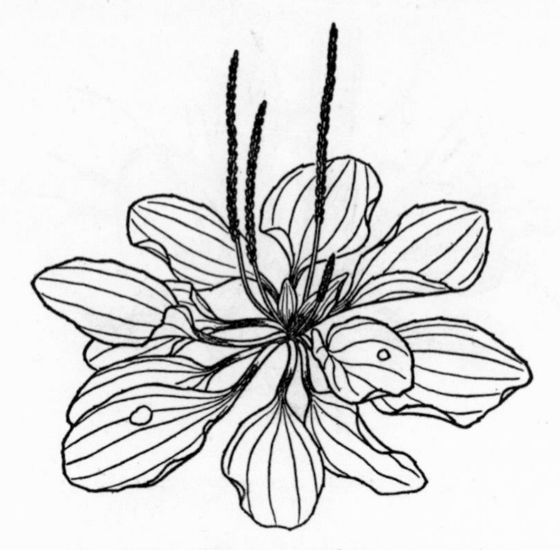

Broad-leaved Plantain (*Plantago major*).

Mouse ear chickweed (*Cerastium vulgatum*).

Common Chickweed (*Stellaria media*).

The strongest defense against weeds is, simply, to practice the principles of good lawn-keeping as explained in detail earlier in this chapter:

Feed the soil properly.

Mow your lawn frequently, but never cut the grass too short.

Promptly re-seed bare spots.

Preventing weeds is easier than to get rid of them once they are entrenched.

Yet, if weeds manage to invade your lawn, you can enlist one more weapon: chemical weed killers.

These are, of course, no substitute for the sound lawn-culture methods just listed. Rather, chemical weed killers should be looked upon as devices to help you clear weeds from your lawn so that you can renew the principles of lawn care. In using these weed killers, remember these important points:

1. Chemical weed killers, like chemical fertilizer, can "burn" your grass and, therefore, it is important you water the lawn thoroughly after each application to wash the chemicals off the grass into the soil. Also, because of the danger of such burns, do not apply these chemicals while the grass is wet from rain, dew or prior watering.

2. Watering your lawn immediately after application of weed-killing chemicals is also important for another reason: these chemicals cannot work in soil without moisture. In fact, weeds on hot, dry soil are practically resistant to these chemicals.

3. If your lawn is newly planted, delay use of chemicals until after the grass has been mowed several times. Chemicals can harm very young grass.

Here are some of the most common lawn weeds and what you can do to prevent or get rid of each:

CRABGRASS is such a regular, though unwelcome, visitor on home lawns that many a suburban dweller braces himself each spring for this annual "Battle of the Crabgrass." Part of the key to the problem is in the word "annual." Crabgrass is an annual plant, meaning it lives for only one season. The first frost each fall usually kills all crabgrass plants. But before the plants die, they spread seed which brings forth a new crop in spring.

A single crabgrass plant can produce as many as 300,000 seeds. No wonder crabgrass is loathed so fiercely by home gardeners. Any neighbor's crabgrass plant can supply your whole neighborhood with seed. These seeds need no more for their growth than some rain, temperatures above 65 and a bare spot on the soil.

Pulling crabgrass out of the soil by hand or with a small dandelion rake is one effective way of getting rid of the plants as well as their seed heads. But, since the plants die each fall anyway, all you really need accomplish is to keep the seed from spreading. Earlier in this chapter, the section on mowing advised you to leave your mowed grass clippings on the lawn to replenish soil nourishment. Here is an exception to that rule: if your lawn has crabgrass, use a grass catcher on your mower in July and August when the crabgrass forms its seed heads. Then, throw away all clippings along with the crabgrass seed heads among them.

Five chemical crabgrass killers are in use for "pre-emergence" control, meaning they are applied early in spring, usually in June, before the crabgrass seeds germinate.

These chemicals include lead arsenate, arsenic trioxide and chlordane, but their use in this way is controversial because tests have shown less than half the crabgrass being destroyed by them so that it is still necessary to apply "post-emergence" controls after the seeds germinate.

The most dependable crabgrass killers are phenyl mercuric acetate, disodium methyl arsenate and calcium arsenate. Use one fluid ounce of one or these in two to four gallons of water for each 1,000 square feet. Three to five applications are usually needed at six- to ten-day intervals. Wash hands and equipment after each use. If grass shows any damage, cut the dosage in half, but continue application until crabgrass is eliminated. The calcium arsenate has been shown to be effective for a second year's protection from crabgrass by applying a booster of only 1/4 the original dose early in the second year. Once crabgrass plants are deeply rooted, however, best results can be obtained with potassium cyanate in the same dosage given for the above chemicals.

All of these chemicals are available at your garden supply store under a variety of trade names. Read the labels on the containers carefully and follow the directions shown there. And once you have eliminated crabgrass from your lawn, remember this most important point: re-seed the spot vacated by the crabgrass at once before another weed seed catches hold there.

DANDELION, PLANTAIN, BUCKHORN, CHICKWEED AND BUTTERCUP as well as certain other weeds can easily be destroyed with a weed killer known as "2,4–D." It comes in dry and liquid form. Add an ounce of it to 12 quarts of water.

However, 2,4–D is not effective on crabgrass, quackgrass and other grasses which are narrow-leaved. It kills broad-leaved plants only. And here is something else to watch for: 2,4–D will set clover back, although the clover will survive the 2,4–D treatment. If weed killers contain 2,4–5–T or 2,4–5–TP, you can be pretty certain the clover will be killed outright. Any of the above weed killers will also kill shrubs and nearby vegetation and, for that reason, should be applied only on days when there is little wind so that it will not drift to those plants. Because of these disadvantages, some home gardeners will only "spot apply" it by dipping a sponge tied to a stick into the solution and then rubbing the sponge against the weeds. If, however, you apply 2,4–D with a sprinkling can, mark that can so that you or someone else will not mistakenly use that same can to sprinkle flowers.

VERONICA (also called "Creeping Speedwell") is a creeping perennial with dime-size scalloped leaves. It produces tiny, pale-blue flowers each April on slender, thread-like stalks. It is a stubborn, fast-spreading weed which remains unharmed by the chemicals mentioned so far. But it can be destroyed by applying a solution of four ounces of Endothal in 12½ gallons of water.

GROUND IVY (Nepeta) is a flat-growing vine also known as "Gill-over-the-ground" and "Creeping Charlie." It has leaves the size of a quarter and forms mats on the ground as its roots spread wherever the stems touch the ground. Control it by mixing potassium cyanate with 2,4–D or arsenical compounds.

MOSS on your lawn is a signal the soil is undernourished and the

Courtesy Du Pont Co.

Dipping tip end of poison ivy or other weed in a jar of weedkiller sometimes works well. Plants absorb the weedkiller through the leaves, causing plant to commit suicide. This is especially useful when weeds are near trees or other plants where spraying would injure other vegetation.

grass is starving. That's why moss often occurs under shallow-rooted trees. There, the tree's roots invade the top foot of soil, the same layer from which grass must draw its nourishment.

To get rid of moss, simply rake off the green moss coating with an iron-toothed rake and then rebuild the depleted soil with a generous serving of lawn food. Then re-seed grass.

If you want to eliminate moss growing between stones or in cracks on your driveway, douse it with gasoline, oil or even salt or, if you prefer, with a solution of one pound of Ammate weedkiller in a gallon of water. This solution will eliminate most types of weeds from driveways, but be careful not to spill any of this solution on your lawn or the grass will die too.

MUSHROOMS and TOADSTOOLS sometimes grow in a circular arrangement called "fairy rings" on lawns, depriving the grass within the circle of nutrients. These rings measure anywhere from 2 to 25 feet in diameter.

Mowing mushrooms will spread their spores to other areas. Although it's a rather tedious job you can handpick the mushrooms and burn them before they discharge spores. Or, apply dolomitic limestone to your entire lawn at a rate of about 25 pounds for each 1,000 square feet. Repeat this application at double the rate in late autumn.

If the rings persist the following year, perforate the area with a spade and apply two ounces of corrosive sublimate on each 1,000 square feet. Mix at the rate of 2 ounces per gallon of water. Also helpful is repeated soaking of the soil at two-week intervals with a solution of a pound of iron sulfate in 1½ gallons of water. Another effective treatment consists of using a solution of about ¼ of a tablespoonful of bichloride of mercury in a gallon of water.

LAWN DISEASES—AND HOW TO CURE THEM

Lawns are prey to more than 100 different diseases, although they are not likely to be serious except on Bentgrass and highly managed lawns. No single chemical can cure all of them. Mercury compounds are effective against many. But prevention is to be preferred over treatment.

An application of 3 to 5 ounces of calomel-corrosive sublimate mixture (deadly poisonous) for each 1,000 square feet in late fall is a useful preventative for some lawn diseases. It can be applied diluted in water or dry by mixing the amount with a quart of dry sand and then mixing the sand with a finely screened fertilizer mixture.

Here are some of the most frequently occurring lawn diseases and what to do about them:

SNOW MOLD, also known as "winter scald," spreads while snow is covering the lawn. When the snow melts, patches of dense, cotton-like growth show the presence of the disease. It is usually more severe on lawns in low-lying areas, especially when large piles of snow have covered the grass for long periods. Most lawns will recover from snow mold, without treatment, when the grass dries and the ground warms. If treatment is desired or needed, 3 or 4 ounces of mercury chloride (calomel-corrosive sublimate mixtures) in a gallon of water for each 1,000 square feet is recommended. Sulfur compounds are also effective. You can decrease the susceptibility of your lawn to this disease by fertilizing the grass no later than September (because late fertilizing leaves lawns more susceptible) and by keeping the lawn well-mowed and keeping leaves and other ground coverings off the lawn before snow covers it. Also refrain from piling heavy accumulations of snow on the lawn.

GOING-OUT DISEASE, which hits mostly Bluegrass, shows itself through the yellowing and thinning of grass in April and May. Apply mercurial compounds, Thiram or Actidione with Thiram.

FADING-OUT DISEASE, also known as black mold, produces off-color, yellow-green patches on the grass. A white cloth rubbed over the grass will show sooty black smudges. Apply mercurial compounds, according to manufacturer's directions.

BROWN PATCH, also called summer blight, occurs when night temperatures remain above 70 degrees Fahrenheit and when the relative humidity approaches 100 per cent. The disease shows itself with circular "smoke rings" on the lawn. Apply any mercury compound preparation or cadmium.

DOLLAR SPOT occurs during cool, wet periods in spring, summer or fall. Brown circular patches, about the size of a silver dollar, appear on the lawn. Cobwebby growths appear whenever there is dew. Tiny yellow spots on the grass blades soon thereafter turn bleached or off-white. Apply mercury compounds of cadmium preparations.

TURF BLIGHT, known as helminthosporium and curvularia, causes discoloration of grass which is often mistakenly blamed on drought or improper nutrition. The disease kills grass by attacking the roots and crowns. Spray with phenyl mercurial compound.

INSECTS—AND HOW TO GET RID OF THEM

A wide variety of insects living below the surface of the soil are liable to attack the grass, chewing its roots or sucking juices from the leaves. When a well-fed, properly watered lawn turns brown despite the care you give it, chances are underground insects are active. Telltale signs that such pests may have invaded your lawn are dug-up turfs, mole tunnels and runways and visits by skunks who feed on these insects. You can check the presence of insects or their grubs by rolling back some loose sod in suspected areas and seeing whether grubs are there.

Chemicals which kill insects or their grubs are called insecticides. Effective insecticides include Chlordane, DDT, Dieldrin and lead arsenate which usually kill grubs within about four, six and twelve weeks, respectively. Many insecticides are available at your garden store as sprays or in granular form, or as powders for "dusting" the lawn. Your selection is a matter of choice, but experience has shown sprays to be somewhat more effective. Once applied, these chemicals usually give protection against grubs from three to five years.

Early spring, about April, is about the best time to de-grub your lawn. At that time the grubs are still dormant and it is far easier to fight them in that stage than when they have become active. Most insecticides are poisonous and you should therefore avoid inhaling them either as dust or sprays. Clean your hands and face and other exposed parts of your body after applying any insecticide. Water your lawn thoroughly *after* each application to wash the chemicals into the soil. Keep children and pets off the lawn until it is dry following the watering.

Here are the names of some of the most common insects and how to fight them:

JAPANESE BEETLE, CHINCH BUGS, EUROPEAN CHAFER and WHITE GRUBS ("June bug" larvae) can best be controlled by what may be called "standard treatment for making a lawn grub-proof," namely by the use of any of the following chemicals: DDT, Chlordane, lead arsenate or Dieldrin. For proper dosage see the chart below:

GRUB-PROOFING

DRY MATERIAL	RATE PER 1,000 SQ. FT.
DDT 10% wettable powder	10 oz.
Dieldrin 1% granular	8 lbs.
Dieldrin 10% granular	1 lb.
Chlordane dust (5%) or granular	5 lbs.
Lead Arsenate	(follow instructions on label)
WET OR SPRAY MATERIAL	
Dieldrin 25% wettable powder	5 oz.
Dieldrin 18% concentrate	6 oz. liquid
Chlordane 40% wettable powder	10 oz.
Chlordane 75% emulsifiable concentrate	4 oz. liquid

* Apply in accordance with manufacturer's directions.

CLOVER MITES are tiny brownish-red creatures (about 1/50 of an inch long) which feed on grass and other plants in summer, but in cold weather seek shelter and are then often seen in swarms of thousands at windows and on walls and foundations. Mites multiply rapidly, through as many as six generations in a season, and produce most prolifically on new, well-growing lawns as well as on lawns and shrubbery which have been treated with DDT or the other insecticides mentioned earlier. Mites are not affected by these insecticides. As a result, their heaviest invasions are sometimes into the best-kept homes.

Effective chemical mite-killers are Malathion, Pyrethrum, Kelthane, Dimite, Aramite and a sulfur-rotenone mixture. See "Insect and Animal Control" chapter for more information on this pest.

ANTS can cause lawns to dry. For control spray anthills with Chlordane and water the area thoroughly after application, as outlined in "Insect and Animal Control" chapter.

GREEN THUMB TIPS

After grading your lawn, give it time to settle before sowing. Loam soils often settle 20 per cent, or 1/5 of their original depth.

There is no perfect grass. Watch out for "wonder" grasses. You buy them, plant them and "wonder" why they don't grow.

Temporary lawns cost money. Invest more in a permanent lawn and have green grass as long as your house lasts.

Grass seed sowed on snow is for the birds! Wait and sow the seed on a good, well-prepared seed bed.

Mow grass as soon as you have something to mow. Mowing encourages filling out at the base.

Don't lime your lawn every year! It does more harm than good. Once every four years is safer, but feed twice a year.

Don't be a lawn crank. If grass starts to dry in hot weather, it'll bounce back after the first rain, if the grass is a permanent type.

Don't water a lawn unless you do it right. An average soil loses 50 gallons (barrel) per 1,000 square feet a day. Six days of this would be 300 gallons, or 1/2 inch of rain. It'll take three hours of steady sprinkling to replace this amount of water on each 1,000 square feet.

Sprinkling during a hot sun is harmless.

2

Flowering Annuals

Why do so many gardeners grow annuals? The answer is simple. In the first place, annuals are the cheapest, yet showiest of all garden flowers. A 25-cent packet of seed produces hundreds of dollars' worth of enjoyment, with a minimum of effort. The price you pay for one evening's outing can fill a large flower bed around your home with annuals that bloom throughout the summer. There are many other reasons why gardeners grow annuals. The annual list is long and variety is so great it's possible to have color from spring until frost.

What Is It? An annual is a plant which completes its growth in one year. It is started from seed each year. Annuals are divided into three groups, according to the time when the seed is sown—tender, half-hardy and hardy. Hardy annuals are those you can sow directly in the open ground as soon as the soil can be prepared. Examples: Sweet Alyssum, Calendula, Larkspur, California Poppy, China Pinks and Sweet Peas.

Half-hardy annuals are sown in February and March in a hotbed or warm window. Plants are "hardened" off in a coldframe before planting in their permanent quarters outdoors. Examples: Sweet Sultan, Lobelia, Sweet Scabiosa.

Tender annuals need more warmth and protection and a longer growing season. Start these in January or February in a warm greenhouse or window, but don't plant outdoors until danger of frost is over. Examples: Ageratum, Petunia and Salvia.

How To Use Annuals: In planting annuals, put the taller-growing ones behind those of medium or low growth. An elaborate color scheme is not necessary. Select two or three good combinations and place them where they'll show off best. All one color in masses is very striking, although many prefer an old-fashioned mixture. Scattered single plants of any one kind of flower give a spotty effect. Three plants of a kind in a group should be the minimum. In making beds for annuals, don't make them too wide. If against a fence, 4 or 5 feet is handy, and in the open 6 or 7 feet is sufficient. Over greater distances it's difficult to pick the flowers or work the beds.

Time To Start Annual Plants: You can sow most annuals out of doors after danger of hard frosts, but those that should be started indoors vary in their rate of germination and development. Other annuals are fall-sown and these are discussed later.

Outdoor Sowing: Fast-growing annuals such as zinnias, marigolds, portulaca and cleome can be sowed outdoors. Since they do not suffer the shock of transplanting, they will get off to a quick start and often bloom sooner than plants started indoors. Not all annual flowers may be sowed directly in the garden, yet there are many that should be, because they are difficult to transplant. These include candytuft, clarkia, California poppy, godetia, kochia, leptosyne, linaria, lupine, matthiola (evening-scented stock), nasturtium, dwarf phlox, poppies, portulaca and salpiglossis.

Fall Sowing Outdoors: It isn't generally realized that many annuals can be successfully planted in the fall to produce better plants than when sowed in the spring. To fall-sow, work up the soil after the first heavy frost. You can plant any time until the ground freezes. If you sow after October, there's little likelihood that the seed will germinate until spring.

Sow rather thickly, since some seeds will be lost to birds, mice or rot. If germination is good in the spring, you can thin and transplant to other parts of the garden. For complete directions for sowing seed of annuals indoors and outdoors see the chapter on "Plant Propagation."

Here is a list of annuals and the approximate times to start indoor growing. For an extra-early crop, you can start most varieties about two weeks earlier than the time specified. The table is based on conditions for Central New York State and planting time will vary according to the section of country you're in. A general rule is to start slow-growing kinds eight to ten weeks before setting outdoors in midwestern, northern and eastern areas. Look on the seed packet for extra instructions on starting seed indoors.

Plant	Sow Seed Indoors	Transplant Seedlings in	Suitable for Starting Outdoors
Ageratum	March	April	No
Amaranthus	April	May	Yes
Anagallis	April	April	Yes
Babysbreath	April	May	Yes
Balsam	April	May	Yes
Bachelor's Button	April	May	Yes
Calendula	April	May	Yes
California Poppy	April	May	Yes
Calliopsis	April	April	Yes
Candytuft	April	May	Yes
China Aster	April	April	Yes
Chrysanthemum	April	May	Yes
Clarkia	April	May	Yes
Cleome	April	May	No
Cockscomb	April	April	Yes
Cosmos	April	May	Yes
Cynoglossum	April	April	Yes
Dahlia	March	March	Yes
Dianthus	April	April	Yes
Dimorphotheca	April	April	Yes
Gaillardia	April	May	Yes
Godetia	April	April	Yes
Gomphrena	April	May	Yes
Hunnemannia	April	April	Yes
Kochia	April	May	Yes
Larkspur	April	April	Yes
Lavatera	April	May	Yes
Lobelia	March	April	No
Marigold	April	April	Yes
Mignonette	April	May	Yes
Mimulus	April	May	Yes
Morning Glory	April	May	Yes
Nasturtium	April	May	Yes
Nicotiana	April	May	Yes
Nierembergia	March	April	Yes
Nigella	April	April	Yes
Petunia	March	April	No
Phlox	April	April	Yes
Poppy	April	May	Yes
Salpiglossis	April	April	Yes
Salvia	March	May	No
Scabiosa	April	May	Yes
Schizanthus	April	May	Yes

Plant	Sow Seed Indoors	Transplant Seedlings in	Suitable for Starting Outdoors
Snapdragon	March	April	No
Statice	April	April	Yes
Strawflower	April	April	Yes
Sunflower	May	May	Yes
Sweet Alyssum	April	April	Yes
Verbena	March	April	No
Vinca	April	April	Yes
Zinnia	April	May	Yes

See list of annuals for fall sowing later in this chapter. You can experiment with dozens of others.

DISEASES AND INSECTS OF GARDEN FLOWERS

Annuals and perennials have practically the same pest problems. To fight them you can use all-purpose pesticides, either home-mixed or purchased.

All-Purpose Sprays: To lick all insects and diseases you can buy combination pesticides at your garden store or you can make your own. Try my formula: 4 tablespoons Malathion, 25 per cent wettable powder; 4 tablespoons Methoxychlor, 50 per cent wettable powder; one tablespoon of Captan, 50 per cent wettable powder; Karathane (or Mildex), ½ tablespoon. Or you can use sulfur instead of Karathane, 2 tablespoons of the 95–100 per cent wettable powder.

Mix these with 1 gallon of water for an excellent disease- and insect-control on all your flowers. It will kill every insect and most diseases on your plants (virus, alternaria, fusarium excepted). Keep your plants sprayed before bugs and diseases appear. Don't wait until plants become infected because it may be too late!

Other Materials To Use: Sulfur is still one of the best fungicides and is an excellent powdery mildew-fighter. Used in a spray with Ferbam, Zineb or Captan, it increases their effectiveness against certain diseases like black spot of roses, and rusts. It also acts as a miticide and is helpful against tarnished plant bug, leafhopper and thrips.

Copper dusts are also helpful in combatting blights, leaf spot and mildew, but under cool, wet conditions, they may burn certain plants.

Whatever commerical preparations you use, be sure to read the label carefully and follow the manufacturer's recommendations.

If you spray, get a compressed-air sprayer, holding between 1 and 3 gallons, or one of the new hose sprayers. Agitate frequently while spraying and be sure to cover the undersides of the foliage. Wash and clean your sprayer as soon as the job is finished.

For dusting, get a good plunger-type duster, holding 1 to 3 pounds, with a spoon nozzle which allows the dust to be directed to the undersides of the leaves, a good meeting place for bugs and disease organisms.

Personally, I prefer spraying to dusting, because sprays stick to the foliage longer than dusts and can be applied at any time during the day (but with less danger of plant injury if applied in early morning or late afternoon). Dusting is appealing to the small gardener, because dust is all ready to use. It sticks better if put on in early morning or late afternoon when the foliage is moist. Apply a thin layer and repeat as often as necessary to keep new growth covered. Don't work on the theory that if a little does a lot of good, a lot will be even better. A heavy dose makes plants unsightly and may be injurious.

Slugs and Snails: These pests can cause heavy damage. They are night marauders and hide under damp boards, leafy trash and stones in the daytime. Control: Scatter 10 per cent metaldehyde and 5 per cent chlordane dust in infested areas. You can trap snails by placing boards in areas where they hide during the day. Then scrape them off and destroy them. (See "Animal Control" chapter.)

SOILS AND FERTILIZER

A sandy loam soil, well supplied with organic matter, is best for most flowers. Use lime only when a test shows a need for it. For plants like daisies, lupines, salvia and others which prefer an acid soil, use aluminum sulfate, iron sulfate, sulfur or acid peat.

To sweeten the soil, ground limestone is the best form of lime. An acidity test should be made every two or three years. (See "Soils" section for more information about liming.)

The soil should be well drained; and if it is heavy and has a tendency to bake or is sandy and dries out quickly, the addition of organic material such as leaf mold, compost or peat will be beneficial. Coal ashes are recommended for heavy clay soils. The more organic matter you can add to a heavy or sandy soil, the better it will be for flowers. This is explained in detail under the "Compost Soils" section.

Fertilizer: The rate of application is based on the fertilizer concentration and, as a rule, the soil should be moist before the fertilizer is applied. If plant food is applied in liquid form, the foliage should not be wet with the solution, unless you are using a type especially designed for foliage feeding. They will not burn when applied according to directions. "Ra-pid-Gro," with its 23–21–17 formula, has been a favorite in our greenhouse and nursery operations for years because it's safe and can be used with our pesticides.

Any dry fertilizer should be measured accurately and spread uniformly over the surface of the soil, keeping it about 4 inches away from the stems of the plants.

Make the first application in the spring when growth is 4–6 inches high, and a second application a month later. For a detailed chart on feeding the flower garden see the "Soils and Fertilizer" section.

SUMMER CARE OF ANNUALS

Pruning: Just about all annuals will perform much better if you give them a summer pruning or pinching. This means simply shortening the growth to make them bushy. At the base of every leaf are one or more dormant growth buds or "eyes." When you snip off the tops, you force them to grow into side shoots. If you pinch the tips of these side shoots again, you will get still more shoots. Pruning will delay flowering a little, but without it the plants will be tall and gangly. The extra care will repay you with more bloom and better plants.

Pinch the tip back with thumb and forefinger when plants are 3 or 4 inches high and continue to snip and prune all summer long. Do only a few branches at a time and begin before the plants look ragged, picking off flowers as soon as they fade to prevent seed pod formation. Your plants will stay fresh-looking and full of bloom much longer with this extra attention.

MY 21 BEST ANNUALS

Here are the annuals I consider best for the home garden. There are many more to try, but, generally speaking, these will give you plenty of show, color and performance with the least amount of effort.

AGERATUM (Floss Flower)

Description and Uses: This is one of the few good blue flowers, popular for borders, edgings, rock gardens; also indoor pot plants, and porch boxes. Grows 8 to 12 inches tall.

Green Thumb Care: Cut off faded flowers to keep plants looking handsome. In dry soils, plants will wilt, but soon after watering they revive. Plant 6 to 8 inches apart in full sun or half shade.

Propagation: Seed started indoors.

Problems: Red spider. Use Malathion.

ALYSSUM

Description and Uses: A dainty little plant, recommended for use in borders, edgings, baskets, pots and rock gardens and for cutting. The white alyssum is a prolific plant that sows seeds which live over the winter. The pink and purple varieties do not often self-sow. Growing to a height of 3 to 6 inches, there are two types—the dwarf upright, such as Little Gem, Violet Queen and Rosie O'Day, and the procumbent type like Carpet of Snow and Royal Carpet.

Green Thumb Care: When plants become "seedy-looking," clip them back within a few inches of the ground. They come back quickly with renewed beauty.

Propagation: A fast-growing annual and can be sown out of doors. Seed is small and should be covered lightly if at all. Some gardeners cover the row with a strip of newspaper after sowing. Anchor it down with soil along the edges and take it off as soon as the seedlings appear. The newspaper keeps the soil moist and insures a good stand. Alyssum will produce bloom in six weeks if sown outdoors.

Problems: None.

ASTERS (*Callistephus chinensis*)

Description and Uses: A fine late-summer and early-fall cut flower. Colors come in all shades of lavender, salmon, crimson, light pink, deep rose, white and cream. Grows 2 to 3 feet tall. Ideal for bouquets, bedding plants.

Green Thumb Care: Likes full sun, does well in partial shade where insects will not work. Should have well-drained, fairly rich soil. Spray with DDT or Malathion to check leafhoppers, tarnished plant bugs and blister beetles, three villains that cause trouble with asters. Rotate the spot you grow asters in each year.

Propagation: Sow indoors in April. After seedlings are about 2 inches high, transplant to a seed flat or to the garden after frost.

Problems: Aster wilt or fusarium causes asters to wilt suddenly, turn yellowish green and die. The wilt organism lives in the soil from one year to the next, so you should grow the flowers in a different spot each year. The use of wilt-resistant asters is helpful but there are many different strains of wilt organism and no one variety of asters is resistant to all of them. You should always buy wilt-resistant strains in preference to the non-resistant type, however.

Aster Yellows: If leaves get yellow and sickly with a spindly growth, although they do not die, your plants are infected with aster yellows. Yellows is caused by a virus spread by leafhoppers, so partial control can be had by spraying. Also since the virus is known to winter-over in certain biennial and perennial plants, such as thistle, daisy and some mums, it's a good idea to plant asters at least 200 feet away from weed borders.

CALENDULAS (Pot or Scotch Marigold)

Description and Uses: One of the best annuals for the home garden. Once used as a remedy for sore teeth, the name became "Mary's Gold," and this was slurred into Marigold. Ideal for bouquets, combines well with mums and snapdragons. Grows 2 feet tall.

Green Thumb Care: Will withstand hot weather quite well, although flowers are larger in cool weather. Cut off seed heads, and flowers will come after frost. New Pacific beauties produce uniformly large, well-formed flowers with longer and straighter stems.

Propagation: Seed started indoors, then transplanted to open garden after frost. Make a second sowing in early July and you'll have flowers in late summer and fall.

Problems: None.

CLEOME (Spider Plant)

Description and Uses: Outstanding for summer bloom. The Pink Queen variety develops huge heads of delightful true pink. There is also the equally showy, pure white Helen Campbell. Cleome is a tall, bold annual, growing from 4 to 5 feet tall and blooms from June until frost. The four-petaled flowers have an airy appearance because of their unusual long-stemmed stamens and pistils (male and female floral parts) which protrude several inches from the flowers. The plant has a rather peculiar odor and does not lend itself too well to arrangements, but is striking as a garden flower in the background of the border. Because the plants sometimes get leggy and leafless at the base, it's a good idea to plant other annuals in front of them. A mass planting is most effective.

Green Thumb Care: Grows in poor soils, but flowers are fuller if plants are watered twice a week or so. Very easy to grow.

Propagation: Seed may be started indoors. When you transplant, set the plants at least 2 feet apart. Some gardeners sow outdoors when the weather warms up. Cleome self-sows readily.

Problems: Self-sows and may grow like a weed.

COCKSCOMB (*Celosia*)

Description and Uses: A red-hot flower for gardeners who are constantly in search of something different. The new red Toreador is a flashy annual with a different look. Plant has attractive bright red-crested flower heads resembling cockscombs, 6 to 8 inches across, and on stiff-stems 18 to 20 inches high. Use fresh or dried like strawflowers. *Celosia plumosa* has plumed spikes and is called "feathered cockscomb." Flowers are yellow, red and pinkish, feather-like spikes, good for contrasts in the garden.

Green Thumb Care: Needs plenty of space (12 to 18 inches), since close spacing decreases size of heads. This is a good feature if you use them in bouquet work.

Propagation: Seed started indoors.

Problems: Cockscomb will bloom prematurely with small heads if growth of young plants is checked.

Cosmos

Description and Uses: An attractive, airy, background plant. If you are a new home owner and want a quick-growing item while your small woody ornamentals are getting established, consider the cosmos. It grows 4 feet tall with daisy-like flowers in clear white, pinks, orchid, crimson, orange, and yellow.

Green Thumb Care: After plants are 2 feet tall, pinch back to induce side branches to form. Pinching delays blooming, so don't pinch too late or you won't get blooms. They like a well-drained, gravelly soil, and full sun. Avoid heavy feeding as they don't require too rich a soil.

Propagation: Start seed outdoors in May (after frost). Space plants 18 inches apart so as to get nice husky plants. You can start seed indoors for earlier blooming.

Problems: May break in wind. Staking will prevent this.

Dwarf Dahlia

Description and Uses: Unwin hybrids, annual dahlias. Gardeners who raise the Unwin Dwarf Hybrid dahlias from seed are surprised to find they produce tubers like the large dahlias. These dahlias are earlier to bloom and will form tubers which are handled similarly to the giant or larger dahlias. Flowers are many-colored and double or semi-double, ideal for cut flowers all summer long.

Green Thumb Care: If stems are dipped in hot water for a few minutes after cutting, the cut flowers will last for days. The tubers of colors you like may be saved, since separate colors of these hybrids are not possible from seed. The Coltness hybrid is a single-flowered form.

Propagation: Sow the seed directly outdoors after danger of frost or for earlier bloom start indoors or in a coldframe.

Problems: Tarnished plant bug and leafhopper. Spray with DDT.

Larkspur (annual)

Description and Uses: Lovely branchy stalks of single or double florets, with white, pink and shades of lavender. Ideal for cut flowers. 3 feet tall.

Green Thumb Care: Needs cool weather, otherwise plants will be stunted. Will bloom all summer unless hot weather intervenes. New varieties do not shatter as easily as older types. Hardy larkspur is delphinium, a perennial.

Propagation: Early-spring sowing indoors, or sow seed in fall for June blooms.

Problems: None.

MARIGOLD (*Tagetes*)

Description and Uses: Gardeners have a bewildering number of marigolds to choose from—tall mum types, carnation-flowered and ball-flowered, dwarf single- and double-flowering types, the African (*erecta*) and the French (*patula*). Ideal for urns, porch boxes, background plantings, edgings along drives and walks. Few annuals are more satisfactory.

Green Thumb Care: Thrives in almost any kind of soil, blooming continuously in summer heat, especially the dwarf and semi-dwarf types. Foliage is strong-smelling, but there are odorless types you can use. Pick off seed heads for continuous bloom. Some large-flowering marigolds bloom too late, so be sure to buy early-flowering types.

Propagation: Seed sown outdoors.

Problems: Leafhoppers and red spider. Control with Malathion.

MORNING GLORIES (*Ipomea*)

Description and Uses: Ipomea (Heavenly Blue and similar kinds are *convolvulus*) is the most popular annual vine. Thrives in poor soil and grows almost anywhere so long as it has sun. In dull weather the flowers stay open most of the day, but on sunny days they close up about noon, and really hot weather wilts them. A good screening vine.

"Moonflowers" are a form of Morning Glory with larger vines, larger leaves and huge, fragrant white flowers. They start to open in late afternoon, stay open all night and close in the morning.

Green Thumb Care: Likes a soil not too fertile and does well without too much moisture. They need a trellis or strings to climb on. Cloudy wet weather produces lots of runners and leaves, few or no blooms. Will bloom more freely if growing tips are nipped out before buds form. This forces the growth of side shoots which bloom profusely.

Other good annual flowering vines are the scarlet runner bean—which has bright red, pea-like flowers—and the climbing nasturtium.

Propagation: Seed. Morning Glories have a hard seed coat. To aid germination, soak seed overnight in warm water. You can also file a notch in the seed. Sow outdoors, after danger of frost, in the place where they are to remain, as they do not transplant too readily. With care they can be transplanted, however, taking them up when they have their first set of true leaves. They can be started indoors in pots or paper containers. Seed germinates irregularly so don't give up too easily.

Problems: None.

NASTURTIUMS (*Tropaeolum*—pronounced Tro-pee-o-lum)

Description and Uses: An old-fashioned plant which remains popular. Ideal for poor, hot soil and tolerates semi-shade. The tall type is ideal for trellises and window boxes and to cover walls and stumps. Flowers are orange, yellow, red. They will climb to considerable height during the summer if given support.

There are also the dwarf semi-double types, such as Gleam, with short runners and the globe type which makes a compact plant. Cherry Rose is one of the best in this class.

Green Thumb Care: Don't sow in too rich a soil or you will get mostly leaves and few or no flowers. Folks who like to use leaves for sandwiches are disappointed to find flowers full of aphids or lice which secrete a honey-dew material.

Propagation: Sow outdoors in late spring.

Problems: Aphids. Nicotine sulfate and soap, or Malathion alone will knock out this pest; but bear in mind that these are poisonous materials, and be sure to wash the foliage well if you eat it.

PETUNIAS

Description and Uses: No doubt about it, the petunia is the most wanted annual in America. The new hybrids are revolutionary, since this technique of plant breeding produces plants that stand hot, dry summers better, flower much more freely, and generally make a more compact growth. They are produced by crossing two inbred parent lines which are hand-pollinated and will not reproduce true in the second generation.

Petunia classification has been so confusing that even expert gardeners have a hard time deciding which kind to select. Here is a general grouping to guide you, prepared with the cooperation of Fred Statt of the Joseph Harris Company:

Grandiflora (Giant Flower)—The larger flowered kinds, including those with fringed, waved and plain edges. This class includes both F_1 hybrids and open-pollinated varieties. Examples: Ballerina and Snowstorm.

Multiflora (Many-Flowered)—Smaller-flowered or bedding F_1 hybrids. Blooms in greatest profusion. Examples: Red Satin and Dream Girl.

Dwarf Bedding or Nana Compacta—Open-pollinated, smaller-flowered types. Usually flower less freely, are not as uniform as F_1 hybrids. Examples: Celestial Rose and Snowball.

Balcony Type—Denotes a use rather than a single class, as all taller-growing varieties (14 inches or more) can be used. Examples: Seaform (grandiflora), Pale Moon (multiflora), Burpee Orchid (double), and Tall Giants of California.

Double-Flowered—These have more than one row of petals. They include both the large double varieties with flowers up to 5 inches across, and the smaller kinds, sometimes called carnation-flowered (2- to 3-inch flowers).

Examples: Sonata (large), Cherry Tart (small).

Giant Ruffled—These have double the normal number of chromosomes and are known as tetraploids. They produce the largest flowers (up to 6 inches) in a limited color range. Because they do not flower freely, they are not satisfactory for the garden and are grown primarily for specimen blooms.

Green Thumb Care: Petunias like full sun, ample water in summer. Remove more than the faded blooms—pinch off the seed pods too to maintain plant vigor. Keep faded blossoms and pods picked off and the plants keep right on blooming.

Propagation: Start indoors in early spring. Seed is fine, so be sure to use a light soil. We often use pure muck. Sow thinly and *do not cover;* press the seed in lightly and water by submerging the seed flat in a shallow pan. Do not water from above. If you cover the seed box with newspaper or glass pane, remove immediately after the seeds have germinated.

Double petunia seedlings develop a little more slowly than the singles and seed should be sown indoors about two months before outdoor planting time.

Problems: Petunias are often attacked by snails which eat holes in blooms and leaves. Metaldehyde baits scattered among plants will check them. Flea beetles and other pests can be controlled with DDT.

Damping off is a real problem in raising petunias. Try sterilizing your seed soil (see chapter on "Starting Seed") and sow thinly. When crowded, seedling plants do not get enough air and rot sets in.

Botrytis, another form of damping off, is air-borne. The leaves take on a watery, glassy appearance and the whole plant suddenly dies. Control by providing good air circulation and dust with 50 per cent Ferbam.

Rhizoctonia and pythium are controlled by soil sterilization.

PHLOX (*Drummondii*)

Description and Uses: Among the showiest of our bedding annuals. We like the new Twinkle, a starred variety with dainty flowers in an unusually wide assortment of colors. It stands heat well, and the dwarf, neat plants are fine for bedding and highly effective in masses, likes full sun and blooms all summer long.

Green Thumb Care: Cut off faded blooms so seed pods cannot form. This extends blooming period and makes plants more compact. Feed and water regularly. Some gardeners shear the plant back after the first blooms fade.

Propagation: Easy to grow and self-sows readily. Fall-sown seed will bloom next May or June. You can start indoors in March or sow outdoors in April or early May, as it is quite hardy.

Problems: None.

PORTULACA (Rose-moss)

Description and Uses: Here is a gay and accommodating garden flower. We like it because it grows in the poorest and driest ground as long as it gets plenty of sun. It seeds itself and is unrivaled for brilliancy among plants of low growth. The flowers open only when in full sun, closing at night and on cloudy days. The flower is ideal for lining sidewalks, driveways, around garages, on sunny banks and even between stepping stones. Some gardeners broadcast the seed over rock gardens to fill them with color. Grows 3 to 6 inches tall. Single and double flowers in red, pink, rose, yellow, white and shades in between. Plants have a spreading habit. Good also to cover for bare spots, rock gardens and hollow stumps.

Green Thumb Care: Keep weeds out. Avoid heavy watering.

Propagation: Sow seed outdoors after soil is warm. Blooms in 6 weeks, continuing until frost. Plant self-sows, but the doubles revert to singles even though colors remain of good quality. Scatter seed on surface and thin plants later to 6 inches apart. Can also be started indoors in May.

Problems: None.

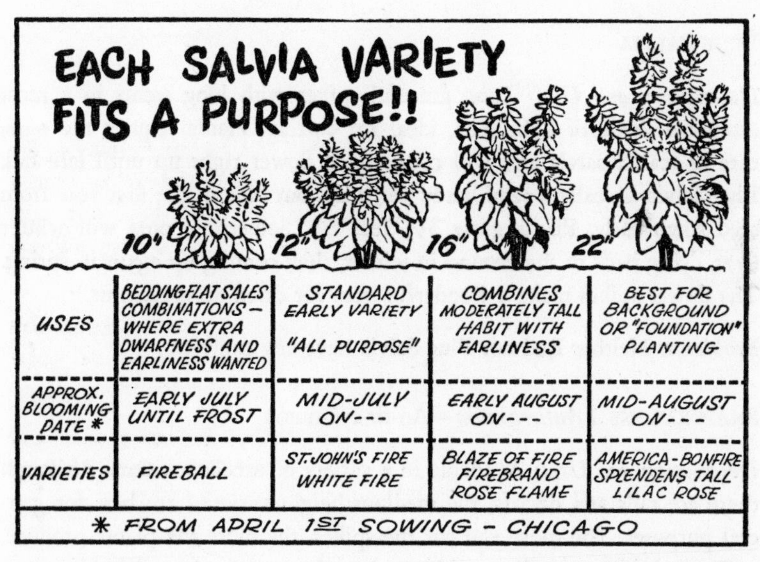

USES	BEDDING FLAT SALES COMBINATIONS — WHERE EXTRA DWARFNESS AND EARLINESS WANTED	STANDARD EARLY VARIETY "ALL PURPOSE"	COMBINES MODERATELY TALL HABIT WITH EARLINESS	BEST FOR BACKGROUND OR "FOUNDATION" PLANTING
APPROX. BLOOMING DATE *	EARLY JULY UNTIL FROST	MID-JULY ON---	EARLY AUGUST ON---	MID-AUGUST ON---
VARIETIES	FIREBALL	ST. JOHN'S FIRE WHITE FIRE	BLAZE OF FIRE FIREBRAND ROSE FLAME	AMERICA-BONFIRE SPLENDENS TALL LILAC ROSE

* FROM APRIL 1ST SOWING — CHICAGO

Courtesy George J. Ball Co.

Ever wonder why some salvia plants blossom ahead of others? The reason is that some naturally bloom early. Select the variety you need. The shorter varieties bloom ahead of the taller types. The above chart tells you which do best in the times you want them to bloom.

SALVIA (Scarlet Sage)

Description and Uses: Few plants in a mass are more striking than a bed of salvia. You'll like the brilliant red flowers planted among evergreens, in borders or masses. But there is a world of difference in the habit of growth and blooming dates of the several types available, since there are three to select from—the early dwarf, the intermediate and the tall types which are usually later.

The early dwarf (12 inches tall) blooms from mid-July until frost. The intermediate type grows about 16 inches high, blooms from early August till frost. The late salvia blooms from mid-August until frost and grows 24 to 30 inches tall.

Green Thumb Care: Keep watered in summer.

Propagation: Start indoors in early spring. Do not plant outdoors until all danger of frost is over.

BLUE SALVIA

Description and Uses: Long graceful spikes with long stems in a most attractive shade of light blue, ideal for cutting. Plants require the same care as scarlet salvia and will continue to flower right up until late fall. Blue Salvia is really a semi-hardy perennial but blooms the first year from seed sown early. Plants grow 3½ feet tall. Sometimes ours will winter over, dying back to the ground in winter, then coming up again in spring. The flower spikes make a wonderful item for dried arrangements.

Problems: Neither Red nor Blue Salvia have any troubles.

SNAPDRAGONS (*Antirrhinum*—An-tir-rye-num)

Description and Uses: Available in a variety of excellent colors. Although there are talls and dwarfs, the medium height varieties are best for general purposes. The more you cut the spikes, the more the plants produce.

The hybrids are earlier to bloom, branch more freely and have an upright and stiff-stemmed habit of growth, enabling them to withstand moderate winds without support. Try the new tetraploids ("tetras"), a group which has larger flowers and taller, stronger stems than regular varieties. They are not rust-resistant, however.

Green Thumb Care: Plants will be "leggy" unless you pinch them back when 3 inches high. For husky seedlings, grow them cool. They will withstand frost after hardening.

Propagation: Sow indoors in March for outdoor planting. Sow in loose soil and cover lightly. Just sift fine peat moss or muck over the seed, otherwise you'll get poor germination. The seed is fine and has little "pushing up" power.

Problems: Rust. Reach for your dust gun if you see chocolate-brown puffs on the undersides of the leaves. Rust is the most serious disease of indoor and outdoor snaps. Dust with Ferbam, sulfur, Parzate or Zineb. If you use sulfur, try to keep it off the blooms as it bleaches or burns them. Weekly dusting during periods of rain, and fortnightly doses during dry weather will do the trick. It's always a good idea to dust when plants are young, to prevent rust from getting a foothold. Use rust-resistant varieties also.

Verticillium Wilt. If plants suddenly wilt, pull them up and burn them. Plant in a new location in well-drained soil.

Aphids. Spray with malathion.

STOCKS (*Matthiola*)

Description and Uses: Also called Ten Weeks Stock. Everyone likes the high, spicy fragrance of Stocks, but not everyone can get this plant to bloom outdoors. Stocks like cool weather and must be started indoors or they may not bloom when warm weather rolls around. Plants grow 15 to 18 inches high and are well branched. The so-called Double Ten Weeks Stock is a favorite for outdoor growing and blooms ten weeks after sowing. Flowers are ideal for vase arrangements and last a long time.

Green Thumb Care: Pound the stems with a hammer to help them take up water better. No pinching is necessary. Remove spent blossoms.

Propagation: Seed sown indoors or outdoors.

Problems: None.

SWEET PEAS (*Lathyrus*—Lath-ihr-russ—*odoratus*)

Description and Uses: Here's one of our most useful annuals. The Cuthbertson variety, a spring flowering strain, is quite heat-resistant. Zvolanek's

Floribundas and Multifloras are free-flowering and long-stemmed. Spencer types are good for the home garden, especially where summers are not too hot.

Green Thumb Care: Sweet peas need sunlight and plenty of water. Being a legume they need lime, applied at rate of ½ pound to a 15-foot row. Also add 1 pound of complete plant food to a 15-foot row. Pick flowers daily, otherwise vines will wither. If a single seed pod forms, the vine will die. Cut flowers in the morning before sun hits them. If blooms wilt after picking, hold stems under warm water and cut off an inch or two. They'll recover in thirty minutes. Support your vines early, when 4 inches high, because if they topple over they seldom do as well again. Chicken wire or twiggy branches stuck in both sides of the row give good support.

Propagation: Seed sown in fall or early spring. Dig soil deep, work in generous amounts of humus, but never manure. Sow seeds 2 inches apart in a furrow 2 or 3 inches deep, and cover lightly with loose soil. After plants are 4 or 5 inches high, give a side dressing of 5–10–5 fertilizer. A feeding of liquid plant food when they are in bud gives a longer blooming season.

Problems: Seed rot. Treat the seed with Captan, Spergon or other good fungicide. White seeds seem to rot more readily than the tinted ones, and very dark seeds usually have a harder coat and take longer to germinate. You can "nick" each seed with a file before sowing, or soak the seed in pure sulphuric acid for three minutes to hasten germination. If you try this, be sure to wash the acid off before sowing. If your seed rots in the ground, try "pre-sprouting" it. Place the seed in a moist medium, such as wet cotton or shallow pans of water for three to five days at 70 to 80 degrees.

Anthracnose. After a good start, leaves suddenly wilt and dry up before the blooms have a chance to develop. Control: First, it's a good idea to treat the seed in a 5 per cent formaldehyde solution for five minutes before planting; also, plant in a new spot. Burning debris in fall removes a fertile source of spores in the spring. Spray young plants with Captan.

Black Root Rot. Infected plants are dwarf, yellow and sickly. Diseased plants linger for long periods but fail to bloom. Control: Sterilize soil, use a new spot for growing.

Rhizoctonia Root Rot. Young plants are completely destroyed by damping off, causing uneven stands. Older plants are dwarfed and die, producing no blooms. Roots are decayed, becoming brown, not black as for Black Root Rot. Control: Same as for Black Root Rot.

Root Knot. Small galls on roots give a gnarled appearance. Plants dwarf and yellowish. Control: Sterilize the soil with methyl bromide.

Mildew. White, powdery growth on upper leaf surfaces, causing leaves to shrivel and fall. Control: Spray with Captan.

Mosaic. (Virus) Spread by aphids. The leaves curl and take on a distinct yellowish, mottled effect. Flower stalks short and color of blooms is broken. Control: Remove infected plants, spray with nicotine sulfate or Malathion to control aphids.

Bud Drop. Caused by lack of light or improper fertilization. Feed Balanced Plant Food.

Zinnia

Description and Uses: The zinnia is perhaps the best all-purpose annual we have in our gardens. In its native country, Mexico, it was called the "eyesore" plant because the original flowers were a dirty orange or a washed-out magenta color. The plant has been streamlined and hybridized so that we now have a bewildering color range and types to choose from. They bloom all summer.

Zinnias have been badly classified but, in a nutshell, here's a guide to go by:

Dahlia-Flowered Types—The most popular class. Large flowers with broad petals, resembling dahlias in appearance.

California Giants—Large flowers, essentially the same as dahlia-flowered.

Cactus Flowers—Large flowers with curled or twisted petals.

Cut-and-Come-Again or *Pumila*—Intermediate-sized flowers, very symmetrical heads, borne in profusion.

Pompon or *Lilliput*—Miniature 1- to 2-inch flowers, produced freely. Excellent for cutting.

Mexican—A distinct type with narrow leaves. Grows 18 inches tall, producing small button-type flowers in shades of crimson, mahogany, yellow, orange and bicolors. Flowers resemble small marigolds.

Green Thumb Care: The crown flower (first to appear) can be cut early, forcing the blooms on the side branches to grow larger. Give them full sun, almost any soil.

Propagation: Seed. Zinnia seeds germinate quickly from four to ten days, giving you flowers in about forty days after sowing. Seed started indoors and potted up in bands may even bloom quicker, although most gardeners have good luck sowing outdoors and transplanting. You can save your own zinnia seed after a frost has blackened the plants. Do not save hybrid seed. Store seed in glass jars until spring when they can be sown.

Problems: Alternaria Leaf and Blossom Blight. Dust with Sulfur or Parzate.

Mildew. A white, powdery discoloration of the foliage, starting in late summer. Sometimes causes leaves to curl up or plants to shrivel in dry weather. Control: Dust with sulfur, Bordeaux or Mildex regularly. Start early enough, before the disease strikes in the cooler days of fall when it's harder to lick. Add DDT or Malathion to the fungicide to kill the leaf-chewing insects also.

Tarnished Plant Bug. If blossoms open only halfway, chances are the trouble is due to tarnished plant bugs. This pest injects a poison into the plant whenever it stings, dwarfing or stunting the plant in the area of the sting. Control: Dust or spray with DDT for these, as well as for the leaf-chewing insects.

OTHER BONUS ANNUALS WORTH GROWING

The preceding list of annuals was shortened for the sake of brevity. There are dozens of other "blue ribbon" annuals I'd like to see you grow in your garden. These include Amaranthus (Joseph's Coat); Anchusa (Summer-forget-me-not); Balsam (Ladyslipper); Candytuft (Annual); Centaurea (Bachelor's Buttons); Centaurea (Dusty Miller); Chrystanthemum (Annual Painted Daisy); Clarkia; Datura (Angel's Trumpet); Dianthus (Annual Pinks); Eschscholzia (California poppy); Gaillardia (Annual Blanket Flower); Gomphrena (Globe Amaranth); Gypsophila (Baby's Breath); Helianthus annus (tall-growing sunflower); Helichrysum (Strawflower); Hibiscus (Annual mallow); Kochia (Summer cypress); Lavatera (Loveliness); Lobelia; Lunaria (Honesty, a biennial); Mirabilis (Four-O'clocks); Molucella laevis (Bells of Ireland); Nicotiana (Flowering tobacco); Nierembergia (Cup-flower); Papaver (Shirley poppy); Reseda (Mignonette); Ricinus (Castor bean); Salpiglossis (Painted tongue); Sanvitalia (Creeping Zinnia); Scabiosa (Pin-cushion flower); Schizanthus (Poor Man's Orchid); Statice (Sea Lavender, a half-hardy annual); Tithonia (Mexican Sunflower); Verbena; Vinca (Periwinkle).

Annuals for Poor Soil

Alyssum
Amaranthus
Balsam
Calendula
California Poppy
Calliopsis
Cornflowers
Four-O'clocks
Godetia
Nasturtium
Poppies
Portulaca

Annuals for Hot, Dry Places

Arctotis
Calliopsis
Centaurea (Cornflower)
Eschscholzia (California Poppy)
Gaillardia
Ipomoea
Phlox drummondii
Portulaca
Salvia
Statice
Zinnia

Annuals Which Tolerate Semi-Shade

Note: All annuals must have some sun. None will do well in full shade.

Alyssum
Aster
Balsam
Calliopsis
Coleus
Centaurea (Cornflower)
Cynoglossum
Godetia
Lobelia
Impatiens
Lupines
Myosotis (Forget-me-not)
Nasturtium
Nicotiana
Pansy
Petunia
Phacelia
Snapdragon
Salvia
Virginia Stock
Vinca
Viola

Annuals Which Do Well in Window Boxes

Ageratum
Alyssum
Centaurea (Dusty Miller)
Lobelia
Marigold
Nasturtium
Pansy
Petunia
Phlox (dwarf)
Portulaca
Salvia (dwarf)
Verbena
Zinnia

Summer Blooming Annuals for Rock Gardens

Alyssum
Gypsophila
Linum
Lupines
Pansy
Petunia
Phlox
Poppy
Portulaca
Silene
Statice
Verbena

Some Good Annual Vines

Balloon Vine
Cardinal Climber
Cobaea Scandens
Cypress Vine
Gourds
Hyacinth Bean
Moonflower
Morning Glory
Nasturtium
Scarlet Runner Bean

Annual Flowers for Cutting

Anchusa
Antirrhinum (Snapdragon)
Arctotis
Aster
Calendula
Calliopsis
Centaurea (Cornflower)
Chrysanthemum, annual
Clarkia
Cosmos
Cynoglossum
Gaillardia
Gypsophila
Larkspur
Marigold
Nasturtium
Nicotiana
Petunia
Phlox drummondii
Scabiosa
Statice
Stocks
Sweet Peas
Sweet Sultan
Verbena
Zinnia

Annuals for Fragrance or Odor

Alyssum—Sweet, delicate.
Garden Pinks
Heliotrope—Considered the par excellence of fragrance.
Marigold—Intolerable to some, agreeable to others.
Mignonette—Delightful to all.
Nasturtium—Admired by some.
Nicotiana—A delight in the evening.
Pansy—A refreshing fragrance.
Petunia—Heavy.
Phlox
Stock—Fresh, unusual fragrance.
Sweet Peas—Delicate, enjoyed by all.
Sweet Sultan—Delicate.
Verbena—Some have fragrance of trailing Arbutus.

The Following Annuals May Be Sown in the Fall

- Alyssum
- Anchusa
- Antirrhinum (Snapdragon)
- Aster
- Calendula
- California Poppy
- Candytuft
- Centaurea (Cornflower)
- Cleome
- Cosmos
- Cynoglossum
- Datura
- Dianthus
- Larkspur
- Portulaca
- Sweet Peas
- Shirley Poppy

It is wise to place a light evergreen mulch over beds of fall-sown plants. Let it be only an inch or so thick for it must not choke out the seedlings.

Low-Growing Annuals—6 to 8 Inches

- Ageratum, dwarf
- Alyssum
- Anagallis
- Lobelia, dwarf
- Lupine
- Marigolds, miniature
- Nemesia
- Nemophilia
- Nierembergia
- Phlox, dwarf
- Portulaca
- Verbena
- Virginia stock

Medium Annuals—1 to 2 Feet

- Ageratum, tall
- Aster
- Balsam
- Brachycome (Swan River Daisy)
- Calendula
- Calliopsis, dwarf
- Celosia, dwarf
- Clarkia
- Cynoglossum
- Dianthus (Pinks)
- Dimorphotheca (Cape Marigold)
- Eschscholzia (California Poppy)
- Four O'Clock
- Gaillardia
- Gilia
- Godetia, dwarf
- Gypsophila (Baby's Breath)
- Hunnemannia (Tulip Poppy)
- Iberis (Candytuft)
- Larkspur
- Marigold, dwarf
- Petunia, medium
- Salpiglossis
- Salvias
- Schizanthus, dwarf
- Statice
- Stock
- Zinnia, dwarf

Tall Annuals—2 to 3½ Feet

- Antirrhinum, tall (Snapdragons)
- Campanula (Canterbury Bells)
- Celosia, tall
- Centaurea
- Godetia, tall
- Gomphrena (Globe Amaranth)
- Helichrysum (Strawflower)
- Lupinus (Lupine)
- Marigold, tall
- Scabiosa
- Schizanthus, tall
- Shirley Poppy
- Zinnia

Very Tall Annuals—4 to 12 Feet

Amaranthus
Castor Bean
Cleome (Spider flower)
Cosmos
Helianthus, tall (Sunflower)
Hollyhocks (certain varieties)
Nicotiana (Flowering Tobacco)
Tithonia

Some "Hedge" Annuals

Balsam (Lady Slippers)
Celosia
Cosmos
Helianthus
Hollyhock
Kochia
Mirabilis
Moonflower
Ricinus
Tall Marigolds
Tithonia

Annuals Which Self-Sow

Anchusa
Balsam
Calendulas
California Poppy
Clarkia
Coreopsis
Cornflowers
Cosmos
Cynoglossum
Gypsophila
Larkspurs
Morning Glories
Nicotiana
Petunias
Portulaca
Shirley Poppy
Snow-on-the-Mountain
Sunflowers
Sweet Alyssum

Annuals for Sandy Soil

Balsam
California Poppies
Cockscomb
Coreopsis
Gaillardia
Marigolds
Nasturtiums
Petunias
Poppies
Portulaca
Summer Cypress
Sweet Sultan

Annuals Which Produce Foliage Effects

Amaranthus
Castor Bean
Cockscomb
Ornamental Grasses
Prickly Poppy
Snow-on-the-Mountain
Summer Cypress

Annuals Which Produce Everlasting Flowers

Acroclinium
Bells of Ireland
Blue Salvia
Cockscomb
Globe Amaranth
Rhodanthe
Strawflower
Thrift
Winged Everlasting

Annuals Which Bloom Throughout the Season if Successive Sowings Are Made

Baby's Breath
Bachelor's Button
Candytuft
Cape Marigold
Coreopsis
Forget-me-not
Love-in-a-mist
Mignonette
Petunias
Poppies

Frost-Proof Annuals

Bachelor's Button
Calendulas
California Poppy
Carnation
Dianthus
Larkspur
Lavatera
Mignonette
Nierembergia
Pansy
Petunias
Phlox
Scabiosa
Snapdragons
Stocks
Verbenas

Annual Plants for a Seashore Garden

Alyssum
California Poppy
Candytuft
Centaurea
Coreopsis
Dianthus
Gaillardia
Geranium
Larkspur
Nasturtium
Phlox drummondii

If you have fairly good topsoil you can grow practically all annuals successfully.

GREEN THUMB TIPS ON ANNUALS

"Pre-planted" flower gardens coming in various lengths of thin batting are no substitute for the old-fashioned way of starting and growing plants. Starting your own seeds in boxes or open soil is more fun and more practical than growing them in a plastic dish or a roll of batting.

Annuals are ideal for growing in among a foundation planting of both evergreens and non-evergreens.

Pinching out the centers of your annual seedlings after they are 3 or 4 inches high develops stockier, stronger plants.

Don't work in your flower beds on damp, cloudy days when your clothing may brush against plants and help spread disease.

Scattered single plants of any one kind of flower give a spotty effect in the garden. Three plants of a kind in a group should be the minimum even in the smallest grouping.

Most low-growing annuals which flower early (such as alyssum) should be sheared off when the seed heads start to appear "ragged." You'll get a second bloom.

Annuals in window boxes need water daily, and you should also remove faded blossoms for greater mileage.

Don't allow most plants to go to seed. It's a strain on the plants.

Flowers cut for indoors should be gathered in late afternoon and arranged in hot water (110 degs.).

Some annual seeds are fine and difficult to sow. A good idea is to mix the seed with five times its bulk of fine dry sand. Sow sand and all.

Hard-coated seeds such as sweet peas and morning glories start faster if soaked overnight in a teacup of water.

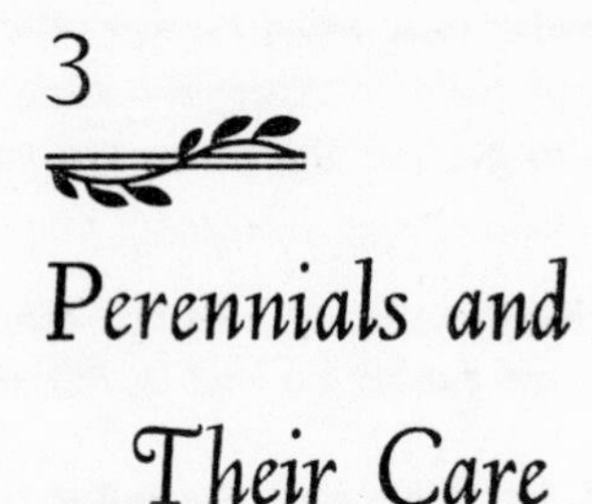

3

Perennials and Their Care

A perennial is a plant whose roots live in the ground year after year, even though the tops die down each fall. These nearly ever-living plants are treasured not only for their long life but for their early response to warm spring days which quickly produce a luxuriant growth of leaves, covering the bed with a welcome green color and serving as a natural background for the flower display.

Gardeners should keep in mind that there are hundreds of different kinds, and for best show you must do some careful selecting. Choose for size of plant and flower color; foliage habit is important, too, as are season and length of bloom. It takes time and effort to keep a perennial bed neat, so the main idea is to select a few of the best and easiest to grow.

Beginners might start with the seven so-called "backbone" perennials for a continuous flower display. These, in order of bloom, are: daffodils, tulips, iris, peonies, delphinium, perennial phlox and hardy mums. To these you may add others, governed by your space and energy. Don't be too enthusiastic to start with, because a perennial border can be like a runaway horse if you let it get the best of you.

Planning: Fall is an ideal time to get the perennial bed in shape for spring planting. Dig up the soil thoroughly, mixing in plant food and compost or any available humus. The more organic matter you can incorporate into a sandy soil (or clay) the better it will be. Soils that bake hard in the summer or which are poorly drained are apt to give you trouble later on if not corrected beforehand.

Make the perennial bed 4 or 5 feet wide and curve it for effect. A bed

5 feet wide is as large as can be worked without getting into it. Remember that perennials in masses are showier than when set out in a hit-or-miss fashion. And it doesn't do a bit of harm to repeat the same variety in a perennial bed. It will take years to get just the plants you want, so don't try to do it all in one year.

Soils: Hardy perennials thrive in a wide diversity of soils and conditions, but most of those preferred for the home garden do best in full sunlight and deep loamy soil.

Spade as early as the ground allows, but don't work the soil if it is too wet. If it adheres in a lump when squeezed in the hand, it's too wet to work. Tile drains are good for heavy water-logged soils or wet spots. Work coal ashes, sawdust, peat or similar materials into heavy soils, as described in our chapter on "Soils."

Green Thumb Care: Transplanting. A good general transplanting rule to follow is: Flowers that bloom in the fall are transplanted in the spring, and flowers that bloom in the spring are transplanted in the fall. If transplanting in early spring, do so before growth has started so they can become re-established before summer's heat overtakes them. Avoid late-fall planting, because the plants cannot become well established before freezing weather sets in. Flowers that bloom in mid-summer may be transplanted in spring or fall. In transplanting, keep as many roots as possible, digging a good-sized ball of soil with each plant, so that the roots are less disturbed.

Set plants firmly in the soil with the roots spread out to a depth slightly greater than they originally grew, and water well. Avoid hot windy days for transplanting. If the perennials have long tops, cut them back about ½ to ⅓ size so they won't droop and look messy.

Feeding. At dividing time it's a good idea to add a new supply of compost, manure, peat or other forms of organic matter to the soil. Use about 3 bushels per 100 square feet and work it in thoroughly. At the same time, add a balanced plant food such as 5–10–10 or similar analysis at about 3 pounds per 100 square feet. Liquid feeding is discussed in our chapter on "Liquid Plant Foods."

To feed a well-established perennial bed, make an application in early spring and another in mid-summer. Scatter dry plant food around the plants but don't get any on the foliage. Many gardeners like the liquid fertilizers applied to the foliage with sprinkling cans or hose attachments.

PROPAGATING PERENNIALS

Perennials are increased in many ways. For a detailed discussion see section under "Plant Propagation."

Dividing: Division is the simplest process for increasing and it helps to keep most perennials vigorous. The best time to divide is the proper time for transplanting—that is, fall-flowering plants in the spring and spring-flowering plants in the fall. Many, like garden mums, need division annually while others, such as phlox, iris and astilbe, should be divided every three years. If you find a hard, woody center when you lift the plants, discard it and use the younger sections, usually found on the outside edges.

Some perennials shouldn't be disturbed unless they are really overcrowded. These include Gas Plant, Bleedingheart, Oriental Poppy and Lupine. If they are doing well for you, don't molest them.

From Seed: This is a good way to get fine plants at low cost. Many can be sown in late fall, if you have a coldframe to keep them over winter where they will remain dormant for an early start in the spring. Don't sow in early fall, since the seed will germinate before winter sets in and you'll have many losses. Wait until October, November or even December. August is probably the latest date for planting perennial seeds outdoors for bloom the following year if a coldframe is not used.

Many perennial seeds, such as dictamnus, delphinium and certain rose species, germinate sooner and better if "stratified." This is done by mixing the seed with moist peat, sand or vermiculite and keeping it in the refrigerator for two or three months at a temperature of 35 degrees or so. This gives the same effect as planting the seed in a coldframe for the winter.

Rooting Cuttings: A simple and practical means of increasing plants. Take stem cuttings when the growth is young and tender, selecting shoots about 3 inches long. With a sharp knife, cut at or just below a node where a leaf joins the stem. Remove the bottom leaves and, if you wish, dip the ends in a root-inducing hormone powder. Place the cuttings about ⅓ their length in washed sand, perlite or vermiculite, press firmly around the base and water well. Encase the rooting pot or flat in a plastic bag (such as your dry cleaner brings you), which acts as a miniature green house. After the cuttings have rooted, pot them up or set them directly in the garden or coldframe.

Root Cuttings: Lift the plant and cut the best roots into pieces 2 inches long, place them in a sand-peat mixture and cover 1 inch deep. Some kinds which are originally nearest the parent stem will develop shoots at that end and roots at the opposite end. Others will throw out roots and shoots anywhere along the cutting.

Layering: Many perennials can be increased by "layering," which consists merely of placing stems in contact with the ground. Covering them with soil encourages rooting. You'll find more information on this process in the chapter on "Plant Propagation."

COLOR AND TEXTURE

The colors you select will vary greatly in their effect. For example, orange and scarlet are stimulating colors that will attract great attention. Greens are quiet and restful. Yellows are warm and invigorating. Blues are cool colors with greatest appeal in the warm midsummer months. There's no rule for arranging colors harmoniously, but one thing you can be sure of—white is the peacemaker in the perennial garden and makes other colors blend together better. You should have no more than two or three colors predominating at one time.

As for texture, the only point to keep in mind is that large-leaved, coarse-branched plants don't look well mixed with small-leaved, fine-twigged plants. One of the real pleasures of a perennial garden comes from rearranging plants from time to time and place to place to get better harmony of color, form and texture, as well as better seasonal effects.

CULTIVATING THE PERENNIAL BED

While many perennials are well adapted for naturalizing (that is, growing them without cultivation), most need timely care for best development. Frequent but shallow cultivation is best for keeping weeds down and the surface soil loose.

Mulching the Bed in Summer: A summer mulch not only makes the bed look sharper but cuts down on the need for weeding and watering. Where water is not available, a 3-inch summer mulch retains soil moisture and aids growth. (See section on "Mulches.")

Winter Mulching: Most hardy perennials like a winter mulch, although a good many gardeners who don't take the trouble still have good success. A winter mulch prevents the alternate freezing and thawing of the soil which causes your plants to "heave." Young or newly set plants are more likely to be affected. Protect them with hay, straw or evergreen branches right around the time of freezing weather.

Watering Perennials: Perennials do best in wet seasons or when plenty of water is made available. An inch of water a week is enough to maintain growth, and a lawn sprinkler can supply this amount in from 3 to 6 hours, moistening the soil to a depth of 8 inches or so, enough for a week's growth (except in unusually hot and dry weather). Avoid heavy daily waterings which make the ground soggy, as well as light sprinklings which encourage shallow root development. Apply as a heavy mist, only as fast as the soil can absorb it. Heavy sprinkling packs the soil and causes water to stand on the surface. Sprinkle during late afternoon rather than in the heat of the day when the sun evaporates much of it. Night watering is to be discouraged, since wet foliage at cool tempeartures encourages fungus diseases.

Pruning and Trimming Perennials: You can lengthen the blooming period of many perennials by removing old flower heads when they fade. Some early-flowering types often produce a second crop if tops are cut back following bloom. Any perennial which tends to grow out of bounds should be sheared back to keep it trim. When fall comes, tops are best cut and burned, since many insect and disease pests may harbor over winter in them.

(To control flower garden pests, see the section on "Insects and Disease" under annuals.)

BIENNIALS

A biennial is a plant that takes two growing seasons to complete its life cycle. It makes part of its growth one year, blooms the following year, sets seed and dies. Examples include Hollyhock, English Daisy, Canterbury Bells, Digitalis and Pansy.

Most biennials are started in a seedbed or coldframe in June or July, although some, such as Pansies, are best started in August. This gives a long enough season to grow good husky plants for bloom the following year. Biennials usually self-sow, and it's a good idea not to cultivate too vigorously around the plants if you want to save the seedlings. They are generally winter-hardy and need little if any protection, but a coldframe or straw mulch helps to keep young plants through the winter.

SOME OF THE BEST-KNOWN BIENNIALS

Botanical Name	Common Name	Color	Height (Ft.)	Bloom Date
Althaea rosea	Hollyhock	Various	6	July, August
Campanula medium	Canterbury Bells	Blue, pink, white, purple	3	June, July
Delphinium grandiflorum	Chinese Delphinium	Blue, white	2	June, July, August
Digitalis purpurea	Foxglove	Lavender, purple, white		June, July
Lunaria annua	Honesty	Purple, white	3	May, June
Salvia sclarea	———	Pink, blue	3	July, August
Verbascum (various species)	Verbascum	Pink, yellow	3	June, July
Viola tricolor var. *Hortensis*	Pansy	Various	½	May to September

PERENNIAL FAVORITES

While there are hundreds of perennials available, here are some you might want to consider first. Gardeners interested in an excellent book on perennials can find none better than *Contemporary Perennials* by Robert E. Lee and Roderick W. Cumming.

ALTHAEA ROSEA (Hollyhock)

Description and Uses: A biennial or semi-perennial. Must have full sun and lots of room, since it grows to 6 feet or more. Hollyhocks show to best advantage when grouped together in bold masses. Self-sows readily.

Green Thumb Care: Prefers rich, well-drained soils but does well in clay soils too. Since young plants are more vigorous, seed of the semi-perennial types can be sown each summer. Established plants resent being disturbed, but you can transplant young seedlings in the spring.

Propagation: By seed self-sown in August, or you can sow in the coldframe in February. After transplanting into open ground, plants will flower the same year. Seed can be obtained for extra-large, fully double flowers in lovely, delicate shades.

Problems: Hollyhock Rust. Causes leaves to turn yellow, wither and die. Spreads rapidly up the stalk in wet weather and shows badly when it's hot. Control: In fall, cut down and burn old stems. In spring, dust thoroughly with Zineb as soon as leaves start to show and continue once a week throughout the summer. Rust overwinters in dead leaves and a weed known as mallow or "cheeseweed." Eliminate these from the garden or lawn.

AQUILEGIA (A-kwee-*lee*-gee-a—Columbine)

Description and Uses: Grows 2 or 3 feet tall and blooms in May and June. Flowers are blue, yellow, pink, red and white. Ideal for border or rock garden. McKana's Giant Columbine is an All-America medal winner which we like. It has flowers 4 inches across and spurs almost as long. Good for cut flowers.

Green Thumb Care: Columbines have a tendency to peter out after two or three years. Pinch off the seed heads before they set, as this is one reason why the plant "disappears." However, you can allow a few seed pods to set to save for planting elsewhere.

Propagation: Increased by seed or by division of clumps in spring.

Problems: Leafminer insects may tunnel between the upper and lower leaf surfaces. Spray with lindane once a week.

CAMPANULA (Bellflowers)

Description and Uses: There are several Campanulas well worth trying. Canterbury Bells is a biennial. *Campanula persicifolia* (Peach-leaved Bellflower) is a noble plant for borders. Blue or white spikes of large, bell-shaped flowers from June to August, ideal for cutting.

Green Thumb Care: Give lots of water during the flowering period for giant stalks blooming at the same time as Foxglove, Sweet William and Garden Pinks.

Propagation: Seed is sown in outdoor seed beds in late spring or early summer. Move the seedlings to their flowering quarters by early fall.

Problems: Aphids. Spray with Malathion.

CHRYSANTHEMUM COCCINEUM (Pyrethrum or Painted Daisy)

Description and Uses: Red, pink and white flowers in June and July. Produces ideal cut flowers when grown in full sun. 2 to 3 feet tall.

Green Thumb Care: September is a good time to transplant. Keep faded flowers cut and you'll extend the flowering season. Likes a well-drained, moderately fertile soil.

Propagation: By seed and division. Oddly enough, the double-flowering pyrethrum will often produce single or semi-double flowers the first year after transplanting, but the following year the flowers will be fully double. No serious troubles.

CHRYSANTHEMUM MORIFOLIUM (Garden Mums)

Description and Uses: No other perennial gives us so much variation of color and plant type in the fall, after the blossoming period of most other flowers has passed. Hundreds of good varieties are available, so you shouldn't try to grow mums that bloom too late and freeze before the buds have a chance to open. Mums may be grouped according to the blooming period as follows: (1) Very early, starting in August. (2) Early, beginning between the middle and end of September. (3) Medium early, beginning the first of October. (4) Medium late, beginning the first and second week of October and (5) Late, starting to bloom after the middle of October. The largest and most colorful mums grow in October when nights are cool and humidity is high. 2 to 3 feet tall.

Green Thumb Care: They like a loose, sandy soil that's neutral or slightly acid, lots of sun and good drainage. Spade in plenty of humus such as compost or well-rotted manure (3 to 5 bushels) per 200 square feet. Have the soil worked up loosely with a little peat before transplanting. I like to feed outdoor mums liquid plant food when I set them out, and later when in bud stage.

Pinching Mums: The most neglected operation in growing mums is pinching. Without it they grow tall and spindly. Briefly, here's all there is to it—when plants are about 6 inches tall, pinch off the top 2 inches of new growth. This stimulates new growth to break out from the first several leaf nodes so that each stem has many stalks. Pinch again when new

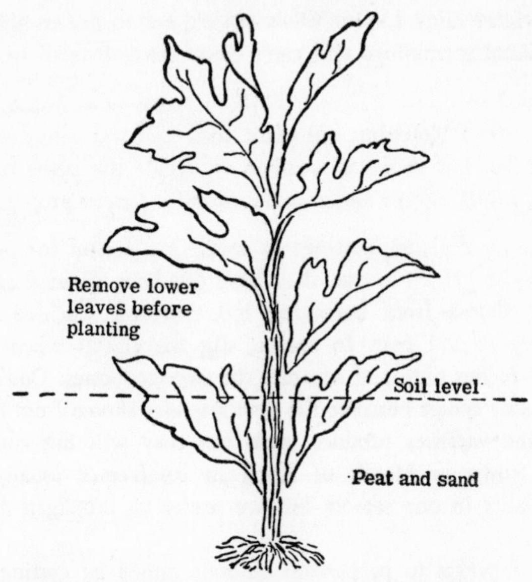

Pot your rooted cuttings in a loose mixure.

shoots are 6 inches long, but don't pinch after late July, as they may not bloom before frost. Cushion types and so-called Azalea-mums need no pinching since they branch naturally.

Protect Blooms from Early Frost: Even though garden mums can withstand cold weather, frost will damage open blossoms. You can prevent this by covering plants with sheets, old burlap sacks or plastic mulch on frosty nights. When you see the frost starting to melt in the morning, remove the covering.

Wintering Your Mums: It's been our experience that mums come through the winter with no mulch at all. Although they are not altogether hardy, it's not the cold that kills them, but rather excessive water around the roots and fluctuating temperatures. If your soil is well drained, your plants will probably winter over successfully without any extra care. If it is heavy and poorly drained, lift the plants with the soil clinging to the roots and place them in a cool, dry place, such as under the eaves of a building or a coldframe where they can remain until spring. Some gardeners, when their soil is heavy and wet, just dig their clumps and place them on top of the ground. It's a good idea to mulch these lifted mums in case of winter rains. Do not allow the clumps to dry completely, however. Occasional sprinklings will carry them through until spring.

Care of Potted or Florist's Mums: Florist's mums need lots of water and bright light. After blooming, cut plant back half-way and keep in cellar until spring. Set out in warm weather, or divide the plant and grow in pots. In fall, bring indoors and they'll flower for you at proper time.

Propagation: By division, cuttings or seed. One reason for poor growth of mums in the garden is that they have not been divided each year to prevent the shoots from becoming too crowded. Cushion mums are divided every second year. In spring, dig the clump when the young shoots are 3 inches high and separate the strongest ones. Don't use those from the woody center but save the young tender shoots from the outside.

Seed: Some varieties produce seeds but they will not come true to type. Seeds sown in March or April in coldframes usually produces flowering plants in one season, but we prefer to propagate by cuttings or division.

Cuttings: I prefer to perpetuate outdoor mums by cuttings taken in March or April from plants heeled in an unheated greenhouse or coldframe all winter. Simply cut tips 2 or 3 inches tall from husky growing shoots, making your cut a bit below a leaf joint, and remove the bottom leaves. Insert cuttings in a box of sand, perlite, vermiculite or other rooting mixture and keep moist. They will root quickly and can be set outdoors or transplanted into pots and allowed to grow larger before planting in the garden. Do not allow them to get dry.

Problems: Foliar Nematode. Probably the worst pest of garden mums, Nematodes are microscopic eelworms which readily spread from one plant to another, causing the lower leaves to turn bronze, then black, and die. Nematodes are worse in wet seasons when they spread more freely. Once inside the leaf, they are difficult to reach, so the best way to deal with them is to avoid splashing water from the soil and to remove dead leaves and burn them before they fall. Branches containing a number of dead leaves should be removed and burned.

Tarnished Plant Bug. Punches many "shotgun" holes in leaves, stings growing tips and flower buds. Control: Keep new growth protected with DDT or Malathion.

Aphids. Soft-bodied lice, cause twisting and curling of shoots. Control: Nicotine sulfate, 1 teaspoonful in 2 quarts of water to which a pinch of soap has been added, or Malathion.

Leafrollers. Small worms feeding on undersides of leaves. Upper part of leaf is untouched, appears as a parchment-like film. Control: DDT.

Red Spider Mites. Hard to see with the naked eye. They infest the tips of shoots and cause curled leaves and stunted growth. Control: Aramite or Malathion.

Leafminer. Larvae feed within tissues. Mines appear as white lines or blotches. Control: Malathion, 1 teaspoonful to a quart of water.

Leaftier. Larvae eat soft tissues on underside of leaves, feeding between lightly woven silken webs. Control: DDT, Lindane or Malathion.

Corn Earworm. In fall, corn earworms often eat buds. Control: DDT, 50 per cent wettable powder, as soon as the worm is seen.

Chrysanthemum Midge. Maggots bore into the stem or flower, causing cone-shaped galls ½-inch long. Control: Nicotine sulfate, 1 teaspoonful to 2 quarts of water, or Malathion.

Thrips. They rasp leaf tissue and are troublesome especially if gladiolus or onions are grown nearby. Control: Keep lightly covered with DDT or Malathion.

Spittlebug or Froghopper. Small yellowish-green insects live inside a mass of froth which they generate to protect themselves. They suck plant juices, reducing the vigor of the plant. Control: Lindane dust or spray is effective.

Leaf Spot. If mum leaves are peppered with dark brown or black spots, the trouble is due to leaf-spot disease. It usually appears in July and becomes increasingly worse until fall. Control: Start spraying early in July and repeat at seven- to ten-day intervals until bloom. Use Ferbam or Captan. In the fall, rake and burn all parts of the plants above ground, since the fungus winters over in debris. Drench plants and soil with Bordeaux or Ferbam.

Rust. Chocolate brown pustules on the undersides of the leaves mean rust is present. Control: Spray with sulfur or Captan at weekly intervals.

Mildew. If leaves look floury, the plant has mildew, common in the cool moist weather of fall. Control: Sulfur spray or dust, maneb or bordeaux mixture to which is added 2 teaspoonfuls of Malathion per gallon. This kills aphids and controls many fungus diseases of mums.

Verticillium Wilt. Infected plants show yellowing, wilting, dying of leaves from base upward. Plants may be stunted, killed. Brown streaks can be detected inside the stems. Control: Plant-resistant varieties, propagate from disease-free cuttings rather than by root division. Sterilize infected soil with formaldehyde. Do not grow susceptible types.

Septoria or Black Spot. A fungus disease, serious enough to defoliate some varieties. Foliage shows black spots or blotches. Control: Use Ferbam or Bordeaux.

Stunt. A virus disease, very slow to express its symptoms. Destroy all stock of a variety which shows dwarfing, lighter green foliage and flowering seven to ten days prematurely. Pink, red or bronze flowers are faded in comparison to healthy plants. No control known, but keep aphids in check as they spread virus diseases.

Grey Mold (Botrytis). Causes brown, water-soaked spots on flower petals. Control: Spray plants daily with Captan.

Crown Gall. Swollen growths on stems near soil level. Control: Use clean stock and a new soil location. Avoid splashing tops of plants. Prune out infected stems, using a knife or scissors dipped in formaldehyde or anti-freeze alcohol.

Yellows. Flowers become entirely or partly green. Plants are stunted, leaves show slight yellowing, especially the margins. Control: This is a virus spread by leafhoppers, so spray plants with DDT or Malathion. Try not to grow mums near annual asters.

Ray Blight. Causes a high proportion of diseased flowers to open lopsided. Half the petals turn brown or black and stick together, and rot may progress from ½ inch to several inches downward into the flower stalk. A characteristic symptom: falling of the petals when the blossom is shaken. Attacks only chrysanthemums, so far as is known. Control: Bury or burn all debris. Sterilize the soil with steam, chlorpicrin or methyl bromide. Leave infected gardens or fields idle for a year or two, preferably fallow, so that no volunteer mums or other possible hosts will keep the fungus growing. Do not propagate from infected plants.

DELPHINIUM ELATUM (Common Delphinium)

Description and Uses: A superb, tall accent plant for border or background. Flowers are blue, purple and white, pure colors with some pink shades. Grows 4 to 6 feet tall in rich soil and sunny location. Many gardeners get the terms "delphinium" and "larkspur" confused. Strictly speaking, "larkspur" is the common name for all species of delphinium, but in everyday horticulture, "delphinium" is used as the common name for the perennial species and "larkspur" for the annuals.

Green Thumb Care: Any soil that's well drained is suitable for growing delphiniums. Root rot is worse in heavy soils, and those containing high amounts of organic matter should be avoided. More important is regular feeding with a balanced plant food, either in dry or liquid form. When preparing the soil, work in about 4 pounds of a 5–10–10 brand in each 100 square feet.

Plants can be moved in spring, summer or early fall, and still make good growth. Your best bet is to move them with a ball of earth and set them in a hole large enough to accommodate the entire clump. Cover the crown lightly (1 inch of soil) and press down firmly. Water each clump thoroughly. Feed delphiniums in early spring and again about June or July when the shoots start growth for the second bloom. Or you can use a liquid feeding about once a month. Most delphinium will bloom a second time if plants are cut back to a foot from the ground after first flowers have withered. After cutting a bloom for indoor arrangements, bend over the end of the cut stalk to prevent rainwater from entering the crown. Moisture held around the crown will encourage disease .

You cannot grow good delphinium spikes without staking or fencing the plants. I stake mine with tomato stakes, just when the plants begin to bud. Delphinium stalks are hollow and winds or rains are sure to break your spikes if you do not stake them.

Propagation: Mostly by seeds but also by division and sometimes by cuttings. Good results are obtained by planting seeds in coldframes or deep flats filled with a 50–50 mixture of garden loam and sand. We like to sow in the ground in spring for husky plants next year. Seed germinates best at a temperature of 55 degrees and takes about 21 days. For this reason, summer-sown delphinium will require a two-week refrigerator treatment. Store the seeds in the refrigerator at a temperature of 40 to 50 degrees or sow the seed in a small pot and place pot and all in the refrigerator. Faulty germination is due to old seed as it loses its viability in a few months unless stored under proper conditions.

Heavy soils should not be used. Sow in midsummer as soon as fresh seed is available. Plant ¼ inch deep. The soil surface may be kept moist by covering with clean burlap or by shading with burlap or muslin. Subirrigation of flats with Fiberglas wicks is excellent. When seedlings have reached their first true leaves, they are potted or "flatted" (planted in boxes) and placed in a coldframe for the winter. Larger seedling plants are left outdoors for winter. They are perfectly hardy, although highly susceptible to wet feet. Coldframe plants can be transplanted into their permanent location, the sunniest part of your garden. Shade is taboo because of mildew which turns the leaves brown.

Clumps of delphinium can be divided by digging clumps and cutting them into sections, each of which has at least one good eye and well-developed roots. This is preferably done in early spring or late summer.

Problems: Sclerotium or Crown Rot. A very destructive disease which causes the plant suddenly to wilt and die. The infected spike is blackened at the base and there may be a web-like fungus at the crown. Control: Infected plants should be dug up and destroyed. Other delphinium plants should not be set in the same place. Setting the plants on a low ridge so that water drains quickly away from the crown helps to prevent infection. When only a part of the plant is diseased, sterilize the soil around the clump, drenching with Semesan or bi-chloride of mercury solution.

Cyclamen Mite. One of the worst pests. It causes distortion of shoots and blackening of infested spikes. Control: Cut off infested spikes and spray plants with Malathion.

Mildew. Delphinium is susceptible to mildew disease, infecting the leaves. Control: Keep plants dusted with sulfur or Karathane and don't let them grow too close together. If they are in shade, move them to full sun.

DIANTHUS BARBATUS (Sweet William)

Description and Uses: Handled as a biennial, seed is sowed in spring and seedlings are transplanted in early fall to their flowering quarters. It may self-sow freely, grows 18 inches tall, and flowers in June or earlier. A medley of color and form, doing best in full sun.

D. LATIFOLIUS (Garden Pinks)

Another member of the carnation family, worthy of trying. Grenadin is a strain of hardy carnations in mixed colors and is larger-flowered than many of the older varieties. Even the annual types are hardy enough for sub-zero weather if protected with evergreen boughs. 10 to 12 inches tall.

D. PLUMARIUS (Cottage Pinks)

Description and Uses: Sweet-scented, double, semi-double and single flowers ideal for rock gardens, if in full sun. A delight in any garden. 12 inches tall.

Green Thumb Care: Garden Pinks and "Carnations" love cool weather. They do not make good house plants, and summer flowers are not ordinarily as handsome as fall blooms, but if you keep the roots cool by mulching and watering, you'll get a good crop of blooms. They prefer a well-drained soil, full sun and a chance to ripen off in fall. Don't feed them after August so that the plants can harden up for winter. They need winter protection, and the best material is evergreen boughs which allow air to circulate.

Propagation: By seed in spring or fall, also by cuttings or division. Seed sown outdoors in early July will bloom the following summer, or sow indoors in March in shredded sphagnum moss or a soil mixture of ⅓ sand, ⅓ leafmold and ⅓ loam. Seedlings are transplanted into boxes, spacing about 2 inches apart or into small peat pots. In May, peat pot and all may be set outside. Water after planting and pinch out growing tips to induce branching.

Problems: Red spider. Use Malathion.

DICENTRA SPECTABILIS (Bleeding Heart)

Description and Uses: Grows 3 feet tall with red and white flowers, appearing in May and June. Best in semi-shade but tolerates full sun. Ideal for planting in clumps. Blooms from spring to mid-season, then dies down to the crown. Many other species are available for the home gardener.

Green Thumb Care: Large bushes with no bloom mean that plants are getting too much shade or possibly that soil is too rich or moist.

Propagation: By division. In fall or early spring, chop the clump with an axe into divisions. Replant, supplying ample water. Mulch the first winter with evergreen boughs to prevent heaving, especially if there is clay in the soil. You can also make root cuttings in spring or fall. Root in sand or a sand and peat mixture.

DIGITALIS (Foxglove)

Description and Uses: Grows 3 to 4 feet tall with big, bell-shaped flowers in heads 3 feet long. Colors range from white to pale pink to deep rose in June, and many of them are spotted.

Green Thumb Care: Thrives in full sun or partial shade and is benefited by a straw mulch after freezing weather sets in in the fall. If foxglove does not bloom the second year, they often bloom the third. The drug (digitalis) is poisonous in overdoses and is obtained from the second year's young leaves. To gather seed, pick capsules from the lower part of the stem as soon as brown and before they shed. Excelsior hybrids are a great improvement over the old Shirley hybrids.

Propagation: By seed sown out of doors in late spring and transplanted in early fall to its flowering quarters. The coarse foliage remains green all winter.

Problems: Leaf spot. Dust with Captan.

GAILLARDIA ARISTATA (Blanket Flower)

Description and Uses: One of the best perennials. Grows 3 feet high in full sun. Ideal for cut flowers from June through September. Tolerates hot weather.

Green Thumb Care: If old flower heads are removed and the plant fed and watered regularly, you have one of the most productive plants for cut flowers. It fails to survive the winter if grown in rich, heavy clay soils. Good drainage is the most important factor here.

Propagation: By seed in spring for bloom the same year. Also by division in the spring.

Problems: None.

GYPSOPHILA PANICULATA (Babysbreath)

Description and Uses: Grows 3 feet tall with white flowers in July and August and has fine-textured opposite leaves. Bristol Fairy has great clouds of starry flowers in feathery panicles, ideal for cutting. Blooms all summer. 3 feet tall in full sun.

Green Thumb Care: The generic name Gypsophila or "chalk plant" refers to its preference for lime soils. If soil reaction is lower than pH 6, ground limestone should be added so that the reading is pH 7 or more.

Propagation: Both single and double Babysbreath may be started from seed in spring. Of the double varieties, about 50 per cent will be double flowers. You can transplant young plants early in the spring, but be sure to get a big ball of earth. If transplanted in the fall, they are apt to heave out of the ground. No serious troubles.

HEMEROCALLIS (Daylily)

Description and Uses: Daylilies have advantages not found in any other plant. They are easy to grow; they resist heat and dry spells, and wet seasons do not injure the roots. They are disease-resistant and you don't have to spray them. If you neglect them, they outdo the weeds. A good selection of varieties will produce bloom from early spring to late fall. 2 to 3 feet tall.

Common daylilies come in a variety of shades of red, orange, yellow and brown. The flowers last only a day but are replaced by new ones the next morning. Give them plenty of room, 2 feet per plant. Dividing them every third year promotes bloom.

Green Thumb Care: Although daylilies are toughies, they do respond to feedings, so apply a little plant food, such as 5–10–5 fertilizer, about 2 pounds per 100 square feet to improve bloom size. They get better and better each year, but they like to be kept from overcrowding each other, so if yours are matted together, separate them and they will reward you with better plants and blooms.

Propagation: By division any time. Do not plant too deep and water well after setting them out.

Problems: None.

HEUCHERA SANGUINEA (Coral Bells)

Description and Uses: A prolific bloomer, fine for hardy border or rock garden. Grows 1½ feet tall with tiny red, pink and white flowers from May through September. Excellent for cutting and lends an airy gracefulness to bouquets.

Green Thumb Care: Likes a moist, rich, sandy soil in full sun or partial shade. Transplant every three years or when the center of the clump starts to die out. Straw mulch in winter may be needed. Does well in a variety of soils with no special treatment. Blossoms have good keeping qualities when cut and are ideal in floral arrangements.

Propagation: By seed or division in early spring.

Iris

Description and Uses: "German" or tall Bearded Iris (Fleur-de-lis) offers broad masses of blue, purple, white, yellow, red and intermediate hues, coming on in May and June. They can be planted any time from June through September, and you'll get better results if you divide the clumps and reset them every four years. Iris like a sunny, well-drained spot. If your soil is mostly clay, add organic matter to encourage fast drainage.

Green Thumb Care: These plants don't need much feeding. Bonemeal is good, but don't use manure or a heavy nitrogenous fertilizer, because of the danger of soft growth which eventually leads to rot. Superphosphate applied two or three weeks before flowering, plus a side dressing of bonemeal in late June, will help your iris. Bearded types are referred to as "Pagoniris." If you set out iris in the summer, give some covering with evergreen boughs for winter, removing the covering when growth starts in the spring. The wide-spread belief that iris need lime is erroneous. They do well in neutral or even slightly acid soils. Repeated heavy applications of lime seem to promote iris rot and we see no need for it.

Whenever your iris fails to bloom, chances are the plants are overcrowded. Thin out every three or four years by digging up crowded rhizomes here and there. Those you do not disturb will bloom profusely if others are thinned.

Propagation: In cutting the divisions, remove the old growth, trim the roots back some and cut the foliage in fan-shaped fashion to make the planting job neater. Avoid deep planting. Set the rhizomes just barely below the surface of the ground, within reach of the sun's rays, with roots well spread out. Plant from 8 inches to 2 feet apart.

Problems: Leafspot. Oval spots with watersoaked margins. Control: Dust with fermate and remove and burn the old leaves in the fall. This is an important factor in growing iris, since the foliage carries over disease spores and insect eggs.

Iris Borer. Overwinters in eggs pasted to dead leaves. The eggs hatch in May and the larvae crawl up the plants, and make pin-prick holes in the leaves, gnawing their way through them, down the stalks and into the rhizomes, where great tunnels are made, causing serious damage to the plant. Control: Look for "sawdust" on the stalks or rhizomes. It shows

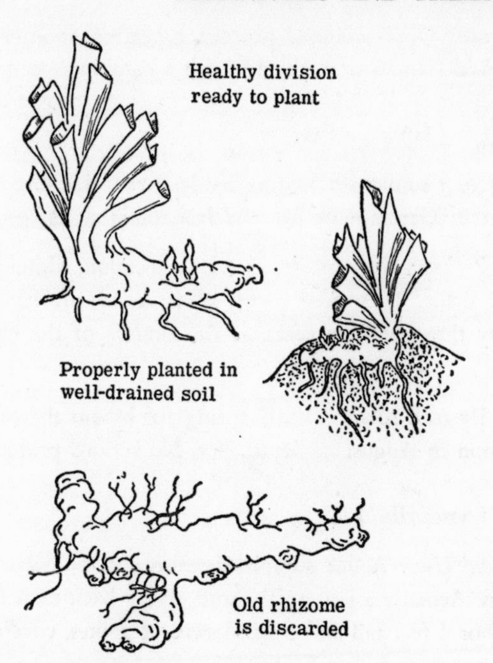

Best time to divide iris is after the blooming season has finished. Divide and replant every 2 or 3 years for best results.

the borer is there, and it can be cut out with a knife. Then apply Ferbam and Chlordane around the roots.

Soft Rot. This disease causes the whole rhizome except the outer skin to become mushy. Bacteria live from year to year in infected rhizomes and most new infections take place through wounds. Usually the iris borer paves the way for infection. Control: Cut the leaves back in a fan shape to about 6 inches, and burn the trimmings. Lift the clumps and cut out and destroy all rotted portions. Soak the rot-free parts in a 1 to 1,000 corrosive sublimate solution (¼ tablespoon to a gallon of water) for ten minutes, then plant in a new location or drench the soil with the solution, using one pint per square foot and repeating in ten days. Shallow planting retards rot.

While you have your iris dug, cut out any borers in the base of the leaves or in the core. It's a grub-like worm, cream to pinkish in color. It overwinters as eggs on old dead leaves. Dust the rhizomes with DDT, Captan or Ferbam. In May or earlier, spray plants when 6 inches high with 50 per cent DDT wettable powder, repeating at intervals of seven to ten days. Add Captan or Ferbam or use a combination spray.

IRIS KAEMPFERI (Japanese Iris)

One of the best summer-blooming hardy perennials. Grows 3 feet tall, blooms after the "German" or Bearded Iris and is at its best in July.

Green Thumb Care: They prefer a sunny location, although they may exist in some shade. They need plenty of water up until flowering time. Separate every three or four years, as the centers of the clumps usually start to die.

Propagation: By seed sown in early spring for bloom the following year. Also by division in August or September. No serious problems.

LYTHRUM ("Loosestrife")

Description and Uses: A fine summer-flowering perennial with pink and purple flowers. Actually a perennial shrub, dying back each fall. Morden's Pink grows 3 or 4 feet tall and bears dozens of spikes, covered with deep pink florets from June to late September.

Green Thumb Care: Good for sunny spots, poor soils or partial shade. Easy to grow with no disease or insect problems.

Propagation: Readily accomplished by root division.

LUPINUS

Description and Uses: Thrives in almost any soil, but it must be well-drained. Pea-like flowers—rose, orange, deep yellow and blue—grow 3 to 4 feet tall on long spikes.

Green Thumb Care: The tall spikes wilt in arrangements but cutting spikes in early morning and using warm water makes this less likely. After the first bloom is gone, you can cut the plants back and often get a second showing of flowers.

Propagation: Sow seed in June for bloom the following June or start indoors in pots of sand and peat in early spring. As soon as the roots start to fill the pot, shift them to their permanent location. Soaking seed overnight before planting is helpful. Lupines are tap-rooted and do not divide or transplant well.

Problems: Root Rot. When lupines wilt and the roots turn brown or black and rot, the trouble is due to root rot disease, a condition more prevalent in periods of wet weather and in soils that are poorly drained. Lupines must have a well-drained soil. Control: Once wilting starts there's no control. Change to a new spot where the soil is treated with Captan or Zineb.

Leaf and Stem Rot. The bottom leaves and stems are first attacked and become spotted, turning yellowish green. The leaves die rapidly from the base upward. Control: Cut back the plants and burn all fallen leaves. Spray with Captan.

Aphids can be a problem to lupines also, but they are easily licked by spraying with nicotine sulfate, 1 teaspoonful to 2 quarts of soapy water, or Malathion.

PHLOX PANICULATA (Garden Phlox)

Descriptions and Uses: A perfectly hardy perennial and one of the easiest to grow, blooming in late summer and fall. Flowers are in various colors: reds, purples, salmons, white and orange. In fact, so many horticultural varieties have been introduced that it would bewilder the average gardener when it comes to selection. Plants usually grow 4 feet tall.

Green Thumb Care: When a phlox changes color, baffled gardeners believe the plant reverts, although this is not true. When blues or pinks change to a lighter color, it is because the faded blooms have been allowed to go to seed, and the seedlings, which never come true with any plant, have crowded out the parent plant. Remove the blooms as soon as they are past their prime, also divide the plants every three years to keep them in a healthy growing state.

Propagation: Division is preferred, since they will not come true from seed. Plants are divided in the spring. To separate the clumps, lift them and shake the soil loose. They can then be pulled apart, and each stem with its roots, separated from the others, is ready for replanting. Or you can simply cut the clump into four or more sections with a spade or sharp knife, making sure each division has about four eyes or buds. Reset at the same depth they grew and water thoroughly. These divisions will bloom for you next year.

Set phlox about 1½ feet apart and just about an inch below the surface. The roots should be planted straight down. When the plants lose their vigor and the flowers their brilliance, divide the clumps again.

Problems: Powdery Mildew. A whitish mold on leaf surfaces is telltale evidence of this pest. It thrives best in damp weather. Control: Dust with sulfur or spray with wettable sulfur, 2 tablespoons to a gallon of water, plus ⅓ teaspoonful of detergent. Mildex is also a good mildew killer. The secret is to start early in the season. Cut old stems back early in the fall and burn them, as the fungus overwinters in old infected leaves.

In spring, just as new growth is coming out, keep it protected with a copper spray repeating once a week until the blooms appear; or use sulfur.

Red Spider. When leaves curl under, look for red spider. This minute pest cannot tolerate moisture and drowns easily. A strong hose spray from below breaks up their webs and does a good job of eliminating this tiny marauder. Sulfur dust kills them too, as will Malathion.

Leafspot. Appears as brown spots, first on the lower leaves which turn brown and die. It works its way gradually up the stem. Control with maneb or sulfur.

Nematodes. Cause stems to swell and crack and leaves to become brown and crinkled. May prevent blossoming. Control: Remove plants and surrounding soil and destroy.

PHLOX SUBULATA (Moss Pink or Creeping Phlox)

Description and Uses: Masses of magenta, pink, purple, red and white flowers. Thrives in dry, unfertile soils in exposed situations and is excellent for rocky slopes or rock gardens. 4 inches high.

Propagation: Readily propagated by cuttings or by dividing the clumps any time in spring or fall.

PAEONIA (Peony)

Description and Uses: There are two broad types of peonies: (1) herbaceous, whose colors range from pink, white, red, and even a yellow with single, double, semi-double, Japanese, and anemone-type flowers; and, (2) the tree peony, or the wood shrub type, growing 5 or 6 feet tall.

Green Thumb Care: Peonies like a well-drained soil. Heavy soils can be loosened with peat or compost before planting. The best time to plant them is in September or October. Depth of planting is important. Do not cover eyes too deeply (about 1 inch). Go easy on plant food for peonies. Too much feeding makes lush growth and weak stems, with few or no flowers. You get your best stalks if plants are supported with a wire fence. Best blooms are on plants in full sun, but colors last longer when given some shade. Disbudding is not necessary, although if you want larger flowers it's simple. Just remove the side buds (near the base of the large end bud) when they are pea-size, leaving the one center bud.

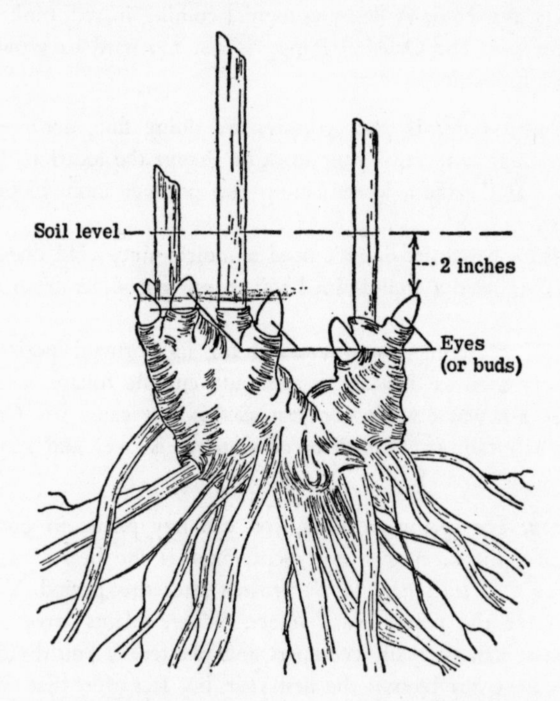

Peonies are best divided in autumn. Avoid deep planting as it produces lots of top growth, usually few or no flowers.

Propagation: By seed or division in fall. Peonies are plants that do not need to be divided frequently. About every eight or ten years is enough. Make sure each division has an eye or two.

Problems: Botrytis blight, causes buds to dry or blast. Avoid use of manure. Spray plants in spring with Captan, Ferbam or Parzate. Cut yellowed foliage down in fall and burn.

Ants. Harmless, feeding on honeydew material secreted by bugs and aphids. Control with chlordane.

Leaf spot. Controlled by sanitation in fall.

Failure to bloom. Due to shade, deep planting. Heavy heads due to rains, requiring supporting the bushes. Some cultivars are notoriously weak-stemmed.

PAPAVER ORIENTALIS (Oriental Poppy)

Description and Uses: A flashy perennial coming in red, pink and white, 2 to 3 feet tall. The Oriental Poppy is not too hard to grow once you understand its habits.

Green Thumb Care: If your poppies are doing fine, don't touch them unless you want to increase your stock or change the location. They resent disturbance and make a larger clump and produce more blooms as they grow older.

This tough perennial doesn't need a mulch, since cold does not affect it, but it does need a well-drained soil to prevent water from rotting the crowns.

Hot, baking summers are required for its dormant period. Remove seed pods as soon as they are formed and cut the foliage when it turns brown. Do not water while dormant as this may cause rot. Green leaves appear in the fall, after the heat of summer is over and stay green all winter.

Propagation: For spring planting, you can buy plants in pots to avoid transplanting shock. August and September is the best time to handle them, since they start next year's growth after this period. You can dig up and move the entire plant intact. Where plants have some small crowns, these can be easily cut apart and planted. If you divide severely, you won't have any blooms the first year, but lots after that. When roots are 12 to 14 inches long, cut them off 6 inches below the crown and plant these cuttings also. You'll get double the number of plants this way. A 6-inch root as thick as a lead pencil will produce one bloom next spring. Set the pieces about 2 feet apart, making sure the end of the piece nearest the crown is uppermost and about 1 inch below the surface. Fresh green leaves will show up in about a month.

Problems: Bacterial Blight. Causes black lesions on stems, leaves, floral organs and seed pods. Tissues between the spots turn yellow, then brown, and the leaf falls. Stems are often girdled and die. Control: Destroy plants as soon as you see this. Use clean soil.

Aphids and other pests can be controlled with Malathion.

PAPAVER NUDICAULE (The Iceland Poppy)

Description and Uses: One of the best of the smaller perennial poppies and a very early-flowering type. It is not hardy enough to be a good perennial in cold areas, however. Two feet tall with wide range of colors and flowers, 2 to 3 inches in diameter.

Green Thumb Care: If blooms are cut early in the morning and the stems are seared, they make good cut flowers. They will bloom all summer if not allowed to go to seed.

Propagation: By seed sown in the spring outdoors. Blooms the first year.

Problems: None serious.

PRIMULA (Primrose)

Description and Uses: Clusters of small flowers in lavender, white, pink and red. Plants grow 1 to 2 feet tall and tolerate shade. They are excellent for the shaded, moist corner or north border.

Green Thumb Care: Primroses prefer shade, a soil rich in organic matter and reasonably cool weather. The crowns of the plant should be kept high and dry, but the roots should always be able to reach moisture. Abundant moisture during the summer is essential to good growth for future flowering. Plant is trouble-free.

VERONICA LONGIFOLIA VAR. SUBSESSILIS (Speedwell)

Description and Uses: An excellent item for the border, rock garden or flower garden. Grows 2 to 3 feet tall and blooms from June through September. Its spikes of deep blue flowers are ideal for floral arrangement.

Green Thumb Care: Will grow in ordinary soils and withstands hot weather well. Some varieties have weak stems that need support. Veronicas tend to raise their crowns when left in the same place for three or four years, so it's a good idea to dig the plant every third year and replant to get the crowns closer to the ground.

Propagation: Seed sown in late spring. Also divisions in fall or spring.

No troubles.

PERENNIALS WHICH WILL GROW IN SEMI-SHADE

(Nearly all perennials need some sunshine)

Botanical Name	Common Name	Bloom Season	Height (Ft.)	Color
Aconitum (various species)	Monkshood	June–Sept. (according to species)	3½–4½	Yellow, blue, purple
Ajuga reptans	Bugleweed	May, June	¾	Purple, white
Anemone hybrida (*japonica*)	Japanese Anemone	Aug., Sept.	4½	Pink, white
Aquilegia (various species)	Columbine	May, June	2½–3	Various colors
Aubreita deltoidea	Aubreita (Rockcress)	Apr., May, June	½	Purple
Bergenia cordifolia	Saxifraga cordifolia	Apr., May	1½	Pink, purple
Campanula carpatica	Harebell	July, Aug., Sept.	1	Blue, purple, white
Campanula lactiflora	Bellflower	July, Aug.	3½	Blue
Campanula persicifolia	Peachbell	June, July	2–3	Blue, white
Cimicifuga racemosa	Snakeroot	July, Aug.	6	White
Convallaria majalis	Lily-of-the-valley	May	1	White, pink
Dicentra eximia	Wild Bleedingheart	May, June, July	1¾	Pink
Dicentra spectabilis	Bleedingheart	May, June	2¾	Red, white
Epimedium (various species)	Epimedium (Barrenwort)	May, June	1½	White, red, yellow
Eupatorium coelistinum	Mist Flower	Aug., Sept.	3	Purple
Geranium maculatum	Wild Geranium	May, June	2	White, blue, purple
Helleborus niger	Christmas Rose	Nov.–Apr.	1	White, purple
Hemerocallis (various species)	Daylily	June–Sept.	2–4	Yellow, orange, red

Heuchera sanguinea	Coralbell	June–Sept.	1½	Red, pink, white
Hosta (various species)	Plantain Lily	July–Sept.	2–2½	Blue, white, lavender
Iberis sempervirens	Candytuft	May, June	1	White
Liatris scariosa	Gayfeather	Aug., Sept.	5	Purple
Lobelia cardinalis	Cardinal Flower	Aug., Sept.	4	Red
Lysimachia clethroides	Gooseneck Loosestrife	July, Aug.	3	White
Lythrum salicaria	Purple Loosestrife	July, Aug.	4½	Purple, red
Mertensia virginica	Bluebells	Apr., May	2	Blue
Monarda didyma	Beebalm	July, Sept.	3½	Red, pink, white
Myosotis scorpioides	Everblooming Forget-me-not	June, July, Aug.	1	Blue, pink
Primula (various species)	Primrose	Apr.–June	½–1¼	Various colors
Ranunculus repens (var. *florepleno*)	Creeping Buttercup	May, June	1½	Yellow
Veronica spictata	Speedwell	June, July	1¾	Blue, pink
Viola cornuta	Viola	May–Sept.	¾	Purple
Viola odorata	Violet	May, June	¼	Purple, white

PERENNIALS FOR MOIST PLACES

Botanical Name	Common Name	Bloom Season	Height (Ft.)	Color
Aruncus sylvester	Goatsbeard	June, July	5	White
Astilbe arendsii	False Spirea	July	4	Pink, white
Bergenia cordifolia	Giant Rockfoil	Apr., May	1½	Pink, purple
Hibiscus hybrids	Rose-mallow	July, Sept.	5½	White, red, pink
Iris kaempferi	Japanese Iris	June, July	3	Red, purple, white
Lobelia cardinalis	Cardinal Flower	July, Aug., Sept.	4	Red
Lysimachia clethroides	Gooseneck Loosestrife	July, Aug.	3	White
Lythrum cultivars	Purple Loosestrife	July, Aug.	4½	Red, purple
Monarda didyma	Beebalm	July, Aug.	3½	Red, pink, white
Myosotis scorpioides	Everblooming Forget-me-not	June, July, Aug.	1	Blue
Trollius europaeus	Globeflower	May	2	Yellow
Trollius ledebouri	Globeflower	June	2	Yellow, orange

PERENNIALS FOR A SEASHORE GARDEN

Botanical Name	Common Name	Bloom Season	Height (Ft.)	Color
Aconitum (various species)	Monkshood	June–Sept.	3–4½	Blue, purple, yellow
Alyssum saxatile	Goldentuft	Apr., May	1¾	Yellow
Arabis caucasica	Rockcress	Apr., May	1	White
Armeria maritima	Sea Pink	May, June	1	Red and pink
Coreopsis lanceolata	Coreopsis	June–Sept.	2½	Yellow
Coreopsis verticillata	Coreopsis	June–Aug.	3	Yellow
Dianthus barbatus	Sweet William	June, July	2	Various colors
Dianthus deltoides	Maiden Pink	May, June	1	Red, pink, white
Dianthus plumarius	Cottage Pink	May, June	1	Pink
Dictamnus albus	Gasplant	June	3	White, purple
Gaillardia aristata	Gaillardia	June–Sept.	3	Yellow, red
Helenium autumnale	Sneezeweed	Aug., Sept.	3	Yellow, red
Hemerocallis cultivars	Daylily	June–Sept.	2–4	Yellow, red, orange
Heuchera sanguinea	Coralbells	May–Sept.	1½	Red, pink, white
Iris (various species)	Iris	Apr.–July	1–3	Various colors
Lupinus polyphyllus	Lupine	June–July	4	Various colors
Lychnis chalcedonica	Maltese Cross	June–July	3	Red
Lychnis coronaria	Mullein Pink	June–Aug.	2	Red, purple, white
Rudbeckia lacineata	Goldenglow	July–Sept.	6	Yellow
Rudbeckia triloba	Black-eyed Susan	Aug.–Sept.	4	Yellow
Sedum spectabile	Sedum	Aug.–Sept.	1¾	Purple, red
Veronica (various species)	Speedwell	May–Aug. (according to species)	1½–2½	Blue, pink, purple, white

PERENNIALS FOR CUT FLOWERS

Botanical Name	Common Name	Bloom Season	Height (Ft.)	Color
Achillea ptarmica	Sneezewort	July, Aug., Sept.	2½	White
Anemone hybrida (*japonica*)	Japanese Anemone	Aug., Sept.	4½	Pink, white
Aquilegia hybrida	Columbine	June, July	3	Various colors
Aster frikartii	Aster	July, Aug., Sept.	2¼	Blue
Boltonia latisquama	Violet Baltonia	July, Aug., Sept.	4	Lavender
Campanula carpatica	Carpathian Harebell	July, Aug., Sept.	1	Blue, white, purple
Campanula persicifolia	Peachbell	June, July	3	Blue, white
Chrysanthemum coccineum	Painted Daisy	June, July	2½	Red, pink, white
Chrysanthemum maximum	Shasta Daisy	June, July, Aug.	3	White
Chrysanthemum morifolium	Hardy Mum	Aug., Sept., Oct.	3	Various colors
Convallaria majalis	Lily of the Valley	May	1	White
Coreopsis verticillata	Tickseed	June, July, Aug.	3	Yellow
	Golden Shower			
Dianthus barbatus	Sweet William	June, July	2	Various colors
Dianthus plumarius	Grass Pink	May, June	1	Pink
Echinacea purpurea	Purple Coneflower	July, Aug., Sept.	4	Purple
Gaillardia aristata	Gaillardia	June–Sept.	3	Yellow, red
Gypsophila paniculata	Babysbreath	July, Aug.	3	White
Heuchera sanguinea	Coralbells	May–Sept.	1½	Red, pink, white
Iris germanica	German Iris	May, June	3	Various colors
Liatris Species	Cattail Gayfeather	July, Aug.	2–4	Purple, white
Lilium candidum	Madonna Lily	June, July	4	White
Monarda didyma	Beebalm	July, Aug.	3½	Red, pink, white
Paeonia lactiflora	Peony	May, June	3½	Red, pink, white
Phlox paniculata	Summer Phlox	July, Aug.	3	Various colors
Physostegia virginiana	False Dragonhead	July, Aug., Sept.	3½	White, lavender, purple

TOUGH PERENNIALS FOR DRY SITUATIONS

Botanical Name	Common Name	Bloom Season	Height (Ft.)	Color
Achillea ptarmica	Sneezewort	July, Aug., Sept.	2½	White
Alyssum saxatile	Golden Tuft	Apr., May	1¾	Yellow
Anthemis tinctora	Camomile (Chamomile)	June–Aug.	3	Yellow
Arabis caucasica	Rockcress	Apr., May	1	White
Baptisia australis	False Indigo	June	4	Blue
Centaurea macrocephala	Showy Centaury	July	3	Yellow
Cerastium tomentosum	Snow-in-Summer	May, June	1	White
Dianthus plumaris	Grass Pink	May, June	1	Pink
Gaillardia aristata	Gaillardia	June–Sept.	3	Yellow, red
Gaura lindeheimeri	Blanket Flower	July–Sept.	4	White
Gypsophila paniculata	Babysbreath	July, Aug.	3	White
Helianthus decapetalus (var. *multiflorus*)	Thin Leaf Sunflower	Aug., Sept.	3½	Yellow
Linum perenne	Flax	June, July	2	Blue, white
Lychnis chalcedonica	Maltese Cross	June, July	3	Red
Lychnis coronaria	Mullein Pink	June, July, Aug.	2	Red, purple, white
Oenothera missouriensis	Giant Sundrop	June, July, Aug.		
Rudbeckia laciniata			1	Yellow
(var. *hortensis*)	Goldenglow	July, Aug., Sept.	6	Yellow
Rudbeckia triloba (*Bi*)	Black-eyed Susan	Aug., Sept.	4	Yellow

EVERGREEN PERENNIALS

Botanical Name	Common Name	Bloom Season	Height (Ft.)	Color
Dianthus barbatus	Sweet William	June, July	2	Various colors
Heuchera sanguinea	Coralbells	June–Sept.	1½	Red, pink, white
Iberis sempervirens	Hardy Candytuft	May, June	1	White
Sedum spectabile	Sedum	Aug., Sept.	1¾	Purple, red
Teucrium chamaedrys	Germander or Teucrium	(grown for foliage)	¾	
Yucca smalliana (filamentosa)	Bayonet Plant or Adam's Needle	July, Aug.	5	White
Asperula Odorata	Sweet Woodruff	May, June	¾	White

Of the evergreen perennials mentioned above, probably *Sedum spectabile* is the showiest. It blooms in late August and September and is an excellent border plant. I like the form with variegated foliage. Flowers vary from rose to purple, pinkish to almost white. The stems and stalks dry up in early winter and in early spring new rosettes appear above ground, later elongating to make dense clumps a foot or more high.

PERENNIALS FOR APRIL SHOW

Botanical Name	Common Name	Color
Alyssum saxatile	Basket of Gold	Gold
Anemone pulsatilla	Pasque Flower	Purple, white, pink
Anemone sylvestris	Snowdrop Anemone	White
Bellis perennis	English Daisy	White, pink
Bergenia cordifolia	Bergenia	Pink
Brunnera macrophylla	Siberian Bugloss	Blue
Dicentra cucullaria	Dutchman's Breeches	Pink
Eranthis hyemalis	Winter Aconite	Yellow
Helleborus orientalis	Lenten Rose	White, pink
Hepatica (various species)	Hepatica	White, pink
Primula polyantha	Polyanthus Primrose	White, pink, red
Primula hybrids	Dwarf Primrose	White, pink, red
Pulmonaria saccharata	Lungwort	Blue
Sanguinaria canadensis	Bloodroot	Pink, white
Viola odorata	Violet	Pink, white

PERENNIALS FOR MAY SHOW

Botanical Name	Common Name	Color
Ajuga reptans	Bugleweed	Blue
Alyssum saxatile	Goldentuft	Golden
Anemone pulsatilla	Pasque Flower	Pink, white
Anemone sylvestris	Snowdrop Anemone	White
Aquilegia canadensis	Wild Columbine	Various colors
Arabis caucasica	Rockcress	White
Armeria maritima	Sea Pink, Thrift	Pink
Aubrieta deltoidea	Aubrieta	Pink
Bellis perennis	English Daisy	Pink, white
Bergenia cordifolia	Bergenia	Pink
Brunnera macrophylla	Siberian Bugloss	Blue
Convallaria majalis	Lily of the Valley	White
Dianthus deltoides	Maiden Pink	Pink, white, red
Dicentra canadensis	Squirrel Corn	White, pink
Dicentra eximia	Wild Bleedingheart	Pink
Dicentra spectabilis	Bleedingheart	Pink, white, red
Dodecatheon meadia	Shooting Star	White, pink
Epimedium (various species)	Barren Wort	White, red
Euphorbia cyparissias	Cypress Spurge	Yellow-green
Euphorbia epithymoides	Euphorbia	Yellow
Geum (various species)	Geum	Red,yellow,orange
Hepatica (various species)	Hepatica	Pink, white
Hesperis matronalis	Dames Rocket	Purple, white

PERENNIALS FOR MAY SHOW (*Continued*)

Botanical Name	Common Name	Color
Heuchera sanguinea	Coralbells	Pink, red, white
Iberis sempervirens	Candytuft	White
Iris chamaeiris	Dwarf Iris	White
Iris cristata	Crested Iris	Lilac, white
Iris germanica	German Iris	Various colors
Iris pumila	Dwarf Iris	Yellow, blue, purple
Lamium maculatum	Spotted Deadnettle	Purple, rose
Mertensia virginica	Bluebells	Blue
Paeonia lactiflora	Peony	Various colors
Paeonia suffruticosa	Tree Peony	Various colors
Phlox divaricata	Blue Phlox	Blue
Phlox subulata	Moss Pink	Pink, white, rose
Polemonium reptans	"Creeping" Jacob's Ladder	Blue
Polygonatum caeruleum	Solomon's Seal	Blue
Primula denticulata	Primrose	Lilac, white, violet
Primula polyantha	Polyanthus Primrose	Various colors
Primula sieboldii	Japanese Primrose	White rose, purple
Pulmonaria saccharata	Lungwort	Blue
Trollium europaeus	Globeflower	Orange, yellow
Trillium grandiflorum	Trillium	Pink, white
Viola cornuta	Tufted Pansy	Various colors
Viola odorata	Violet	Various colors

PERENNIALS FOR JUNE BLOOM

Botanical Name	Common Name	Color
Achillea tomentosa	Woolly Yarrow	Yellow
Aconitum vulparia	Yellow Monkshood	Yellow
Aethionema grandiflorum	Persian Stonecress	Pink
Ajuga reptans	Bugleweed	Blue
Alstroemeria aurantica	Peruvian Lily	Orange, yellow
Alyssum murale	Yellowtuft	Yellow
Amsonia tabernaemontana	Amsonia	Blue
Aquilegia hybrida	Longspurred Columbine	Various colors
Aquilegia vulgaris	European Columbine	Various colors
Ameria maritima	Sea Pink, Thrift	Pink
Aruncus sylvester	Goatsbeard	White
Asperula odorata	Sweet Woodruff	White
Asphodeline lutea	Asphodel	Yellow

Botanical Name	Common Name	Color
Aster alpinus	Rock Aster	Purple
Aubrieta deltoidea	Aubrieta	Pink
Baptisia australis	False Indigo	Blue
Bellis perennis	English Daisy	Pink, white
Campanula glomerata	Danesblood	Pink
Campanula rotundifolia	Harebell	Blue, white, violet
Centaurea dealbata	Persian Centaurea	Lilac
Centaurea montana	Mountain Bluet	Blue
Cerastium tomentosum	Snow-in-Summer	White
Chrysanthemum coccineum	Pyrethrum, Painted Daisy	Various colors
Chrysanthemum maximum	Shasta Daisy	White
Clematis integrifolia	Clematis	Blue
Corydalis lutea	Corydalis	Golden
Dianthus barbatus	Sweet William	Various colors
Dianthus deltoides	Maiden Pink	Purple, rose, white
Dianthus plumarius	Cottage Pink	Red, pink, white
Dicentra eximia	Wild Bleedingheart	Rose, pink
Dicentra spectabilis	Bleedingheart	Pink
Dictamnus albus	Gasplant	White
Digitalis grandiflora	Yellow Foxglove	Yellow
Digitalis purpurea (*Bi*)	Foxglove	Purple, pink
Dodecatheon meadia	Shooting Star	Pink, white, purple
Eremurus (various species)	Foxtail Lily	Pink, yellow, white
Euphorbia cyparissias	Cypress Spurge	Yellow-green
Filipendula hexapetala	Dropwort	White
Gaillardia aristata	Gaillardia	Yellow, white
Geranium sanguineum	Cranesbill	Purple, red
Geum (various species)	Geum	Red, yellow, orange
Gypsophila repens	Creeping Babysbreath	Pink, white
Hesperis matronalis	Dames Rocket	Lilac, white
Heuchera sanguinea	Coralbells	Pink, red, white
Iberis gibraltarica	Candytuft	Purple
Iris germanica (*Pogoniris*)	Bearded or German Iris	Various colors
Iris kaempferi	Japanese Iris	Various colors
Iris sibirica	Siberian Iris	Blue, white
Linum perenne	Blue Flax	Blue
Linum narbonense	Blue Flax	Blue
Lunaria annua (*Bi*)	Honesty	White
Lupinus polyphyllus	Lupine	White, purple
Lychnis viscaria	Catchfly	Rose, pink

PERENNIALS FOR JUNE BLOOM (*Continued*)

Botanical Name	Common Name	Color
Lysimachia punctata	Yellow Loosestrife	Yellow
Myosotis scorpioides	Everblooming Forget-me-not	Blue
Nepeta faassenii (*mussinii*)	Catmint	Blue
Oenothera pilosella	Sundrop	Yellow
Paeonia lactiflora (*albiflora*)	Peony	Various colors
Paeonia suffruticosa	Tree Peony	Various colors
Papaver nudicaule	Iceland Poppy	Various colors
Papaver orientale	Oriental Poppy	Red
Polemonium caeruleum	Jacob's Ladder	Blue
Primula japonica	Primrose	Pink, white
Salvia haematodes	Salvia	Blue
Salvia pratensis	Meadow Sage	Blue, rose-pink
Saponaria ocymoides	Soapwort	Pink
Stachys olympica (*lanata*)	Woolly Lambs-Ear	Pink, purple-red
Symphytum asperum	Prickly Compfrey	Light blue
Thalictrum aquilegifolium	Meadowrue	Lilac-purple
Thalictrum minus	Maidenhair Meadowrue	Yellow flowers
Thermopsis caroliniana	False Lupine	Yellow
Thymus serpyllum	Thyme	Rose-lilac
Tradescantia virginiana	Spiderwort	Violet-purple
Trollius ledebouri	Globeflower	Orange-gold
Tunica saxifraga	Tunic Flower	White, rose-pink
Verbascus (Various species) (*Bi*)	Verbascum	Rose
Veronica latifolia (*V. teucrium*)	Speedwell	Blue
Viola cornuta	Tufted Pansy	Blue

PERENNIALS FOR JULY BLOOM

Botanical Name	Common Name	Color
Achillea filipendulina	Fernleaf Yarrow	Yellow
Achillea millefolium (var. *rosea*)	Pink Yarrow	Pink
Achillea ptarmica	Sneezewort	White
Aconitum napellus	English Monkshood	Violet
Althaea rosea (*Bi*)	Hollyhock	Various colors
Alstroemeria aurantica	Alstroemeria	Orange-yellow
Alyssum murale	Yellowtuft	Yellow
Anchusa azurea (*italica*)	Italian Bugloss	Blue
Anthemis tinctoria	Golden Marguerite	Gold

BOTANICAL NAME	COMMON NAME	COLOR
Aquilegia hybrida	Longspurred Columbine	Various colors
Astilbe arendsii	Astilbe	Red, pink, white
Callirhoë involucrata	Poppy Mallow	Purple, red
Campanula carpatica	Carpathian Harebell	Blue, purple, white
Campanula glomerata	Danesblood	Purple, blue
Campanula lactiflora	Bellflower	White, blue
Campanula medium (*Bi*)	Canterbury Bells	White, pink, blue
Campanula persicifolia	Willowleaf Bellflower	Blue, white
Campanula rotundifolia	Harebell	Blue, white, violet
Catananche caerulea	Cupid's Dart	Blue
Centaurea dealbata	Persian Centaurea	Lilac
Centaurea macrocephala	Globe Centaurea	Golden Yellow
Centranthus ruber	Red Valerian	Red
Chrysanthemum maximum	Shasta Daisy	White
Chrysanthemum parthenium	Feverfew, Matricaria	White
Cimicifuga racemosa	Snakeroot	White
Clematis integrifolia	Clematis	Blue
Coreopsis lanceolata	Coreopsis	Yellow
Coreopsis verticillata	Golden Shower	Yellow
Corydalis lutea	Corydalis	Yellow
Delphinium cheilanthum	Belladonna Delphinium	Blue, white
Delphinium elatum	Delphinium	Blue, pink, white
Delphinium grandiflorum (*Bi*)	Delphinium (Chinese)	White, blue
Dianthus barbatus	Sweet William	Various colors
Dicentra eximia	Wild Bleedingheart	Pink
Digitalis purpurea (*Bi*)	Foxglove	Various colors
Eremurus (various species)	Foxtail Lily	Pink, yellow, white
Filipendula rubra	Queen of the Prairie	Pink
Filipendula ulmaria	Queen of the Meadow	White
Gaillardia	Blanket flower	Red, yellow
Galium aristatum	Bedstraw	White
Gaura lindheimeri	Gaura	Pink, white
Geranium sanguineum	Cranesbill	Purple, red
Gypsophila repens	Creeping Babysbreath	White, pink
Gypsophila paniculata	Babysbreath	White
Heliopsis scabra	Heliopsis	Yellow
Hesperis matronalis	Dames Rocket	Lilac, white
Heuchera sanguinea	Coralbells	Pink, white
Hosta fortunei	Tall Clustered Funkia	Lavender, white
Hosta ventricosa	Blue Plantain Lily	Blue
Iberis gibraltarica	Candytuft	Light purple
Iris kaempferi	Japanese Iris	Various colors
Kniphofia (various species)	Trochlily, Tritoma, Red Hot Poker	Orange, yellow
Lamium maculatum	Spotted Deadnettle	Purple, rose

PERENNIALS FOR JULY BLOOM (*Continued*)

BOTANICAL NAME	COMMON NAME	COLOR
Limonium latifolium	Sea Lavender, Statice	White, lavender
Linum flavum	Yellow Flax	Yellow
Linum perenne	Blue Flax	Blue
Linum narbonense	Blue Flax	Blue
Lychnis chalcedonica	Maltese Cross	Scarlet
Lychnis viscaria	Catchfly	Red-purple
Lysimachia clethroides	Gooseneck Loosestrife	White
Lythrum salicaria	Purple Loosestrife	Purple
Macleaya cordata (*Bocconia*)	Plume Poppy	Pink
Monarda didyma	Beebalm	Pink, purple
Myosotis scorpioides	Everblooming Forget-me-not	Blue
Nepeta faassenii (*mussinii*)	Catmint	Blue, violet
Oenothera missouriensis	Giant Sundrop	Golden
Penstemon barbatus	Beardtongue	Deep rose
Phlox carolina	Phlox Miss Lingard	White
Phlox paniculata	Phlox	Pink-purple
Platycodon grandiflorum	Balloon Flower	Blue, white
Salvia sclarea (*Bi*)	Vatican Sage	White, rose, purple
Scabiosa caucasica	Perennial Scabiosa	Blue
Scutellaria baicalensis	Skullcap	
Sedum seiboldii	Sedum	Pink
Sidalcea (various species)	Prairie Mallow	Pink, rose
Stachys grandiflora (*Betonica*)	Betony	Purple-violet
Stachys olympica	Woolly Lambs-Ear	Pink, purple
Stokesia laevis	Stokes Aster	Blue
Symphytum asperum	Prickly Compfrey	Blue
Thalictrum dipterocarpum	Meadowrue	Lavender
Thalictrum rugosum (*glaucum*)	Meadowrue (Dusty)	Yellow
Thymus serphyllum	Creeping Thyme	Rose-lilac
Tunica saxifraga	Tunic Flower	Lilac
Valeriana officinalis	Garden Heliotrope	White, lavender
Verbascum (various species)	Mullein	Rose, cream
Veronica incana	Woolly Speedwell	Blue
Veronica spicata	Speedwell	Blue
Veronica longifolia (var. *subsessilis*)	Speedwell	Royal blue
Veronicastrum virginicum	Culvers Root	White
Viola cornuta	Tufted Pansy	Violet
Yucca smalliana (*filamentosa*)	Spanish Bayonet Adam's Needle	Cream

PERENNIALS FOR AUGUST BLOOM

Botanical Name	Common Name	Color
Achillea filipendulina	Fernleaf Yarrow	Yellow
Achillea millefolium (var. *rosea*)	Pink Yarrow	Pink
Achillea ptarmica	Sneezewort	White
Aconitum napellus	Monkshood	White
Althaea rosea (*Bi*)	Hollyhock	Various colors
Anchusa azurea (*italica*)	Italian Bugloss	Blue
Anthemis tinctoria	Golden Marguerite	Yellow
Artemisia lactiflora	White Mugwort	White
Asclepias tuberosa	Butterflyweed	Orange
Aster amellus	Italian Aster	Purple
Aster frikartii	Hardy Aster	Blue
Boltonia latisquama	Boltonia	White
Callirhoe involucrata	Poppy Mallow	Purple-red
Campanula carpatica	Carpathian Harebell	Blue, white
Campanula lactiflora	Bellflower	White, pale blue
Campanula rotundiflora	Harebell	Blue, violet, white
Cantananche caerulea	Cupid's Dart	Blue
Centranthus ruber	Red Valerian	Red
Ceratostigma plumbaginoides	Plumbago, Blue Lead-wort	Blue
Chrysanthemum maximum	Shasta Daisy	White
Chrysanthemum parthenium	Feverfew, Matricaria	White
Clemantis heracleifolia	Clematis	Blue
Coreopsis lanceolata	Coreopsis	Yellow
Coreopsis verticillata	Golden Shower	Yellow
Corydalis lutea	Corydalis	Yellow
Echinacea purpurea (*Rudbeckia*)	Purple Coneflower	Purple
Echinops exaltatus (*ritro*)	Globe Thistle	Blue
Eryngium amethystinum	Sea Holly	Gray
Gaillardia aristata	Gaillardia	Yellow
Galium aristatum	Bedstraw	White
Gaura lindheimeri	Gaura	White
Gypsophila paniculata	Babysbreath	White
Helenium autumnale	Sneezeweed	Yellow
Helianthus decapetalus (var. *multiflorus*)	Thinleaf Sunflower	Yellow
Heliopsis scabra	Heliopsis	Yellow
Heuchera sanguinea	Coralbells	Pink, white
Hibiscus moscheutos	Rose Mallow	White

PERENNIALS FOR AUGUST BLOOM (*Continued*)

Botanical Name	Common Name	Color
Hosta lancifolia	Narrow-leaved Plantain Lily	Lavender
Hosta plantaginea	Fragrant Plantain Lily	White
Kniphofia (various species)	Red Hot Poker, Torch-lily, Tritoma	Orange
Lamium maculatum	Spotted Deadneedle	Purple, rose
Liatris (various species)	Gayfeather, Blazing Star	Purple, white
Limonium latifolium	Sea Lavender	White, lavender
Linum flavum	Yellow Flax	Yellow
Lobelia cardinalis	Cardinal Flower	Red
Lobelia siphilitica	Blue Perennial Lobelia	Blue
Lychnis coronaria	Rose Campion	Red
Lysimachia clethroides	Gooseneck Loosestrife	White
Lythrum salicaria	Purple Loosestrife	Purple
Monarda didyma	Beebalm	Purple
Myosotis scorpioides	Everblooming Forget-me-not	Blue
Nepeta faassenii (*mussinii*)	Catmint	Blue
Oenothera missouriensis	Giant Sundrop	Yellow
Phlox paniculata	Phlox	Various colors
Physostegia virginiana	False Dragonhead	Rose
Platycodon grandiflorum	Balloon Flower	Blue, white
Rudbeckia laciniata (var. *hortensis*)	Goldenglow	Yellow
Rudbeckia triloba	Black-eyed Susan	Yellow
Sedum spectabile	Sedum	Various colors
Sidalcea (various species)	Prairie Mallow	Pink, rose
Stokesia laevis	Stokes Aster	White, lilac
Symphytum asperum	Prickly Compfrey	Blue
Thalictrum dipterocarpum	Meadowrue	Lavender
Veronica longifolia (var. *subsessilis*)	Speedwell, Veronica	Blue
Veronicastrum virginicum	Culvers Root	Blue
Viola cornuta	Tufted Pansy	Violet
Yucca smalliana (*filamentosa*)	Spanish Bayonet Adam's Needle	Cream

PERENNIALS FOR SEPTEMBER BLOOM

Botanical Name	Common Name	Color
Achillea ptarmica	Sneezewort	White
Aconitum carmichaelii (*fisheri*)	Monkshood	White

BOTANICAL NAME	COMMON NAME	COLOR
Anemone hybrida (japonica)	Japanese Anemone	Various colors
Artemisia lactiflora	White Mugwort	White
Aster amellus	Italian Aster	Purple
Aster frikartii	Hardy Aster	Blue
Aster novae angliae	New England Aster	Purple
Aster novibelgii	New York Aster	Blue
Boltonia latisquama	Boltonia	Blue-violet
Callirhoe involucrata	Poppy Mallow	Purple, red
Campanula carpatica	Carpathian Harebell	Blue
Centaurea montana	Mountain Bluet	Blue
Ceratostigma plumbaginoides	Plumbago	Blue
Chrysanthemum morifolium	Hardy Chrysanthemum	Various colors
Coreopsis lanceolata	Coreopsis	Golden
Eupatorium coelistinum	Mistflower	Blue
Gaillardia aristata	Gaillardia	Orange
Gaura lindheimeri	Gaura	Pinkish-white
Helenium autumnale	Sneezeweed	Yellow
Helianthus decapetalus (var. *multiflorus*)	Thinleaf Sunflower	Yellow
Helianthus salicifolius (*orgyalis*)	Yellow Sunflower	Yellow
Heliopsis scabra	Heliopsis	Yellow
Hibiscus moscheutos	Rose Mallow	White
Hosta plantaginea	Fragrant Plantain Lily	Blue
Lespedeza thunbergii	Bush Clover	Purple
Lobelia cardinalis	Cardinal Flower	Red
Rudbeckia laciniata (var. *hortensis*)	Goldenglow	Yellow
Rudbeckia triloba	Black-eyed Susan	Yellow
Sedum spectabile	Sedum	Pink
Tradescantia virginiana	Spiderwort	Violet
Viola cornuta	Tufted Pansy	Violet

GREEN THUMB TIPS ON PERENNIALS

It's better by far to have a few showy perennials than to raise a lot of short-blooming types which require a lot of care.

Many perennials can be started from seed or divisions. Keep an eye on your neighbor's flower garden and swap plants for a bigger collection.

Keep the perennial bed or border neatly edged and weeded.

Water perennials well in hot summer. An inch of water per week is enough to maintain growth, and automatic lawn sprinklers can supply this amount in from three to six hours, enough for a week's growth.

When a perennial starts to get out of hand, keep it in bounds by shearing.

If your garden mums get frosted before flowering, discard them for earlier blooming types.

If your mums bloom ahead of time ("precocious blooming"), cut the entire plant back in first week of July and new growth will come along to flower by the end of September or October.

When mums change colors, it's due to self-sown seeds producing stronger plants which eventually take over.

Peonies fail to bloom for many reasons: (1) Heavy shade; (2) Hard soil; (3) Deep planting; (4) Botrytis blight (dust with Captan); and (4) Dry soils.

Perennials are showier planted in masses or clumps than when planted in a hit-and-miss fashion.

Cleaning up the garden in fall will do a lot to control insects and disease pests the following year.

Keep your perennial borders neat and sharp!

4

House-Plant Culture

PART I

FLOWERING HOUSE PLANTS

Rare is the house without some flowering or foliage plant in it. Quite likely you can tell much about the nature and temperament of a home owner by the plants he has in his home. People who enjoy plants have a much better insight on life, and seem to be more understanding than those who have no use for plants.

House plants are divided into two groups: the flowering types and the foliage types. There's a strong trend toward foliage plants by planters because the selection is so large it's possible to use the foliage to brighten drab corners and add distinction to the modern interior. Flowers on foliage plants are usually inconspicuous and the main interest is the foliage itself.

To get more fun and enjoyment from your house plants you should be able to answer this commonly asked question: "Why do my house plants fail?" There are three main reasons for poor plant growth indoors: (1) Wrong selection, (2) Neglect and (3) Injurious gases. Once you understand the cultural tips on house plants, you should get more mileage from them. I'm going to mention the care of Flowering House Plants first because this is probably the most important of all.

Light: To some plantsmen, no other factor is more important in governing the growth of plants than light. Indoors, most plants do best in a southwest window. Sunlight is needed to produce flowering buds on nearly all flowering plants, some needing less light than others. Most foliage plants, such as Philodendron, are of tropical origin and thus need less light. Some plants need a shorter day to produce blooms, and they are called short-day plants. Others need a longer day before they'll bloom. By influencing the length of day, greenhouse owners can produce chrysanthemums the year around, even though the plants are traditionally and strictly a fall-blooming flower. Mums will not set flower buds, and they bloom only when the day-length is short; hence their profusion in fall months. And that's why your mums do not bloom in June when the day is longer. The recent discovery known as photoperiodism, or ability of plants to be affected by length of day is one of the most important recent developments of the plant world. As we learn more about it, we'll be able to tell you why some plants don't bloom, or produce seeds or bulbs in some areas—but do in others.

Temperature: Plants are like people. Some like it hot, some like it cold. Probably the best temperature for most plants in winter is 70 degrees in day and 55 degrees at night, with a few exceptions such as African violets. A high night temperature causes food in plants to be used up, followed by yellowing of foliage. You can have a day fluctuation between 45 and 80 degrees with no serious results, if your plants have a low night temperature. One reason why our grandmothers grew better house plants than we do now is because the room temperatures then were lower, especially at night. In those days, bedrooms were seldom heated. If your house plants have soft, spindly growth, pale foliage, and the buds blast or drop prematurely, you can often look to the temperature as being too hot. At night put your plants in a cool room, 60 degrees or lower and see how much difference it makes in prolonging their life.

Humidity: Although most of our modern homes are too hot and dry, it's still possible to raise good flowering plants, by resorting to some green thumb tricks. While the proper humidity in the home is from 35 to 40 per cent, the air indoors often goes as low as 12. This is 8 to 11 per cent lower than the average relative humidity in the Sahara Desert in the summertime, and while it may be fine for camels, it's much too dry for human or plant comfort. Plants grow best when the humidity is from 80 to 90 per cent, although we cannot obtain this in our homes. In a greenhouse the relative humidity is 60 per cent or more. This explains why plants start to turn brown around the edges, flowers drop and buds shed, soon after being moved from a moist atmosphere of the greenhouse or even from the garden, in the fall.

You can increase the moisture in the house by putting a pan of water on the radiators or register. Also place a galvanized or zinc tray on the window for your plants, and fill with pebbles. Syringing foliage increases humidity if done once or twice a week. And don't forget the old kitchen teakettle. It used to sing songs and make plants happy because they enjoyed the extra humidity. Plants themselves help release moisture into the room, and thus are healthy for humans. For example, the leaves of an average-sized cineraria gives off as much as three times more water as would be evaporated from the surface of a 4-inch pan of water.

Watering: Watering is an art. A greenhouse man will tell you that the man with the hose determines the profits and losses. One reason home owners have so much trouble watering plants is due to the pots themselves. Plastic and glazed pots are trickier to use than the good old-fashioned florist clay pot. Plastic or glazed pots are non-porous and do not "breathe" or allow air to enter. For that reason the soil does not dry so fast, and when plants are watered with the same frequency as those in clay pots, the result is overwatering. This shuts off oxygen to the roots, water accumulates and causes stunting, yellowing of foliage and shedding of buds.

A good way to water is to set the plant, pot and all, half-submerged in a dish or pan. After the plant waters itself completely, allow surplus to drain off. Keep in mind that pots with drainage openings need more water than those without openings. Glazed pots without drainage facilities can be made more suited for growing by placing small pieces of charcoal or stones in the bottom. Water plants in early morning, from top or bottom. Also if you repot a plant the soil should be watered immediately. Plants in small pots dry out faster than those in larger pots due to smaller volume of soil, so they may need watering many times during a hot day.

WATERING PLANTS WHILE YOU VACATION

Your plants need not go dry while you take a vacation from home. One helpful trick is to set a few building bricks in the bathtub with about 1½ inches of water. Pots placed on the bricks are automatically watered for at least two weeks. Another trick is to place several thicknesses of newspapers in a pan, saturate them well, and place the pots on these. Other gardeners sink their pots in vermiculite, wet sand or sawdust. Saturate these materials and water the plants first before packing the pots to their rims. These plants will keep three or four weeks in this manner. Another trick worth trying: Place a plastic bag over the plants and tie them securely around the pot. This forms a vapor-tight greenhouse which makes a fine "plantsitter" for you for three or four weeks. Some plants do not tolerate the excess humidity inside the plastic sheet, but it's worth the try.

HARD WATER vs. SOFT WATER

Some gardeners depend on rain or melted snow for their plants. African violets, azaleas and other "acid-loving" plants do not like hard water and nearly all water coming from wells in limestone areas will have some degree of hardness. Hardness is caused when water containing dissolved carbon dioxide comes in contact with limestone. How to tell if water is hard: If your soap curdles or doesn't mix well, chances are it's hard. Another simple test is to look for scale inside the teakettle. If you don't own a teakettle, test water with litmus paper. If it turns the litmus paper blue, the water is alkali or hard, and if it turns red, the water is acid and is not likely to be hard. Litmus, obtainable in drugstores, is a purplish coloring matter made from lichens. These lichens are ground to a pulp with water, and mixed with lime.

IS A WATER SOFTENER HARMFUL TO PLANTS?

In most cases water passing through mechanical softeners does have a harmful effect on plant growth. Hard water is hard because it contains large amounts of calcium and magnesium. Softeners exchange the calcium (harmless) for sodium (harmful). Sodium is more harmful than calcium because it has a tendency to puddle the soil (make it sticky) or "deflocculate" it, leaving such soils in poor physical condition. To add to this, sodium is taken up by plants, forming a toxic substance. Our water softener is hooked to the hot-water line only.

Is chlorine or fluorine in water harmful to house plants? Probably not, although many of my friends emphatically state that chlorine-treated water is harmful to plants. Perhaps the greatest concentration of chlorine is noticed early in the morning when the water is first turned on, after standing all night in pipes. To be on the safe side, allow tap water to run a few minutes before gathering water, since chlorine disappears rapidly upon aeration. Allow tap water to remain in a pail before applying to plants.

Soil mixtures: Good soils mean good drainage, an important factor for husky growth. Plants in a heavy soil will turn yellow due to poor drainage and a lack of air. Some authorities recommend dozens of complicated soil mixes. Frankly, there's no need for these because plants just aren't that fussy. Greenhouse operators use just one mix for a wide variety of plants. A good soil mixture for all house plants is made up of 1 part peat moss (or compost) 1 part sand and 1 part garden loam. The only plants to benefit from a larger amount of peat are gardenias, azaleas and other acid-loving items.

Organic matter in some form is important as it provides drainage, helps hold nutrients. You cannot go out in your garden and scoop up soil for house plants. Good soils are made, not born. The earth from rotted stumps is a fine source of humus. You may note that some florists also add vermiculite or perlite in a soil mixture along with peat. Peat holds the moisture whereas vermiculite and perlite add porosity, resist decay and aid in root growth. Charcoal, while it contributes very little plant food nutrients, is a valuable soil conditioner and purifier. Florists use small pieces of charcoal in the soil because of drainage and of its ability to absorb impurities from the soil solution.

"Musty" or moldy soils mean poor drainage and usually additions of charcoal or sand will prevent this. If you're interested in sterilizing soil of house plants, see section under "Plant Propagation," "Starting Plants from Seeds."

FEEDING HOUSE PLANTS

Nearly all plants respond to regular applications of plant food, applied preferably in liquid form and in light doses. Such items as coffee grounds, tea leaves, eggshell water, castor oil, etc. offer very light encouragement to starved plants. Liquid plant foods are increasingly popular for all types of house plants because they are safe and easy to use. All of my house and greenhouse plants are fed with a liquid food (23% N–21% P and 17% K) at the rate of 1 level teaspoon to 2 quarts of water, and applied every three or four weeks.

If you use a dry chemical fertilizer such as 5–10–5, do not apply it dry. Dissolve a teaspoon in a quart of water and feed it in liquid form. While many plants are dormant in winter, it's still a good idea to feed them lightly to maintain color.

SHIFTING OR POTTING HOUSE PLANTS

Some house plants become "potbound" (the roots fill the pot). A little "potboundness" is desirable in that it encourages blooming. Too much is followed by stunted growth, falling leaves and a generally unsightly plant. No hard and fast rule can be made for repotting, since plants vary greatly in their habits. Probably the best time for repotting is in spring when new growth is starting. The pot size is determined by the growth habit. For example, slow-growing items such as cacti do not need large pots, nor frequent potting. Rapid-growing plants such as begonias can be shifted from a 4-inch pot to a 6-inch size if potbound. As soon as you remove the ball of soil and roots from the pot, remove a portion of the old soil and matted roots. This stimulates development of new roots and you should also replenish the old soil with new mixture.

Potting soils should be moist but not wet since such soils often pack too hard. And keep in mind that finely sifted soils are fine for seedlings, but not acceptable for house plants. Finely prepared soils bake, crack and often become hard.

PINCHING PLANTS IS LEGAL

One reason most house plants are tall, spindly and lopsided is that they are never pinched back. Most greenhouse operators would go out of business if they never pinched their snapdragons, mums and other crops. Pinching merely consists of removing the tip of a plant after it has developed anywhere from four to six leaves. To pinch you simply take your thumb and forefinger and pinch out the tip. This makes your plants nice and bushy, so they'll branch out instead of growing straight up. Clipping a hedge amounts to "pinching" the plants. In most instances, the pinched tips of your house plants may be rooted in just plain sand or tap water to make new plants.

SUMMER CARE OF HOUSE PLANTS

Summer's a fine time to give your plants a vacation outdoors, as it helps build up vigor for winter growth. Sink the plants up to the rim in pot, in shade or semi-shade and water them once or twice a week. If you have a shady back porch or terrace, try moving house ferns, gardenias, begonias, and your other plants there. Hosing these items will give them a new lease on life.

HOW TO INCREASE YOUR HOUSE PLANTS

House Plants are increased by three common methods: Seeds, leaf and stem ("slips"), and by division. (For details on seeds, rooting and division, see section under "Plant Propagation.")

BE YOUR OWN PLANT DOCTOR

House plants fall heir to physiological troubles, as well as to insect and disease pests. Armed with a few green thumb facts you can track down most house plant ailments and correct them. I'm listing a few of the common physiological problems you're apt to come across with your flowering plants.

Blindness: This is failure of plants to produce flower buds. Environment is likely to be the cause. Look for poor light, improper nutrition, low or high temperature. Flower buds form on hydrangeas at temperatures below 60 degrees and azaleas form their buds at a temperature above 65 degrees, so you can see that many plants have "hidden" requirements which must be met before buds set.

Chlorosis: A sickly, yellowed condition of plants, often due to a lack of nitrogen or a lack of iron. Balanced feeding or iron chelates corrects this. (See chapter on "Soils and Fertilizers.")

Leaf Scorching: Found among ferns, begonias, and hundreds of other items. This can be a sign of little water, excess fertilizer, sun-burning or not enough humidity.

Stunted Growth: Poor growth accompanied by dark, undersized leaves are often good signs of lack of phosphorus. Balanced feeding corrects this. Also a lack of moisture will cause the same type of growth. Soft growth during winter is generally due to a combination of high heat and insufficient light.

Effect of Gas Fumes on Plants: Artificial or manufactured gas and coal gas have a bad effect on many house plants. Natural gas isn't as hard on plants. Quite often a concentration so small as to be undetected by the human nose will cause carnations to "go to sleep." Many plants will lose their foliage from leaking gas or gas fumes, especially in winter because rooms are poorly ventilated.

Natural gas is more difficult to detect indoors because it works differently on plants. Usually the stems start to harden, or plants make poor or slow growth, as if stunted, and leaves will often yellow or distort. If you cook by gas, light the burner immediately because each time you turn it on before lighting a match you allow some gas to escape into the room. To ventilate as much as possible is your best way to cope with gas fumes.

INSECTS AND DISEASES OF HOUSE PLANTS

House plants are subject to attack from insects and diseases 365 days out of the year, but fortunately we have chemicals to combat them. Probably the safest effective insecticides are Malathion, rotenone and Pyrethrum and DDT. These come in three forms: dusts, liquids and in the handy aerosol containers. Whichever you use, follow instructions of the manufacturer. Malathion is just about the best all-purpose bug killer for house plants. Mix a teaspoon of the liquid to a quart of soapy water (or a pinch of a household detergent) and spray the plants. Some gardeners dip their house plants into a bucket of the solution. Cover the pot with wax paper or aluminum foil to keep soil from falling into the bucket. Two treatments a week apart should control your pests. The new aerosol pushbutton cans are handy but the only precaution here is to make sure the material is for use on plants. The kerosene-base formulations made to kill flies and mosquitoes will burn plants. Hold the spray about 18 inches from the surface of the leaves and cover both top and undersides.

COMMON HOUSE-PLANT PESTS
(Insects)

Pest	What To Look For	Control Measures
Aphids (Plant lice)	Small plump insects (black, brown, green) on tips and undersides of leaves. Secrete a messy honeydew.	Nicotine sulfate or Malathion, 1 teaspoon to 2 qts. of soapy water.
Fungus-gnats	Young are slender, legless white maggots. Hatch from eggs laid in soil by black flies you see buzzing around plants.	Same as for springtails.

Pest	What To Look For	Control Measures
Leaf-chewing pests	Chewed or ragged foliage.	Spray with DDT.
Mealybugs	Oval, white, waxy-coated, sap-sucking insect in leaf axils and on stems. Secrete sticky honeydew.	Swab a matchstick in rubbing alcohol and apply to the cottony masses. Try Malathion also.
Nematodes (soil)	Poor growth, stunted, knotty roots. Affects over 500 different kinds of plants.	Discard plant, pot and all.
Nematodes (foliage)	Cause brown areas in leaves.	Discard plant.
Scale insects	Oval or hemispherical spots on leaves and stems. Secrete honeydew. Do not confuse scale with black dots on back of fern leaves. (They are the "seed" or spore-bearing structures.)	Same as for mealybugs.
Spidermites (Red Spider & Cyclamen Mites)	Nearly microscopic; needle-like mouthparts cause speckled or stippled foliage, bleaching, curling and leaves to be webbed.	Malathion; or try Dimite or Kelthane. Syringing foliage weekly is helpful.
Springtails	Tiny slender-bodied pest which jumps when plant is watered. Not serious unless severe infestation.	Dust 1 teaspoon of DDT, Chlordane or Lindane on surface and water it in the soil.
Symphylids	Small swift-moving pest, ¼″ long, feeding on roots of plants, cause stunting and yellowing. Often brought in with manure.	Same as for springtails.
Thrips	Slim pests which cause gray-speckled foliage; flower buds fail to open.	Malathion or DDT or Aerosol spray.
White flies	Small white-winged insect which flies out when plant is touched. Secretes honeydew.	Same as for thrips.

COMMON HOUSE-PLANT PESTS (*Continued*)

(Diseases)

PEST	WHAT TO LOOK FOR	CONTROL MEASURES
Crown Rot or Stem Rot	Due to fungi or bacteria which cause foliage to yellow, or rot at soil level.	Dust with Ferbam or Captan.
Damping-off	Young plants rot at base and topple over.	Dust soil with Captan, Ferbam or Terrachlor.
Powdery Mildew	White, fuzzy spots on leaves.	Dust weekly with Mildex, Sulfur, Karathane, or Actidione.
Rust	Rusty spots on leaves or stems.	Keep foliage dry. Spray or dust with Zineb.
Virus (mosaic, ring spot, etc.)	Mottled foliage, stunted growth.	Destroy plant.

SOME FLOWERING PLANTS FOR YOUR HOME

Flowering house plants are so numerous it would take volumes to cover the subject. I have selected some of the most common house plants for discussion here. There are several good books on House-Plant Culture you may refer to for further information.

Flowering Plant	Green Thumb Care	Propagation	Problems
ACHIMENES (species and hybrids)	Grow from cone-like root planted in spring. Flower in summer. After flowering, soil should be dried gradually and pot placed in cool, dark place. In Feb., remove old soil and repot.	Division of roots.	Failure to flower due to lack of rest period in summer. Aphids, use Malathion or Nicotine Sulfate.
AFRICAN VIOLET (*Saintpaulia* species and hybrids)	Detests direct sun, will not flower in poor light. Likes humusy soil and 70 degs. temperature. Water from below, making sure of good drainage.	Leaf cuttings and seed. Insert cuttings in water or sand. Seed sown in sand-peat mix.	Aphids. Use Malathion. Leaf or crown rot due to overwatering. Lack of blossoms due to poor light. Spots on leaves due to water splashing.
AMARYLLIS (*Hippeastrum* species and hybrids)	Needs summer rest. In fall, bring indoors and keep in cool basement for 30 days, without water. Then move to bright window.	Bulbs.	Failure to bloom due to lack of 30-day "cure" in fall or no summer rest outdoors.
AZALEA (*Rhododendron indicum* and *R. obtusum "amoenum"*—many hybrids)	Prefers acid soil. If your water is hard, apply vinegar, 1 teaspoon to quart every 3 weeks. Grow outdoors in summer, move indoors in fall, keeping in a cool window until Jan. 1 and move it into living room.	Cuttings in July. Also by seed sown in Sphagnum moss.	Non-flowering due to no cool period in fall. Red spider and Chlorosi of foliage.

SOME FLOWERING PLANTS FOR YOUR HOME (*Continued*)

FLOWERING PLANT	GREEN THUMB CARE	PROPAGATION	PROBLEMS
BALSAM (*Impatiens sultanii* and *I. holstii,* hybrids of same)	Grown as house plant and outdoor annual. Ideal for sun or in shade.	Seed started in sand-peat mixture, also by cuttings in plain water.	Aphids and red spider.
BEGONIA (*Begonia* species and hybrids)	Among the most versatile house plants. All like humusy soil, warm temperature, bright light, but never direct sunlight.	Seeds, cuttings and by tubers. Calla begonia is most trying to root. Try greenest tips under plastic bag.	Leaf scorch, bud drop, due to hot dry rooms.
CALCEOLARIA (*Calceolaria integnifolia*)	"Pocketbook" plant likes full sun, 70 degs. F. in day and 60 degs. at night. Cut plant back to within 4" after blooming for new growth. Keep below 60 degs. for bud formation.	Seeds.	Dropping of buds due to poor ventilation (this item can gas itself and nearby flowers, though harmless to humans).
CALLA LILY (*Zantedeschia aethiopica*—white; *Z. elliottiana*—yellow)	Both yellow and white callas need full sun and ample water. Dry the yellow tubers off in June, repot in Aug. Yellow callas should be left until Nov. before repotting.	Offsets of the fleshy storage organs.	Mealy bugs and spider mites. Nonflowering due to lack of light, or dry soil.
CAMELLIA (*Camellia japonica*)	Not an ideal house plant. Likes a temperature of 50 degs. F. at night and 60 degs. in day.	Cuttings.	Same as gardenias (see).

CHRISTMAS CACTUS (*Schlumbergera bridgesii*)	Likes full sun and night temperature around 65 degs. Should not be kept dry as with other cacti. Buds form in Oct. and will flower through winter. Place plant outdoors in summer.	Cuttings in sand.	Bud drop due to high temperature or low light intensity.
CHRISTMAS PEPPER (*Capiscum frutescens "conoides"*)	This flashy house plant has edible (hot!) peppers, needs full sun and lots of water. Discard after flowering.	Seed sown in June or July.	None.
CHRYSANTHEMUMS (*Chrysanthemum coronarium* and *C. carinatum*)	(See Perennials) May be dug in garden and potted for indoor flowering. Plants need full sun and ample water. Potted florist-mum is often late and should be discarded, unless brought indoors.	Division and cuttings.	Red spider, aphids and white flies.
CINERARIA (*Senecio cruentus*)	Prefers full sun, lots of water, cool night temperature (50 degs.). Discard after flowering.	Seeds.	Aphids.
CITRUS PLANTS	A large group including lemon, orange, grapefruit, limes and others. Flowers, fruits and foliage are handsome. Keep plants outdoors in summer, bring in before frost.	Seeds, cuttings and grafting. Buy grafted types from nursery for large handsome fruit.	Capricious blooming habit, due to hot, dry rooms. Red spider and scale.

SOME FLOWERING PLANTS FOR YOUR HOME (*Continued*)

Flowering Plant	Green Thumb Care	Propagation	Problems
CYCLAMEN (*Cyclamen indicum*)	Prefers full sun in day at 70 degs. and night temperature of 50 degs. Keep soil moist at all times. After blooming, dry corm off and place in cellar until summer when it can be repotted for another show.	Seed takes 18 months to make a new plant.	Yellow leaves and buds blasting, due to high room temperature or lack of light.
EASTER LILY (*Lilium longiflorum*)	Prefers bright light and a good supply of water. After flowering, plant bulb outdoors in permanent place in garden and it will bloom year after year.	Bulblets, scales, and seed.	Leaves turn yellow due to lack of light, root rots, poor aeration, high soluble salts.
FLOWERING MAPLE (*Abutilon megapotamicum*)	So called because of maple-like leaves. Likes a cool room, is a fast grower. Must be pinched to induce squattiness. Deserves renewed interest.	Cuttings and seed in sand-peat mixture.	Yellow leaves due to lack of nitrogen.
FUSCHIA (mostly hybrids of species)	Will grow in full sun or part shade. Likes a moist, humusy soil, temperature of 70 degs. Flowering stops in summer due to high temperature. Ideal for window boxes and hanging baskets.	Cuttings from young growth, inserted in sand. In fall, cut old plant back and start new plants.	Flower drop due to high room temperature or poor light, or poor drainage. Heir to white flies, aphids and red spider.
GARDENIA (*Gardenia jasminoides "fortunei,"* hybrids of same)	Not a satisfactory house plant, though a challenging one. Needs full sun, night temperature of 60 degs., day temperature of 70 to 80 degs. Feed ammonium sulfate, 1 teaspoon to quart of water, once monthly from Mar. to Nov. Grow outdoors in summer.	Cuttings in sand taken in winter.	Bud drop due to high night temperature. Yellow foliage due to non-acid soils and low temperatures. Mealybugs.

GERANIUMS (*Pelargonium hortorum* and *P. domesticum,* hybrids of *hortorum* and many species)	All like a cool temperature (60 degs. or so), full sun and plenty of water. Too much shade and high temperature causes spindly plants. Pinch back the growing tip to make them bushy. Available in many varieties, some most valuable for odor of foliage. Plants may be kept over winter by hanging upside down in cellar, in polyethelene bags.	Seed sown in a shallow box. Also cuttings taken in autumn and stuck in sand. Pour boiling water on sand first to sterilize it. Plastic bags over cuttings favor rooting. Ideal for storing mother plants over winter.	Failure to flower due to lack of light, low moisture content, or too high a room temperature. Yellow leaves, due to lack of light, dry soil, too little nitrogen or poor drainage.
GLOXINIA (*Sinningia speciosa*)	Prefers humus soil, with charcoal for drainage. Night temperature 62 degs., day temperature 70 degs. Avoid direct sun, but provide bright light. Tubers planted in Mar. will bloom in summer. After flowering, soil can be kept dry until foliage wilts and dies, then store in basement until next fall or spring when it can be repotted. Some gardeners grow them the year round without a rest period.	Tubers do not multiply, rather get larger as they get older. Split tubers so each piece has eye. Or root stems in water. Small tuber will form at end with roots. Sow fine seed in box of peat.	Leaf curl due to poor drainage or red spider. Bud failure due to overwatering, botrytis blight, thrips and lack of humidity. Failure to bloom is due to lack of light as is spindly stems. Rotate plants every 3 or 4 days to prevent lopsidedness.
HANGING BASKETS	Ferns, ivies, fuschia, begonia, Episcia, Hoya, and many other trailing items are suitable. Use ⅓ each of sand peat and loam. Water daily by dipping basket in pail of water. Repot every 2 years.	Cuttings, seeds and by divisions.	Red spider, aphids. Put basket on porch and spray. Remove dead leaves and cut out poor dead growth as soon as you see them.

SOME FLOWERING PLANTS FOR YOUR HOME (*Continued*)

Flowering Plant	Green Thumb Care	Propagation	Problems
HYDRANGEA (*Hydrangea macrophylla*)	Prefers bright window, lots of water. After blooming, cut tops back 2″ above pot and plunge into garden until Sept. when it is brought in and left in cool, dark basement until Jan. 1, when it can be brought into living room.	Cuttings and by divisions.	Changing colors due to soil acidity. If you want to change yours from pink to blue, water with aluminum sulfate solution several times during growing season. Only pink varieties will turn blue. Plants not hardy outdoors. Non-flowering due to pruning. Prune *after* flowering or not at all. Yellow between veins means alkaline (sweet soil).
JERUSALEM CHERRY (*Solanum pseudo-capsicum*)	Likes cool bright window and lots of water. Give 70 degs. daytime temperature and 60 degs. at night. Fruits poisonous when eaten.	Seeds and cuttings taken in summer.	Fruit dropping, due to old age, lack of water or poor light. If plants get too leggy, prune them back for size and shape.
KAFIR LILY (*Clivia miniata*)	Does well indoors in same pot for years. Likes cool room and good light in winter, and should be outdoors in summer.	Start new plants, divisions.	Failure to flower due to lack of light.

SCARLET KALANCHOE (*Kalanchoe blossfeldiana*)	Handsome, tough little house plant which should be raised more for its glossy green leaves, pink or red flowers. Flowers in bright light from Thanksgiving until May.	Seeds and leaf cuttings any time of the year. Sow seed in sand-peat mix.	Failure to flower due to poor light.
LANTANAS (many species)	Ideal for hanging baskets, porch or patio. Need full soil and average soil. 55 to 65 degs. temperature.	Cuttings from outdoor plants will bloom in winter.	Lack of blossoms due to rich soil.
LEOPARD PLANT (*Ligularia kaempferi*)	Grandma grew this handsome plant for its spotted foliage and yellow flowers. Likes cool temperature, full sun or part shade, moist peaty soil.	Dividing old plant, or by taking stem cuttings in the spring.	May get leggy if not pruned. Also subject to red spider.
LILY-OF-VALLEY (*Convallaria majalis*)	"Pips" (Rootstocks) are dug from garden after foliage dies, stored at 30 to 40 degs. until Jan. when they can be planted in sand or moss and forced to flower merely by keeping them wet.	Divisions.	Failure to flower due to poor light or lack of cool storage period.
OLEANDER (*Nerium Oleander*)	Tubbed plant grown for foliage and white, pink or reddish-purple flowers in spring. Keep outdoors in summer, bring indoors in fall and keep dry until Mar. 1. Give bright light and ample moisture.	Cuttings.	Failure to flower due to lack of moisture. Tall plants get out of bound. Nip back old growth *after* flowering.

SOME FLOWERING PLANTS FOR YOUR HOME (*Continued*)

Flowering Plant	Green Thumb Care	Propagation	Problems
ORCHIDS (many species and varieties)	Orchids are more difficult to nurse than most house plants indoors. Cattleya is the most popular and easiest. All may be grown if humidity is high. Likes full sun in winter, and shredded bark for potting soil. Likes bright light but not full sun in summer.	Seeds and by division of "pseudo-bulbs."	Failure to flower due to poor light or low humidity. Orchids grow without sun, but will seldom, if ever, bloom. Red spider, scale and aphids. Use Malathion.
PASSION FLOWER (*Passiflora* species and hybrids)	In early winter plant likes to rest so give cool window and withhold water. In late winter give more water and temperature of 72 degs. Keep plant watered in summer outdoors. In fall, cut vine back to 10″ and bring indoors.	Cuttings in water, sand or perlite. Also seed sown indoors in Feb. or Mar. Seed is slow to germinate.	Yellow foliage due to red spider. Failure to flower due to early winter rest period.
POINSETTIA (*Euphorbia pulcherrima*)	Likes bright window at 70 degs. and plenty of water. After blooming, cut to 5″ in May and set pot in garden all summer. Bring indoors Sept. 1. Put plant in dark room each night until after Thanksgiving.	Cuttings taken in summer.	Leaf drop due to poor light, drafts, or high temperature. Failure to flower due to lack of long-night treatment.
RED HOT-CATTAIL (*Acalypha hispida*)	Has heart-shaped leaves and red "tails" for blooms. Prefers bright window. Shade during hot summer. Pinch soft foliage to make them branch.	Cuttings in sand-peat mixture.	Legginess. Pinching soft growth produces compact plant.

ROSES (Potted for Easter)	Prefers full sun and ample moisture. Plant outdoors after flowering. Hardy.	Cuttings under a fruit jar in summer.	Thrips and red spider.
TWELVE APOSTLES (*Neomarica northiana* and *N. gracilis*)	Flowers 2″ to 3″ across and iris-like, short-lived. New flowers unfold in quick succession over period of several weeks. Bright window and ample moisture.	Set old plant in garden in May. Bend flower stalk to earth and anchor. By autumn it'll be rooted and can be separated from the old parent plant.	Failure to flower due to dry soil, poor light.
WILD ORCHID (*Bletilla striata*)	"Oriental Orchid" of Japan. Potted in November, will bloom in Feb., with 6 or 8 dainty orchid blooms on a 12″ stem. Blooms for 6 weeks.	Rhizomes.	None.

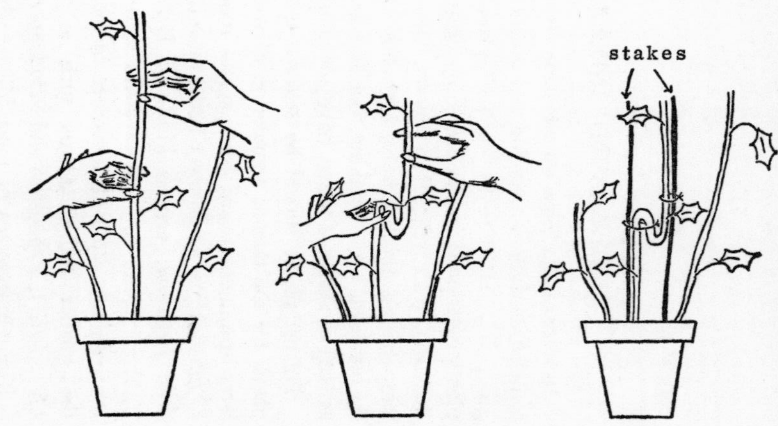

If your poinsettia grows out of bounds try this trick of shortening lanky stems. (1) Mash stems gently with thumb and index finger for a distance of one inch at two points shown. (2) Gently fold down, then up. (3) Stake and tie stem.

PART II

"HARD-LEAVED" INDOOR FOLIAGE PLANTS

In recent years home owners have turned to "hard-leaved" foliage plants to brighten drab corners and add distinction to the modern interior. This group is referred to as "foliage" plants, in contrast to the "flowering" plants mentioned in the preceding chapter. Foliage plants are grown for their leaf effect rather than flowers. They thrive under conditions of warm temperature, diffused light, high humidity and moist soil. Most homes do not have high humidity, but foliage plants on the whole are tough, as long as they are warm, have adequate moisture and a little heat.

Foliage plants should be selected with as much care as you'd select plants for the outside foundation of your home. Some foliage plants are large specimens suited for spacious rooms. Of these, *Monstera deliciosa* (*Philodendron pertussum*) is the most common. Others include *Philodendron hastatum,* various kinds of *Dracaena* and *Ficus* (the common "rubber" plant) and old favorites such as *Aspidistra.* "Dish gardens," a relatively new kind of adventure in indoor gardening, is making use of the smaller foliage plants such as Chinese Evergreen, *Syngonium* (*Nepthytis*), *Peperomia* and *Scindapsus* (*Pothos*).

The requirements of most foliage plants are simple: a humusy, well-drained soil, diffused light and the highest humidity possible. Probably more foliage plants die in dish gardens and planters from overwatering than underwatering. Plastic or metal containers are trickier to use because they do not dry out as fast as clay pots and therefore are usually over-watered. Water standing in them causes stunted growth, yellowed leaves and musty soil. For the most part, the soil and water requirements for foliage plants are similar to flowering plants. The big difference in culture is that the foliage plants need less light than do the flower-producing plants.

GROOMING "HARD-LEAVED" FOLIAGE PLANTS

If you've wondered how to make foliage on your vines and other indoor plants look shiny and well-scrubbed, try a trick that florists use. Put a few drops of glycerine on a cloth and swab the leaves. This gives the plants their desired natural colors and appearance, and at the same time eliminates the dull, dusty look found on most plants. Glycerine is safe to handle, does not harm plant life, and is also usable on gourds, for brighter effect. Never use olive oil as it collects dust and plugs up the pores in the leaves.

GROWING VINES ON TOTEM POLES

"Moss sticks" or "totem poles"—slabs of bark with moss wrapped around them—are used for growing house ivies such as philodendrons, grape ivy, English ivies and dozens of others. Roots grow into the bark and moss and receive added nourishment. To water the plant you simply add water (with liquid plant food added) to the bark and moss, and any excess water will drain to the pot, since the moss stick is sunk deep into the soil where it is anchored.

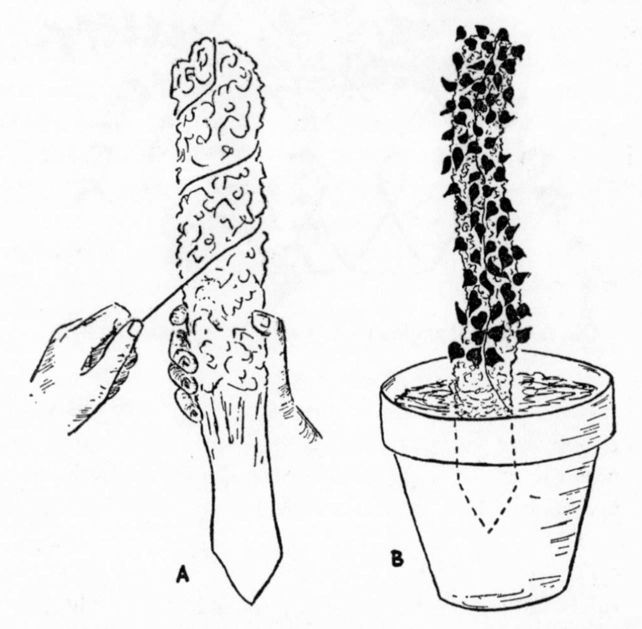

Totem poles made from a slab of wood and covered with sphagnum moss are good supports for philodendrons and other vines. (A) Shows how to wrap copper wire around the moss. (B) Shows vines growing luxuriantly in the moss.

SELECTING FOLIAGE PLANTS FOR THE HOME

Designed to help bring the garden into your home, indoor planters add a great deal to the view through low windows, whether you're on the outside looking in, or on the inside looking out. There are literally hundreds of foliage plants to use for interior decorating. Some that I'm listing are not strictly "hard-leaved" foliages, but may be admired for their leaf effect.

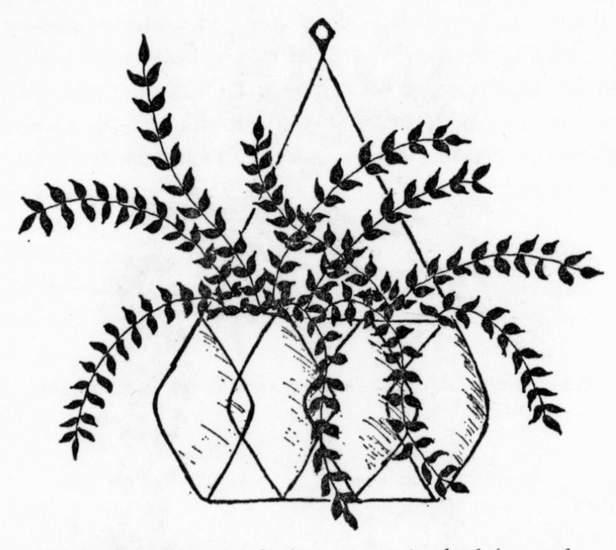

Old-fashioned hanging baskets are coming back into style.

Another type of hanging basket in use in the modern home.

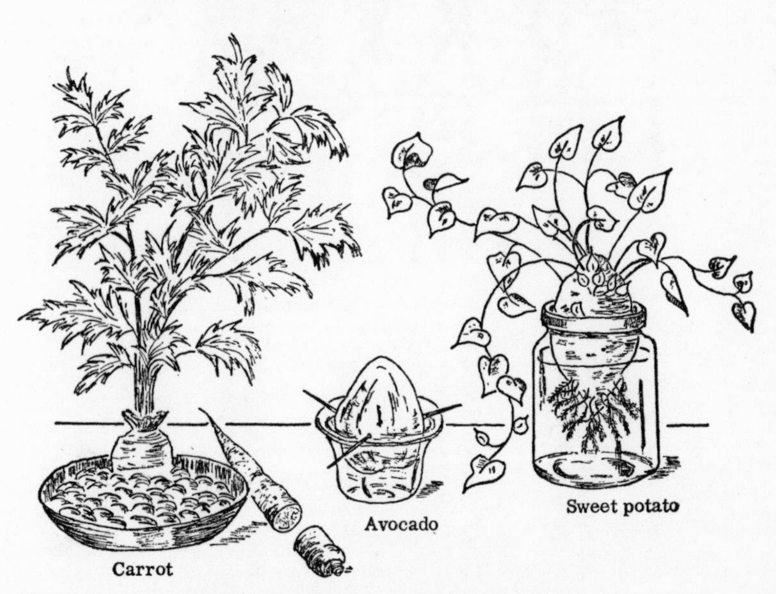

Simple methods of starting plants indoors.

Foliage Plant	Green Thumb Care	Propagation	Problems (For control see flowering plants)
ALUMINUM PLANT (*Pilea cadierei*)	Silver blotches as if aluminized.	Tips cuttings.	Rotting of stems due to poor drainage.
ARTILLERY PLANT (*pilea microphylla*)	Anthers (male elements) burst open and discharge little puffs of pollen, resembling smoke. Likes ample water, bright light.	Seeds and cuttings.	Light foliage due to lack of nitrogen.
GOLD DUST TREE (*Aucuba japonica*)	Variegated leathery leaves, some with yellow spots. Likes cool, bright window. Keep dry.	Cuttings.	Browning of edges due to hot, dry rooms.
BABY'S TEARS (*Helxine soleirolii*)	Pronounced Helk-sy-nee, this rambling plant makes a solid mat, often called "Paddy's Wig." Likes bright light, ample moisture.	Cuttings.	None.
BIRD OF PARADISE (*Strelitzia reginae*)	Nice foliage but hard to get flowers. Prefers 60 degs. at night, 70 in day. Takes up to 3 years for plants to bloom. Avoid excess watering in winter as plants are semi-dormant.	Seed in sand peat mix, also by divisions.	Failure to flower due to immaturity.
CACTUS (many genera)	Most cacti like 70 degs., bright light and a dry soil. Avoid plastic or glazed containers and excess watering. Sandy soil is best.	Seeds, grafting and cuttings.	Rotting due to excess water or poor drainage. Water from below, and make sure plants are well drained. Mealybugs; and scale.

CHINESE EVERGREEN (*Aglaonema modestum*)	Grows well in water, soil, light or dark room. Is tolerant of dry living rooms, does not like to be overwatered.	Cuttings and division.	Yellow leaves due to too much light and overwatering. Mealybug and scale; use Malathion.
CHRIST-IN-MANGER (*Phyllocactus*)	A close relative to Christmas cactus (see). Name comes from flower parts. "Manger" is the pistil (female parts) and the "Hovering Angels" are the stamens or male elements.	Cuttings.	Mealybugs, scale. Use Malathion.
COLEUS (*Coleus blumei;* many varieties)	Likes warm room, rich soil and ample moisture. Bright light or shade.	Seeds or tip cuttings rooted in water.	Mealybugs, use Malathion. Pale color due to lack of light. Tall plants, due to failure to pinch.
CORNCOB DISHGARDEN	Interesting foliage effect can be had by placing cob upright in dish of water until well soaked. Scatter grass seed over cob and in a week cob will be green. May be trimmed or grown in a shaggy manner.	Seeds.	Yellowing of grass due to lack of nitrogen. Soak with liquid plant food.
CROTON (*Codiaeum variegatum pictum*)	Highly ornamental foliage, likes rich soil, lots of heat, and a high humidity. Good light for best coloring.	Cuttings.	Leaf burn due to direct sun. Wilting foliage due to dry soil or dry air.
DUMB CANE DIEFFENBACHIA (many species)	One of the best foliage plants. Leaves have acrid juice which can cause temporary loss of speech if chewed. Bright window, ample moisture and 70 deg. temp. is best.	Cuttings. Cut stem in 3" pieces and root in pan of peat.	Tall plants. Cut top off and root in moist sphagnum moss.

Foliage Plant	Green Thumb Care	Propagation	Problems (For control see flowering plants)
EPISCIA	Ideal for hanging baskets, with culture same as for African violets. Rich loam soil, bright window for bronze-green foliage.	Cuttings.	Rotting due to excess moisture.
FERNS (many genera)	All ferns like a peaty, moist soil, a cool window and freedom from direct sun. Remove dead twigs and blind runners. Hose off fern in summer, and apply weak liquid plant food every 3 months. Repot yearly.	Division of roots, done any time of year. Spores from black spots on back of leaves (do not confuse these with insect pests!).	Scale, red spider. Use Malathion. Brown tips due to hot dry rooms. Yellowing of leaves due to poor drainage, standing in jardiniere, lack of nitrogen or too much sun.
FITTONIA (*Fittonia verschaffeltii*)	A real darling of the plant world, having handsomely veined foliage. Likes plenty of moisture and semi-shade, 70 degs.	Cuttings stuck in sand.	Wilts badly in dry soil, turns brown in direct sun, yellow in temp. below 55 degs.
IVY	Includes English ivy, Wandering Jew, Grape ivy, Sweet Potato and most trailing types. Most like bright windows, without direct sun. Grow in soil or water, temperature around 70 degs.	Cuttings stuck in water.	Drying of foliage due to hot rooms. Red spider, aphids and scale. Use Malathion.

JADE PLANT (*Crassula argentea*)	Old favorite will tolerate shade and neglect, but does best in bright windows and in moist soil. Place outdoors in summer; bring in in fall.	Leaf cuttings in sand.	Leaf drop due to poor light or excess water. Mealybugs and thrips, use Malathion. Wilted leaf due to anthracnose, dust with Captan. Root rot due to poor drainage.
KALANCHOE (*Kalanchoë blossfeldiana*)	Flowers are brick-red and numerous, leaves green and leathery, making it an ideal foliage plant. Needs full sun and moist humus soil.	Seeds and leaf cuttings.	Lack of flowers due to poor light or high temperatures. Mottled foliage due to thrips. Use Malathion. Dropping of foliage due to poor light or old age.
KANGAROO VINE (*Cissus antarctica*)	Has 3 leaflets resembling poison ivy (unrelated). One of the most durable foliage plants to grow.	Cuttings in sand or water.	Leaves turn brown or are scorched at edges, due to lack of water, or red spider.
KENILWORTH IVY (*Cymbalaria muralis*)	A delicate vine ideal for hanging baskets. Grows in sun or shade.	Cuttings and it also self-sows.	None.
MIGNONETTE Maderia Vine (*Boussingaultia gracilis*)	Tall, fast-growing item with tuberous roots, leaves are heart-shaped and tiny white flowers are fragrant.	Seed, root divisions and small tubercles found on stems.	Free from troubles.
GARDEN NASTURTIUM (*Tropaeolum majus*)	Here's a fast climber for indoor use, in sun or semi-shade.	Start seeds or cuttings.	Aphids. Spray with Malathion or nicotine sulfate.

Foliage Plant	Green Thumb Care	Propagation	Problems (For control see flowering plants)
NIGHT BLOOMING CEREUS (Cacti family: *Hylocereus undatus, Selenicereus undatus, Nyctocereus serpentinus*)	There are several night-blooming plants. Most all detest overwatering. Prefer bright light, well-drained soil. Take many years to bloom. Flower in summer, rest in winter.	Cuttings.	Stubborn blooming habit. Give good light and plenty of water in summer, less in winter. Don't force it during winter rest period.
NORFOLK ISLAND PINE (*Araucaria heteraphylla*)	A charming evergreen for indoor culture. Likes cool window, ample moisture and a fairly heavy soil.	Seeds, or cuttings taken from tip growth and rooted in sand.	Open space between whorls makes plant less graceful. Greenhouse-grown plants are preferred to home-raised types.
PALMS (many genera)	There are many true palms, but one used often is Paradise Palm (*Kentia*), found in hotels, lobbies, florists' shops. All have same culture. Soak well when watering, give filtered light. Syringe foliage regularly to rid dust.	Seeds; slow to germinate (3 to 16 months). Buy fresh palm seed because it does not mature properly indoors.	Yellow leaves from poor drainage, or bright sun. Burning at tips or edge of leaves due to hot, dry room or fertilizer injury.
PEPEROMIA (many species)	Will not tolerate heavy soggy soils, prefers loose peaty type. "Little Fantasy" is a hybrid with crinkled leaves. All prefer filtered or subdued light, dry soil.	Leaf and stem cuttings.	Stem and crown rot due to overwatering or poor drainage, or heavy soggy soil.

PHILODENDRON (many species)	A large group and one of the most popular. They prefer subdued light, and temperature of 60 to 70 degs. Humus soil is best and they prefer to be grown on "totem poles" (see).	Tip, cuttings in sand or water.	Smaller leaves due to lack of light, hard soils. Failure of slit-leaved types to develop holes or slits; due to age. Yellow leaves due to overwatering, dry soils or too much plant food. Tip-burn and leaf-scorch, due to dry room or dry soil. Overwatering is cause of most troubles here.
PICK-A-BACK PLANT (*Tolmiea menziesii*)	"Youth-on-Age," endures dry air, dust and gas fumes in most homes. Likes bright light and ample moisture. Regular house-plant soil is suitable.	A self-propagating type, producing small plantlets which will root if pinned on surface of soil in a pot.	Leaves turn yellow due to direct sun or lack of nitrogen.
PRAYER-PLANT (*Maranta leuconeura*)	Oval dark green leaves with brown spots, leaves folding up at night. Likes it warm; avoid direct sun.	Divisions or cuttings in sand.	Scorched foliage due to dry air or hot sun.
ROSARY VINE (*Ceropegia woodii*)	String of heart-shaped leaves make this ideal for hanging baskets. Does best on dry side, likes warm room and filtered sunlight.	Root cuttings in sand or water.	Rotting due to overwatering or poor drainage.
"RUBBER" PLANT (*Ficus* species)	Glossy green leaves elliptical or fiddle-shaped. Plants like full sun, rich soil and lots of water during growing season. Slow growers resistant to dry air in the home.	Tip cuttings and air-layering.	Leaf-drop due to poor light, too much water. Spots on edges due to dry soil or leaf spot disease.

Foliage Plant	Green Thumb Care	Propagation	Problems (For control see flowering plants)
SCINDAPSUS (*Scindapsus aureus*)	Heart-shaped leaves, solid green or splashed with yellow. A handsome trailing vine, to me more handsome than philodendron. Keep out of direct sun. Likes humus soil.	Leaf or stem cuttings.	Crown rot due to poor drainage or overwatering.
SCREW PINE (*Pandanus veitchii*)	Stiff spikey leaves need ample room. Tolerates shade, should be watered sparingly and soil must be well drained. A rugged foliage plant for the "Everything-I-touch-dies" gardener.	Offshoots or suckers.	Scorched leaves or burning around edges, due to hot sun or dry air.
SENSITIVE PLANT (*Mimosa pudica*)	A curiosity valued for its ability to droop when touched. Likes loose soil, ample light and warm temperature.	Seeds, which are tricky to start. File a notch in the seedcoat to hasten germination.	Yellowing of foliage due to excess water.
SHAMROCK (*Oxalis* species)	Term Oxalis is common name for both Oxalis and white clover. No such thing as a true shamrock. Oxalis is a bulbous perennial grown in pots. Loose soil and good light are main requirements.	Seed and bulbs. Bulbs started in October will produce by spring.	Avoid overwatering.
SNAKE PLANT (*Sansevieria* species)	Most common foliage plant today, grows in most soils, bright light or shaded window. Blossoms when given good care.	Cuttings and divisions. Divide every 3 or 4 years. Cuttings from variegated type will not come true. Divide these plants.	Yellowing of leaves due to overwatering. No pests to trouble it.

SPIDER PLANT (*Chlorophytum capense*)	Numerous bright green leaves make it a different sort of foliage plant. Prefers cool temperature, good drainage and loose soil. O.K. in sun or part shade. *C. comusum* is another leaved variety.	Division.	Red spider, checked with Malathion. Yellow foliage due to heavy soil or poor drainage.
STRAWBERRY "GERANIUM" (*Saxifraga sarmentosa*)	Leaves round, or heart-shaped. Known as "Mother-of-Thousands," it is happy in a cool, lighted window without sun. Rich soil with ample humus.	Planting the young plants.	Leaf-scorch due to bright sun.
SYNGONIUM (*Syngonium podophyllum* "Trileaf wonder")	Leaves rich green and arrow-shaped; prefers moist soil and indirect light.	Cuttings.	Yellow leaves due to poor drainage, scorched tips from direct sunlight.
TERRARIUMS	Glass container used to grow small plants from the woods and fields. Use ⅓ each of sand, peat and loam to grow seedlings, lichens, bits of bark, moss, etc. Avoid overwatering.	Get the small plants in fall in woods, fields and meadows.	Rotting due to too much water. Ventilate in day if rotting does start.
TREE IVY (*Fatshedera lizei*)	Ivy grows upright, leaves resemble maple foliage. Does well in sun or dull window. Soil must be kept moist.	Cuttings.	May get scale. Use Malathion. Yellow foliage due to wet feet.
TROPICAL FRUITS	Avocado pears, dates, olives, figs, grapefruits, etc., all prefer a humus soil, ample light and a warm temperature.	Seeds and cuttings. Buy started plants from a nursery for most items.	Failure to set fruit is natural, as they are meant for outdoor growing. Red spider and scale, checked by syringing and Malathion.

Foliage Plant	Green Thumb Care	Propagation	Problems (For control see flowering plants)
WANDERING JEW (*Zebrina* and *Tradescantia* species)	Ideal for porch boxes, planters, terrariums and hanging baskets. Shade from bright sun. Likes loose soil.	Root shoots in water.	Tips take on a scorched appearance, due to dry soil.
WAX PLANT (*Hoya* species)	Prefers full sun, rich, well-drained soil. If pot-bound somewhat, plant will bloom well. Keep cool and dry in fall and winter.	Cuttings.	Failure to bloom. Due to lack of light or rest period in fall.

5

Bulbs, Tubers and Corms

To the gardener, the term "bulb" includes all plants grown from corms, and tubers as well as bulbs. All of these are food storage organs. A busy gardener should not concern himself with the correct term for each of these underground storage organs, although the botanist would take a different view. To most of us, a dahlia "toe" is a swollen root. The canna has an underground stem called a rhizome. The gladiolus "bulb" is a swollen stem technically known as a corm. Narcissus, tulip and hyacinth plants produce bulbs which are buds (or an embryo flower) surrounded by scaly, fleshy leaves. All of these parts of plants are lumped into a large group called bulbs, for the sake of simplicity.

These are divided into hardy and non-hardy bulbs, the term here again being used to include corms, rhizomes and bulbs as well. For hardy bulbs, see that section.

PART I

NON-HARDY BULBS

A non-hardy bulb is one which will not live outdoors over winter. These are usually dug in fall, stored in winter and started into growth again the following year. Here are some of the most common types, with special green thumb tips to guide you.

AMARYLLIS: (*Hippeastrum*)

Description and Uses: The flowers are similar in form to the Easter lily, coming in assorted colors with various shades and markings of red, pink, scarlet and rose. The plant often bears flowers before the foliage appears. Ideal for pots indoors.

Green Thumb Care: Place in a 6-inch pot, removing all dead roots. A mixture of sand, peat and garden loam, with a teaspoon of bonemeal for each 6-inch pot is ideal. Plant so neck of bulb is above soil surface; water and place in cool light room, but not in full sun.

A temperature of 50 degrees is ideal while roots are forming. Warmer temperature causes top growth, with no roots, giving poor flowers or none at all. A dark room is not necessary. After roots have formed, keep in a room at 70 degrees. Avoid overwatering before growth starts. After growth starts, they need plenty of water. A liquid feeding every three weeks is good, from April to August 1. After danger of frost is over, set the pots at earth level in a semi-shaded spot in the garden and continue watering all summer. The amaryllis usually flowers only once a year.

Fall Care: Bring the bulbs indoors before frost, and place in a cool basement, gradually withholding water until earth in the pot is absolutely dry. This will cure them and give the bulbs the 60-day rest period they need prior to starting new growth. This is the secret for getting the amaryllis to bloom indoors. Incidentally, leave the bulb in the same pot year after year.

Propagation: By seed and small bulbs ("offsets"). Sow seed in January in a sand-peat mixture. Allow plants to grow for two years before giving them a rest period. Take offsets from old bulbs at potting time.

Problems: Failure to bloom. This usually indicates a need for plant food. Scrape soil from top surface and add a loose soil mixture.

BEGONIA: (Tuberous Rooted)

Description and Uses: Called the "mockingbird" flower because the blossoms have so many forms resembling other flowers such as camellia, rose, hollyhock, daffodil and others. The camellia-type begonia is the most popular, ranging in colors from white, yellow, bronze and reds, with blooms 5 inches in diameter. The tuberous begonia makes a poor house plant but an ideal flowering plant for a semi-shaded part of the garden or border.

Green Thumb Care: Tuberous begonias like a rich soil composed of ⅓ sand, ⅓ peat and ⅓ light loam. This shade-lover will tolerate morning sun and late afternoon sun, but should be protected from the hot mid-day sun. They like water and should be kept constantly moist, never waterlogged. Don't be fooled by tuber size or shape. The tubers are flat, shaped like a door knob. The size is not affected by age, nor does the age of the tuber affect the quality. I've seen some reach the age of 20 years.

Some growers start the tubers indoors in pots in February. If you've had trouble with rot, place the tubers upside down and cover with ½ inch of peat moss. Keep in a cold room (50 degrees) for a few days, giving the tubers a chance to take on moisture slowly. Then move into a room of 70 degrees or so for 2 weeks. As soon as they start to form roots on their upturned bottoms, turn tubers right-side up and pot in a humus soil, covering the top with about ½ inch of soil. If rotting hasn't been a problem, plant tubers right-side up with the surface of the bulb showing. If you have long growing seasons, plant tubers directly outdoors.

Outdoors the plants may be given a liquid feeding once a month. If you cut flowers for use in a corsage, cut only half the stem. The other half will mature and fall off by itself, leaving no wound.

Single flowers are pistillate (female) and double flowers are staminate (male). Keep spent flowers picked off.

Digging: Dig the tubers after a light frost has nipped the stalks and allow to ripen off in an airy, sunny spot. After a month of slow ripening, clean the tubers, dust with sulfur and store in a half-and-half mixture of dry sand and peat moss at 40 to 50 degrees until the end of February.

If tubers are grown in pots outdoors, simply store pot and all in the cellar until late February when they can be repotted.

Propagation: From cuttings, seed, and division of tubers. To make cuttings, start the tubers indoors and when sprouts are a few inches long, sever the fleshy stem and root them in warm, moist sand. These rooted shoots are potted up and planted outdoors where they'll bloom the first year. Young cuttings will form tubers that can be stored away for another year.

You can cut an old tuber into two or more pieces, but make sure each one has one or more "eyes." Place the tuber in moist peat moss in February, allow sprouts to form enough so you can see them. Then take a sharp knife and divide.

Tuberous begonias raised from seed will bloom in seven months. Sow in January in a light soil mixture. Plants from seed are more compact than those from tubers and you can buy separate color strains that are 90 per cent or better true to color. Buy seed from a florist since your own tuberous begonias usually carry incomplete and nonviable seed. The seed is fine and must not be covered. Merely press it into the soil.

Problems: Mildew, a white furry growth on leaves. Avoid wetting foliage in late afternoon. Dust with Mildex, Karathane or sulfur.

Leaf-scorch and leaf-curl are due to too much sun.

Bud- and flower-drop means dry soil, too much water.

Lots of growth but no flowers can mean too much shade or too much nitrogen in the soil.

Leaf spot disease shows up as round, dead spots followed by premature leaf-drop. Dust with Captan.

Red spider causes leaves to curl and turn pale. Dust with Kelthane or Malathion.

Caladium (Fancy-leaved Caladiums)

Description and Uses: Here's a striking decorative foliage plant valued for its ornamental veins and marbled foliage. It can be grown outdoors as a bedding plant, but is more popular in the home since its brilliantly marked leaves go well with modern decorations. Good for sunless room, terrace or shaded garden.

Green Thumb Care: Caladiums are shade-lovers. Dry soil, too much sun and dry air may cause leaf-burn. Apply a liquid summer feeding and give lots of water at all times. Syringing the foliage once a week keeps plants nice and fresh.

Propagation: By tubers. Caladium tubers have "eyes" similar to potatoes. The larger the tuber, the more eyes that will develop sprouts and leaves. To increase your plants, cut the tubers into pieces, in spring, allowing one or two eyes per section. Dust the cut surfaces with Ferbam, Captan or sulfur.

Many commercial growers plant tubers in clean sand, peat or vermiculite at 80 degrees F. with plenty of water until root action has started. Caladium roots start from the top of the tuber, near the growing point. For that reason, some florists start tubers upside down so that roots start from the part of the tuber deep-set in the soil. They say this gives larger plants. As soon as the roots show, the tubers are potted right-side up in 4-inch pots, using half-peat and half-loam mix. In fall, dry the tuber and store in peat or sand and leave in a cool cellar until spring when you can repot in a humus mixture.

Problems: Wilting and dying of foliage. Due to overwatering. This shuts off oxygen from roots. The aluminum-wrap-around pots will sometimes trap water and cause this. Punch a hole in the bottom to make sure water is drained. It's natural for leaves to turn yellow in fall.

CANNA (Canna)

Description and Uses: The modern canna is a highly hybridized plant 4 feet tall with broad leaves colored green or bronze, and with a wide range of flower colors. The canna has outlived its boycott by gardeners and has staged a comeback in newer and better colors. This member of the *Cannaceae* family looks best in masses or groups rather than planted singly.

Green Thumb Care: Cannas like full sun, rich soil and plenty of water during dry spells. There are two ways to handle the bulbs: (1) Plant directly outdoors or (2) start them indoors in pots for early bloom. I start mine indoors in 4-inch pots in February, using a half-peat, half-loam mix. Water sparingly until growth has started, and then give plenty of water. Outdoors, plant the tuber with the "eye" about an inch below the surface.

Cannas are tropical herbs and cannot tolerate much frost. Dig the same as you do dahlias, following a black frost. Lift roots and allow to dry in sun for a few hours. Cut stalks to within 5 or 6 inches of roots and store the fleshy roots upside down in orange crates in the cellar. I dust mine with sulfur and cover with vermiculite to prevent drying. Every now and then take a look to see if they are shrivelling or rotting. If too dry, sprinkle lightly with water.

Propagation: Division of roots in spring. Take a sharp knife and cut each division with one good eye on each piece. Plant divisions in 4-inch pots after dusting with sulfur.

Problems: Non-flowering. Usually due to too short a growing season. Start plant indoors, about five weeks before planting time. Non-flowering may also be due to lack of phosphorus, or too much nitrogen. Also excess shade will cause it. There's a bacterial bud rot which ruins the flowers and leaves. Control for this comes by treating dormant tubers for 2 hours in a solution of corrosive sublimate.

CLIVIA (Kafir-Lily)

Description and Uses: This popular member of the Amaryllis family has narrow evergreen leaves and showy 3-inch blooms of orange and scarlet in early spring. Plants have fleshy roots which shouldn't be allowed to dry out completely.

Green Thumb Care: Place the bulb in an 8-inch, florist's clay pot to allow for growth. In summer, leave pot outdoors until first frost threatens and then bring into cool room or cellar for resting period until January. Give just enough water to prevent drying out, and after January move it to a warm room and feed it liquid plant food. After buds start to show, increase the water supply. *Clivia miniata* hybrids produce flowers in large trusses any time from March to May. After blooming, reduce watering gradually and place outdoors in summer until fall.

Propagation: Bulbs.

Problems: None serious.

DAHLIA (Common Dahlia)

Description and Uses: The common dahlia has come a long way within the past twenty years. There are all types, sizes and colors to suit any fancy. Dahlias are ideal for cut flowers, in beds and borders.

Green Thumb Care: Dahlias do well in a wide variety of soil, so long as drainage is good. If soil is clayey, work in some form of humus in fall and also an application of 5–10–5 plant food.

Dig holes 4 to 6 inches deep, 4 inches in heavy soils, 6 inches in light soils. Place the tuberous root flat in hole in a horizontal position, with eye facing upwards. At time of planting, put a 4-foot garden stake 1 inch from end of root. The young plant can thus be given support all the time until it reaches full growth. Cover the root with soil. As plants grow, tie the stem to stake using pieces of cloth. Tubers should be planted about 3 feet apart, especially the tall vigorous varieties. Incidentally, don't condemn a small tuber. Many of the best varieties make small tubers.

Cultivation: Early in summer, hoe to keep weeds down. About ten weeks after planting, do no more cultivation, especially when plants are in bud or bloom. I apply a sawdust mulch around our plants in summer to keep weeds down.

Pinching and Disbudding: Both terms are used by dahlia growers who grow top-quality flowers. To get symmetrical plants, pinch when about a foot high, by nipping out the top just above the second set of leaves. Pinching gives a better show of flowers in the pompon, mignon and bedding types. If large exhibition flowers are desired, the plants should be disbudded, and side shoots removed. To disbud, you pinch out all the buds except one central one in each group. Buds usually appear in groups or clusters of three, so you remove the side two. As other buds form, remove these. Pinching, just as for mums, develops a shorter, more branched plant, and is done before the flowers begin to develop, early in the season. Pinching retards flowering, but disbudding does not. Most gardeners neither pinch nor disbud and they still get lots of blooms. More important to them is keeping insects and diseases from their plants so they'll blossom before frost.

Cutting Blooms: As cut flowers, some dahlias are often discouraging, while others make excellent cut flowers. Large-flowering types usually wilt if cut during the day. Cut after sundown or very early in the A.M. Dipping the ends of stems in boiling water for a minute helps keep flowers longer. We use many cactus-flowering types and pompons in our floral work.

Digging: Dahlias can be dug any time after the first killing frost. This checks the growth and causes the stalks, limbs and leaves to blacken. Leave them this way for a couple of weeks so that juices can flow back to the toes. Then take a digging fork and lift the entire clump without bruising the slender necks of the tuberous roots. When the neck is broken, you usually have a "dud" tuber. Cut the tops off so that one or two inches of the stem remain attached to the crown. Some gardeners leave the soil attached, others hose it off and then allow tubers to dry a few hours before storing in wooden trays or orange crates. A cool, well-ventilated cellar is ideal and helps to cover the roots with peat moss which has a moisture content of 50 per cent. This can be done easily by weighing out 10 pounds of peat moss and adding it to 2½ quarts of water. Work the peat over thoroughly.

Incidentally, sometimes new shoot growth may come after heavy black frosts. When this happens, break off the shoots before storing tubers, since this "de-sprouting" operation will save strength for toes next year.

Some gardeners do not dig their dahlias each fall. Mrs. Maude Wohlschlegel of R.D. 3, Naples, N.Y., has left hers in the ground for seven years. She cuts her stalks back to the ground in the fall, covers clumps with a foot of leaves and places chicken wire over the pile. Her dahlias start flowering earlier and she doesn't worry about storage problems. With protection, some of her clumps have come through winters of 29 degrees below zero.

Propagation: Dividing roots in fall or spring, seed and by indoor cuttings. The best way to divide dahlias is to wait until the eyes really start and then with a sharp knife, cut the clump or roots into divisions. The tuberous roots are connected to the main stem at the region known as the crown, where new buds or eyes are produced. Each division should be detached so that an eye or bud remains connected with it. To increase stock by indoor cuttings, pot the tubers in January and allow shoots to grow. As soon as a shoot with a second or third set of leaves develops, cut off at soil surface and place cuttings in a flat of coarse sand, or vermiculite and keep moist. In three or four weeks they will root and can be potted up for planting outdoors in shirtsleeve weather.

Outdoor Cuttings: You can root shoots by breaking off leaf stalks and inserting them in the open ground. Branches broken by wind or rain can be rooted this way.

Seed: Dahlias do not produce seed in areas with short growing season, but you can buy seed for starting plants. The odds are 1,000 to 1 against any one seed producing an outstanding new plant. Sow seed in March, using vermiculite, peat or a mixture of sand and peat. Cover lightly and place a pane of glass over the seed box and store in a room at 60 degrees. As soon as seed has sprouted, remove glass and place the seedbox in a bright window. After seedlings have first set of leaves, transplant into 3-inch pots and grow on until shirtsleeve weather when they can be set outdoors. For raising annual dahlias from seed, see section under annuals.

Problems: Premature budding, when plants are only a foot high. Cloudy weather in late spring will initiate flower buds. So will hot dry days. When this happens, cut plants back in July and you'll get all new growth for the fall show. Or, you can remove most of the buds or blossoms so plants can develop.

Failure to Bloom: This is due to too much shade or too rich a soil, factors which sometimes are responsible for no tubers.

Stunt: This is a virus which causes leaves to curl and turn yellow. Stunted plants seldom flower, tuber development is repressed and the disease causes tubers to rot in storage. Destroy such plants.

Insects: Tarnished-plant bugs. An insect 1/4 inch long causes buds to blacken, or grow lopsided, flowers open one-sided or not at all. Thrips feed on open flowers and leaves. Leafhoppers cause leaves to turn pale along the edges and curl, gradually dying. Cornborers cause the stalks to suddenly wilt. For all these pests, use Malathion, an all-purpose bug killer. Snails sometimes eat blooms and foliage during the night. Clean up rubbish around plantings. Scatter a metaldehyde bait around the base of your plants.

Change in colors: Dahlias often change colors by a process known as mutation, more commonly called "sporting" or "breaking." Mums, azaleas and many other plants often do this. The cause of mutation is unknown, but it can be induced artificially by use of X-ray, heat treatment and use of a gout remedy known as colchicine.

Freesia

Description and Uses: This is a fragrant indoor or greenhouse bulbous herb grown for its white or yellowish flowers, popular among florists who use them in wedding and vase arrangements.

Green Thumb Care: Plant the corms an inch deep, about a dozen in a 6-inch pot, using plain garden loam. Set pot in a cool, light place free from frost, moderately watered until tops are 1 to 2 inches high. Then increase water gradually. When tops are 6 inches high, increase the room temperature. After flowering, dry off gradually to allow natural growth to be completed. When foliage yellows, place in frost-proof, sunny spot to ripen bulbs. After two weeks, store bulbs in cellar until fall.

Propagation: By bulbs.

Problems: None.

Gladiolus

Description and Uses: "Glads" are the most important bulb plant grown in America. Their long period of bloom and usefulness in floral arrangements makes them highly desirable as a cut flower. If you're wondering about the correct spelling, whether it's gladiolus, gladiola, or gladioli, you'll be interested to know that the American Gladiolus Society put an end to this confusion by polling glad-growers throughout America and an overwhelming majority voted to call the flower "gladiolus," both singular and plural.

Green Thumb Care: Plant your corms as soon as you can work the soil. A series of plantings will spread the blooming over a longer season. Early varieties may take from 65 to 75 days to bloom; mid-season varieties 75 to 85; and the late ones 90 days or more, sometimes taking as long as 120 days.

Corms are graded in six sizes: No. 1., 1½ inches and larger; No. 2, 1¼ inches to 1½ inches; No. 3., 1 to 1¼ inches; No. 4., ¾ to 1 inch; No. 5., ½ to ¾ inch; and No. 6., ½ inch and under. Large corms will bloom about 4 days earlier than medium-sized ones and from 10 to 14 days earlier than small ones. Unless you plant to grow for exhibition purposes, you can buy the medium corms, which are often cheaper and will flower well the first year. The bloom from these will be almost as large as that from the larger and more expensive ones.

Plant glads in rows 18 to 30 inches apart and at a depth of 4 inches in heavy soil, 6 inches in a light soil. Glads do not exhaust the soil if you return humus and plant food. The biggest danger of not rotating the land is building up diseases. Do not plant glads near beans as glads sometimes get bean mosaic. By planting corms of various sizes and varieties of different maturity, you'll have blooms from the middle of July until the fall freeze.

Watering: First-class spikes come when glads are given an abundance of water. Water applied to the soil is less apt to spread disease than is overhead watering.

Feeding: Apply a balanced food between rows while the plants are growing. About ⅓ of the fertilizer can be used just after the shoots come up, the remainder being used in two or three top dressings about 3 weeks apart. Many growers feel that the fertility under which the glads grew the year before has much more to do with the growth of the plants than the fertilizer you give them *while* they are growing.

Cutting Blossoms: If blossoms are cut in the bud stage, or when two or three florets show color, they'll open up nicely indoors. Spikes can be cut in early morning or late afternoon with a sharp knife. Remember that next year's flowers will be determined by the growth made in the new corm after the flower spike has come and gone, therefore leave as many leaves on the plant as possible.

Weeding and Cultivation: Shallow cultivation is best for keeping weeds down. There are chemicals you can use when applied to a moist, packed soil, just prior to emergence from the soil. This treatment kills the germinating weed seeds as these are more sensitive to weed killers than the more developed weeds. Post-emergence treatments, those applied after the glad shoots are up, should be directed at the bases of the plants and not used when the spikes are just emerging. I've had wonderful luck with Crag Herbicide. This material works on weed seeds, having no effect on weeds an inch or taller. Gladiolus plants tolerate this chemical both before they emerge and up to the time they are about 10 inches tall, so the chemical may be used 8 to 12 days after planting, and again about 5 weeks later. Use 1 level tablespoon in a gallon of water for a 100-foot row, and apply with a sprinkling can.

Winter Storage: The corms may be dug any time when the foliage is still green (it's not necessary for foliage to yellow off). Cut the stalks tight to the corm. Dry the corms in a warm part of the cellar for a couple of weeks. Then dust the corms leaving the tissues on. Place corms in paper bags or wooden trays and store in temperature of 40 degrees or so.

Propagation: By seed. Gather pods and store in sealed glass jars until spring. Sow seeds in loose soil in spring. If you do not want to use the seed, be sure not to allow spikes to develop seed pods.

By cutting corms in half. In spring select corms with two or more buds, then cut the corm through the middle between the two buds. Dust with sulfur and plant.

By bulblets. Save the pea-like bulbs or cormels clustered around the large corms. Store in winter and plant in rows in spring.

Problems: "Changing colors." Glad bulbs do not change colors. Some colors are strong physically and send up a number of flower spikes, and each spike produces a usable corm. It's a case of the survival of the fittest, the stronger outproducing the weaker ones. Sometimes a gladiolus will revert or "mutate," producing a sport of a different color.

Crooked stalks (Saxophone spikes). This is an inherited trait. Select varieties which do not develop crooked spikes.

Mosaic. Causes mottling, spotting, specking, twisting and crinkling of flowers. Blossoms become hood-shaped. Control: Rogue (pull up) diseased plants and burn.

Scab. Causes deep circular pockmarks on the surface of corms. While it appears ugly, it's not a serious disease. Treat infected corms with one tablet of corrosive sublimate (deadly poisonous) to 7½ gallons of water. Soak corms for two hours.

Thrips. The worst enemy of gladiolus. Look for white transparent spots on the leaves and blooms. They cause buds to blast (fail to open). Keep plants dusted regularly using 5 per cent DDT dust and starting when leaves are 6 inches high.

Tall and short plants. No one knows why a variety will grow 4 feet tall one year and only 2 feet the next year. Weather, fertility, insects and other factors enter the picture.

HYMENOCALLIS (*Ismene Calathina*) Spider Lily, Peruvian Daffodil.

Description and Uses: This tropical member of the lily family has white flowers 6 to 8 inches long, making an ideal pot plant or outdoor plant.

Green Thumb Care: This summer-bloomer prefers full sun and ample water. Set bulbs out in spring in shirtsleeve weather and feed once or twice during growing season. In fall, dig bulbs and store them in the hottest room in your cellar. Cool storage prevents or delays blooming.

Propagation: Bulbs.

Problems: Failure to bloom. Due to too much shade, cold storage temperature in winter, or lack of moisture during summer.

ORNITHOGALUM THYRSOIDES (Chincherinchee or South African Wonder Flower)

Description and Uses: This is the plant commerical firms offer free in their advertisements as an inducement to buy their products. I've seen three different spellings for this bulbous herb. Chincherichee, Chinkerichee and Chincherinchee, the last (pronounced Chin-che-rin-chee) being preferred. Bulbs are globe-shaped, 1½ inches thick. The variety Aureum has brilliant long-lasting yellow flowers and you can also buy bulbs with white blooms.

Green Thumb Care: Plant is not hardy and must be grown indoors. Plant bulbs 1 inch deep in pots or boxes in a mixture of loam and peat or compost plus sand, in September. Avoid overwatering when growth starts and after full growth has been attained, give more water. After the foliage starts to turn yellow, withhold watering and dry the bulbs for another year.

Propogation: Bulbs.

Problems: None.

POLIANTHES (Tuberose)

Description and Uses: These summer-flowering tubers are natives of Mexico and a member of the Amaryllis family. Their waxy white flowers have a delightful aroma in both single and double forms. This old-fashioned outdoor bloomer makes a fine addition to the summer garden.

Green Thumb Care: Being a tender bulb, it should be planted outdoors after danger of frost is over. Start them in pots in early May and plant in a sunny bed for earlier bloom. Dig bulbs in fall and store in warm cellar about 60 degrees.

Propagation: Buy new bulbs each year since bulbs which have flowered are difficult to flower again the following season.

Problems: Failure to bloom. Usually due to a shortage of water during the growing season.

ZEPHYRANTHES (Fairy Lily)

Description and Uses: This tender bulb has delicate funnel-shaped single flowers coming in white, yellow, pink and bronze colors with grass-like foliage. Blossoms come out one or two at a time, fade out and oddly enough you can get three flowerings from your pot of bulbs within a year's time.

Green Thumb Care: Pot bulbs in soil mixture of peat and loam, grow in a sunny window until warm weather comes. Grow outdoors in summer and bring it in before frost.

Propagation: Bulbs divided during dormant period.

Problems: None.

GREEN THUMB TIPS ON NON-HARDY BULBS

Lack of moisture during growing season can cause failure to bloom.

Seed pods can cause a drain on your plants. Keep them removed.

A QUICK GUIDE TO SOME COMMON SUMMER-FLOWERING BULBS

Flower		Type of Soil	Exposure	Time to Plant	Depth	Apart	Dig	Store
Acidanthera	S	Sandy loam	Sun or part shade	Early Spring	3 in.	6 in.	Before frost	45–55°
Anemones de Caen St. Brigid	S	Humus-rich sandy loam	Morning sun	Aug. to Nov. or early Spring	2 in.	12 in.	Leave in Mulch 5 in.–6 in. After first frost	35–45°
Begonia, tuberous	T	Rich, fibrous	Shade	Feb. to Mar. indoors. After last frost outdoors	1–2 in. in pots	12 in.	Dry off in pots (Autumn)	50–60°
Dahlia	T	Rich loam	Sun	After last frost	5–6 in.	24 in.	Before first frost	45–55°
Galtonia (*Hyacinthus candicans*)	T	Rich, sandy loam	Sun or part shade	After last frost	3–5 in.	8 in.	Before first frost	50–60°
Gladiolus	S	Humus-rich sandy loam	Sun	Apr. to June 15	3–5 in.	6 in.	After frost	35–45°
Lilium	H	Well-drained loam	Sun or part shade	Early Spring (or Autumn)	3–12 in.	24 in.	Leave in ground	
Montbretia	S	Rich, sandy loam	Sun or light shade	After last frost	3–5 in.	5–6 in.	After frost	35–45°
Oxalis Deppei	T	Sandy loam	Sun	After last frost Sept.–Oct. in pots indoors	1 in.	6 in.	Before frost Dry off in pots	50–60°
Ranunculus	S	Humus-rich sandy soil	Sun	Spring (or Autumn)	2 in.	6 in.	As Anemone	35–45°
Tigridia	S	Sandy loam	Sun	Early Spring	2–3 in.	8 in.	After first frost	35–45°

Start fine seeds on a brick sitting in a pan of water.

Curling leaves may be due to red spider. Spray weekly with Malathion.

Don't be afraid to buy new stock every year or so.

Poor soils mean poor growth. Spend time to build up soils. (See section on Soils.)

In winter storage, prevent bulbs from rotting and drying. Dust with sulfur.

Watch out for weed killers. Misuse can cause trouble.

Be on lookout for new "sports." You may have something!

PART II

HARDY OR OUTDOOR BULBS

There is nothing more interesting in a gardener's green thumb bag of tricks than his ability to stage a show from outdoor-flowering bulbs. The hardy or outdoor bulbs are a big group which home owners depend on each year for outdoor display. Hardy bulbs are those which can be left in the ground year after year without danger of winterkilling. Here are some of the most common hardy bulbs you can grow for maximum enjoyment and with a minimum of effort.

COLCHICUM AUTUMNALE (Autumn Crocus or Meadow Saffron)

Description and Uses: Flowers appear on bare stems the beginning of September with leaves showing up in spring. Flower color ranges from white to lavender or orchid. This is the so-called "Mystery" bulb which grows without soil or water as advertisements claim. Ideal for rock gardens, in among ground covers and between evergreens.

Green Thumb Care: Plant as soon as received or they'll bloom inside the package. They will grow in any soil, in a sunny spot. Allow leaves to grow so they can form buds for fall flowering.

Propagation: Dividing bulbs in spring or fall.

Problems: None.

CROCUS (Common Crocus)

Description and Uses: Crocuses have white, blue, yellow and striped flowers, appearing in spring, later than snowdrops. Often planted in evergreen border and in lawns.

Green Thumb Care: If grown in the lawn, do not cut the leaves until they've turned yellow. If mowed when leaves are green the bulbs will die. To plant in a sod, take a plug of grass roots out, dig a hole 3 inches deep, using a narrow trowel. Set bulb in and cover with loose soil. Be prepared to replace half of your crocus bulbs each year. Divide every three years.

Propagation: Plant new bulbs in fall.

Problems: Vanishing bulbs. Due to cutting leaves when green.

ERANTHIS (Winter-Aconite)

Description and Uses: Bright yellow flowers, 2 inches high, resembling marsh marigolds. Good on slopes, rock gardens and under trees. Appearing same time as snowdrop.

Green Thumb Care: Plant bulbs anytime in fall, 2 or 3 inches deep and same distance apart.

Propagation: Division.

Problems: Prefers to be undisturbed.

FRITILLARIA IMPERIALIS (Crown Imperial)

Description and Uses: Grows 2 to 4 feet high with purplish, yellow-red or reddish-brown flowers 2 inches long. Blooms in May. Good in beds where a tall spring bloomer is desired.

Green Thumb Care: Plant in rich humus soil 4 to 6 inches deep. Will grow in shade.

Propagation: Division.

Problems: Capricious bloomer. Avoid crowding with other plants.

FRITILLARIA MELEAGRIS (Guinea-Hen Flower, Checkered Lily)

Description and Uses: Checkered purple or maroon bell-shaped flowers are interesting. Grows 12 to 14 inches high and is used to good advantage in rock gardens. A little-known variety comes in white but the purple shades are more showy.

Green Thumb Care: Plant 3 inches deep in a loose soil which does not bake in summer. Can be grown in semi-shade.

Propagation: Division.

Problems: Has fickle blooming habits. Leave undisturbed.

GALANTHUS (Snowdrops)

Description and Uses: Fine little white flowers usually appearing in February or March in spite of snowy weather. Ideal in foundation plantings, under trees and along a shady walk.

Green Thumb Care: Plant in fall, 3 inches deep and 3 inches apart. They do well in all types of soil and will grow in semi-shade.

Propagation: Division in fall.

Problems: None, leave undisturbed.

HYACINTHUS (Hyacinths)

Description and Uses: Everyone is familiar with this common, squatty spring bloomer with clusters of fragrant pink, white, blue or cream bell-shaped flowers. Ideal in borders, masses, around trees and especially suited for indoor forcing.

Green Thumb Care: Plant in fall in loose soil, 4 to 6 inches deep. Bulbs often "peter out" and usually have to be replaced every other year. Outdoor culture is similar to tulips (see).

To force indoors, pot the bulbs in fall in 5-inch pot, water well and bury in a trench or storage pit or store in refrigerator for eight weeks. After that, bring to semi-dark room for a week so shoots can turn green and "lengthen." After that, bring into direct sunlight in a temperature of 65 degrees. Many home owners use a hyacinth glass for forcing. Just add a small piece of charcoal in the bottom, set a bulb in the glass so its base almost touches the water. Twist a sheet of paper into a cone, fasten with a pin and cover bulb. Place in refrigerator for eight weeks. After that, give same treatment as above.

Propagation: Multiply by dividing in fall. You can increase your stock by cutting the bulb in sections. Buy new bulbs each year for fall planting. There's no truth to the idea you can produce various-colored blooms by cutting the base of the bulb. (See *Narcissus.*)

Problems: "Blindness," or no flowers, due to overcrowding. Dig bulbs each year. Indoors, if flowers come before stems, it means too much light and heat after you bring them out of the cold-storage (root-forming) period. Forced plants should be replanted outdoors after blooming, where they may or may not bloom the following year.

Lilium (Lilies)

The lily family is a large one. There are many kinds I've not grown or even seen, yet each year they become more commonly known and grown.

Green Thumb Care: Lilies may be planted any time from autumn until spring, some as late as June. However, fall planting is best. Many foreign-grown bulbs do not arrive here until late in fall and this makes fall planting impossible. Some lily bulbs cannot stand much freezing unless well rooted, so if your bulbs arrive late, it's best to hold them over winter and plant in spring. Store the bulbs in sawdust or peat if you plan to carry them over. Dust with Ferbam, Arasan or Captan at the rate of a heaping tablespoon to a quart of peat or sawdust and keep them in a cool cellar.

Bulbs planted in fall need a light covering of straw or peat to prevent their being heaved out of the ground. The first season of bloom is often the poorest, as lilies do not flower at their best until bulb has become well established.

Lilies are heavy feeders, preferring a fertile, well-cultivated, well-drained soil. Depth of planting depends on whether the lilies are stem-rooting species, or those rooting from the base of the bulb. Stem-rooting kinds need deeper planting. The general rule is to plant stem-rooting varieties 3 times the depth of the bulb. Bulb-rooting sorts may be planted about 4 inches deep. Even in a well-drained soil it's a good idea to set the bulb on a cushion of sharp sand. Make the hole sufficiently large so that the bulb may be surrounded by sand. Some of the popular bulb-rooting species are: *Canadense* (Meadow lily); *Candidum* (common madonna); *Giganteum, Testaceum, Chalcedonicum, Pardalinum* and *Martagon.*

Most popular of the stem-rooting species include the *Auratum, Concolor, Hansoni, Henryi, Japonicum, Longiflorum, Regale, Speciosum, Tenuifolium, Tigrinium, Umbellatum, Willmottiae.* Latin names are mentioned because lilies have so many different common names in different areas. Most catalogs list lilies by their botanical names.

Care of the Florist or "Bermuda" ("Easter lily"), botanically known as *L. longiflorum.* There are several varieties grown by florists, including *giganteum, harrisii, formosum, Erabu* and Creole. This Easter plant likes plenty of water, a sunny window and a temperature of 65 to 70 degrees. For best mileage pull out the yellow floral parts (anthers, the male elements) to keep the blooms longer, flowers fresh-looking. After blooming, set bulb in a permanent spot in the garden and it will bloom again for you in fall. It's hardy outdoors and needs no winter covering.

Indoor Forcing: If you want to grow the lily for Easter, buy "pre-cooled" bulbs, those already given a special cold storage treatment. If bulbs are not pre-cooled, they must be refrigerated six weeks at 35 degrees before potting.

Propagation: Increase by seed, scales, and division of bulbs. Seed may be sown in fall in mixture of sand and peat in pots or flats. Do not plant deeply. A flour-sifter makes a fine device for sprinkling soil over seed you sow. You can get a Regal lily to flower nine months after sowing. Others may take longer. Transplant the seedlings to pots and set outdoors in shirt-sleeve weather.

None of the hybrid lilies come true from seed so you can start these from bulb scales, a more rapid method. All lilies grow from bulbs composed of overlapping scales. Each scale is a special form of leaf attached to the bulb. Simply break these scales away and plant them in a sandy soil. Best time is after flowers have faded. Small bulblets will form along the bottom of the scale and grow into flowering-sized bulbs. It's not necessary to dig up bulbs to get the scales. Simply remove soil so as to expose the bulb, then pry off the scales you want and cover again with soil. I prefer to lift the bulb, remove half the scales and replant the heart of the mother bulb. In autumn, before freezing, a covering of dry leaves is placed over the flat in a coldframe where the scales are left until spring. The following July the scales will be large enough to plant in the garden. Many will flower the following year.

Many gardeners use plastic bags for starting lily scales. Put a couple of handfuls of slightly moist shredded sphagnum moss in the bottom, and then set the fresh plump scales in the bags.

Shake well to cover the scales. Fold the tops to shut out air. Keep in a dark cabinet at room temperature for three weeks, when you'll notice from one to four or five small bulbs will form at the bases of the scales. By late September or early October these may be placed in a sheltered coldframe for winter rest. Or you can set them out directly from the plastic bag to the border where they are to flower. A 2-inch covering of leafmold or peat is helpful. By the scale method you can make one healthy bulb yield up to a hundred flowering-size bulbs within a period of two years.

Problems: Botrytis Blight (gray mold disease). Telltale evidence is brown spots all over blossoms and leaves. This is the same villain which hits tulips and peonies. Control: Dust weekly with Zineb or a copper compound. Zineb alone, 1 tablespoon of 50 per cent grade to a gallon of water, plus ½ teaspoon of a detergent makes a good spray. The secret is to keep new foliage and buds covered from the start. In fall, cut back dead stalks and drench plants and soil with Zineb.

Mosaic. The most serious and widespread disease of lilies, Mosaic is spread by the melon aphid. Affected plants are stunted, twisted and mottled. Remove and destroy mosaic-infected plants. Spray lilies with Malathion regularly to check aphids.

Chewing insects. Malathion will banish most of them.

Missing lily bulbs. Due to basal rot, nematodes and probably some type of insect injury.

Wilting. Due to borers and ants. Chlordane checks both.

LYCORIS SQUAMIGERA (Hardy Amaryllis, Autumn Amaryllis, Magic Lily)

Description and Uses: Sometimes listed as *Amaryllis Hallii,* this item has green, strap-like leaves appearing in spring. These die down and completely disappear by June. In August, lavender flower spikes 3 feet long and fragrant, pop up out of the ground. While a poor keeper in vase arrangements, Lycoris does make a fine perennial when grown in a mass by itself.

Green Thumb Care: In spring or fall, plant bulbs 5 inches deep in rich, humus soil. They prefer sun or partial shade. The best time to move *Lycoris* is in spring or fall, although it will bloom in the same spot year after year without disturbance. A winter covering is unnecessary.

Propagation: Division of bulbs in spring or fall.

Problems: Failure to bloom. This is due to deep planting or overcrowding. Separate bulbs in spring and plant 5 inches deep.

NARCISSUS (Daffodils)

Description and Uses: The first major flowers of spring are daffodils, following crocuses in March or April. Daffodils are a species of narcissus. The latter is the Latin name, and daffodil is the English. Recent introductions by daffodil breeders have given us beautiful types. They range in size from the miniatures which produce tiny blossoms on 3-inch stems, to those reaching a height of 2 feet or more with blooms 4 inches across. Ideal for naturalizing, growing in beds, borders and forcing. Plant in drifts near shrubs, or in woodlands.

Green Thumb Care: Leaves and flowers may cause irritation of skin. If you are sensitive to daffodil poison, wear rubber gloves while handling leaves and blossoms. Plant large bulbs in fall 5 to 6 inches deep. Smaller bulbs 4 inches. Space 8 to 12 inches apart.

Closer spacing will result in quicker mass effect, but will also mean you'll have to separate the bulbs sooner. Feed a balanced plant food at planting time and again in fall. After plants finish flowering, keep them growing green as long as possible to build up food for next year's crop. Lift and divide the bulbs every 3 years to avoid overcrowding. After foliage has yellowed ¾ of the way from the top, dig, divide and replant. Bulbs may be stored in basement during summer or planted back in ground. Never keep them in basement over winter.

For indoor forcing, the paperwhite narcissus are easiest of all to make bloom, requiring no special cool storage treatment, as needed by trumpet daffodils. Plant bulbs in soil, gravel or shells and keep at room temperature. Other daffodils need cold storage treatment. Plant bulbs with "noses" just sticking out of surface. Place them in a cold place (50 degrees or less) for eight weeks to develop roots. Keep them moist and, around December, bring pots into a room with temperature of 60 to 65 degrees in partial light to "green up" and make stem growth. Then move to a bright window and water as needed.

After flowering, potted daffodils can be planted in border or outdoor flower bed. Do not force them again indoors. The treatment above applies to tulips, hyacinths and other hardy bulbs.

Propagation: Separating bulbs and planting small ones.

Problems: "Blasting" or drying of flower buds. Due to violent changes in weather, especially hot sunny days in spring, accompanied by drying winds. A mulch of straw, peat or sawdust conserves soil moisture.

Botrytis blight is another cause of blasting. Cut and burn leaves when they turn yellow. Keep plants sprayed with Captan or Ferbam starting in early spring. Overcrowding is another cause of failure to bloom. Dividing and replanting every two or three years will check this.

SCILLA (*Scilla hispanica*—Spanish Scilla)

Description and Uses: Numerous blue, white, purple or pink flowers appearing in May. Ideal in beds and borders. Grows 10 to 15 inches tall.

Green Thumb Care: Plant 4 to 5 inches deep.

Propagation: Division of bulbs.

Problems: None.

SCILLA SIBERICA (Siberian Scilla or Squills)

Description and Uses: Blue, long-lasting, six-petalled flowers appearing in early spring on 4- to 6-inch stems. Good for edging or in masses. Can be had in white, but blue is more popular. They are easily naturalized and grow well among shrubs.

Green Thumb Care: Plant 2 or 3 inches deep. Tolerates a wide variety of soils.

Propagation: By division of bulbs.

Problems: None.

TULIPA (Tulips)

Description and Uses: Spring isn't spring without tulips, a flower everyone knows. Ideal for beds, borders, mass plantings and forcing indoors. Combine with early flowering perennials such as creeping phlox, myosotis, alyssum (Basket of Gold); pansies, violas, perennial candytuft, arabis and the old-fashioned bleeding heart. They are ideal in foundation plantings of evergreens.

Green Thumb Care: Plant in fall as soon as you receive bulbs. If ground isn't frozen, you can plant as late as mid-December. Plant 4 to 6 inches deep, 8 to 12 inches apart. They must have full sun, will do well under trees or shrubs which leaf out after the bulbs have started their growth. Tulips look best planted in clumps rather than in a single row. Good drainage is essential.

Old-timers still mix bonemeal in soil, 10 pounds per 100 square feet. I never use manure because it spreads botrytis blight. After bulbs are planted, add 5 pounds of a balanced plant food such as 5–10–10 to each 100 square feet. Bonemeal, made of animal bones, attracts dogs which dig up bulbs in search of a juicy bone. The phosphorus in bonemeal is slowly available and never burns. However, sometimes the phosphorus is so locked up in the bonemeal it's so slow that flowers and bulbs will not benefit from the application. I suggest superphosphate instead, because on the basis of the phosphorus which plants can take up, you're paying nearly three times as much for bonemeal as you would pay for superphosphate, available in farm supply stores. Feeding liquid plant food in spring will do a lot to give bigger blooms. Mulching with straw is not necessary, and it may attract mice. (For indoor forcing, same as for hyacinths.)

Remove seed pods unless you want to save seed. Pick blossoms before fully open for cut flowers. A few drops of wax on the inside petals keeps blooms from opening wide. We find the double varieties and the Parrot types make excellent cut flowers since the blooms are much longer-lasting than blooms of other varieties.

Propagation: Multiply by dividing in fall, also by seed sown in sand-peat mixture. Takes three or four years to produce blooms from seed-sown plants. Plant tiny bulblets in garden row in fall.

Problems: Botrytis (Fireblight) or "blasting out" of buds. Comes sometimes from using manure. Keep bulbs dusted or sprayed with Captan or Ferbam. Spindly flowers or none at all means bulbs need transplanting. Dig yours every two years or so to avoid overcrowding. Replant those having a diameter of 1 inch or more for blooms that following spring. Smaller-size bulbs can be planted in a row in the garden to grow for bloom later on.

Cut off old stalks below soil level and burn. Do not place on the compost pile if tulips had Fireblight.

Mosaic. A virus which causes variegation in color, twisted stems, yellowed or mottled foliage. Aphids transmit the virus. Plants showing this peculiar pattern should be pulled up. Do not confuse mosaic with the new parrot tulips which have bizarre patterns.

Rodents. Moth balls among bulbs will discourage mice and moles. Dust bed with dieldrin to kill insects which moles are after.

Small flowers. Due to dry soils, overcrowding, insufficient plant food.

Rotted bulbs. At transplanting time, remove bulbs and burn.

Dug bulbs. Due to dogs (looking for bones) or skunks (looking for grubs). Use superphosphate instead of bonemeal, use Dieldrin for grubs.

GREEN THUMB TIPS ON HARDY BULBS

Failure to bloom is usually due to overcrowding. Most hardy bulbs should be dug and separated every two or three years. Buy new bulbs each year to complement your old stock. It'll pay you in extra blooms.

If you can't get manure for your bulbs, be glad! Use balanced plant foods and you won't introduce botrytis and other diseases found in manure. (See section on "Compost.") Soak your bulbs in a liquid plant food such as RA-PID-GRO, 1 tablespoon per gallon of water for 1 hour before planting.

Hot pepper and mothballs scattered in a border do a lot to discourage rodents and dogs which bother tulip bulbs.

Don't plant hardy bulbs in outdoor planters. They'll freeze.

Fireblight of tulips can be prevented by dusting early in spring using Zineb, Ferbam or Captan.

After tulips, daffodils and other bulbs have died down, remove foliage and fill in spaces with asters, begonias, violas, dwarf phlox, petunias, salvias or marigolds.

Tulips coming up with only one leaf in spring means they need dividing.

Plastic bags make good containers for starting bulbs from seed or scales.

BULBS FOR A ROCK GARDEN

Spring Blooming

*Camassia**
*Chionodoxa**
Crocus
Eranthis—Winter Aconite*
Erythronium—Dogtooth Violet*
Fritillaria meleagris
Galanthus—Snowdrop*
Hyacinth
Iris—dwarf forms
Leucojum—Snowflake*
Muscari—Grape Hyacinth
*Narcissus**
*Scilla**
Tulips, especially species

Summer Blooming

Lycoris squamigera—Resurrection Lily

Fall Blooming

Colchicum—Fall Crocus*
Sternbergia

* Tolerate partial shade.

Below is a chart of some of the most important minor bulbs. With the exception of Ornithogalum the minor bulbs listed resent transplanting, and so should be planted where they are to be left permanently.

Flowers (*in order of appearance in garden*)	Planting Time	Flowering Time (*in the Northeast*)	Height in Inches	How to Plant	Where to Plant	Color
WINTER ACONITE (*Eranthis*)	Aug.–Sept. 15	March	2–3	2 in. deep 3 in. apart	Light shade rock gardens	Yellow
GALANTHUS (Snowdrops)	Aug. 15–Sept. 15	February March	7–12	3 in. deep 3 in. apart	Some shade, groups, rock garden, or sheltered corner	White
CHIONODOXAS (Glory of the Snow)	Aug. 15–Oct. 1	March	6	3 in. deep 3 in. apart	Rock garden, groups near spring-flowering shrubs	Blue
LEUCOJUM VERNUM (Snowflakes)	Aug. 15–Oct. 15	April	9–12	3 in. deep 4 in. apart	Rock gardens, large groups	White dotted green
ORNITHOGALUM UMBELLATUM (Star of Bethlehem)	Aug. 15–Oct. 15	April	about 6	3 in. deep 6 in. apart	Rock gardens, groups, near spring shrubs (tends to be weedy)	White
FRITILLARIA MELEAGRIS (Guinea Hen Flower)	Aug., Sept.	April	12	3 in. deep 3 in. apart	Light shade, rock gardens, groups	Checkered reddish brown & purple

HARDY-BULB-PLANTING CHART

FLOWERS (*in order of appearance in garden*)	PLANTING TIME	FLOWERING TIME (*in the Northeast*)	HEIGHT IN INCHES	FOR INDOOR CULTURE	HOW TO PLANT	WHERE TO PLANT
CROCUS	Sept. 1–Dec. 15	March 15–30	5	Yes	3 in. deep 3 in. apart	Rock garden, border, lawn
GRAPE HYACINTHS	Sept. 1–Dec. 15	March 25–April 10	5	Yes	3 in. deep 3 in. apart	Rock garden or border
TULIP Species For Rock Gardens	Sept. 15–Dec. 15	April 1–30	5–15	No	4 in. deep 5 in. apart	In rock gardens
DAFFODILS—Large Trumpet	Sept. 1–Dec. 1	April 10–25	18–20	Yes	6 in. deep 6 in. apart	In beds, groups or borders
DAFFODILS—Medium Trumpet	Sept. 1–Dec. 1	April 10–25	16	Yes	6 in. deep 6 in. apart	In beds or groups
DAFFODILS—Short Cups	Sept. 1–Dec. 1	April 10–25	14	Yes	6 in. deep 5 in. apart	In beds or groups
TULIPS—Fosteriana	Sept. 15–Dec. 15	April 15–30	20	No	4–5 in. deep 6 in. apart	In groups

TULIPS—Early	Sept. 15–Dec. 15	April 15–30	14	Yes	4–5 in. deep 5 in. apart	In beds or groups
HYACINTHS	Sept. 15–Dec. 15	April 15–30	10	Yes	6 in. deep 6 in. apart	In borders or groups
TULIPS—Triumph	Sept. 15–Dec. 15	April 25–May 5	20–24	Yes	5–6 in. deep 6 in. apart	In beds, groups or borders
TULIPS—Darwin	Sept. 15–Dec. 15	May 5–20	26–32	Yes	5–6 in. deep 6 in. apart	In beds, groups or borders
SCILLA hispanica	Sept. 15–Dec. 15	May 5–20	10–14	No	4 in. deep 3 in. apart	Rock garden or border
SCILLA siberica	Sept. 15–Dec. 15	May 5–20	4–6	No	3 in. deep 3 in. apart	Rock garden or border
TULIPS— May flowering (Cottage)	Sept. 15–Dec. 15	May 5–20	28	No	5–6 in. deep 5 in. apart	In beds, groups or borders
TULIPS—Parrot	Sept. 15–Dec. 15	May 10–25	22–28	No	5–6 in. deep 6 in. apart	In beds, groups or borders

SOUTHERN CLIMATE—If you live in a warm region, store bulbs in a cool spot till planting time. Plant deep; add 4 inches to recommended depth for daffodils, hyacinths and all tulips except species. Plant in partial shade. Water frequently. You can plant from early fall through January. (Based on information supplied by Associated Bulb Growers of Holland.)

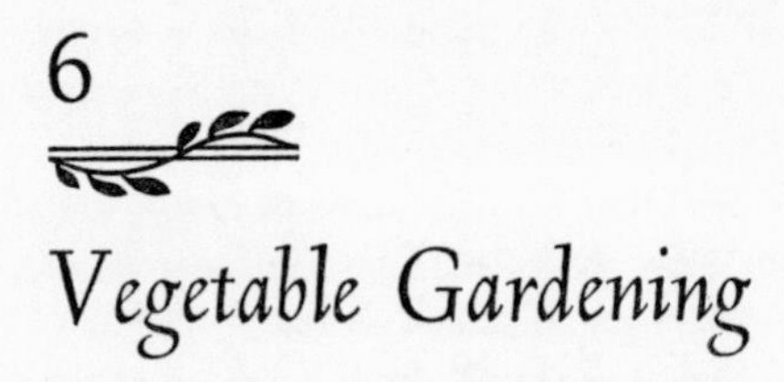

Vegetable Gardening

Early Vegetables: Most of our vegetables today found places on the menu centuries before the Christian era, and are among the oldest foods cultivated by man. During the twenty years required to build the gigantic pyramid at Gaza, Egypt, in the Fifth Century B.C., the workers consumed about $2 million worth of onions, garlic and radishes. The Bible tells us that the exiled Israelites complained to Moses that they missed the cucumbers, melons, leeks, onions and garlic which were part of their Egyptian diet.

Few enterprises about the home give as much satisfaction and as big a net return as the vegetable garden. Studies show that for every minute you spend in the garden, you get a net return from $2.00 to $5.00 an hour. This doesn't allow anything extra for the high-quality crops you pick right in your own backyard—when you want them. A plot 50 feet x 50 feet (that's 2,500 square feet) will be sufficient for a small family, but if you have a larger family—say five or more members, then you'll need a garden 50 feet x 100 feet, or even larger, especially if you want to have vegetables to can or freeze, besides all the fresh ones you want to eat.

One state college figures that the average farm garden in its state will be worth $165. The average gardener will spend $34.50 on his garden, and that means he'll be getting back about $4.75 in produce for every $1.00 he spends. So you can figure that it pays to plan and plant a garden!

Planning the Garden: It makes no difference which way the rows run, although running them lengthwise of the garden makes it easier to cultivate. If they run east and west, plant your large crops on the north side of the garden so that they will not shade the small crops. Get your garden in shape as soon as the ground permits and select the best plants and seed.

Fitting the Soil: This operation starts with turning the soil over to a depth of 8 inches as soon as it's dry enough. Here's a simple green thumb test for soil fitness. Grab a handful of earth and squeeze it tightly for ten seconds. If the soil breaks in several places when dropped from a 3-foot height, it's workable. Soil that forms a mudball is too wet to work. Heavy soils (clay types) are slow to dry out in spring and should not be worked when wet. To improve such soils add plenty of humus or mix in 1 or 2 inches of coal ashes each year. Sandy loam soils are ready to work early in the year because they are better drained. (For details see "Soils" section.)

Treating Your Soil: If you've been plagued with soil pests such as wireworms, centipedes, white grubs and other pests, treat the soil before you plant. For small areas, use Dieldrin, Chlordane or Aldrin, following directions of the manufacturers. Labels now must give recommended rates to use. I mix ½ cup of the emulsifiable concentrate to 2 gallons of water and spray it on each 1,000 square feet after plowing, but before it's worked the final time prior to planting. There's no danger of vegetables absorbing the chemicals if the materials are worked into the top 3 or 4 inches of soil.

Feeding the Soil: Good growth of plants is dependent upon ample amounts of nitrogen, phosphorus and potash in the soil, elements offered in a complete plant food. With "average" weather conditions, most gardens produce best when a balanced fertilizer such as 10–10–10 is added at the rate of 4 lbs. per 100 square feet. Half of this can be applied before planting in spring, the other half applied as a "side-dressing" (along the rows) during the growing season. Lime helps make better use of fertilizer (see section under "Lime") and should be used every three or four years at rate of 5 pounds per 100 square feet. A simple soil test is your best guide.

Most gardens enjoy a "summer snack," since plant growth and rains combine to take food nutrients from the soil. A popular way to boost droopy, parched plants along in midsummer is to irrigate and apply a liquid plant-booster for quick and larger plant growth. Complete plant foods are available which are mixed with water and applied along the soil row, or on the plant foliage itself. Home-made plant-boosters are apt to burn roots and leaves if care is not taken. If you use a handful of nitrate of soda to a 12-quart sprinkling can of water, and apply it to the soil, little burning is likely, or use 1 level tablespoon of a balanced fertilizer such as 5–10–5 or 10–10–10 with each gallon of water. The figures given stand for pounds of nitrogen, phosphorus and potash nutrients available in 100 lbs. of fertilizer. Dig a ring around each plant and apply a cup of solution, or apply in a stream along the row so it will penetrate the soil.

Commercial mixtures of liquid fertilizers such as 23%N–21%P–17%K are available for the home gardener and these are safe enough to pour on top of the plant, the foliage absorbing some of the nutrients, as well as the roots. (See "Foliage Feeding.")

Varieties: Remember that many vegetable diseases can be prevented by using the right varieties. For example, sweet corn is susceptible to bacterial wilt, but if you plant such varieties as Golden Cross Bantam, Spancross, and others, troubles from bacterial wilt disappear. Most hybrid sweet corn varieties are resistant to bacterial wilt. Mary Washington and Washington selections of asparagus are rust-resistant, and a number of cabbage, tomato and celery varieties are resistant to Fusarium yellows or wilt. Many seed catalogs list varieties safe to plant in infected soil.

Obsolete Varieties: The American Seed Trade Association performed a notable service by compiling a list of obsolete varieties. In looking over your seed catalog don't be disappointed if you can't find a certain old-time variety. Chances are it has been discarded and replaced by a better one.

Starting Your Plants: Vegetables, as flowers, are started readily from seed. This is discussed in full under "Plant Propagation." I'll only repeat here that the secret for getting a good start is to use a sterile starting material such as vermiculite (heated mica) or perlite (volcanic ash) or sphagnum moss. I still use a sand-peat mixture because the seedlings are moved from it so readily. Never use soil for starting seed, unless you cook it for 45 minutes in a 200-degree oven. (See "Plant Propagation" for more on starting seed.)

Most greenhouses have plants already started and often it's cheaper to buy the started plants, unless you're willing to go to the trouble of growing them from seed. Usually seed is treated, but it's still a good precaution to treat your own seed with Arasan, Spergon or Semesan. After treatment, sow seed in a mixture you prefer and cover *lightly.* Do not water from above but rather water the container by setting it in a shallow flat pan of water; this method of watering is called sub-irrigation and it prevents "damping-off," the disease which kills young seedlings. If your seeds fail to germinate, it may be due to covering too deeply, or old age.

Testing Your Seed: Saving seed of your favorite vegetables is often desirable but never save hybrid seed as it will not come true. Test your seed before planting. It's simple. Place a known number on a piece of moist blotter, and keep them moist between two plates, at room temperature. Check daily to be sure blotters are moist. The germination of most seeds can be checked in 5 to 7 days, and it should be at least 80 per cent. If you put 100 seeds in a paper towel and ten of them sprout, that means 10 per cent germination, which is very low.

Handling Young Plants: You don't need greenhouse facilities for getting a good catch of seedlings, since a sunny window, attic or sunporch are adequate if the temperature is around 65 to 75 degrees. The seedlings should be moved into small pots (peat pots or clay pots) and allowed to become established. In a greenhouse or in a home, growth is apt to be soft and "leggy," so your job is to toughen or "harden" off the plants in a coldframe before planting outdoors. By subjecting them to a cooler temperature and giving them less water, seedlings slow down in growth and are better able to withstand the shock of transplanting into the garden.

Plants Like Elbow Room: Whether you start your plants indoors and transplant them, or whether you start them directly in the garden, remember each must have room enough for natural growth. A weed is a plant out of place. If you leave two plants to occupy the space needed by one, each is likely to produce poorly. Hand thinning is a slow but necessary step. It's impossible to avoid the need for thinning by sowing just the right amount of seed. Even with high-germinating seed it's a good idea to sow more than you need. To thin your plants, just pull out every other one, leaving the most promising ones to mature.

Weed Control and Cultivation: The best weed killer you can have in the vegetable garden is a hand hoe or cultivator. Some gardeners prefer to use a mulch of straw, old hay, shredded cane, sawdust, wood shavings or chips and plastic sheets. These keep the soil warm, weeds down and water in. (For detailed discussion, see "Mulches.") A garden plot 50 feet x 50 feet has about 170 pounds of weedseeds in it and the best way to lick these future bandits is to get them while they are small. In hoeing, you don't gain a bit from deep cultivating. Just enough to break the crust is all you need. Never hoe or cultivate too close to the plants, especially in a season of plenty of rain. When there's lots of moisture in the ground, roots are likely to be near the soil surface. That's why deep cultivation near the plant may cut off as many as half of the feeder roots. A good rule of thumb: cultivate shallow, just deep enough to cut off the weeds, below the surface of the ground, then apply a mulch.

WATERING THE VEGETABLE GARDEN

All growing plants must have water, and throughout the hottest part of the season most garden crops benefit by at least 1 inch of water a week. Sprinkling is good but not exactly a necessary way to irrigate the garden. If it does not wet down at least 3 or more inches it's likely to do little good and may be even harmful. To apply the equivalent of 1 inch of rainfall requires about ⅔ of a gallon of water to each square foot of soil.

The canvas-hose soaker is a good way to prevent washing of soil as it keeps leaves dry. Whichever method you use, apply water sufficient to wet down several inches into the soil. Incidentally, did you know dew works for you? Dew can often total as much as 10 inches of water a year, so even if your soil seems bone dry, the plants may still be getting some moisture in the form of dew.

FIGHTING DISEASES AND INSECT PESTS

The secret of growing pest-free vegetables is to apply chemicals as soon as plants are large enough, and continue once a week. The reason is that these materials are effective for only about 7 days. Use an all-purpose pesticide containing Methoxychlor and Malathion (for insects) and Zineb or Captan (for diseases). This will give you the best general-purpose combination at the present time. You can buy this combination or make it yourself. Dust or spray both top and bottom side of leaves—as many foliage diseases enter the plant from the undersides, and most insects spend the greater part of their feeding life there as well. Do not apply these materials to edible portions of vegetables within 7 days of harvest.

Fall cleanup is a fine way to reduce pest population in the garden. Early removal of crop residues and fall burning do a lot to reduce insect population. But don't count on cold winters to kill insects. They won't, because the bugs are too tough! For small-animal damage see section on "Animal Control."

SOME IMPORTANT VEGETABLES FOR THE HOME GARDEN

The following vegetables are the easiest to grow, or are most generally liked and are favored because they produce the greatest food value from a given area. Refer to your seed catalog or seed packet for spacing distances.

ASPARAGUS

Green Thumb Care: Asparagus does best on a well-drained soil. Spring is the best time to set out a patch and a 15-foot row will furnish enough spears for one person a season. One- or two-year-old plants are best for planting. Dig a trench 10 inches deep and place plants 6 or 8 inches below ground level if soil is sandy. Shallower planting is needed if soil is clayey. Firm soil around the roots but do not fill trench completely at one time. Cut no spears the same season of planting. Wait until the second or third year. Stop cutting after first week in July. Snapping off the spears increases yield and is recommended over cutting. In fall, after foliage has yellowed, cut stalks back to ground, or wait until spring.

Problems: Asparagus beetle lays black eggs on stalk. Control with 1% rotenone dust during cutting season. Use DDT *after* cutting season is over.

BEANS

Green Thumb Care: Snap beans are a tender crop, yielding heavily in the area occupied. Easily killed by frost, seed should not be planted until the soil is warm. After last killing frost in spring, make your planting, then plant more at intervals of two or three weeks if a constant supply of beans is wanted. Pole beans do best if vines are supported on poles or trellises. Lima beans need a longer and warmer growing season. The bush or dwarf type of lima matures earlier than the pole type. All beans like a well-drained soil.

Problems: Mexican bean beetle, the beans's No. 1 pest, is controlled by dusting with Sevin or rotenone. The bean weevil troubles stored beans. Store beans in cans in an unheated building. Bean "rust" (anthracnose) can be avoided by not working in the plants when they are wet with rain or dew.

BEETS

Green Thumb Care: A "double-header" vegetable because of its edible tops and fleshy roots. Easily grown, yielding heavily, beets are hardy enough for sowing in the ground as early as you want. Caution: Each seed has one to four seeds within it, so avoid heavy seeding. Six or seven seeds to every foot is plenty. When plants are small, thin them to four or five plants per foot. Beets are lime-lovers, so if yours appear yellow, stunted or off-color, test soil for acidity, and add lime if needed.

Problems: All tops, no bottoms, due to close planting, lack of thinning or lack of boron.

BROCCOLI

Green Thumb Care: Broccoli is hardy, nutritious and easy to grow. Seed may be sown direct or started indoors six weeks before they are to be planted in the garden. The edible heads should be picked just before the yellow flowers come out of the green buds. Plants will produce green flower buds way into fall. Plant Green Mountain for a spring crop or Waltham 29 for a fall crop.

Problems: Aphids, cabbage worms (see "Cabbage").

BRUSSELS SPROUTS

Green Thumb Care: Not as easy to grow as cabbage, but will be productive if plants are started early indoors or in hotbed. When sprouts have formed, break off the lower leaves and stems. Pick the largest sprouts at the bottom, and eat them as soon as ready. Sprouts have best quality if frozen once or twice in the open ground. When severe freezing weather comes, pull the plants or cut them close to the ground, and pack tightly together in a cool cellar.

Problems: Same as cabbage.

CABBAGE

Green Thumb Care: Cabbage is valued for its high vitamin content as well as its ability to cure some stomach troubles. The only requirements are ample moisture and plant food, plus a non-acid soil. Cabbage roots run shallow, good reason why cultivation should be light. Seed may be sown direct or start plants indoors. A wise selection of varieties give you cabbage for several months and the time may even be lengthened by cold storage.

Problems: Clubroot "Finger-and-Toe" disease, a fungus that persists for many years in acid soils and which attacks all members of the cabbage family (broccoli, brussels sprouts, cauliflower and kale). Control by dipping roots in Calomel solution (poisonous!), ½ level teaspoonful to a gallon of water, just before planting. Terraclor is also ideal for clubroot control. Cabbage worms and aphids can be controlled with Malathion or DDT. Cabbage maggot attacks the roots of plants in the cabbage family. Control by mixing 1 teaspoon of Dieldrin or chlordane or methoxychlor to a gallon of water, and wet the soil of newly set plants in spring. Make a second application two weeks later. Split heads are due to a soaking rain following several weeks of late summer drought. Also excess fertilizer and insects are responsible. All varieties are susceptible, although the later varieties have less tendency to burst open. You can prevent bursting by seizing a stalk of the plant and giving it a slight pull until you feel the roots tearing out of the soil. By not pulling it all the way out of the ground, the cabbage will resist bursting.

CARROTS

Green Thumb Care: Here's one vegetable that takes only a small spot in the garden for a season's supply. Carrots prefer a deep, sandy soil well supplied with moisture. Young carrots are more tender and thrive best during cool season. For fall use and in storage, sow seed in July or early August. Store carrots in a pit in the garden, covered by leaves. Sand makes a poor storage place.

Problems: Carrot rust fly which burrows into the carrots. The best control is to harvest carrots in early September, also use Chlordane. Forked roots is due to gravelly soils, use of fresh cow manure, a high water table or any compacted soil.

CAULIFLOWER

Green Thumb Care: Cauliflower grows best in the cool moist weather, and unlike cabbage it will not withstand severe freezing or extreme heat. If you like the white "curds" of edible heads you must blanch the edible part by tying the outside leaves together over the curd when it has reached a diameter of 2 or 3 inches. Harvest the curd when they are still compact, not open and "ricey." You'll have more luck with a late crop than one planted for early harvesting.

Problems: Heading when plant is only 2 or 3 inches tall. This is due to hot, dry weather, regardless of soil moisture.

CELERY

Green Thumb Care: Celery is a "problem" vegetable for the average gardener because it likes a rich, moist soil well supplied with organic matter. Seed may be started indoors and planted out in warm weather, or better still, buy plants started by your florist. Celery is slow-growing, has a small root system, which means frequent cultivation is needed as the plants cannot compete with weeds. Watering is essential for a good celery crop, and the soil around the roots should be soaked each week in July and August. Watering several days prior to harvesting is desirable because it produces a crispier product. There's no need to "blanch" celery stems by banking with soil or boards during the growing period. Green celery which now dominates the consumer market proves there's no need for blanching.

Problems: Bitter, dwarfed, yellow plant is due to a yellows disease. Control leafhoppers, also grow resistant varieties to avoid these problems. Early and late blights spot the foliage. Spray plants with manzate and Malathion once every week.

CHARD

Green Thumb Care: If you don't like spinach try this summer "green" because it takes to heat better than does spinach whose culture it resembles. If only the outside leaves are removed in harvesting, you can make a single planting produce all season.

CORN (Sweet)

Green Thumb Care: Fresh-picked corn from the garden has far more sweetness and flavor than any you can buy. Corn loves hot weather, yet will withstand more cold than will cucumbers, muskmelons, pumpkins or squashes. Sweet corn is best planted in small blocks of at least 3 rows side by side, rather than in a single row, for better pollination and full kernels. By selecting early, midseason and late varieties, home gardeners can make successive plantings and have a constant supply of fresh corn for the table from midsummer on until frost. Corn is a "gross-feeder," and should be fed about 10 pounds of a balanced plant food per 100 feet of row in summer.

There's no advantage to "suckering" (removing side shoots from the base of the stalk) or removing tassels for earlier corn. Sweet corn loses 50 per cent of its sweetness when kept a day at 86 degrees and only 8 per cent when stored at 32 degrees, so try to eat your corn an hour after picking. Maximum sweetness develops when kernels have filled out but still spurt "milk" when punctured with the thumbnail. Don't overcook corn ears! Four minutes of boiling is ample and if you want something really different try buttering the ears, wrapping them with aluminum foil and broiling in the oven. If you like to freeze corn on the cob, select small ears and blanch in boiling water for 6 minutes, and cool immediately in ice water. Place the ears in cellophane bags and place into the freezer. Later, to prepare for table use, remove ears from the bags, place in a shallow tin and heat in a 350-degree-F. oven for 30 minutes until ears are warmed through to the center.

Popcorn and Indian ornamental corn are both popular items for home gardeners. You can plant an early sweet corn variety with popcorn without fear of contamination because popcorn is usually a later pollinator.

Problems: Smut boils on ears and stalks. Pick them off and burn. Ear worms and cornborers. Cut down and burn infested stalks following harvesting. Dust ears or tassels with DDT, directing the chemical into the silks. Start treatment as soon as the corn is 12 to 18 inches high, and as soon as it comes into silk. Don't worry about DDT poisoning because husked ears do not accumulate the spray or dust. Ants on tassels or silk do no harm. They are seeking out honeydew food secreted by aphids. Spray with Malathion to check the aphids.

Birds can strip corn ears, and about the only relief from them is the old-fashioned scarecrow. (See "Animal Control.")

CUCUMBERS

Green Thumb Care: Cucumbers are a warm-season, frost-sensitive crop admired by all because a few plants produce such a large number of fruit.

Seed may be sown in hills or rows, with soil types making very little difference in growth or yield. Long varieties are used for slicing and pickling if the fruit is removed when small. Pickling varieties, being blunt-ended when small, are preferred by most gardeners who like to pickle. Provide ample moisture and do not disturb vines while harvesting a crop.

Problems: A poor set and "nubbins" (misshapen fruit) due to improper pollination.

Striped cucumber beetle may wreak havoc if Malathion dust is not applied.

Shrivelling of vines is due to bacterial wilt or anthracnose ("blight"). Rotating with other crops and keeping vines covered with Zerlate or copper spray are sound practices for control.

A yellow-green leaf color means mosaic, a virus spread by aphids and leafhoppers. Pull up and burn infected plants since no chemical control is available. Mosaic-resistant varieties are available. A bitter taste to a certain degree may be expected, but if the bitterness is intolerable blame a sharp drop in temperature following a warm spell.

EGGPLANT

Green Thumb Care: Eggplant, considered a difficult vegetable, has about the same culture as peppers. Six plants will produce all the fruits an average family of five will need. A rich warm, sandy soil produces the best eggplants and the most fruit. Start plants indoors, as it takes about 8 weeks to grow plants to proper size before setting out.

Problems: Verticillium causes plants to wilt and flop over, and there's no control for it. Leaf spot and fruit rot are encouraged by excess nitrogen. A covering of copper fungicide prevents these diseases. Poor set and blossom-drop are due to low night temperature, hot dry winds and lack of water.

GOURDS

Green Thumb Care: A few cents worth of gourd seed brings bushels of fruit for a fall show, and pin money besides. Gourds have about the same culture as pumpkins. They must be allowed to mature before picking or they'll rot. Don't use the "fingernail" test for maturity, as the scratch on the shell of an unripe gourd destroys its future use. Leave gourds on vines until frost threatens, and harvest in the afternoon of the first clear day that portends frost. Cut stems with sharp knife, leaving a few inches of stem attached to avoid bruising. The stem usually drops off as the gourd dries. Wash gourds in warm soapy water, with household disinfectant added, dry each one in warm place (takes a week) and paint with shellac, varnish or floor wax for glossy effect.

Problems: None.

LETTUCE

Green Thumb Care: Lettuce is one of the easiest home-garden vegetables to grow, with loose-leaf and head lettuce being the two principal types. Although a cool season crop, it may be sown any time from early spring until July. If you have trouble getting seed to germinate in hot weather, try putting it in a refrigerator for 24 hours prior to planting. Loose-leaf varieties are easiest for the inexperienced green thumber, and Salad Bowl is ideal because it holds up well in dry weather, will not "bolt" (go to seed) or become tough and bitter. Head lettuce may be either the "crisp" or the "butter" (Boston) types. To form heads plants need plenty of room (15 inches apart) and lots of water. Your chances for swell heads are enhanced if you can start plants indoors and set them in the garden early in spring.

Problems: Tough leaves. Harvest daily, water frequently and make successive sowings for new crops.

Bitterness and browning of leaf edges, due to hot dry weather. Plant resistant varieties.

MUSKMELONS AND WATERMELONS

Green Thumb Care: You can raise sweet, tender melons if plants are started indoors in plant bands, berry boxes, fertile pots or similar growing containers. Place 3 or 4 seeds in each container covering lightly with peat, vermiculite or perlite. Water well and keep in 75–80 degrees temperature. Heat is important for germinating muskmelon seeds. Never disturb the roots of any cucurbits (melons, cucumbers, squash) as it checks growth. After all danger of frost is past, set plants (pot and all) in the ground. From eight to ten hills are needed for the average family. You can also start seed outdoors if you cover them with "hotcaps" or plastic bags. Pick melons when the body color turns to a yellowish green and the netting of the skin becomes rounded. Don't test skin with your fingernail as rot may set in. When a melon slips easily from the stem, then that's the signal to pick.

Problems: Tasteless melons may be due to disease, or a lack of magnesium or boron in the soil. Melon growers have found such soils can be corrected by giving them a dose of Epsom salts and ordinary household borax. Mix 6½ tablespoons of Epsom salts to 3½ tablespoons of the borax to 5 gallons of spray water and apply when vines start to run and again when fruit is about 2 inches in diameter. Melons do not cross with cucumbers or pumpkins, so you cannot blame flat taste on cross-pollination.

Aphids, striped cucumber beetle, may be troublesome insect pests. Malathion banishes these. Damping-off, bacterial wilt, downy mildew and blossom-end rot are troublesome pests, but Captan added to the above spray will do a lot to check these.

MUSHROOMS

Green Thumb Care: You won't get rich raising mushrooms in your cellar, although it can be a satisfying experience. Mushroom spawn is available in prepared trays, or you can buy tobacco process spawn, which is more economical since ½ lb. will spawn 35 square feet of bed. Your cellar temperature must be between 50 and 60 degrees and darkness is not essential. Mushrooms are a fungus having no chlorophyll. The most common failure with mushrooms comes from high temperatures or dry air. If held over 75 degrees for as much as 24 hours, failure will result. Never allow the beds to dry out. Sometimes spent spawn discarded on the compost will produce mushroom buttons, even outdoors! If you're a mushroom enthusiast, be leary of the wild types popping up in fields. Some are edible and some are not, and there's no dependable test for determining which is which. For more information write to the U.S.D.A., Washington, D.C. and ask for *Farmer's Bulletin 1875,* on mushroom growing.

Problems: Failure to produce can be attributed to drying-out of spawn, or high temperature.

ONIONS

Green Thumb Care: Onions are started from plants or from "sets" (small onions grown from seed during the previous season). Both are planted early in the spring and if you want tender green onions, plant sets close together in a trench. The Sweet Spanish "Hamburger" onions are grown from plants.

The practice of rolling onion tops down is not recommended as it not only leads to lower yields, but also to poor storage quality, and increased losses from diseases. Allow onions to ripen naturally before harvesting if you want them to keep well. The tops will fall over and dry down during the ripening period. See that the outer skin of the bulbs are dry before the onions are pulled.

Problems: Onion maggot. Treat soil with Dieldrin prior to planting, one cup of 15 per cent emulsifiable concentrate to 2 gallons of water and sprayed on after garden has been spaded or plowed.

PARSLEY

Green Thumb Care: Parsley takes little space in the garden and is always appreciated for garnishing and flavoring. Sow in spring or summer where plants can be left until following spring. Some plants can be transplanted into pots and grown indoors for winter use. Leaves may be dried for winter use also.

Problems: Outdoors, none; indoors, yellowing of leaves due to over-watering or high room-temperature or lack of light. (See "Herbs" section if you are an herb enthusiast.)

PARSNIPS

Green Thumb Care: A welcome addition to the list of "winter-vegetables," parsnips need a longer growing season than beets or carrots. Sow seed shallow as it has little "pushing up" power. We sow radish seed with it to break the crust of earth. Parsnips are usually left in the ground until late in fall or even throughout the winter. They have a better flavor and keeping quality if exposed to low temperatures.

Problems: Parsnip poisoning comes not from eating the roots but from contact with leaves, especially in the second year of growth. Some gardeners contract skin poisoning by touching the green parsnip leaves when wet by dew or rainfall.

Rust spots are due to a fungus canker which is controlled by hilling parsnips with soil during the latter part of the growing season.

PEAS

Green Thumb Care: Peas are a cool-season crop. The best way to get a succession of peas is to plant three or four varieties of different maturing dates. Wando is a heat-resistant pea which can be planted as late as July 1 and still give good tender peas even in the fall. Dwarf peas are preferred over tall-growing sorts. Harvest peas when in prime condition and eat or preserve them as soon as possible after harvest. High temperature changes quality fast and it may spoil your efforts.

Problems: Enation wilt, seed rot and root rot. Treat seed before planting, and rotate planting site. Plant resistant varieties. Aphids are checked with Malathion.

PEPPERS

Green Thumb Care: Pepper culture is similar to that of tomatoes. Plants are started indoors in March because peppers are slow growers. There are few varieties which can be depended upon for heavy bearing year after year. Weather, temperature and locality all make a difference in crop performance. Peppers are self-pollinating and should not be planted close together for "rooster" effect. All red peppers are green before they are ripe, the red pigment being masked by the green. Pepper seed may be saved, provided hot pepper plants are not growing nearby.

Problems: "All bush, no fruit" is due to loss of water from soil, low relative humidity or hot drying winds at blossom or bud time. Irrigation and mulching are recommended.

POTATOES

Green Thumb Care: Because of poor-quality potatoes in stores, many home gardeners like to raise their own. Small potatoes, 1¼ to 2 ounces, are planted whole, or larger ones cut into blocky pieces with an "eye" or bud on each may be used. Plant as soon as possible in spring, covering 2 inches deep.

Problems: Plenty of diseases and insects. Spray regularly with manzate or dithane M–22 and DDT. Scab, manifested by rough lesions on skin, is due to alkaline (sweet) soils. Soil acidity should be below pH 5.4 (see "Soils" for explanation). Plant scab-resistant variety.

PUMPKINS

Culture of pumpkins is the same as for winter squash (see).

RADISHES

Green Thumb Care: Radishes are hardy, easy and quick to mature. They do best in cool weather, become pungent in hot weather. Small round varieties mature more quickly than long ones. Make successive plantings for young, tender radishes, irrigate every third day.

Problems: Hot taste, due to dry soils and hot weather. "All tops, no bottoms" is due to planting close together (without thinning), or lack of boron.

Flea beetles are checked by DDT. To avoid maggots, dust row of seed with Chlordane before covering with soil.

Pithiness, a long-time annoyance, is due to heredity, aggravated by hot, dry soils.

RHUBARB

Green Thumb Care: Pie-plant or rhubarb likes a deep, rich, well-drained soil with plenty of moisture and heavy feeding to keep it tasty. Plant root divisions in spring, setting crowns 2 to 4 inches below soil level. Don't harvest any stalks until after third year. Remove flower stalks as soon as they appear to conserve energy. Never cut stalks, rather *pull* them. Confine feeding to chemical plant foods, as manure brings on a lot of disease problems. Varieties to try: McDonald and Valentine. Divide your patch every 5 or 6 years, by separating the roots. Most gardeners do not bother to do this and they have all the pie-plant they can eat!

Problems: Curculio, a snout beetle attacking stalks. Hand-pick and burn the pest. Also dust with rotenone when stalks are 2 to 3 inches long and leaves have started to unfold.

SUNFLOWERS

Green Thumb Care: While not a vegetable for table use, the tall-growing sunflower (*Helianthus anthus*) is grown for ornamental use and for bird food, and for a "living fence." Seed sown in the ground in spring will quickly germinate and grow into husky plants. You really don't need a green thumb for sunflowers.

Problems: Mildewing of seed heads. Prevent by picking heads when seeds first start to ripen (just before they shed), and hang upside down in any dry place. Better still, dry them off quickly by placing heads in front of an electric fan to drive off moisture.

SQUASHES (Summer and Winter)

Green Thumb Care: Summer and winter squash, pumpkins and gourds have much the same culture as melons and cucumbers. For summer squash, sow seed in hills 3 or 4 feet apart. Plant 8 or 10 seeds in a hill and cover with about 1 inch of soil. Later, thin plants to 3 in a hill. For best eating, pick squash fruits while still small, young and tender. By keeping fruits picked you'll make the vines bear throughout the entire season. Blossoms of squash and pumpkins make delicious fritters when fried. Dip in egg batter and fry in deep fat.

Winter squash needs more space to grow than summer squash. Plant in rows 7 to 8 feet apart for smaller types such as Butternut, Acorn and Buttercup, and in rows 9 feet apart for the larger types such as Hubbard. Plant in hills 4 feet apart in the rows with 8 to 10 seeds to the hill, but thinned to 3 plants per hill after plants are up.

Allow squash and pumpkins to ripen thoroughly before picking, but do not allow them to be frosted, as it will damage their keeping quality. Store in a dry place about 50 degrees.

Problems: Troubles of summer and winter squash and pumpkins are the same. Squash vine borer causes wilting and death of vines. Small piles of a sawdust-like material (frass) on ground indicate presence of borers. Spray vines during late June and early July (after the blossom shucks have fallen) using 2 tablespoons of 50 per cent methoxychlor to a gallon of water, giving 2 or 3 doses, seven days apart. Borers already inside a stem may be stabbed with a penknife. The wounded stalk is then placed on the ground and covered with soil for root formation. Blossoms which dry up are no cause for alarm. Squash and pumpkins produce 5 to 10 male blossoms to 1 female, and only a small per cent of the female blossoms naturally develop into normal fruits.

Squash bugs are a messy nuisance but can be controlled by Malathion. Clean up and burn all vines and trash in fall.

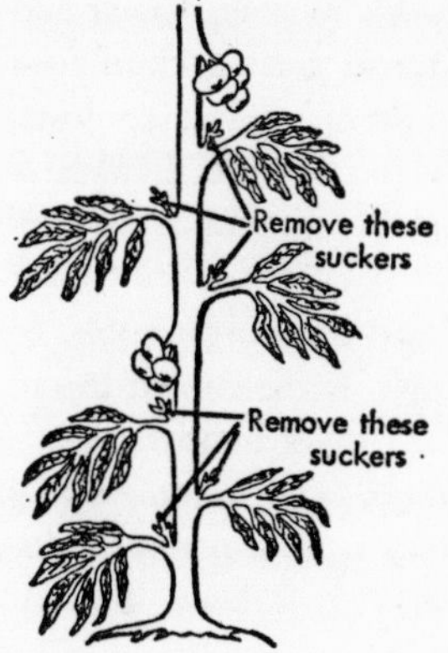

Courtesy Univ. of Missouri

This diagram illustrates how you "sucker" or prune a tomato plant.

TOMATOES

Green Thumb Care: Called "Oranges" of the garden, tomatoes are probably America's No. 1 vegetable after potatoes, mainly because they are so easy to grow and have such wide uses canned, fresh or as juice. Tomatoes grow in almost any well-drained soil. Plants are started indoors or purchased, and set out after frost danger has passed. If you are a smoker always wash your hands with soap and water before handling tomato, pepper, eggplants to avoid spreading tobacco mosaic to this group of plants. Gardeners have a large selection of early, midseason and late tomatoes in both hybrid and non-hybrid groups. Hybrid seed and plants cost more because the seed is produced by controlled pollination, but the price is often justifiable. If you like to stake and prune tomatoes, set them 2 feet x 2 feet. If you let your plants ramble on the ground, 3 feet x 4 feet is a good distance. Staking gives you earlier, cleaner fruit, less snail injury, and they are easier to pick and spray. Disadvantages to staking: more sun-scald, blossom-end rot and a little extra cost and effort. Mulching with straw reduces fruit cracking and dry blossom-end rot.

Some gardeners train tomatoes to a single stem, removing "suckers," shoots arising at the point where a leaf joins the main stem. If space is limited, try growing tomatoes on a cylindrical wire (6″ mesh) trellis, 1½ feet across and 5 feet tall. A single-trellised plant can be trained to climb the wire "corset" and produce over 60 pounds of tomatoes.

Problems: Tomatoes fall heir to many insect and disease troubles, but all can be checked. The secret to getting clean fruit is to keep your foliage covered at all times with maneb sprays or dusts. *Don't wait for diseases to strike because it will be too late.* Maneb is good for most foliage disease, blights, rust and fungi, although ineffective against powdery mildews.

Blossom-end rot is a heart-breaking trouble, forming on the bottom of the fruit during dry weather. A mulch and lots of water will prevent this. Poor fruit set is due to low night temperatures, as well as prolonged hot, dry spells. Spraying blossoms with a hormone will induce setting despite low night temperatures or a lack of natural pollination. Cracked tomatoes occur when a hot dry season is followed by rain. Variety has nothing to do with this.

Leaf-curl is common on pruned and staked tomatoes, is common on hot days and following heavy rains. When tomato plants grow in a shoe-string fashion, you'll know it's a virus for which there's no control.

Snails (see "Small-Animal Control") are another serious pest on mulched tomatoes, less serious on staked ones.

Green or unripened tomatoes can be prevented by starting with early varieties, applying "Blossom-set" hormone sprays and staking your plants.

SWEET POTATOES

Green Thumb Care: While sweet potatoes are generally a warm climate crop, you can grow them almost anywhere tomatoes will grow, if you use a black Polyethylene sheet around the base to raise the soil temperature. Buy sweet potato plants from a seedsman and plant outdoors 15 to 18 inches apart as soon as frost damage has passed. In fall when vines show frost damage, dig the roots and store near a furnace for 15 days to cure. After curing, move them to a cool part of cellar. They need a warm soil and long growing season. Black plastic mulch helps provide the warmth.

Problems: None.

HOME STORAGE OF VEGETABLES

The old-fashioned "root cellar" went out when the freezer and improved preserving methods came in. If you're interested in storing your crops remember this rule: fruits and vegetables are still living parts of plants, and the cooler you can keep them the better. An orchardist-friend

Fruits and vegetables are kept fresh longer if stored in barrels or boxes.

recommends sinking a clean garbage can in the garden for storing crops. The can is fitted with a tight cover and covered with a pile of straw to a depth of 2 feet. Heat from the ground will keep the fruits and vegetables in fine condition. Another trick is to use an old ice box buried backside down in the garden (see picture). Be sure to knock the lock off so no curious child could possibly lock himself in. My neighbor's 8-cubic-foot refrigerator, stripped, holds 5 bushels of produce and has kept apples and vegetables from 20-below-zero weather, although he still covers it with straw for extra protection.

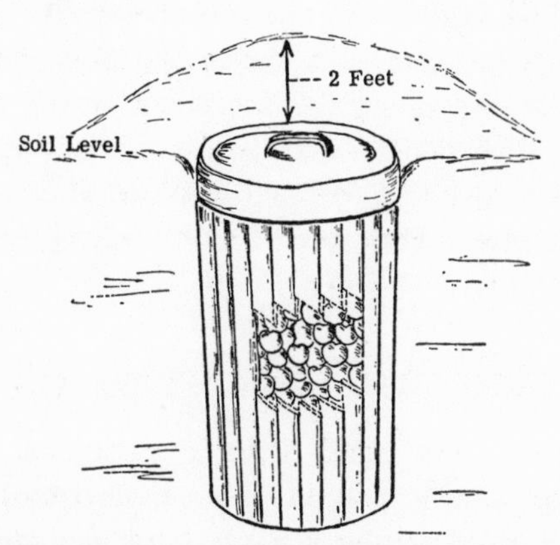

Apples stored in galvanized can keep well when can is buried in garden during winter.

GROWING HERBS IS FUN

Herbs do a lot to pep up a jaded appetite. Their culture is simple and uses are many. If you've ever wondered how to pronounce the word, it's either "herb" or "erb," depending on where you live. In America it's "erb," and in England one is a Cockney if he drops the "h."

Most herbs are started by seed sown in spring or fall. Fall-sown seed lies dormant until spring when it gerimnates earlier and often better. One venture which more gardeners should undertake is growing herbs in the kitchen window. Start seeds in florist's pots or a kitchen window box using a ⅓ sand, ⅓ peat and ⅓ loam mixture. Keep the plants watered uniformly, provide a bright window, and feed them lightly from time to time. A few annuals to try indoors include sweet basil, chervil, dill, sweet fennel, sweet Marjoram and summer savory. For perennials, try lemon balm, chives, parsley, peppermint, rose geranium, rosemary, sage, winter savory, tarragon, thyme and lemon verbena.

Here are some of the most common herbs to grow for fun, food and ornamental effect. You can buy seeds or plants from various seedhouses and get started to build up a herb garden within a short time.

Herb	Green Thumb Tips	Outdoor Uses	Indoor Uses	Harvesting
Angelica (*Archangelica*)	Start by seeds or plants, grow in light shade. Sow in fall and transplant in spring.	Grows 6 ft. tall, ideal for background plant. Cut flower heads off after blooming for longer life.	Use young leaves with fish, seed for cookies and candies.	Cut seed head before dry and keep in warm airy place.
Anise (*Pimpinella anisum*)	Plant seed in May in well-drained soil, full sun. Sow seed direct without transplanting.	2-ft. annual, sprawling and rather slow-growing.	Fresh leaves in salads, soups and stews. Seeds in cake, cookies and fruit pie.	Pick fresh leaves as needed. For seed, clip umbels when gray-green; dry in attic.
Basil (*Ocimum basilicum*)	Sow seed in well-drained soil after frost. Likes full sun and ample water.	Border plant 2 ft. tall. Attracts bees.	Use fresh or dried leaves in eggs, meat, salads and vegetables.	Cut 6 in. above ground when plants flower, and dry. Strip leaves and flower tips and store in opaque jars.
Borage (*Borago officinalis*)	Seed sown in poor dry soil, full sun. Thin to 12 in. apart.	3-ft. annual, star-shaped blue flowers. Good in rock garden.	Herbs, teas, vegetables.	Use fresh. Pick flowers and leaves, dry and store in jars.
English Chamomile (*Anthemis nobilis*)	Sow seed in spring or late summer in sunny spot. Thin to 10 in. apart.	Hardy perennial 12 in. tall. Useful in border or as ground cover.	Herb tea.	Cut flower heads in full bloom and dry in sun. Store in closed containers.
Caraway (*Carum carvi*)	Sow seed in spring or fall in dry light soil. Germination is slow.	A biennial 2 ft. tall, white flowers useful in back border.	Leaves in meat, salad, soup, rye bread and cookies.	Cut seed heads before dry and leave on cloth in attic. Store dried seed after separating.

Herb	Green Thumb Tips	Outdoor Uses	Indoor Uses	Harvesting
Chervil (*Anthriscus cerefolium*)	Sow seed in spring, grows best in shaded, moist spot. Thin to 4 in. apart.	Hardy annual, 2 ft. tall, handsome deep green foliage ideal in back of border.	Use fresh or dried for aromatic garnish or use like parsley.	Cut leaves and dry quickly. Keep in glass jars sealed tight.
Chives (*Allium schoenoprasum*)	Sow seed in spring or fall, or use divisions. Likes full sun, loamy soil indoors or outdoors. Divide clumps every 3 or 4 years.	Onion-like perennial in 10-in. clumps, with lavender blooms. Good in rock gardens.	Use in omelets, salads, cheese, appetizers and soups.	Cut leaves as needed.
Coriander (*Coriandrum sativum*)	Sow seed in late spring, 1 in. deep in well-drained soil; full sun. Thin to a foot apart.	Handsome annual, 12 in. tall; do not disturb by cultivating.	Meats, cheese, salads, soups and pickles.	Snip stalks when seeds are ripe, dry in shade, then separate seeds and store in glass jars.
Costmary (*Chrysanthemum balsamita*)	Start from seed or root division in spring. Likes semi-shade, division every 3 or 4 years.	4-ft. perennial with yellow flowers. Shade produces nice green leaves, but will not bloom unless in full sun.	Use in linen closet; flavors cakes and meats.	Cut leaves before flowering and dry in dark, airy room.
Dill (*Anethum graveolens*)	Sow seed in spring or late fall in full sun. Do not transplant.	4-ft. annual which may need fencing for wind protection.	Cheese, eggs, pickles; seeds in soups, gravies and vegetables.	Pick whole sprays and hang upside down to dry.

Fennel (*Foeniculum vulgare,* var. *dulce*)	Sow in rows in May and thin to 6 in. apart. When plants are half grown, draw earth up to them to blanch the bulbous stalk.	Grown as an annual. Common sweet fennel grows similar.	Valued for its anise-like flavor—cooked or in salads.	Plants mature in 60 days and are then dug. Seeds of common fennel used in cookies, cheese and with vegetables.
Garlic (*Allium sativum*)	Separate cloves and plant base down, 2 in. deep in spring. Likes full sun, ample water.	Bulbous annual, 2 ft. tall with tiny whitish flowers. Ideal as back border.	Used in cooking, meats, sauces and salad dressing.	When top yellows off, pull up clumps and dry in sun 3 days. Remove foliage and store in attic.
Hoarhound (*Marrubium vulgare*)	Plant seeds or root division in spring. Takes poor soil, full sun.	Coarse perennial 2 ft. tall, forms bush for background use.	Cakes, cookies, sauces and meats.	Cut stems just before flowering, dry in shade and store in opaque jar.
Horseradish (*Armoracia rusticana*)	Plant root cuttings in deep, moist soil in early spring 5 in. deep.	Foliage is coarse, so plant in permanent spot at one side of the garden.	Ground roots blended with vinegar, peps up meats and salad dressings.	Dig up in late fall or early spring and grind roots, store in glass jars. Stays hot if kept cool.
Lemon Balm (*Mellisa officinalis*)	Hardy perennial; sow seed in summer, in full sun.	Good border plant 3 ft. tall. May be a pest if allowed to self-sow.	Valuable in seasoning.	Cut tips 2 or 3 times a season. Store in opaque jars after drying.
Lemon Verbena (*Lippia citriodora*)	Start from cuttings in sand; full sun and ample water.	Fine perennial, also good house plant.	Sachets, perfumes, toilet water. Flavors fruit salads, jellies, beverages.	Pick tender leaves and dry.

Herb	Green Thumb Tips	Outdoor Uses	Indoor Uses	Harvesting
Lovage (*Levisticum officinale*)	Seed in spring or fall in moist soil, full sun.	Tall (5 ft.) perennial, ideal as background plant.	Leaves and stems used in soups and stews.	Use fresh or dry the leaves and store in opaque jars.
Sweet Marjoram (*Marjorana hortensis*)	Start early and transplant out in spring; in dry, well-drained soil.	Annual 15 in. high and with gray foliage, white flowers. Front border.	Eggs, sauces, soups, stuffings.	Use fresh, or dry leaves and store in opaque jars.
Parsley (*Petroselinum crispum*)	Soak seed in warm water for day, plant outdoors in rich soil. Full sun.	Neat plant 12 in. tall, used in front border or edge. Bring indoors in fall and keep in bright window. Biennial grown as annual.	Use as garnish, in egg dishes, meats, sauces, salads. High in vitamins.	Cut as needed or dry in oven and keep in tight jar.
Peppermint (*Mentha piperita*)	Plant roots or runners in spring; shade and wet soils are good.	Spreads fast, keep in bounds with metal strips. Set in back border.	Fresh or dried leaves in jellies, desserts, beverages.	Cut stems in bloom, dry and store in tight jars.
Spearmint (*Mentha spicata*)	Same as for peppermint.			
Rosemary (*Rosmarinus officinalis*)	Start seeds indoors in spring, or root cuttings. Full sun, poor limey soil.	Perennial 4 ft. high, blue flowers. Needs winter protection.	Fresh or dried leaves in poultry, meats or seafoods.	Cut leaves just before blooming period, crush and store in tight container.

Sage (*Salvia officinalis*)	Seed or cuttings in spring. Full sun and drained soil. Mulch in winter, remove dead wood in spring.	Shrubby perennial, 2 ft., light, bluish flowers, fine addition to border.	Chopped, fresh leaves in cheese, pickles or sausage. Powdered leaves in stuffings.	Cut young tips, dry over stove, pulverize leaves and store in tight jar.
Savory (Summer) (*Satureia hortensis*)	Seed in spring, in loamy soil, full sun. Grows fast. Winter Savory has same care and uses.	Annual 18 in. high, bushy, and with pinkish flowers.	Fresh leaves in green vegetables; dried leaves in meats, turnips or cabbage.	Pull up plant and dry; store leaves in sealed jars.
Shallot (*Allium ascalonicum*)	Start from new shoots or cloves in spring. Rich, moist soil.	Bulbous annual without much ornamental value.	Use in same manner as onion.	Pull up when tops are yellow; dry 2 or 3 days. Cut off tops and store cloves in trays.
Sweet Cicely (*Myrrhis odorata*)	Seeds planted in fall or spring, or divide parent plant. Partial shade, any type soil.	Fern-like leaves, fragrant white flowers; 2 ft. to 3 ft. tall.	Seeds have spicy taste, used with other herbs.	Pick seeds when green.
Tarragon (*Artemisia dracunculus*)	Root cuttings in spring; well-drained soil, full sun or semi-shade. Divide every 3 years.	Graceful plant with greenish-yellow blooms.	Fresh or dried leaves in salads, vinegar, poultry and appetizers.	Dry leaves and store in tight jars.
Thyme (*Thymus vulgaris*)	Sow seed in spring in full sun. Renew planting every 2 or 3 years as plants get woody.	Handsome foliage enhances the border.	Flavors sauces, salads, seafoods, stuffings.	Cut any time and hang in loose bundles.
Sweet Woodruff (*Asperula odorata*)	Take root divisions in spring, plant 12 in. apart in dense or part shade. Likes moisture.	Creeping perennial 12 in. high; ideal ground cover for shade.	Fragrant sachet, use fresh or dried leaves for garnishing.	Pick and dry stems in spring. Store in jars.

7

Home-Fruit Culture

Many home owners, unfortunately, fail to look into the merits of including fruits in their original landscaping plans, and find out too late that all fruit trees and many of the small fruits can do double duty as producers of food while adding beauty to the surroundings even on very small lots where each square foot is important.

Apples, pears, peaches, plums, nectarines, apricots, sweet and sour cherries, Chinese chestnuts, black walnuts and English walnuts all provide bountiful shade in summer plus delicate traceries of color and grace in early spring when the blooms appear, and require very little more care than trees that are purely ornamental.

The little more care that is required for fruit trees involves spraying for insects and diseases and somewhat more than casual pruning. Recent developments in spray materials makes it possible to reduce this former chore to a few pleasant hours in the yard on a fine day now and again (see "Fruit Sprays"), and the pruning to be done will not only improve the quantity and quality of fruit you can pick in your own yard, but will enhance the beauty of your garden plan.

Small bush fruits such as currants, gooseberries, quince and blueberries may serve as a decorative planting in a sunny corner of the yard; grapes and raspberries (red, black and purple) can do double duty as hedges on property lines if trained to grow on or between wires. Strawberries, the most glamorous of the small fruits to most people, should not be attempted unless the planting can be moved about every two or three years and a minimum of 100 square feet of garden space allotted to each 25 plants to be set out.

The Age of Bearing: Many gardeners have a mistaken idea as to when their newly planted fruits will bear. Most apple trees rarely bear much before they are six to seven years old, the age of the tree being reckoned from the year of planting. Small fruits must have a year to settle in for fruit production. All other fruits you might be tempted to set out will bear sometime between these two extremes. The following list will give you a rough idea of when to expect fruit, as well as the relative planting distances and height for the trees, bushes or plants.

Kind of Fruit	Age of Bearing	Distance Apart	Height
Apples, Standard	2 to 12 yrs.	35 x 35 ft.	25 ft.
Apples, Dwarf	2 yrs.	15 x 15 ft.	15 ft.
Apricots	3 yrs.	20 x 20 ft.	15 ft.
Blackberries	1 yr.	6 x 6 ft.	4 ft.
Blueberries	1 to 2 yrs.	3 x 6 ft.	4 ft.
Cherries, Sour	2 to 3 yrs.	20 x 20 ft.	20 ft.
Cherries, Sweet	3 to 4 yrs.	25 x 25 ft.	30 ft.
Chinese Chestnuts	3 to 4 yrs.	35 x 35 ft.	40 ft.
Currants	2 yrs.	4 x 4 ft.	3 ft.
Gooseberries	2 to 3 yrs.	4 x 4 ft.	3 ft.
Grapes	2 yrs.	8 x 8 ft.	4 ft.
Peaches and Nectarines	2 to 3 yrs.	20 x 20 ft.	20 ft.
Pears, Standard	3 to 4 yrs.	20 x 20 ft.	30 ft.
Pears, Dwarf	2 yrs.	15 x 15 ft.	20 ft.
Plums	2 to 3 yrs.	20 x 20 ft.	20 ft.
Quinces	1 to 2 yrs.	15 x 15 ft.	15 ft.
Raspberries	1 to 2 yrs.	3 x 6 ft.	4 ft.
Strawberries	1 yr.	2 x 2 ft.	1 ft.
Walnuts, Black & English	3 to 4 yrs.	35 x 35 ft.	40 ft.

FRUITS AND NUTS—General Care

Because of their relative similarity in growth and habits, we will consider together the selection of planting stock, the planting, general culture and fertilizing of the tree fruits and nuts. Specifics may be found in the discussions of the fruits which follow the general discussion.

Buying Trees: If you're in the market for new fruit trees this year, don't be misled by pictures of the most beautiful trees drooping with the best-looking fruit you ever saw. Also watch out for the door-to-door peddler who tells you that the older a tree is, the sooner it will come into bearing. Young trees (1- and 2-year-olds) come into bearing sooner than the older ones, and as far as we can see, nothing is gained by planting "bearing age" trees.

Buy the varieties and sizes recommended by your good local nurseryman and trust in his reputation and wisdom to give you the most for your money and effort. Some nurserymen specialize in the propagation, grafting and readying of fruit trees and, should one of these be in your locality, by all means go to him for your purchases.

If you are an average gardener you will be rightly intrigued by the new dwarf fruit trees which number compactness among their virtues—you can plant them 6 to 12 feet apart; their low-growing nature which makes them easy to prune and spray as well as to harvest the fruit from them; and their adaptation to the small lot. Another of their singular virtues is that they bear their fruit sooner after planting than the standard fruit trees. Dwarf apple trees yield up to a bushel of fruit per tree.

Apples and pears are more frequently "dwarfed" than other varieties of tree fruits. Peach, nectarine, plum, apricot and sour cherry trees as ordinarily grown are small in comparison with well-developed standard apple trees and come into bearing sooner, without the dwarfing process to speed production.

In deciding on dwarf fruit trees, some consideration should be given to the rootstocks that have been used to induce dwarfing. Apples grown on the most dwarfing of all the rootstocks, known as *Malling IX,* require bracing or support because the root system is brittle and will break off easily. Apples grown on the semi-dwarfing *Malling VII,* and dwarf peaches and plums, do not require support. Your nurseryman will be glad to tell you the name of the dwarfing stock used in the trees that interest you and to explain that apples dwarfed on *Malling IX* will grow no taller than a man, while fruits dwarfed on *Malling VII* will attain the size of a small peach tree.

Should you be especially interested in the tiny "man-sized" apple trees, do not be put off by the need to support the tree. All that is required is a strong stake driven into the ground near the tree, which is then firmly tied to the tree with a broad band of cloth or rubber hose.

Another novelty in fruit trees which has practical and attractive virtues in the home planting is the so-called Five Fold or 5-in-1 (five varieties on one tree), producing in from 3 to 8 years. However, some apple varieties grow more vigorously than others and one disadvantage of 5-in-1 trees is that one variety will outgrow the others, and unless it is carefully restricted, the entire tree will eventually be mainly that one variety. The most obvious advantage in the multiple variety fruit tree is the readiness of cross-pollination between varieties.

All tree fruits have a sex problem of their own, many needing "rooster" trees for proper pollination. We have found it relatively simple to overcome the pollination problem by borrowing a bouquet of fresh fruit blooms from a neighbor and placing them in water in a sunny spot where the insects like to work. Cut the bouquets when the most advanced blossoms are open, and the sooner you can get them in water, the better. Keep the blossoms fresh, for when they wilt they are valueless. It goes without saying that should you wish to pollinate apples, you must secure apple blossoms for the purpose, pear blossoms for pears, etc. In the case of apples, the Jonathan, Red Delicious and Cortland are good "roosters."

Planting Fruit Trees: Fall is the ideal time to plant fruit trees, and the way you set them out spells the difference between success and failure of your venture. First of all, dig holes large enough to spread the tree roots without twisting or crowding. Put the topsoil you dig up in one pile and the subsoil in another. Dig the holes deep enough to set the tree 2 inches deeper than it grew in the nursery, with the bud or graft about 2 inches below ground level. (Dwarfed trees are an exception to this rule as the bud union must remain above ground level to prevent scion rooting and to permit the dwarfing root system to have its influence throughout the life of the tree.)

Now place 3 or 4 inches of topsoil in the hole you have prepared and prune the roots of your new tree lightly. The idea is to remove all ragged tips and expose firm lively root structure to the soil to encourage the sprouting of new fine roots. If you are planting in fall, leave the top-trimming of the new tree for spring, except to remove one or two branches that might rub together or limbs that grow from the trunk at a narrow angle.

Set your tree in the prepared hole as straight as you can. Some small trees are crooked when dug from the nursery rows, but they will straighten considerably as they grow. Fill the hole ⅔ full of topsoil and tramp it firmly. Pour in a bucket of water. After the water seeps away, fill the hole with soil, leaving a saucer-like depression to catch the rain. Be sure to remove the nursery tag from the little tree as the wire will cut into the wood as new growth is made and will retard or possibly even kill the limb to which it has been attached.

Spring Pruning of Newly Planted Trees: If you are planting fruit trees in spring or have planted in the fall, you should now turn your attention to pruning out the tops. This should be done, of course, before buds swell and start to break. Approach this job with the knowledge that over-

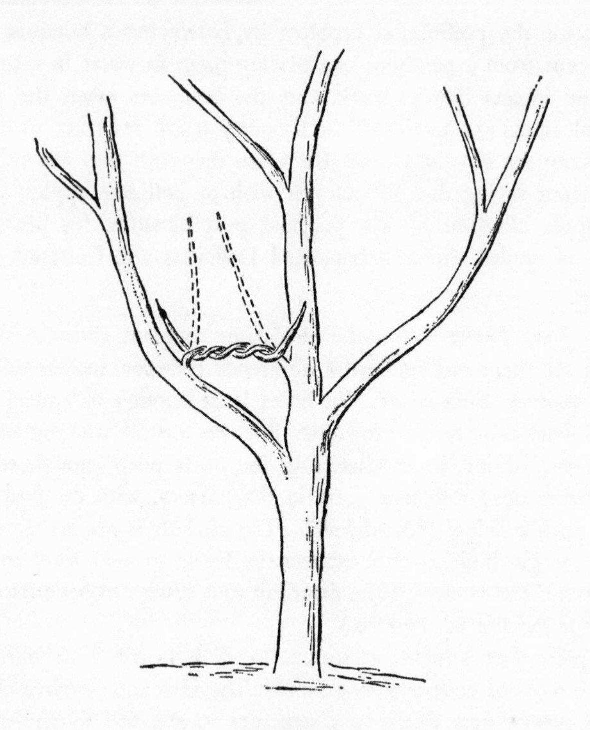

Making a fruit tree support itself. Water sprouts or "suckers" are entwined around each other as shown in the illustration. These unite and form a perfect bond for bracing the tree the rest of its life.

pruning of a young tree will retard bearing and that the purpose of pruning is to shape the tree for both maximum attractiveness and fruit yield. Nut trees require little if any pruning except to remove dead or diseased branches. Peaches are trained to an open center; that is, the main center branch is cut back rather radically to promote a bowl-shaped tree. Other fruit trees are trained to a modified "leader" pattern—the main center branch being allowed to grow upright until the tree reaches bearing age and light is needed at the center of the tree.

Except for these differences, a newly planted fruit tree should be trimmed down to three to five husky side branches that are spaced 6 to 8 inches apart along the trunk of the tree. Branches with wide angles to the trunk are better than those with narrow angles as they are stronger and will make up the "scaffold" or main branches of the tree as it matures. The leader branch is cut off ½ to ⅓ its length and the side branches cut back proportionately. Now remove all other small and spindly branches and your first pruning job has been well done.

Pruning and Training Espalier Trees: This practice, limited more or less to dwarf pears and apples and stone fruits, is a combination of pruning and training the little trees to grow in a limited space, along a wall or trellis. The branches are started low and spread out and up as the tree

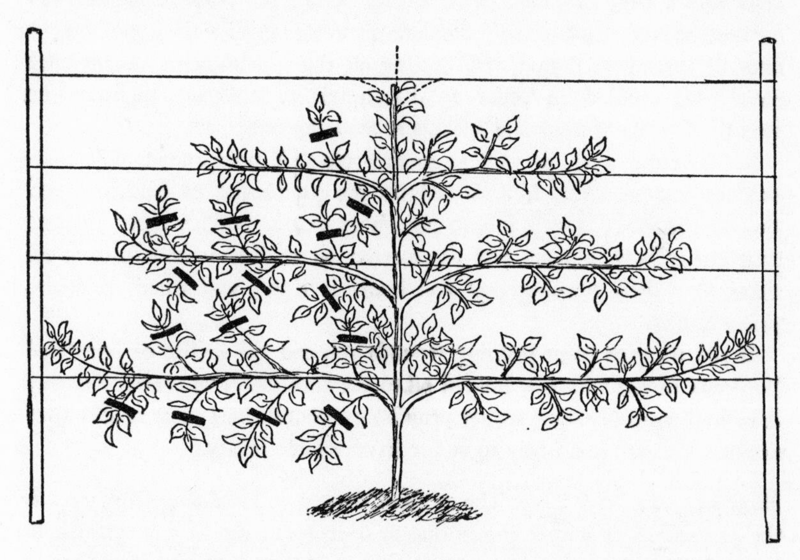

"Espalier" trees are trained to grow flat against a wall. Pinch back the side shoots to about 4 inches from leading branches, or as indicated by the heavy marks on the left side of the drawing.

grows, tying the stems to wire in the shape desired and limiting growth of branches to those that fit the shape. Undesirable shoots are pinched out as they form. The result is not only unusually attractive with small sacrifice of space in the yard or garden, but fruit of exceptionally fine quality is produced.

Pruning Mature Fruit Trees: Why prune at all? You prune to get larger, finer fruit by opening up a tree so sunlight and sprays can get inside it to kill bugs and ripen fruit. Cutting out dead and diseased limbs not only gives the tree relief from pests, it gives the tree a better shape and helps it to develop strong limbs which must carry heavy loads of fruit, sometimes in heavy winds and rain. You can overprune a tree and do much harm thereby, but no pruning at all will defeat the purpose of your efforts too, and your pretty tree will soon become rough and scraggly-looking as well as unproductive.

On mature fruit trees, first remove limbs that are dead, broken, too high or too low and those which rub or criss-cross one another. Skinny, weak limbs come out next along with those that crowd the center of the tree and keep out light and air. All of this job can be done in winter after leaves have dropped, or in spring before the buds break out. On well-established fruit trees, complete pruning should be done over a two- or three-year period, and cutting all the big branches out at once should be avoided in order to discourage an alternate menace—the growth of water sprouts and suckers around the tree.

Small young trees, as well as mature trees, if overpruned, will overproduce foliage which in turn reduces the production of fruiting wood and fruit itself. It is well, too, to remember that a "butcher-type" pruning program is both aimless and destructive, so confine your efforts at all times to a little pruning that you know is right; and when in doubt, prune lightly.

If you want to paint pruning wounds you can use shellac or powdered Bordeaux mixed with raw linseed oil to the consistency of cream. Painting is seldom necessary after spring pruning as wounds heal most readily over summer and are less likely to suffer from winter injury.

Fertilizing the Fruit Tree: The greatest danger in fertilizing fruit trees is the promotion of winter injury due to overproduction of new growth in late fall. Time your feeding program to avoid such late growth, and start as early as December to feed for the growing year ahead.

A complete or balanced fertilizer is used on trees that are not yet bearing. For bearing-age trees, in general, you can use ammonium nitrate, nitrate of soda or a liquid plant food. You can also use a liquid plant food foliage spray applied with the insecticide. If available, you can apply manure around the base of the tree in winter. Generally speaking, here is a good rule of thumb on the amount to use:

Try ¼ pound of 16 per cent nitrate of soda for every year of the tree's growth. So, if the tree is 12 years old, it would take 3 pounds of nitrate of soda. All can be applied over a mulch in the spring. Never put fresh manure in a hole where it will come in contact with the roots of the tree.

The best time to apply nitrogen fertilizers is in April or early May. This early feeding helps set fruit, improves color and encourages bloom. For apples three to five years old, use ½ pound of 10–10–10 fertilizer or nitrate of soda, scattered around the base of the tree. Trees over five years old can get 1 to 2 pounds of ammonium nitrate or 3 to 6 pounds of 10–10–10. Pears one to five years old get ½ pound of ammonium nitrate or 2 pounds of 10–10–10. Peaches and sour cherries five years old can get 3 or 4 pounds of 10–10–10 and prunes five to ten years of age, 1 to 2 pounds.

These materials are readily available in most garden-supply stores, but if you cannot get them, try something close to them, because actually you can feed your trees any kind of plant food and get results. To feed with a substitute is better than not to feed at all. Scatter the food around the base of the tree, going as far out as the spread or the drip of the branches. It is not necessary, incidentally, to punch holes in your ground to feed your trees.

One fruit grower I know uses a liquid plant food (23%–21%–17%) at the rate of about 1 pound per tree. One pound makes 30 gallons of food which he applies equally at three intervals: at the pre-pink or pink stage of blossom formation, in early full leaf, and once more in the summer. (See the "Disease Spray Chart" for ways in which you can apply liquid plant food with other sprays.) Liquid feeding may be applied over the whole tree and what drips to the ground will be absorbed by the roots.

"All-Purpose" Spraying: Commercial growers spray apples anywhere from seven to fourteen times or more a year, to grow clean fruit; but you don't have to spray that much. The introduction of a "home-made all-purpose" formula which will control most of your bugs and diseases has vastly simplified fruit growing for the home gardener. This formula can be used in all applications after the leaves have developed, and on all fruits and ornamental shrubs.

INGREDIENTS—"ALL-PURPOSE SPRAY"

Chemical	*1 gallon of water*	*25 gallons of water*
Malathion (25% Wettable Powder)	2 Tbsps.	½ lb.
Methoxychlor (50% Wettable Powder or DDT)	3 Tbsps.	¾ lb.
Captan (50% Wettable Powder or Ferbam)	3 Tbsps.	¾ lb.
Sulfur	2 Tbsps.	½ lb.

The timing of a spray for fruit pests is important. Try to spray at about the same time commercial grows spray, as shown in the chart below:

TIME TO SPRAY	*Apples*	*Peaches*	*Plums*	*Cherries*	*Pears*
"Green Tip"	X				
"Pre-Bloom"	X	X	X	X	X
"Bloom"	NO	NO	NO	NO	NO
"Petal Fall"	X	X	X	X	X
1st Cover	X	X	X	X	X
2nd Cover	X	X	X	X	X
3rd Cover	X			X	
4th Cover or more	X	X		X	

"Green Tip" means when buds are broken enough to show color.
"Pre-Bloom" means when blossom buds begin to show white, but before petals begin to unfold.
"Bloom" is when blossoms are open. Never spray then.
"Petal Fall" is when last petals have fallen from the blossoms.
1st Cover means 10 days after "Petal Fall".
2nd through 4th Cover—10- to 14-day intervals.

If you're discouraged with the effort involved in the spray program, remember that the most important sprays are "Pre-Bloom" and "Petal Fall" and you *can* do some fertilizing right along with the control program.

This "all-purpose" formula applied through the growing season will check most major pests and, with four or five sprays properly timed, you should be able to eat your fruit in the dark with an easy mind! Methoxychlor controls the plum curculio and other beetles; DDT for leafhoppers, codling moth, fruit moth and other worms. Captan or Ferbam are included to prevent cedar rust and leaf spots, and sulfur to control apple scab, brown rot and mildew.

To control psylla on pears, and aphids on all trees and shrubs, it's a good idea to add nicotine sulfate at the rate of 2 teaspoonsful per gallon. Nicotine is very volatile and will not retain its strength while stored in packages. All of these materials are available at your local feed and seed stores or you can purchase already prepared "all-purpose" formulas. Sometimes you will see chlordane or DDT used in place of methoxychlor; but in the main, the "all-purpose" formulas are pretty much the same.

APPLES

The varieties of apples you can grow in your garden makes an endless list, but for simplification, choose at least one variety from among Red or Golden Delicious, Cortland or Jonathan. All of these varieties are pollinators and necessary—at least one of them—to fruit production. For late apples which will store well, choose from among Baldwin, Northern Spy and Rome Beauty. Red Duchess, Red Astrachan, Lodi and Yellow Transparent are early summer apples. Study your nursery catalog for the best varieties for your area.

Thinning Fruit: Too many sets on apple trees prevent flower-bud formation for the next season, resulting in alternate bearing or a heavy crop of small-sized fruit one year, and no crop at all the next year. This can now be prevented by chemical thinning of the fruit set either when the blossoms are out, or up to two weeks after the blooms have gone. Crop thinning in the home garden is an excellent idea also to prevent an excess of "June drop" which litters the yard with small apples that nature has dropped from the trees in her own attempt to thin the fruit that cannot be nourished by the tree.

There are both hormone- and non-hormone-type sprays that can be used for this purpose. The most popular trade names for the non-hormone types are Elgetol, DN No. 1 and Krenite. The hormone sprays contain naphthaleneacetic acid and may be successfully applied up to two weeks after the fruit has set. Follow the directions on the container, keeping in mind that this is a new and somewhat tricky process and can be overdone. Hand-thinning of the fruit is still the safest method, but somewhat time-consuming. If you decide to hand-thin your apple trees, space the fruit you wish to leave on the tree about 4 to 6 inches apart, or one apple on every third or fourth spur. The result is handsome large fruit and a tidy lawn. Good "garden-keepers" consider the process well worth the effort.

A spray program such as I have outlined earlier in this section will control almost all of the major troubles you might encounter in your backyard apple orchard. And if you want real satisfaction from your tree-fruit efforts, you should make up your mind to spray before you visit the nursery for your planting stock. Home owners further interested in learning more about insects and diseases that attack the tree fruits can write to their State Experimental Station for latest control methods.

Storage: As late apples are being harvested, keep in mind that you may want to store some for winter eating. Your heated basement is not the place to keep apples over winter. A simple way to hold them firm and fresh into the following May is to set a new or very clean galvanized garbage can into a hole in a shady spot of your garden, deep enough so that the lip or rim of the can is just slightly above ground level, or you can use a discarded refrigerator such as I've described under Vegetable Storage. Place your blemish-and-disease-free apples in the can and cover with a pile of straw or leaves to a depth of 2 feet. A board or stone may be placed over this covering to keep it from blowing off. Even though the ground around the can will be frozen during the winter, the apples will not freeze. It's a good idea to keep the apples in an unheated room or garage until the ground temperature gets cold, also keep them moist by spraying lightly with water before placing them in the winter storage can.

BLUEBERRIES

Resistance to low temperatures, varieties that produce plump juicy blue fruit in abundance, and handsome reddish-brown foliage in fall, are working their magic to increase the popularity of home-grown blueberries, only 45 years from the completely wild state and domesticated for easy growing. As a rule, blueberries need no spraying, can thrive in sun or semi-shade and produce fruit the year after planting. They are, however, soil-fussy and demand a humus-rich condition coupled with soil acidity.

You can, of course, have a soil test made to determine the acidity of your land—and this is a subject we touch on under Soils—but for the small home garden, we like the method devised by Michigan State College of growing blueberries in tubs; you are, after all, going to plant at least two, but probably no more than four blueberry plants of at least two varieties for cross pollination: the Concord variety for early, and Rancocas for mid-season, plus a choice between Rubel and Jersey.

For tub culture, you use oil drums cut in half with the bottoms and tops removed. Sink the tubs in the soil and fill with a mixture of either ½ bushel of sawdust or peat moss mixed with good garden soil. This mixture may then be acidified by adding from ¼ pound to 1 pound of ammonium sulfate or sulfur—the former for soils already acid, the latter for very alkaline or nearly neutral soils. Into these specially prepared "tubs" you then set out your blueberry plants, early in spring, trimmed back to little more than half the size the nursery sends you. Trim off ragged root ends also and set the plants just a little deeper in the soil than they were in the nursery row as indicated by the soil line on the plant.

Blueberries are great nitrogen feeders and might show yellow leaves if their nitrogen supply is not up to demand. Ammonium sulfate again is your remedy—as much as one handful around the base of each plant every three weeks until yellow leaves disappear, then cut the quantity to about 2 ounces per plant once or twice during the growing season. Do not use nitrate of soda for blueberries—the plants cannot convert or use the nitrogen in nitrate of soda.

Heavy pruning is important to good blueberry culture, as the plants have a tendency to overbear, producing small fruit. A large number of fruit buds form on new shoot growth and if all these fruit buds, each producing a cluster of from five to eight berries, is permitted to mature, your fruit will be small and inferior.

Do your blueberry pruning in early spring before the bushes bloom. A good rule of thumb is to allow one fruit bud for each 3 inches of new shoot growth, thereafter removing all sucker shoots and twiggy branches. The vigorous new shoots remaining should be about 6 inches in length and well spread.

Blueberries have few troubles, as we have said, but birds are fond of the fruit and can get into the bush before you do. Try using a fibre-mesh netting ("Protecto-Net") over the bushes to salvage the major portion of the crop for the table.

BUSH CHERRIES AND BEACH PLUMS

Bush cherries and beach plums are planted as you would plant any shrub or tree. Make sure that the holes are large enough to accommodate all the roots without crowding. Plant to the same depth as the plants stood in the nursery row. No great amount of pruning is necessary, just enough to shape the plants and remove any dried or broken branches. Trim off about one-third of the tops of the plants before setting.

BOYSENBERRIES

For something different, look to the thornless boysenberry with its giant-sized fruit and smooth canes. In the north, the boysenberry is not absolutely winter-hardy and we cover the canes with straw. The covering is removed in early spring after danger of severe frosts is over.

In spring, cut back one-half the previous year's growth and train the plants to a trellis, 4 to 5 feet high. The new canes that grow up during the summer months should be trained back into the row to facilitate cultivation around the plants. After picking the fruit, the old canes which have borne the crop can be cut back close to the ground and the new canes trained to the trellis.

CHERRIES

Both sweet and sour cherries live on a wide diversity of soils, provided they are well drained. The cherry is sensitive to a poorly drained soil and will not thrive in heavy soil. Cherries may be fall-planted, but take happily to spring planting also—and follow the general rules for all fruit tree planting.

A wrinkle that is little known outside the trade in cherry growing is to spread the branches of the tree with notched boards when the tree is young and supple. This makes a broad and open tree and produces extra fruit. Apple growers do this on varieties which tend to grow straight up.

Sweet cherry varieties range from the pink-fleshed, black-skinned Windsor, and all pink and golden Royal Ann (called Napoleon in most catalogs) to the large, black and temptingly juicy Black Tartarian and Schmidt's Bigarreau. Sweet cherries do not pollinate themselves and need the "rooster" proclivities supplied (in this list) by either or both Windsor and Black Tartarian. In considering sweet cherries in your garden, figure on two trees—one a "rooster," or your best efforts may come to naught.

Montmorency, the leading sour-cherry variety, is self-fertile but may not be used to pollinate the sweet cherries which bloom earlier.

Again, the "All-Purpose" spray program will control most of the major troubles you will encounter in growing your own cherries, with the possible exception of those years in which late frosts (against which there is no practical protection for the home gardener) "take" the blossoms. Should this happen to your cherry program, you will have to resign yourself to waiting for the next year's crop. Birds are often a greater menace to sweet cherries than all the insects, diseases and inclement weather combined.

CURRANTS AND GOOSEBERRIES

Currants grow in any soil, under shaded conditions and do not winter-kill. The culture of gooseberries is so similar to currants that these two fruits will be discussed simultaneously. The Red Lake variety of currant—a large red berry—and Poorman gooseberries are generous yielders for

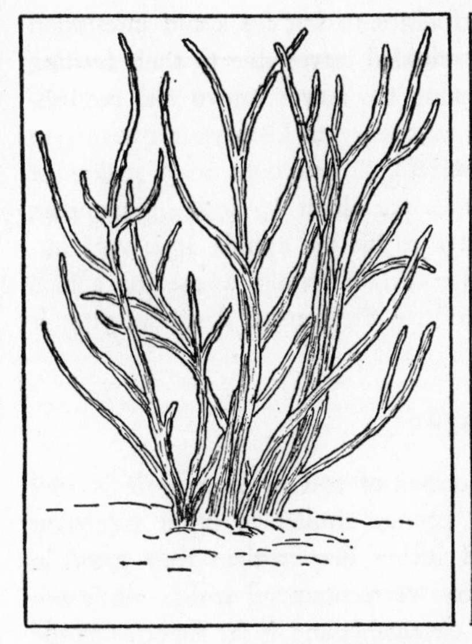
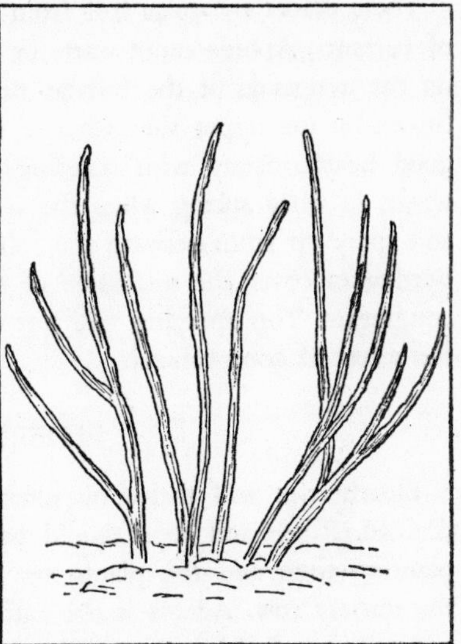

Currant bush before and after pruning.

the home garden. You will want to set out two plants of each per person for the fruit you want.

While currants and gooseberries are relatively free from troubles, there are some states that prohibit the growing of them because the plants serve as host to one stage of the pine blister rust. Before ordering plants from your nursery, make sure to consult the laws of your state on these two fruits.

Plant currants and gooseberries 3 inches deeper than they grew in the nursery, in either spring or fall. Tops should be cut back one half at planting time. After the plants are three years old you should prune out some of the older wood to stimulate growth of the plants and maintain fruit size. The plants are shallow-rooted, so it is necessary to mulch them well with sawdust, peat moss or straw; and for feeding, a handful of nitrate of soda around each bush in early spring will do nicely.

While gooseberries need little more pruning than the removal of dead and low-hanging branches, currants should have old canes removed. The ideal is to have, on each currant bush, three or four canes each of 1-, 2- and 3-year-old growth after the bush has reached maturity. Currant pruning should be done in fall or late winter when the plants are completely dormant.

These plants are quite free from troubles, except for aphid infestation of currants. Aphids cause warts or wrinkled leaves due to their feeding on the underside of the foliage, turning the leaves brown and reddish-brown on the upper side. Control is necessary to keep your currants in good health. Spray with nicotine sulfate, 2 teaspoons to a gallon of water, in early spring when the leaves are about ½ inch in diameter, and spray up from beneath the foliage to hit the aphids. It is very important to cover the *under*side of the currant foliage where the aphids congregate. Top spraying will not control the insects. Early spraying is the secret of good control.

ELDERBERRIES

Elderberries will thrive on most types of soil as long as it is well drained. Roots and tops should be pruned similar to other shrubs at planting time and the plants set 2 inches deeper than they grew in the nursery row. Adams is the variety we recommend which, while not generally handled by all nurseries, is obtainable and is far superior to the wild elderberry plants some gardeners dig up from creeksides and transplant to their gardens.

GRAPES

Since my home is in the very midst of a great grape-growing area of New York State—the Finger Lakes Region—I am particularly enthusiastic about grape culture and the pure delight of grapes as a fruit. I personally feel that no yard or garden should be without at least one or two grapevines.

Varieties: Among the many varieties of grapes you can grow, a few have outstanding qualities with which you should be familiar. Ontario, an early white grape, and Buffalo, a midseason blue grape, have the virtue of needing no spraying. Interlaken Seedless is a semi-early California-type white grape that is utterly delicious and sensational as a conversation piece over the back fence with your neighbors. Delaware and Brighton are excellent red grapes, but do not plant Brighton alone. It is self-sterile and needs another grape variety nearby for pollination. Steuben and Sheridan are Concord-type grapes, bearing late. Sheridan is an excellent keeper and can be held in cool storage sometimes until Christmas.

Grapes are not soil-fussy, but since they live and produce for as long as sixty to eighty years, you will want to do all you can to maintain high organic content of the soil in which you plant your grapes. This can be done by adopting a biennial program of mulching around the plants with waste hay, sawdust, wood chips, compost or peat moss.

Planting: Select either one- or two-year-old grapevines for setting out and locate your vines away from frosty pockets, in full sun and considerably out from under the shade of trees to prevent mildew of the vines. Where growing seasons are short, ripening can be hastened by planting on the south side of a building and training the vine against the wall. Heat radiated from reflected sunlight on the wall will make the fruit ripen as much as a week earlier.

Usual spacing for grapes is 8 feet by 8 feet, but if space is limited you can set the plants on 7-foot centers. Holes should be dug 12 to 14 inches deep and 16 inches in diameter. I like to put some rotted compost in the bottom of the hole before planting the vine. Prune the top back so that you have two buds remaining. If you plant grapes in fall, hold the pruning over until spring; but in either season, trim off broken roots and any roots that are too long to fit without crowding into the hole you have provided.

Set the pruned vine into the hole so that the two buds are just above soil level, tamp soil firmly around the roots and into the hole and water well. You can either mulch or cultivate the first year.

No trellis is needed for the vines the first year since they can be trained on stakes placed next to the base of the plant. The second year, you will need support for the growing vines. I use metal posts about 8 feet long, driven 2 to 2½ feet into the ground. On these posts, two wires should be strung, one 5½ feet from the ground, and the second 2 feet below the top wire. This spacing will provide maximum exposure of leaf area to the sun and promote early ripening of the fruit.

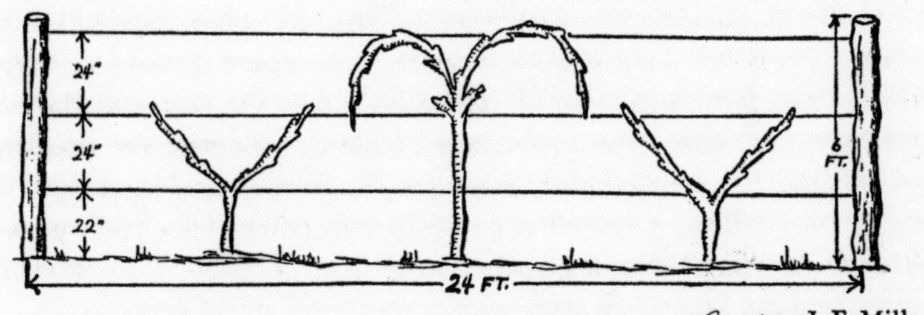

Courtesy J. E. Miller

How to train grapes to grow on a trellis. Wire "twist-ems" are used to secure the vines to the wires.

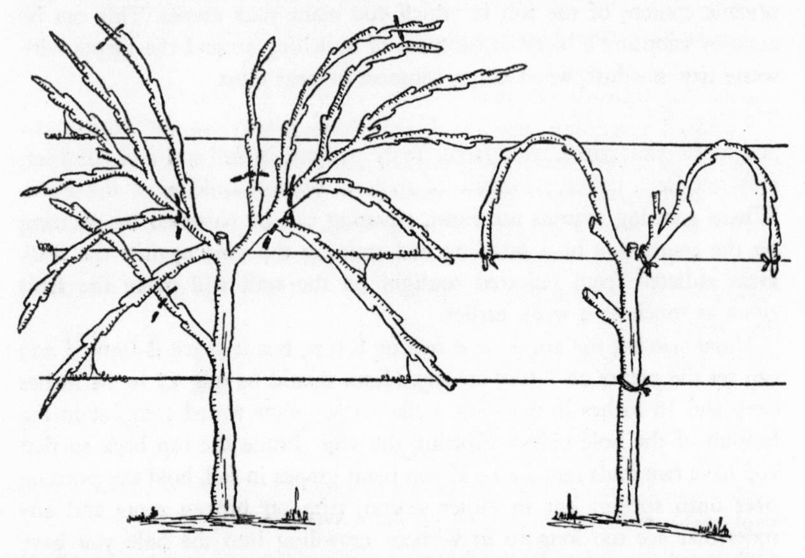

Pruning a mature grapevine. Make cuts where indicated, so that the vine looks like the one at the right.

Pruning Is Simple: So much has been written about pruning grapevines, there is little wonder that the home gardener is afraid to tackle it. But tackle it you must, because there is no one thing that is so completely disastrous to your efforts to grow grapes as vines that have not been regularly and (preferably) properly pruned. Still, let me say this: Better to be brave and hack away at your vines in good spirit than to say "I don't know how to do it" and neglect them entirely. The purpose of pruning is to limit the production of fruit and control cane growth so that cane and fruit are in balance at all times.

In the main, the canes you want to save are those last-year's canes about 5 to 8 feet long and about as thick as a lead pencil, or slightly thicker and fairly short-jointed. Those buds near the center of the cane produce more than those at the base of the cane or near the tip. Thus, cut off the tips of the canes, leaving eight to twelve buds. Remove all unnecessary old wood as well as undervigorous canes of last year's growth. That is the general idea of grape-pruning.

Specifically, here is what you do:

(1) At planting time, prune canes back leaving only two buds.

(2) Second year prune off all growth except one strong cane and leave three to five buds. Tie this cane to the first wire of the trellis or support.

(3) Third year leave two fruiting canes of six to eight buds each, tied to the first wire.

(4) Fourth year, leave two longer fruiting canes of ten to twelve buds each, tying them to the bottom wire of the trellis.

(5) Fifth year, leave three fruiting canes of ten to twelve buds each, tying the longest cane to the top wire of the trellis.

In selecting the fruiting canes to leave, use those which have grown the previous year. You will also want to leave a "spur" for each cane—a "spur" being simply a cane cut back to two buds. The reason for this procedure is that the canes growing from this spur will be the fruiting canes to select from next year, and by following this program, fruiting canes are kept near to the trunk of the vine.

Ordinarily, a total of four canes per vine are enough to leave on. A weak cane can support about forty buds and a thrifty vine about sixty. This is called "Balanced Pruning." If your grapes are a whole mass of vines, don't be discouraged. Your total pruning motivation is this: to select four of the best canes per vine and cut out all the rest, and to select canes of last year's growth which have buds at reasonably close intervals. After you have finished a good pruning job, you should have a lot of "brush" to clear away, which is as it should be, and not a sign that you have just completely ruined your little vineyard.

Feeding: Feeding grapes has just a few tricks to it that you should keep well in mind. On vines that are making exceptionally strong growth, use fertilizers sparingly or you'll get all "brush" and no fruit. On top of that, overfertilized vines won't harden off properly for winter and may kill back. Grape vines have long roots that extend as much as eight feet from the base of the vine with most of the feeder roots 3 to 6 feet out from the base. Therefore, fertilizer applied to the base of the trunk will do almost no good at all. You must fertilize widely for grapes.

Grapes need potash, do not respond to phosphorus, and are fairly nitrogen hungry at all times where yields are wanted. Provide the nitrogen needs of the vines by applying ⅓ pound of nitrate of soda or ⅙ pound of ammonium nitrate to each vine as soon as the buds start to swell in the spring. Potash should be supplied by the application of 2 pounds of potassium sulfate per vine.

Checking Grape Pests: Most of the grape troubles you will encounter in the backyard planting can be controlled by spraying early with Bordeaux mixture to which has been added 2 ounces of 50% wettable DDT and 1/4 ounce of spreader per 6 1/4 gallons of Bordeaux. Spray again with this mixture just before blossoming and a third time just after blossoming. For best results, spray grapevines when the leaves are dry.

One other nugget of wisdom: do not blame bees, wasps and hornets for damage you may find in your grapes. These insects will do no damage to sound fruit, but are simply sharing your enthusiasm for grapes—tempted to the vines by fruit that has popped open due to weather conditions. You will find this condition most often after a long drought followed by heavy rains late in the season. The grapes will build up pressure under these conditions, causing the fruit to pop open and drop to the ground.

PEACHES

Peaches are very easy to grow provided they are given the right care at the right time, and on this will hang the success of your peach production. You start with any type of soil for your peach trees, but be sure the drainage is good. Peach trees will not stand wet feet; therefore, fertile sandy loams are preferable, although heavier soils will do.

Best varieties for your home garden will probably be Golden Jubilee, Hale Haven or Elberta. J. H. Hale is an excellent variety but will need a "rooster" peach nearby of one of the other three varieties to produce fruit.

Pruning: Planted in spring or fall, peaches need very little pruning until they are three or four years old. Then you aim at having an open center tree with three, four or five scaffold branches arising from the trunk, no higher than 36 inches from the ground. Most peach trees bear the third year after planting, and since the fruit is borne from side buds on one-year-old shoots, you'll need to do some regular pruning each year from now on to force out the new shoots. Old, neglected peach trees can be cut back to wood three years old or more and started out from there.

To start the open center formation of your peach tree, the central leader or main branch of the tree should be held down. This is done throughout the life of the tree, beginning the first year after planting. The scaffold branches are allowed to grow with less pruning, the lowest of which may be no more than a foot from the ground. Don't let branches lower than this remain on the tree. Now remove limbs that tend to fill up the center of the tree or make any part of the tree too dense. Head back any tall and ungainly limbs. The best time to prune peach trees is in March.

Thinning: Peaches often set several times as many fruits as the tree can possibly develop. Such overloading should be avoided as it ruins the trees. Thirty good leaves are needed to produce one peach, spaced 6 to 8 inches from its nearest neighbor. So it is part of the culture of peach growing to think in terms of hand-thinning the crop right after "June drop"—the time that nature elects to thin the trees by letting many small peaches drop from the trees that are loaded beyond capacity. At this time you should look over the peach tree, limb by limb, and remove from it any peaches that are small, poorly shaped or damaged or closer together than 6 to 8 inches.

Spraying: The most savage atacks of insects and diseases on your peach trees can be pretty well controlled by the "All-Purpose" spray and program as outlined earlier. Peach-tree borers, leaf curl and brown rot are the most common enemies of good peach production, and each is prevalent enough to make at least a minimum spray program necessary. DDT should be sprayed on the trunks in November to check borer invasion, and Ferbam sprayed on branches during dormant season to prevent peach leaf curl. If it sounds like too much trouble, perhaps you would be better not to attempt peaches—but certainly the tree-ripened fruit you eat out of your own yard is worth some effort.

Picking: There is a trick to picking peaches that a lot of people don't know—and it is this: Don't pick peaches too early! Leave the fruit on the trees at least until it has changed to a greenish yellow color with up to 25 per cent blush color. Delayed picking increases your yield too. One hundred bushels of unripe peaches today will make 109 bushels in two days more, 116 bushels five days from now and 124 bushels next week! Besides an improvement in size and color obtained by delayed picking, the flavor of tree-ripened fruit is far superior to a generally flat taste that peaches have when picked too green.

PEARS

Pears are among the easiest of tree fruits to grow in the home garden, almost as hardy as apples and well acclimated to heavy clay or loam soils.

Pears will even tolerate a little wet feet, but a well-drained soil will produce better growth. But still, a good soil will do wonders for your pear efforts. It is not generally known that the flavor, aroma, texture and keeping qualities of pears are influenced more by the soil than anything else and that pears that are sour, dry and bitter are that way from poor soil conditions more than any other reason. Pears are gritty because they are left on the tree too long before picking. Also give your pear trees good air drainage for disease and frost damage prevention.

Varieties: Bartlett, Bosc, Clapp's Favorite and Seckle are excellent pear varieties, but if you choose Bartlett and Seckle to grow together (a favorite combination), do be sure to provide a pollinator—either in the form of a third pear variety, or by blossom bouquets of a compatible variety as explained elsewhere. Bartlett and Clapp's Favorite are very susceptible to fire blight so if you plant these varieties, be prepared to watch for and deal with this disease.

You should go easy with fertilizing the pear trees. Too much feeding stimulates strong growth and makes the tree more susceptible to blight. Rather, put a screen around the base of the tree and use a mulch of sawdust, ashes, peat moss, etc., to keep weeds down and moisture in.

Spraying: Use the "All-Purpose" spray and program for control of insects and diseases. Fire blight needs much more radical treatment. Fire blight is easily recognizable by dead blossoms, leaves and twigs that turn black and remain on the tree. Cankers and mummified fruit may also be found. Inspect your pear trees and cut out infected wood. Fire blight spreads easily, so disinfect your pruning tools after this chore by thoroughly soaking in 1 part of bichloride of mercury in 1,000 parts of water (¼ tablespoon per gallon).

Picking: It seems almost elementary to say anything about how and when to pick pears, but actually no other fruit requires so much care as this one. Just about every pear we know should be picked long before it is ready to eat. It is hard to say just when green pears should be picked to have the perfect flavor of ripe pears. A fair rule of green thumb is to pick when the stem parts from the branch when the fruit is lifted. Some folks wait until the seeds are brown. If your pears don't keep well, chances are you are picking them too late, causing the fruit to be mealy. You might watch the wormy pears if you have any. When wormy fruit begins to turn yellow, that is the time to pick the green fruit, as injured fruit will ripen first. To ripen your pears after they are picked, cover them with newspapers and keep them in the garage or on a cool porch. They ripen best at 65 degrees and 85 per cent humidity or higher.

PLUMS

The plum is a fine fruit tree, well suited to most conditions in the north, where the tree is hardy. There is some confusion over "when is a plum a prune?" Prunes are a speical class of plum which, because of their sugar content, may be successfully dried on the pit. Most popular for home growing in the northeast are the Stanley prune, the French and German prunes and the Italian or Fellemberg prune which, incidentally, is not self-fruitful and must be grown with another plum tree nearby to pollinate it. For the rough-and-ready gardener, the Stanley is probably the best to try.

There are two Damson-type plums, French and Shropshire, which are blue with green flesh, and two Japanese-type plums, Burbank and Formosa, with red or red-yellow skins and yellow flesh that are popular garden types. Burbank and Formosa need "rooster" trees for pollination and should be grown with one of the other varieties mentioned for fruit production.

Don't be impatient for the fruit from plum trees. It will take anywhere from five to seven years after setting before they start to bear—and they cannot be pushed!

Spraying: Do keep the trees sprayed with Bordeaux mixture regardless of whether they bear. Prune the branches only enough to remove those that are criss-crossing or crowding one another, and wait it out.

Planted in well-drained soil, sprayed with the "All-Purpose" spray plus the Bordeaux mixture and fed about 1/8 pound of ammonium nitrate per tree per year of age, plums will come along with little effort and yield delicious fruit for fresh eating, canning or preserving for many years. If you should see a gummy, gelatinous material on plum fruit, you can be sure that your tree is under attack by the curculio insect. The best way to fight this pest is to gather and burn fallen fruit, since the worm is inside the dropped fruit.

QUINCES

The flowering quince is most often considered an ornamental shrub and referred to simply as "japonica." This is not the same as the fruiting quince. See our section on landscaping for the discussion of flowering-quince culture. The culture of both these types of quinces is similar. As to the fruit of the quince bush, what needs telling here is that quince bears very heavily and, to get large fruit, one must remove the small ones a couple of weeks after the blossoms fade and while the stems are still soft enough to allow pinching them off.

Quinces are not edible out of hand but are popular for a jelly or quince honey. Many people also like to use the fruit for perfuming bedding and linens.

RASPBERRIES

Raspberries probably give the home gardener as good a return in delicious fruit as he can get from any fruit plant. All raspberries do best in a well-drained soil and are not particular as to whether it is largely clay or largely sandy loam. But they need quantities of water and do not like wet feet. Drainage is therefore the important factor.

Red raspberries have different growing habits than the black and purple raspberries and require slightly different care and pruning. It is also well to remember that nothing can get out of hand and into a bramble faster than a neglected raspberry planting! You must be the boss in your raspberry patch, or the plants will quickly take over, become diseased and provide you with nothing but small seedy fruit and you will regret that you ever set a plant.

While raspberries are producing fruit they are also struggling to perpetuate themselves, making, in the case of the red varieties, "suckers" or new shoots and in blacks and purples, "tip-roots." These are the processes that must be watched carefully by the tidy gardener to keep things under control, and can be done by pruning, which we will get at in a moment.

Planting: We feel that raspberries should be planted as early in the spring as possible. They may be set in the fall, in the latter part of October or the first two weeks in November, but the spring planting is usually more successful. Space raspberry plants 3 feet apart in the row, setting them in shallow holes or an open furrow to a depth of 4 inches. Cover the roots with fine, loose soil and firm them in with your hand or foot. Fill the rest of the hole loosely, leaving the top layer loose so that buds growing from the ground level can grow out easily. Water well, but do not place any fertilizer in contact with the roots when planting.

Feeding: Feed the plants with 2 ounces of nitrate of soda or 1 ounce of ammonium nitrate per plant, spreading the fertilizer well out from the plants as raspberries feed 3 to 4 feet from the canes. This feeding should be done early in spring and care should be taken not to feed the plants in the fall, as this might produce soft late growth that will be sure to winterkill.

Pruning: The first thing to know about pruning all raspberries is that the canes that bear the fruit grown on in one year, produce the fruit the next year and then die. Once a raspberry cane has produced fruit, its function in life is over and it should be cut off at ground level, removed from the patch and burned. The burning, while not a total disease and insect control, helps immeasurably.

All raspberries profit by a summer "tipping" or pruning the tops of the new shoots off when the canes have reached a height of from 2 to 3 feet. Black and purple raspberries should be tipped at 2 feet before they make a long, spindly growth which arches over until the end touches the soil. It is at this point that the blacks and purples will get out of hand, for the tip of the long cane will form a new plant and thus a whole new family of canes and arches and new plants. It takes only a couple of years to produce the massive bramble we mentioned earlier if the summer tipping is neglected.

Red raspberries do not tip-root, but make suckers. These sucker plants should be trimmed out every year, allowing the new canes to set no closer than 8 to 10 inches from one another. All raspberries need good air drainage and should not be allowed to grow too thickly.

Clean cultivation of the raspberry planting should be kept up until about the time the blossoms form, then the plants may be mulched with straw or sawdust which does double duty in keping down the weeds and preserving soil moisture for the promotion of large fruit. After harvest of red raspberries, mulch should be thinned to allow the new shoots to come up straight and true for the following year's crop.

Latham, Taylor and Newburgh are good red raspberry varieties, Bristol is a recommended black, and Sodus a favorite purple. There is also a fall-bearing red raspberry called September which does bear two crops of fruit—one in early summer and one on the new canes in the fall. Many people harvest both the crops, but others prefer to cut back the fruiting canes drastically in spring and concentrate on the fall crop. Fall-fruiting raspberries should be supported as the berries are borne high on the cane tips which have a tendency to drag on the ground, bruising and dirtying the fruit.

A new fall-fruiting raspberry of the purple variety is becoming available now and should be tried for both delicious fruit and heavy yield. It is called Purple Autumn.

Spraying: Raspberries fall heir to several insect pests which take the joy out of home-fruit culture. A DDT spray (1½ level teaspoon of 50% DDT to a gallon of water) will check most pests. For Raspberry fruit worm, apply when first blossom buds appear, and repeat just before the blossom buds open. This treatment checks Raspberry sawfly, tarnished plant bug, cane borers, as well as the fruit worm. For red spider, use Malathion, 1 teaspoon to 2 quarts of water, about 2 weeks prior to harvest. If you're bothered by Japanese beetle you'll be forced to use DDT whenever they're attacking.

Diseases of raspberries are best controlled by providing good air circulation around the plants and segregating the reds from the purples and blacks as much as possible. In small plantings, either grow reds alone, or blacks and purples alone. If you must have all three, grow the blacks and purples at least 500 feet from the reds. This will in part prevent the possible mosaic infection in the blacks and purples from travelling by insects to the reds.

STRAWBERRIES

Complete books have been written on the culture of this popular and delicious fruit without completely covering all the ways and means of producing the best strawberries. The home gardener does not need to go into these fine points, however, to raise and pick his own strawberries in season. There are only a few important do's and don'ts involved, but they are important and should be strictly observed.

Strawberries need soils that are well drained and very well supplied with humus. They need water, full sun and protection from the birds (try "Protect-O-Nets") when in fruit; weeds must be kept down in the berry patch, plants should be spaced as they form, the bed should be mulched over winter and some kind of protection against frost should be available when the blossoms are out. Plant food is needed, of course, but care must be taken as to the time and amount applied. In spite of all of this, many people grow strawberries in the home garden with little or no effort, delighted with the fact that any strawberry picked and eaten ripe from one's own patch is a thing of great enjoyment. The persistent plants will give you some fruit no matter how neglectful you are of the things you should do for the best berries.

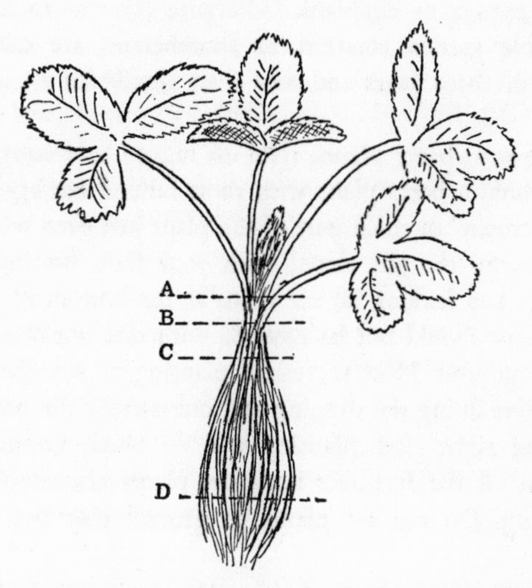

Courtesy J. E. Miller

In planting strawberries don't cover roots too deeply. (A) is too deep; (B) is just right; (C) is planted too shallow. Prune roots at (D).

Planting: Very early spring is the best time to set out strawberries. Buy your plants from a good nursery, preferably a grower, where you can get freshly dug sets. Choose from amongst the heavy-yielding good varieties such as Premier (early), Empire, Catskill, Fairfax and Robinson (midseason) and Sparkle (late). If you can plant only one variety, try Sparkle. Add Premier for a second variety and Fairfax for a third. You will often find nurseries offering a "collection" of these three varieties, twenty-five plants of each.

If you do not intend to spend a lot of time with your strawberry plants, allow 2 feet between each plant and 1½ feet on each side of the plant row. All of this space will be well covered with plants by the end of the first growing season, and you will wonder in the next summer where you can put your feet when picking. Do not underestimate the ability of the strawberry to spread itself wherever there is ground! You should provide twenty-five plants for each member of your family for enough strawberries to eat at any one time. At the height of the season, you will have some extra for preserves or freezing out of this size planting.

For best results, do not set strawberries where you have grown tomatoes, potatoes, green pepper or eggplant. Otherwise you can include the rows in your vegetable garden rotation, as strawberries are seldom fruitful more than two or three years and new rows should be set at least every third year.

When setting strawberry plants, trim off ragged root ends. Make a slit in the soil and hold a berry plant with roots fanned out against one side of the slit, the "crown" or thick part of the plant just even with the top of the slit. Now stamp the slit closed with your foot, firming the soil in around the roots and leaving no air space at the bottom of the slit. The crown of the plant should not be covered with dirt nor should the roots show above the ground. Most successful planting of strawberries is done by two people, one doing the digging and one setting the plants. A good, soaking watering right after planting will do much toward settling in the plants. Hold off the fertilizer until the plants are established in the row and growing. Do not set plants in ground that has been freshly fertilized.

After the plants show signs of new growth in the leaves, you can commence a feeding program, using a complete formula fertilizer, either applied in liquid form or around the plants, about half a handful to a plant, hoed in lightly and then watered. This feeding may be continued at two-week intervals all through the first year.

When blossoms appear on the newly set plants, they should be removed the first year to throw all possible strength into the plants for a good fruit crop the second year. Shortly after the blossoming season, "runners" will spring from the center of the plants, at the end of which, in a few days, a new plant will form and "set" in the ground around the plant you put in the row. If you want highest possible yields of fine, big strawberries, no one plant should be allowed to make more than six of these new runner plants, which you space evenly around the plant in the row. All other runners should be removed as they form. This runner removal should be kept up all summer long. If you do not keep at it, your berry patch will quickly get out of hand, making a matted row of plants which will produce a lot of berries the next year, but very small ones which are difficult to pick and not very nice to eat.

Mulching: In late fall, just before very cold weather when snow begins to fly, cover the entire strawberry bed with a 2-inch blanket of straw or marsh hay. Leaves should be used as a last resort as they tend to mat and may smother the plants. This mulching is very necessary, as strawberries that are not covered over winter tend to heave out of the ground as it alternately freezes and thaws, which will eventually break off at the roots of the plants and kill them.

Early in spring of the following year, the mulch may be gradually removed. You can tell when to take the last of the mulch off by watching the color of the foliage. When it starts to turn a sickly green under the mulch, the plants need light and it is time to fully expose them. Keep the mulch you take off the plants right in the berry rows around the plants. This will serve to keep the fruit off the ground and keep it clean so that you will not have to wash the strawberries before serving them.

Keep fertilizer away from the berry patch until the crop of fruit is off, as feeding at this time tends to make the berries soft and encourages rotting before they ripen. Do supply the plants with frequent watering all through the berry season, soaking the patch after you pick. This increases berry size wonderfully. Should a frost threaten when your strawberries are beginning to bloom, cover the rows over night with newspapers or burlap bags. The blossoms are very sensitive to frost and a late frost can "take the crop" if the patch is not protected.

Renew the Bed: After the patch has produced its first crop of berries, dig out small and unthrifty plants, filling the spaces with the new runners that will again form this second year. Once the spaces are filled, however, again continue the runner removal all through the season—and the feeding program you used in the first year. Some people like to cut the plants back by removing all but a few leaves from each plant after fruit harvest. This is not necessary but does give a cleaner-appearing patch. The winter mulch is again applied to your rows and removed in spring. After the second fruit harvest it is well to dig the plants under and work on a new patch. Some diseases may take hold of an old patch about this time and the plants will be spindly.

There are some very good "everbearing" strawberries which will produce a crop of fruit in the fall of the year you set them out. However, it must be considered that these plants do not attain the size of the regular varieties and therefore do not produce the berries as heavily. Red Rich and Superperfection are two good varieties to try in everbearers, but

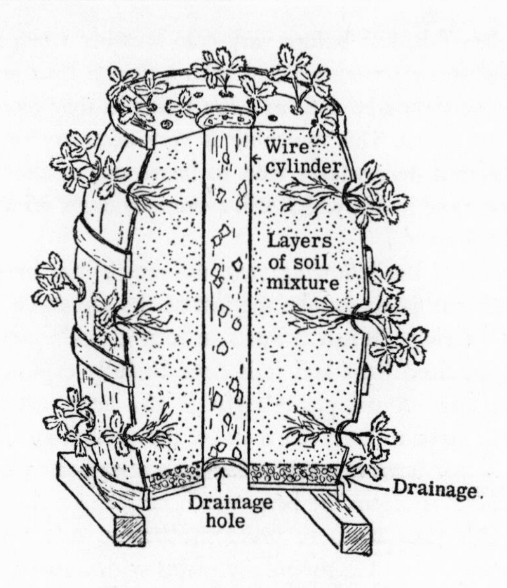

Strawberry Barrel

plant at least twice the number of everbearers as you would of the regular varieties. You can set them much closer together also, making double rows with the plants 10 to 12 inches apart each way.

One of the most serious troubles you will encounter in your berry rows is weeds! The patch should be kept completely clean-cultivated at all times. Summer mulches applied after the plants are well established help a lot in weed control—and for this purpose, sawdust or peat moss are good materials to use. Weed control will also reduce the danger of harboring pests which attack the blossoms and cause "catfacing" or deformation of the fruit. DDT or Chlordane applied just as the first blossoms open will also help in controlling pests which attack strawberries and methoxychlor dust will keep down the spittle bug population which in some summers tends to keep moisture from reaching the berries so they ripen small and deformed.

NUT CULTURE

There's no reason why you can't grow edible nuts right in your own backyard. The trees are ornamental as well as productive, and they don't need spraying for a good crop. Nearly all nut trees have the same cultural requirements, the two most important being a well-drained soil and the presence of a nearby "rooster" tree for cross-pollination. At planting time, dig holes 2 feet across and 2 or more feet deep, so roots will rest in a natural position. Fill around the roots with good top-soil and water well to drive out air pockets from the root area. Prune back the tree before planting to balance the loss of fine root hairs when trees were dug.

Here are some nuts to try: Almonds, similar in culture to peaches; butternuts, chestnuts (Chinese); Filberts (Hazelnuts and English Walnuts).

Starting Trees: Your best bet is to buy trees from a reliable nursery, although with patience you can start your own from seed. Gather nuts in the fall and "stratify" them; that is, pack the shucked nuts between alternate layers of sand in a box (covered with wire to keep out rodents) and sink the container in the ground or in a coldframe for the winter. In spring plant the nuts in a well-drained spot in the garden and watch them grow! They have to have the cold winter treatment before they'll germinate.

GREEN THUMB TIPS

Fruit trees vary in their bearing age. Rusty nails in the soil won't help one bit!

Failure to fruit may be due to early spring frost, or too-cold weather or rain at blossoming time.

All fruit trees bear sooner or later.

Bending the branches downward induces earlier bearing.

Green apples will color up if placed on straw under a tree.

Grafting will convert an undesirable tree into one with top quality fruit.

Don't worry about fruit sprays contaminating your fruit. Washing removes most of it.

Plant young trees! A 1-year-old tree will bear quicker than a 5-year-old tree.

Early fruit drop ("June drop") is nothing serious. It's nature's way of helping you have larger and better fruit.

If space is limited, grow Espalier (Es-pal-yay) trees. These are trained flat against a wall or trellis.

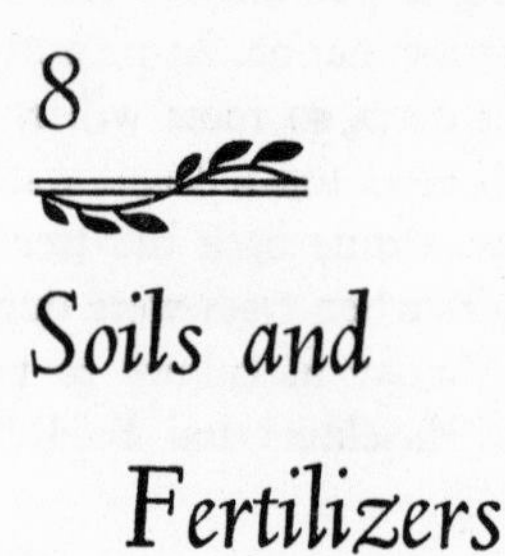

8 Soils and Fertilizers

The soil around your home is full of life! If you went out and scooped up a teaspoonful of it, you'd have as many as 5 billion living organisms in your hand. Keep these helpful workers happy through sound soil management. The information which follows is based on my own work in the greenhouse and in the field. I hope it helps you grow better plants.

Clay Soils: Soils are either "heavy" or "light." A clay soil is heavy because it has finer particles in it than a sandy or light soil. Both types of "problem" soils can be licked, although the clayey soil can be most discouraging at times. If you have a clay soil, your job is to make it "breathe," because a soil not well aerated is unproductive. Many tricks are used to loosen up a tight clayey soil. One is to use various "home-made" soil conditioners such as lawn clippings, corncobs, leaves, garbage, compost, coal and wood ashes, sawdust, peat moss, wood chips, muck, and any other form of organic matter. Humus opens the clay, encourages earthworms to be more active helpers. Earthworms enrich the earth by passing more than 10 tons of dry earth through their bodies annually in 1 acre alone.

Adding sand to a clay-like soil will *not* loosen it, and may result in a concrete-like mixture harder than the original clay. Limestone has a loosening effect on a heavy clay soil, coagulating the fine particles into larger ones, allowing air and water to pass freely. Limestone does not have the same beneficial effect on sand. There is little or no danger of applying too much limestone to heavy soils because it breaks down slowly, and the clay has a "buffer" effect, preventing the calcium in limestone from making the soil alkaline, even when large quantities are used.

Another way to keep a clay soil in top condition is to avoid working it when it's wet. One day's work in a wet clay soil can make it hard the rest of the year. If you're one of those gardeners who likes to whip up a garden soil with a rotary power tiller before planting you'll be surprised to know this working-over is poor for plants and makes a clay soil even worse. Fluffing up a soil breaks down the structure, plugs the soil pores, and as a result the earth will turn to a sticky gumbo after the first rain. Millions of dollars are lost each year by farmers who try to make a lettuce bed out of their fields by overworking the soil.

Nature improves clay soils each time you have a drought. Drying destroys the water film that normally surrounds soil particles, causing them to form granules. This in turn gives soils larger pore spaces which means better aeration, a more workable and productive soil.

Sandy Soils: Sandy soils are easier to work but dry out faster and lose plant foods quicker than clay soils. Fortunately, practices which help loosen up a heavy soil will also "tighten" a sandy soil. The correct way to handle a sandy soil is to apply organic matter in any form available. These materials act similar to a blotter, holding moisture and nutrients. Sandy soils, unlike clayey soils, may be worked earlier in spring, and even while wet, without danger of "puddling" or caking.

Building up the home garden soil bank is a good investment for any home owner. If your soil seems heavy, drains poorly, bakes in summer or seems just plain fagged out, or your crops do poorly each year, then you need a soil bank program of your own.

If there are no other factors involved, such as shade or robber roots from nearby trees, insufficient drainage, or too much acidity, then organic matter is the heart of your soil improvement plan. To date, nothing has been discovered that is superior, on a cost basis, to organic matter as a soil builder and conditioner. When fresh organic matter rots in the soil, slimy materials are formed by millions of soil microbes. These materials bind the soil particles together into loose crumbs, leaving much pore space through which air and water can penetrate easily. Soils well supplied with organic matter remain in good condition to absorb rain throughout the season, and plant roots grow and breathe readily in such soils. The synthetic "soil conditioners" on the market can do about the same things but, generally speaking, are neither cheap nor very practical for this soil building job. Their main value to the home gardener probably will be where short-term treatment of the soil surface is important.

On sandy soils, organic matter has some additional benefits that other "conditioners" can't duplicate. Moisture stored by the soil for plant use increases as the humus content goes up, and fertilizer elements are also retained by the humus instead of being washed out by the first rains.

But how does the home gardener get this organic matter which is to be added to the soil? There are three ways: (1) save it, (2) haul it in, or (3) grow it.

(1) Save all crop residues such as cornstalks, tomato and pea vines, etc., as well as leaves, lawn clippings, sawdust and wood shavings and leafy garbage for use in a compost pile which is described elsewhere.

(2) Obtain organic matter such as peat, manure, straw, sawdust, leaves or similar materials and use as a mulch. This is described later in detail under "Mulches."

(3) Grow organic matter in the form of a "cover crop" and let plant roots work on your soil. Later plow it under for humus

WHAT IS A COVER CROP

The term "cover crop" comes up in garden publications quite often, but not all gardeners know what it really means. A cover crop is merely a temporary planting made to add organic matter to the soil and help keep it in good physical condition. The addition of a commercial fertilizer to produce a heavier cover crop will usually benefit the garden crops which follow. If you have plenty of garden space, a good plan is to put a third or a half of your garden into a cover crop each year, then alternate or rotate the cover crop with your vegetable planting. This method plus the addition of fertilizer and lime should produce a garden soil that's hard to beat. These cover crops are often called "Green Manure" crops, a good substitute for barnyard manure.

Oats, buckwheat and hardy domestic rye grass are a few common crops sown. We like to sow domestic rye grass about August in the corn or tomato patch or vineyard. It develops a root system that holds the soil over winter and adds many pounds of humus to the garden. Cover crops also hold nitrogen and other plant foods that might be leached away during the winter. Their tremendous root systems loosen heavy soils, whereas the added humus will help hold the particles of sandy soils together.

If you want to plant sweet clover, first add about 50 pounds of limestone per 1,000 sq. ft. unless the soil is already above pH of 6.5 (see

Soil Acidity). Sow seed in spring, and this will give you a "green manure" crop, roots and tops, which can be plowed under in fall or next spring.

Alfalfa, another legume, can also be used as a green manure crop, if the soil is sweet (has enough lime). The advantage of alfalfa over sweet clover is that you can make two or three cuttings during the growing season. This would allow you to mulch your early vegetables from your first cutting and use later cuttings on crops such as tomatoes, strawberries and others. Keep in mind that the different kinds of roots do different kinds of jobs. Fine grass and clover roots are ideal for developing soil crumbs in the upper 6- to 12-inch layer. Alfalfa and sweet clover taproots extend deeper and, when they die and rot, leave channels for air and water movement.

Hardy domestic rye grass makes a fine cover crop and soil builder because it develops heavy tops and large root systems. Sow the seed in among the corn, tomatoes or other crops at the rate of 3 pounds per ¼ acre. Loosen the soil up first with hoe or cultivator, then sow seed. We sow it at time of last cultivation, thus doing two jobs at once. DO NOT COVER THE SEED. Just sow it on freshly cultivated soil. It is a cool weather grass and makes most of its growth late in fall after your corn and other crops are harvested. Sown in July or August, domestic rye grass does not go to seed that year and is plowed under before it seeds the following year. Hence, no danger of it becoming a weed.

Among other possible cover crops is buckwheat, which can be sown in July. It dies down in fall, and is plowed under in spring or fall.

SOOT, COAL, WOOD AND INCINERATOR ASHES

Coal Ashes: Coal ashes have very little or no plant food value, although in sufficient amounts they do improve the mechanical condition of a soil which packs hard. They can be used with manure without harm. Scatter them over the garden and plow in.

They are dry and more or less antiseptic and discourage snails, snakes and worms. Hence, screened coal ashes are good for greenhouse aisles, benches, and under potted plants, or you can use them in the bottom of borders or beds to protect roses and other plants which do not like "wet feet."

Soot: Coal soot is a limited source of nitrogen and some potash and phosphorus. It repels wireworms, maggots, and cutworms and snails. Do not use soot and lime together, otherwise the nitrogen will be lost.

Incinerator Ashes: Ashes from burned papers and garbage will vary greatly in composition according to the amount of vegetable refuse and paper. They are not harmful and can be spread on the garden or lawn. They'll be alkaline, due to the calcium, magnesium, and sodium from the original materials. Their nutritive value will be chiefly in the phosphorus and potassium, with traces of many additional elements. There are some toxic metal compounds that might get into the ashes, such as zinc from batteries, metal polishes, waste borax, etc., but ordinarily these are not abundant and can be kept out of the home gardener's incinerator. Roughly speaking, incinerator ashes should be more or less equivalent to wood ashes and can be used wherever liming would not be objectionable.

Wood Ashes: Wood ashes, unleached, contain all the mineral elements that were in the original wood. The most abundant elements are lime and potash. At one time wood ashes were the chief source of potash, which is the plant food that gives stiff stems and imparts increased vigor and disease resistance to plants. Besides potash, wood contains about 2 per cent phosphorus, the plant food that stimulates growth and root formation. Various woods differ greatly in value as a plant food. Twigs are richer than mature wood. Both hardwood ashes and softwood ashes are all right to use in the flower or vegetable garden. If you have a stubborn peony or iris bed, sometimes ashes scattered on them will force flowers into bloom.

Don't use wood ashes with manure, unless it is well rotted. They can be used in the compost pile with leaves to hasten decomposition.

Since wood ashes contain lime, don't use on soils for potatoes—and keep them away from "acid-loving" plants such as azaleas and rhododendrons.

Generally speaking, scattering ashes on the garden is a satisfactory method of getting rid of ashes, although a rather meager way of building up fertility. An 80-pound sack of lime, where needed, and one bag of 10–10–10 fertilizer will do more for the home garden than several bushels of ashes. But, if you've got them, use them. Also, keep in mind that if you add ashes year after year, the soil should be tested to make sure it's not overly sweet, or so saturated with ashes as to cause drying out of the soil.

Few things are less understood than the practice of mulching. When you mulch you borrow a tip from nature and cover the soil to keep soil moisture in and temperatures from fluctuating. The purpose of a summer mulch is to save moisture and choke out weeds. A winter mulch is placed on *after* the ground is frozen (it's better for plants to freeze wet than dry). Such a winter mulch is not designed to keep out cold, but rather to prevent a phenomenon known as "heaving," due to freezing and thawing, which forces plants upward and out of the ground. You might say that a summer and winter mulch act similar to a thermostat in the soil, maintaining a more constant temperature.

Newly planted trees, shrubs and evergreens respond to a 4-inch mulch because it traps moisture in the soil, favoring the growth of roots. There are many mulch materials available, and there's no danger of using too much of any one of them. Here are some of the most common mulches used for the vegetable garden, flower beds, lawns and for trees and shrubs.

Buckwheat Hulls: These are light, clean, do not mat or freeze and may be dug into the soil where they decay slowly to build up a supply of humus. Apply 3 inches thick.

Cocoa Bean Shells: Contains 92 per cent organic matter, 3.2 per cent N, and 2 per cent potash. This mulch has a chocolate odor which disappears in a week. Ideal for new lawns, rose beds, in composts, around trees and shrubs, there is little danger from fire. On new lawns, use 150 pounds per 1,000 square feet. As a mulch, apply 1 to 3 inches thick in the flower border, around trees or shrubs.

Coffee Grounds: Valuable as soil conditioner and mulch, although low in nutrients (2 per cent nitrogen, .4 per cent phosphoric acid and .5 per cent potassium). Non-toxic to soils, coffee grounds are acid, making them valuable around azaleas, rhododendrons and other acid-lovers.

Corn Cobs: Excellent for rose beds, flower borders and vegetable garden. Have your farmer-neighbor grind some extra cobs for you.

Dust Mulch: Created by shallow surface cultivation, a layer of dust (pulverized earth) prevents upward movement of water from evaporating. When the moisture hits the broken soil surface it stops, to be absorbed by plant roots.

Evergreen Boughs: All kinds are suitable. Since they allow air to enter and prevent smothering, evergreens are ideal for soft perennials such as mums, foxgloves, and carnations in winter. Needles are useful as summer mulch although they present a fire hazard.

Excelsior: Free from weed seed, insects and disease, it is more difficult to apply than most materials. However, it does last for years, and if you have access to it, by all means use it.

Glass Wool: Makes a good mulch but tends to tear or blow away. Use chicken wire to cover it.

Gravel Mulch: Gravel stone comes in various colors, is easy to weed and maintain around trees or shrubs. It makes a fine lawn substitute under shaded trees, and in spots where eaves drip and splash mud against the foundation. My objection is that children like to scatter it around the house and lawn, making it a problem for lawn mowers.

Leaves: They make a poor mulch because of packing down and preventing the escape of moisture. They are excellent on the compost, however, and can be useful around evergreens, trees or shrubs.

Newspapers: Place 4 or 5 thicknesses around the plants and cover with peat moss to hide the papers. Paper ashes can be used as a mulch and on the garden. Being alkaline, they should not be around acid-loving plants such as azaleas, rhododendrons, holly and others.

Plastic Mulches: Strips are available in various thicknesses and widths. Rolled out over beds, plants are allowed to grow up through slits. Or you can roll strips between the rows to keep weeds out. Ideal in strawberry patches where they cause less rot (sometimes 50 per cent) and easier picking.

Peat Moss: The shredded moss you see in the woods is sphagnum, and the common brown moss found in bales is called peat moss. There are many different-size bales, but you can figure that one cubic foot of compressed baled peat will fluff out to 2½ cubic feet, and about 5 cubic feet will equal 4 or more bushels. Most peats are acid, and are ideal around azaleas, rhododendrons, evergreens and just about all other plants. Use a 3- or 4-inch thickness as a mulch. During dry weather peat moss tends to form a crust which is more or less waterproof. Stir up this crust from time to time so rainwater will enter more readily. A bale of peat is compressed, sometimes gets lumpy and is slow to take up moisture at first. Once you wet it, the material becomes soft, loose and absorbent.

Salt Marsh Hay: This is a clean, highly sought-after material because it does not contain grass and weed seeds, does not mat down or become soggy. It can be gathered up in the spring and used year after year. Salt marsh does not break down readily, hence it cannot be used as a cover crop or source of humus.

Sawdust: Good gardeners will tell you that sawdust is not the "debbil" many think it is. Contrary to belief, sawdust is not acid, nor is it toxic to plants or soils. Sawdust is organic matter, and is beneficial both as a mulch and a soil conditioner. Sawdust can be either weathered or unweathered, and from hardwood or softwood. It's ideal for fruit trees, shrubs, perennials, around evergreens and in border plantings, when used 3 inches thick. It has no value on lawns.

Sawdust sometimes turns plants yellow, as will manure, leafmold and other carbonaceous materials. This is because soil fungi and bacteria that decompose sawdust consume so much nitrogen that temporarily none is left for the plants, and leaves turn yellow, a hunger sign for the plants. This can be prevented and controlled by adding extra nitrogen, such as a cupful of nitrate of soda for each bushel, or by watering the mulch with a liquid plant food such as 23%–21%–17%, mixed at the rate of ½ pound to 11 gallons of water.

Shredded Bark: Tree bark, formerly a waste product, is used for mulch purposes. Upon decomposition it has a rich, dark appearance. The bark retains moisture and has little tendency to dry up and blow away.

Snow: "Poor Man's Manure," snow is about the best mulch you can get, having small amounts of ammonia, nitric acid and other elements.

Straws: Wheat, oats and buckwheat straw are good mulches, but have some disadvantages, especially as weeds and a fire hazard. Use straw 4 to 6 inches thick.

Sugar Cane: Shredded sugar cane ("Bagasse") commonly sold as chicken litter, is coarse-textured, stays in place, remains loose and springy, admits passage of rain and melting snow, and thus makes a fine mulch. It has excellent insulation value.

Wood Chips: Several manufacturers are putting out a portable wood chipper which chews up logs and limbs into chips. These chips may be used 3 inches thick, but be sure to add some nitrogen as you would for sawdust.

HOW TO MAKE A COMPOST PILE

The backbone of any soil is humus, the jelly-like susbtance derived from organic sources such as leaves, lawn clippings, sawdust, evergreen needles, garbage, coffee grounds and dozens of similar materials. These materials should not be discarded but placed on the compost pile, which is similar to putting money into the bank.

How to Start a Pile: As materials become available, start piling them in a spot away from the house, where it can be screened off by plants. Add materials in such a way that the center is depressed to catch rainwater. From time to time add a layer of balanced fertilizer, 1 pound over a 6-inch layer, where the compost is 10 feet long and 5 feet wide. Apply a plant food such as RA-PID-GRO (23–21–17) using a handful in a sprinkler can, for a 10-square-feet area. This fortifies the compost and hastens decay. A liberal sprinkling of lime from time to time is helpful.

One of the best materials for the compost is leaves. A ton of them is worth $10.00 in nutrients alone. People with sandy or clayey soils should save all the leaves they can rake up, for leafmold has a miraculous ability to hold moisture. Subsoil can hold a mere 20 per cent of its weight, good topsoil will hold 60 per cent, but leafmold can retain 300 to 500 per cent of its weight in water. Leafmold from non-evergreens is richer in nutrients than that from conifers. They are all good property, so don't believe the story that leaves are acid or harmful to crops. Oak leaves are acid and are recommended for azaleas, rhododendrons, laurel, holly and other acid-loving plants. Yet, they are still usable for non-acid plants.

Stirring the Pile: Stirring "ripens" the pile (hastens decay) and aids in destroying insect pests, but it is not essential. The latest wrinkle in composting is to cover the pile with polyethylene plastic film. You make the compost in the regular manner, alternating leaves, clippings, sawdust, soil, garbage and other materials with a scattering of lime and plant foods. Then the pile is watered down thoroughly and a sheet of black polyethelene is spread over the pile. Use a piece large enough to allow about 18 to 20 inches of flap on each side. Cover the flaps with soil so the pile is completely enveloped. The beauty of plastic is that you do not have to fork or turn over the compost. Leave it alone for eight months and you'll find the plastic hastens decay by trapping heat inside and preventing loss of moisture. There's no magical material which converts raw organic matter into humus overnight in a compost.

Diseases and Insects: Are they a problem to compost gardeners? Because of danger of infecting the pile with plant diseases and insects, there are some materials to be avoided. These include iris leaves, if borers have been a problem and peony tops if botrytis blight blasted the buds. Also avoid refuse from cabbage and other crucifers (cabbage family), and corn stalks if borers or smut were present. If a compost is allowed to stand for two seasons with occasional forking over, it is doubtful if diseases and insects will persist any more than they do in the garden where plants have been grown for years. Flies may congregate but a plastic sheet keeps them out, as it will a stray dog or two.

How to Use Compost Soil: For potting, screen through ½ inch mesh wire to remove coarse material, then mix with sand or garden loam or both. If used in the garden or as a mulch, no screening is necessary. Compost doesn't replace fertilizer. You still should fortify it with plant food to achieve maximum use from it.

Use of Lime: Gardeners often use either too much lime or not enough. Cornell University analyzed several hundred home-garden samples and found that ⅓ needed lime, ⅓ were just right, and ⅓ had too much lime. The common garden crops are happy with a slightly acid soil, so if your garden is in that condition, don't change matters. The majority of surface soils in eastern U.S. are naturally acid, however, and require some liming for best production.

Here's what liming acid soil does: corrects soil acidity, supplies calcium and magnesium, speeds the decay of organic matter and the liberation of nitrogen. It increases the efficiency of plant foods like phosphorus that may be otherwise unavailable to plants, promotes the growth of legumes such as clover, controls certain diseases like black leg of cabbage, and to a limited extent helps loosen up heavy clay soils.

The natural acidity of a soil is determined by the type of rocks from which the soil was originally derived. For example, quartz, granite, sandstone and shale usually produce acid soils. But, marble and limestone produce sweet or alkaline soils. Often the lower subsoil is much less acid than the surface soil unless lime materials have been added.

Rainfall and removal of plant material from the soil tends to make surface soils more acid. On the other hand, soils around our houses sometimes have become alkaline or "sweet" because grading may have uncovered limey subsoils, or lime-rich fill may have been added. Continuous watering with water that is "hard" because of calcium and magnesium adds to the sweetness of a soil. These are factors to keep in mind, especially when acid-loving plants such as rhododendrons, azaleas, mountain-laurel, blueberries, trailing arbutus, trilliums, and most lilies are to be grown. These must have acid soils. When planted on alkaline or neutral soils, they quickly become chlorotic (yellowed) and die. If you want to plant these in a limey soil, you will have to convert it to an acid condition by adding sulfur or aluminum sulfate as described later.

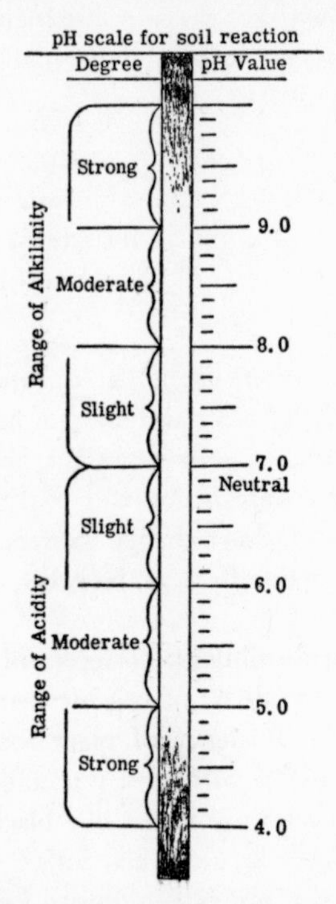

This scale is a "yardstick" for measuring soil acidity. A pH reading of 7 is neutral; that is, neither acid nor alkaline. The smaller the number the stronger the acidity.

CHEMICAL TESTS TELL IF SOIL IS SWEET OR SOUR

What's pH? Gardeners often come across a two-letter term, pH, before a number and it baffles them. pH is a term used to measure soil reaction—whether it is "sweet" or "sour." Let's say soil sweetness or sourness is measured by a pH yardstick. A pH of 7 in the yardstick means the soil is *neutral*—neither sour nor sweet. A soil with a pH below 7 is acid or "sour," and one with a pH above 7 is alkaline, or "sweet." It's a simple matter to test your soil to see if it is acid or alkaline. (See illustration.) There are kits on the market which are simple to operate and fairly accurate.

A soil test alone is not the answer to all your garden- or house-plant problems. Actually there are two types of useful soil tests: (1) Soil Acidity and (2) Major Elements. To me, the first is the most important, but if your lawn or garden is producing well, you won't need a test. Carrots and beets are good indicators. If they grow well, you don't need lime.

The test for major elements is best made through your county agent or State College of Agriculture testing service, but keep in mind that a soil test can do no better than the soil sample you take. For this reason, I feel that in many cases a soil test can be a waste of time. If the soil sample is not representative of the soil in the garden, *the results are meaningless.* Let me cite an illustration: The plow layer of soil on each acre weighs about 2 million pounds. The average soil sample weighs about 1 pound. This means that if a sample is taken from 5 acres, *that 1 pound of sample sent for testing must represent some 10 million pounds of soil in the field!* You just can't go out, scoop up a can of soil, and send it in for a test!

HOW TO TAKE A SOIL SAMPLE

Gather the soil in a clean container and use a proper sampling tool. A garden spade or auger is fine. If you use a spade, first dig a V-shaped hole to plow depth. Second, cut a ½-inch-thick slice of soil from face of hole. Third, trim away soil from both sides of spade, leaving a 1-inch strip of soil down the middle of the spade. Fourth, place this in a clean pail. Take 15 samples from various sections in this manner and mix in a pail. After mixing all samples together, select 1 pint of the entire mixture, throw the rest away.

Don't take samples from unusual areas. Avoid wet spots, lime piles, areas near trees, burned areas, or spots where fertilizer, etc., has been lying in piles. Your fertilizer store has soil-test cartons for you to mail the sample in to your state college. Or you can use a clean plastic bag. Send along as much information as possible, such as crops grown last year, plant foods used, and troubles involved with crops. State colleges determine plant-food deficiencies by chemical analysis of soils, plant-tissue testing, and some use "quick" soil tests. If you plan to have a soil test made, talk to your local fertilizer dealer, your county agent, or a successful neighboring farmer.

WHICH KIND OF LIME TO BUY

Four kinds of lime are commonly sold: burned lime, hydrated lime, ground limestone and dolomitic limestone. (1) "Quicklime" is another term for burned lime (calcium oxide). In general it should not be used because of its caustic action on the skin. (2) Hydrated lime is a fluffy white powder formed from burned lime and water. It is faster acting than ground limestone, but more expensive for the same end result. (3) Ground limestone (calcium carbonate) is a grayish, gritty, very finely ground lime rock. This is the material most commonly used for counteracting acidity. It is slower to dissolve than hydrated lime and takes longer to work. Supply stores sometimes sell a mixture of hydrated lime and limestone combining benefits of both. Ground limestone is less expensive, keeps better, is easy to apply. (4) Dolomitic lime has 20 to 30 per cent magnesium, plus 30 to 50 per cent calcium, and is available in both hydrated and ground stone types. Because magnesium is another element needed for plant growth, we recommend dolomitic limestone, which is just about as inexpensive as the older forms. You may not be able to get it from your dealer—if not, use the others.

Actually, any form of lime can be used, but keep in mind that the more concentrated forms such as the hydrated or burned-lime forms should be used in lesser amounts. The big problem most gardeners run into is using the three forms in equivalent amounts. Roughly speaking, 100 pounds of ground limestone is equal in action to about 74 pounds of hydrated lime, or 56 pounds of burned lime.

We want to remind gardeners who use the burned or slaked lime to be careful not to allow it to sift inside your shoes, since the moisture of perspiration is enough to blister tender skin. And wash *immediately* if it gets in your eyes.

HOW MUCH LIME TO USE AND WHEN

A fair rule of thumb is: If no lime has been added during the past four years, then your garden (or lawn) probably needs it. An application of 50 pounds of lime per 1,000 sq. ft. is a good rough-and-ready treatment. Then for regular applications, use 25 to 30 pounds per 1,000 sq. ft. every

4 years. Apply either hydrated or ground limestone in fall or spring before plowing. I like fall application because it enables you to take advantage of the weather. Winter rains and snow will help carry the lime down into the soil where it can go to work quickly. In the spring, when this ground is plowed, the lime will be turned under close to the subsoil and will help roots grow better.

If you have had your soil tested and the soil test shows a pH reading between 6 and 6.8, don't add lime. If pH is between 5.5 and 6, use 3 pounds of ground limestone to each 100 sq. ft. on sandy soils, 5 pounds on heavier soils.

If pH reading is between 5 and 5.5, use double amounts. If pH is too high and crops do poorly, dust 1 pound of sulfur per 100 sq. ft. to make soil acid. Or, you can add ½ pound of manganese sulfate and about 1 ounce of borax to each 100 sq. ft. of garden. These can be broadcast on the soil, or you can apply them to growing plants if dissolved in water and sprinkled on the foliage. Use 1 gallon of the solution for 100 sq. ft.

Dangers of Overliming: Some minor but necessary elements such as boron, iron, manganese and zinc become less available to plants when soils are heavily limed. Excess liming may result in chlorosis (yellowing of leaves) and poor growth. Correct this by acidifying (see below). Never put lime in contact with manure because it causes loss of nitrogen. Don't mix lime and fertilizer in a single application, as lime may cause loss of nitrogen and reduction in available phosphate.

Making Soils More Acid: As previously mentioned, soils may be too sweet for acid-loving ornamentals such as azaleas, rhododendrons, laurel, lilies, blueberries and others. Then the soil must be acidified with sulfur, ammonium sulfate, aluminum sulfate or even iron sulfate (ferrous sulfate). Sulfur is much the cheapest way, but also the slowest, whereas the sulfates have the full action in the first season. Apply sulfur at the rate of 1 to 2 pounds per 100 sq. ft., depending on the acidity at the beginning. Use sulfates according to the following table:

ACIDITY OF SOIL AT START (as determined by pH test)	AMMONIUM or ALUMINUM SULFATE/SQ. YD.
Medium acid (pH 5 to 6)	¼ lb.
Slightly (pH 6.5 to 7)	½ lb.
Neutral to strongly alkaline (pH 7 to 8)	¾ lb.

Spread the sulfur or sulfates uniformly and mix throughly with the soil. Acid soil in our acid-loving plant beds does not always remain that way, because the water in the soil is apt to become limey and rise from below. Also, angleworms are likely to mix the soil near the plants. On acidified soils, avoid use of all alkalizing materials, such as wood ashes, hardwater, and composts made with lime.

High-lime soils are impossible to acidify, or nearly so. If you must grow acid-loving plants, consider other methods, such as replacing soil in beds, or building raised beds with surface layers of acid soil or peat. Or, you may be able to overcome the high-lime chlorosis in such plants with iron-chelate applications.

What is chelated iron? Most gardeners are familiar with the term "chlorosis." At least they've seen it on plants such as azaleas, gardenias, hydrangeas, roses and many others. Simply stated, chlorosis is yellowed leaves with greenish veins, the entire plant being a sick-looking specimen. This is often due to a lack of iron in the plant and it is most common on "sweet" (alkaline) soils.

For iron-hungry plants we now have a new, easily absorbed material: iron chelate (pronounced key-late). It is a powder which is mixed with water and applied either to the leaves or soil. The amounts needed are unusually small. For example, greenhouse operators mix one ounce of iron chelate to 25 gallons of water and apply this solution to 100 square feet of bench crops.

LIQUID PLANT FOODS

Liquid fertilizers have come such a long way, many predict that shortly half of all the fertilizer used in America will be applied in liquid form. Much of this change has been brought about by the advantages of liquid feeding, which is applied either on foliage of plants or at the base. Foliar or foliage feeding ("non-root") was pioneered by a nurseryman named Thomas Reilly of Dansville, N. Y. He was one of the first to note that plant roots are not the only organs of plant nutrient absorption. Twigs, leaves, branches, buds, fruits and even flowers have the ability to absorb nutrients. One advantage of foliar feeding is the ease of application. Plant men can correct certain deficiency problems by spraying chemicals on leaves of pin oaks, azaleas, citrus and countless other plants. Home gardeners who spray plants with pesticides can add liquid plant food to their solution and do two jobs in one; spraying and feeding. In my greenhouse, I use a liquid plant food with a 23%N–21%P–17%K formula on all crops, mixed with pesticides, and it never burns even the tenderest plants. I prepare a stock solution of 1 cup of the concentrated 23–21–17 nutrients to 2 gallons of water. A Hozon applicator is inserted into this and attached to the water faucet. As I water the crops it automatically feeds them. To foliage-feed, always buy a plant food made especially for spraying on the leaves.

Starter Solutions: Liquid plant foods make ideal "starter" or "booster" solutions, helping young transplants get off to a better start. You simply place a teaspoon of the concentrated fertilizer I mentioned in a couple of quarts of water, and as you set out the cabbage, tomato, pepper, or flowering plants, dip the roots and plant while wet. A word of caution: if you make a home-made booster solution, try it first on a few plants because it may burn. You can make one from a common grade of fertilizer such as 5–10–5 brand (any garden store has it), by dissolving 1 pound in 5 gallons of water. This liquid is applied in the row at the rate of 1 gallon to 20 feet of row, before planting or later.

Liquid plant foods have many extra uses. (1) Soak bulbs in them one hour prior to planting. (2) Hastening decay of compost. (3) Coloring up evergreens. (4) Feeding fruits and flowers. (5) In greenhouse feeding on both benched and potted crops, applied with sprinkler or Hozon applicator. (6) Starting seeds in non-organic materials such as perlite, vermiculite, or similar items. (7) Soil-less culture (hobby) to replace lost solution. There is no known plant which does not respond to feedings of liquid plant foods.

ORGANIC VS. "COMMERCIAL" PLANT FOODS

Will we get better crops, more nutritious food and do a better job of conserving our soils by fertilizing with organic composts rather than commercial fertilizers? I'll answer this controversial question by saying we grow crops by both organic composts *and* commercial fertilizers. I feel that good points about each method should be briefly mentioned.

Organic plant foods are of plant or animal origin. Examples include bonemeal, cottonseed meal, and dried blood, as well as composts and manures. The inorganics or "chemical" fertilizers are either mined or made chemically, sometimes as a by-product from industrial processes. Both organic and inorganic forms supply the essential elements required for plant growth; that is, nitrogen, phosphorus, potassium, magnesium, sulfur and others.

The inorganics are much more concentrated and often are much cheaper sources of these plant nutrients. Humus from organic matter is vital to good soil conditions, and we do all we can to incorporate all organic materials available. We use chemical fertilizers along with organics to get the best results. There is no evidence that there would be less trouble with insects or diseases if commerical plant foods were not used. This is one of the main arguments among the "organic folks," and the one probably stirring up the greatest amount of trouble. Some hold that the commercial fertilizers, having been made through the use of strong acids like sulfuric, are corrosive to soil bacteria and earthworms, or even give rise to crops of inferior food value, causing disease in animals and humans. There is no scientific value to support this. In fact, commercial fertilizers tend to increase the number of beneficial bacteria and earthworms in soils.

What Commercial Plant Foods Do: The most important plant foods in a commercially mixed fertilizer are nitrogen, phosphoric acid, and potash. Nitrogen gives dark green color to plants, promotes increased leaf, stem and fruit growth, and improves the quality of leafy crops as well as hastening growth. Phosphorus stimulates early root formation and growth, gives rapid and vigorous start to plants, hastens maturity, stimulates blooming and aids in seed formation. Potash imparts increased vigor and disease resistance to plants, producing strong, stiff stalks. This reduces lodging (falling over) of plants.

What's in the Fertilizer Bag? Home gardeners are often baffled when they find a recommendation calling for 5–10–5 or 5–10–10 grade of fertilizer, or a similar analysis. Every mixed fertilizer sold has a guaranteed analysis, stating the nitrogen (N), phosphoric oxide (P), and potash (K), the "big three" elements required by state laws to be on the label. This analysis tells the buyer what he's getting in terms of "N–K–P." So let us take a 5–10–10 grade and see what it means. Such an analysis contains 5% Nitrogen, 10% phosphorus and 10% potash, or 25 pounds of the 3 primary nutrients in a 100-pound bag of fertilizer. The question you'll ask is: "What constitutes the other 75 pounds of fertilizer you bought?

The 75 pounds remaining is inert material known as "filler." It is necessary for manufacturers to add filler to dry fertilizers because pure forms of nitrogen, phosphorus and potassium cannot be used as plant foods. Nitrogen is a gas, and phosphorus and potassium are two of the most active chemicals known and wouldn't be safe to use in pure form. Fertilizers therefore must contain their nutrients in "diluted" forms that are safe to plants and man, economical and easily assimilated by plants. (See "Liquid Fertilizers" elsewhere in this chapter.)

MANURE: GOOD OR BAD?

Value of Manure: Several years ago some readers of my garden column told of a fight they had over a pile of elephant manure deposited along a railroad track near Buffalo, New York. This is an indication of what some folks do to get manure. In this age of horseless carriages, sputniks and mechanization, manure has become a thing of the past for many home gardeners, but you can make artificial manure which is just as good as the natural stuff. A ton of barnyard manure has about $3.00 worth of plant food if bought in the form of commerical fertilizer. But much of this may be lost by the time you get it from a farmer. As much as 50 per cent of the nitrogen and 95 per cent of the potassium may be lost through leaching and by conversion of the nitrogen to ammonia, which escapes as the manure dries. The liquid part of the manure contains 45 per cent of the total nitrogen and 65 per cent of the potassium, and that's usually gone by the time you get that "well-rotted" stuff from Farmer Jones' stock pile. Yet, gardeners still clamor for it.

There's another unfavorable side to manure. It may carry plant diseases as well as weed seeds. For example, it's suicidal to put manure on a tulip bed as it causes fireblight disease of tulips. And it's bad business to put manure on peonies because of botrytis blight. Only if you're equipped to sterilize your soils, then manure can create no problems.

For the home gardener, the value of manure is not for plant food, but for the organic matter. Organic matter is the backbone of soils, promoting good structure and aeration.

There's no reason why you can't make your own organic supply house through compost piles, peat moss, sawdust, ground corn stalks, and leaves. Leafmold can be of great value for conditioning a heavy soil, or improving a light soil. Leafmold has the same effect as peat moss and usually is neutral in reaction unless from oak and pine leaves which are acid.

So, if you cannot get farmyard manure, don't worry about it. With fertilizers you can make composted material which is disease-and-weed-seed-free, and which will do the same things manure will do.

Manuring the Garden: If you can get cheap manure, use it liberally on your vegetable garden. A coat of manure adds humus to the soil and increases its water-holding ability even though it is a rather poor fertilizer. One ton of ordinary barnyard manure equals about 100 pounds of a 10–5–10 fertilizer. Manure is low in the plant food, phosphorus. To correct this, gardens should receive about 30 pounds of a 5–10–10 fertilizer for each 1,000 square feet of area, in addition to the manure. Or, you could add superphosphate, about 100 pounds of the 20% grade to each ton of manure. Superphosphate and 5–10–10 are available at your feed and seed store.

Never put fresh strawy manure to a garden that's ready to plow and seed. Broadcast fresh manure over the soil at least six to eight weeks before plowing. Then add a high-nitrogen fertilizer over the manure at the rate of 300 pounds per acre to help decompose the straw. Manure, as with commercial plant foods, is gradually consumed and should be replenished.

SOME MANURES GARDENERS ASK ABOUT

Hen Manure: Hen manure is higher in nitrogen, phosphorus and potash than barnyard manure and should be used whenever possible. Fresh-poultry manure can burn plants, but can be used safely if spread in the fall. About 2 tons of poultry manure can be applied to a 50-by-100-foot garden. Like other manures, this is unbalanced in plant-food content and needs additional phosphate. This can be supplied by 100 pounds of 20 per cent superphosphate to each ton of manure.

Rabbit Manure: Rabbit manure is valuable, being high in nitrogen and humus. You can mix it with peat moss, straw, or put it in compost. Leave it exposed for a month or so, then apply to soil at the rate of 8 pounds per 100 sq. ft. Well rotted and mixed with peat, rabbit manure becomes a safe material. If fresh, apply as a light covering between the rows, but make sure it doesn't touch plants, as it is one of the strongest animal manures.

Sheep and Cow Manure: These are fairly quick-acting organic fertilizers, good for house plants. Sheep manure has about 2 per cent nitrogen, 1 per cent phosphorus, and 2 per cent potash. Cow manure has lower plant food content. Both are ideal for mixing with the soil to add humus.

Horse Manure: This has roughly the same composition as cow manure and those gardeners who live near riding stables or race tracks should take advantage of it as a soil conditioner.

Bonemeal: Some gardeners still prefer bonemeal as a plant fertilizer. Because it is so slow-acting, there is no danger of its burning plants. It penetrates the soil so slowly, about an inch per season, that it's best to work it into the soil rather than sprinkle it on. Steamed bonemeal, which contains about 1 to 2 per cent nitrogen and about 22 to 30 per cent phosphoric acid, is more quickly available to plants. Raw bonemeal takes longer to break down so plants can absorb it. Bonemeal is good for bulbs of all sorts, but an objection is that it often induces dogs to dig around in tulip beds in search of phantom bones. Superphosphate is generally used instead of bonemeal in modern flower-garden practices, since the phosphorus in superphosphate is more readily available and the cost is less.

Sewage Sludge: Sludges make good soil improvers. They are equal to low-analysis fertilizers containing from 1 to 3 per cent nitrogen, phosphorus and potash. To us, the two important things are that the nitrogen is in the long-lasting organic form and the organic-matter content is high enough to warrant use as a mulch or a substitute for farm manure.

As for the sanitary status of sludge, there are many widely different opinions regarding its safety. If you use the *heat-treated* sludges there is nothing to worry about from a sanitary standpoint. Such treatment is normally provided for material that is marketed. These sludges are useful as mulches around certain kinds of flowers, shrubs, and in vegetable gardens.

Digested Sludge: Not heat-treated, should be used with some caution. One way is to incorporate it in the soil several months before vegetables to be eaten raw are grown. According to the U.S.D.A., all danger is thought to be removed after the sludge has been in the soil for 3 months of a growing season. It's reasonable to assume that digested sludges are satisfactory for lawns, shrubs, flowers and ornamental crops.

Raw sewage sludge is not sterile, and has undergone *no* process to kill any harmful organisms that might be in it.

My former teacher at Cornell University, Dr. L. H. McDaniels, a fine gardener, assisted me with this chart for feeding the garden.

THE RATE OF APPLICATION OF FERTILIZERS AND SOIL AMENDMENTS FOR THE FLOWER AND VEGETABLE GARDEN

Materials	Method of Application	Rate of Application
Leaf Mold		Same as for peat
Lime	Dry	Apply to correct acidity (See chapter on Lime)
Liquid Plant Food (23%N–21%P–17%K)	Solution only	1 tsp. to a qt. of water for root or foliage feeding every 2 or 3 weeks
Manure (Rotted: cow or horse)	As fertilizer	From 10 to 50 tons per A. or 4 bu. per 100 sq. ft. of soil
	As mulch	1 in. deep on top of soil
Manure (poultry, rabbit or hog)		5 tons per acre, or 1 bu. per 100 sq. ft. of soil
Mixed fertilizer (5–10–5; 5–10–10)	Dry	From 2 to 3 lbs. per 100 sq. ft. of soil, or 3 in. pot to 3 bu. of soil, or 1 tsp. to a 5 in. pot of soil
Mixed fertilizer (10–20–10; 15–30–15)	Dry	1 lb. or less per 100 sq. ft. of soil, or 2 in. pot to 3 bu. of soil, or ½ tsp. to a 5 in. pot of soil
	Solution	1 oz. to 2 gals. of water
Muriate of Potash	Dry	300 lbs. per acre, or ½ lb. per 100 sq. ft. of soil
	Solution	½ lb. in 10 gals. of water applied to 100 sq. ft. of soil; or ½ cup of solution to 5 in. pot of soil
Nitrate of Soda	Solution	Same as sulfate of ammonia
Peat or Compost	Incorporated in topsoil	5 bu. to 100 sq. ft. of soil for garden
	Mulch	1 in. layer

MATERIALS	METHOD OF APPLICATION	RATE OF APPLICATION
Sulfate of ammonia	Dry	1 lb. to 100 sq. ft. of soil
	Solution	1 lb. in 30 gals. of water applied to 100 sq. ft., or 1 cup of solution to 5 in. pot of soil
Sulfate of potash		Same as for muriate of potash
Superphosphate (16 or 20%)	Dry	1,000 lbs. per acre, 5 lbs. per 100 sq. ft., 3 in. pot to a bu. of soil
Tankage or Sewage	Dry	4 in. pot to 3 bu. of soil; 5 lbs. per 100 sq. ft.
Urea	Solution only	5 oz. to 35 gals. of water applied to 100 sq. ft. of soil or 1 cupful of solution to 5 in. pot of soil

GREEN THUMB TIPS ON SOILS AND FERTILIZERS

You can make a good flower or vegetable garden wherever weeds will grow.

Good soils are usually made, not born. You can tame the wildest soil into a productive one by following the tips in the preceding chapters.

Don't be discouraged if you have a heavy soil. It can be as productive as a sandy loam. Crops on sandy soils suffer quicker from dry spells than do those on heavier soils.

Never work a heavy soil when it's wet.

When spading or plowing the garden soil, go to a depth of 8 inches. Over that brings up undesirable subsoil.

Removing stones from the garden each year is hardly worth the effort (unless you remove rocks), as more keep coming to the surface.

Don't be afraid to use lime, fertilizers and compost to fortify your soils. Organic gardeners need not fear that plant foods are harmful to themselves or to their crops.

High-potency fertilizer mixtures, soluble in water, do a lot to get your young plants off to a fast start and increase the survival rate.

Watch out for advertisements about wonder-growth stimulants. They are not a substitute for good cultural practices such as feeding, spraying and cultivation.

Vegetable gardeners plant seeds in drills or hills. A drill is a single row of plants spaced more or less evenly. A hill is a cluster of plants and not a mound of soil. Do not plant in mounds as the soil in them dries out faster than if kept level.

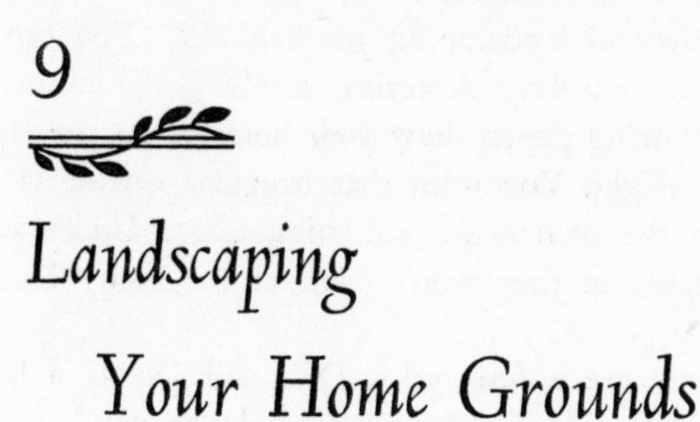

9

Landscaping Your Home Grounds

Trees and shrubs help make a house into a home.

Americans take great pride in beautifying their homes, not only on the inside, but also outside. An estimated $4 billion is spent each year in this country on yards, lawns and gardens. Experts suggest that 10 to 30 per cent of the cost of a new home be spent for landscaping. With that much money, and the appearance of your home at stake, it should be well worth the effort to plan landscaping work with care.

There is more to gain from landscaping than merely the esthetic. Good landscaping cuts down on your fuel bills in winter and makes your home cooler in summer. A properly located shade tree can reduce summer room temperatures as much as 20 degrees. Trees not only eliminate the "attic furnace," but will cut your fuel bill by as much as 30 per cent, by acting as a wind-break. To heat an ordinary house, it takes twice as much fuel at a temperature of 32 degrees and a wind of 12 miles per hour as it does for the same temperature and a wind of three miles per hour.

Trees also help purify air by taking in carbon dioxide and giving off oxygen. One authority suggests America plant 10 trees for every 100 automobiles and 100 trees for every truck on the road. And trees, unlike most things you buy, increase in value. A tree that costs you $5.00 today may be worth $100 to $200 or more in ten to fifteen years.

Planning for your home beautification is not difficult because there are such tremendously numerous varieties of trees and shrubs to meet every need. Your nurseryman will help you make selections. This chapter covers some pitfalls amateurs often encounter in do-it-yourself landscaping, and stresses lasting beauty with a minimum of care.

Foundation Planning: Aside from the lawn, your foundation planting is the most important piece of landscaping you can have. You can spruce up your home front by selecting flowering shrubs listed in my charts later. On a piece of drawing paper, draw your home front and sketch in plants which vary in height. You want that irregular skyline silhouette, with tallest plants on the corners for softening effect. Under windows place the spreading types so they won't obstruct the view. That's how simple it is.

Before you buy, here are a few quick Do's and Don'ts a budgeted home landscaper should consider for that "million-dollar look."

DON'TS

(1) Don't overlook the shrub's mature size.

(2) Don't try to rejuvenate relic evergreens.

(3) Don't plant one variety in a straight row.

(4) Don't have too great a variety of plants.

(5) Don't be afraid to start with small plants.

(6) Don't be afraid to combine evergreens with non-evergreens. (If you like evergreens alone, see Evergreens.)

(7) Don't plant tall shrubs under a window.

(8) Don't plant sun-loving plants in shady places.

(9) Don't be impatient if newly set shrubs don't start fast. It takes some weeks for buds to break.

(10) Don't prune shrubs late in summer or fall.

(11) Don't be a butcher; be a barber when you prune.

(12) Don't hesitate to study nursery catalogs.

DO'S

(1) Do plant shrubs at least 3 feet from the wall and about 3 feet apart.

(2) Do make holes large enough.

(3) Do use annuals and perennials in among your foundation plantings.

(4) Do mix humus and use plant foods in soil for growth.

(5) Do let part of your foundation show.

(6) Do "heel" your plants in ground if you cannot set them out immediately.

(7) Do water all shrubs copiously, at least once a week.

(8) Do prune tips of roots back at planting time.

(9) Do practice moderate annual pruning.

(10) Do have neat, sharp borders in front of your planting.

(11) Do keep your shrubs sprayed.

(12) Do feed your shrubs at least once yearly.

Planting Shrubs: Fall and spring are the best times for planting trees and shrubs. If you are moving the shrubs from another location, be sure to dig up all the roots possible. You can do this by digging a circular trench around the plant, thrusting your spade as deep as necessary. Roots usually extend as far out from the plant under the soil as the spread of branches above the soil. But, just as moving into another home is a somewhat unsettling experience for you and your family, so the experience of being moved disturbs a plant. Roots are especially affected by the change. To make up for this disturbance, you can make the job of the roots easier after the re-planting by cutting the branches of the moved shrubs by about one third.

Give plant food to your shrubs at least once a year and water them at least once a week in dry weather. Most flowering shrubs look their best if allowed to grow in their natural shape. For this effect, it becomes necessary to prune jutting shoots irregularly. Do this pruning very gently—like a barber rather than a butcher. Shrubs which blossom in spring should not be pruned until after the blooming or else the buds will be destroyed. Shrubs which blossom in late summer or fall should be pruned in early spring before the growth of buds begins.

Here are lists of suitable shrubs classified for particular uses. Nurseryman John Kelly has kindly helped us with these listings of the most popular trees and shrubs for the do-it-yourself landscaper.

SHRUBS WITH COLORED STEMS—If planted among evergreens, these shrubs with colorful stems will add variety to the landscape. Usually the color is most pronounced in the young stems. It is therefore desirable to prune the stems sharply each year to encourage new and young growth. Shrubs in this category include Tatarian Dogwood (*Cornus alba*) with blood-red stems; Siberian Dogwood (*C. alba sibirica*) with red stems; Red Osier Dogwood (*C. stolonifera*) with red stems, though not as beautifully colored as the two mentioned first; Golden

SHRUBS FOR YOUR HOME'S ENTRANCE

These shrubs with colorful foliage, fruits or flowers will help make the entrance into your home more attractive.

Plant Name	Maturity Height at	Color of Bloom	Time of Bloom	Comments
Lily of the Valley Flowering Shrub (*Andromeda*)	6 ft.	Waxy White	April–May	Compact, glossy leaf, bell-shaped flowers
Beauty Bush (*Kolkwitzia*)	6–8 ft.	Shell Pink	June–July	Upright growing
Buddleias—Charming, Dubonnet, Ile-de-France	4–5 ft.	Pink, Lilac, Wine	July–Aug.	Long flower sprays
Burning Bush	5–7 ft.	Yellow	May	Red autumn fruits and foliage
Golden Privet	4–6 ft.	White	June	Bright yellow foliage
Golden Syringa	4–5 ft.	White	May–June	Golden yellow foliage
Philadelphus, Belle Etoile	5 ft.	White	May–June	Star-like flowers
Philadelphus, Minnesota Snowflake	6–8 ft.	White	May–June	Large double flowers
Philadelphus virginalis	6 ft.	White	June–Aug.	Fragrant double flowers
Rosa Hugonis	4–6 ft.	Yellow	May	Fine shrub rose
Rosa Rugosa	4–6 ft.	Pink	May thru Summer	Rich green foliage, large red fruit
Scarlet Quince	4–5 ft.	Red	April–May	Early spring blooms
Spirea van Houttei	6 ft.	White	May	A national favorite

Sweet Shrub (*Calycanthus*)	6 ft.	Reddish-brown	June–July	Spicy flowers
Viburnum carlesii	4–5 ft.	Pink and White	April–May	Fragrant flowers
Weigela, Eva Rathke	4–5 ft.	Red	May–June	Trumpet-shaped flowers
Weigela, Variegated	4–5 ft.	Pale Pink	June	Green and white foliage
Winterberry (*Radicans erecta*)	4–5 ft.	Red Berries	Fall and Winter	Evergreen foliage

SHRUBS FOR UNDER WINDOWS

Reaching heights of no more than 5 feet, these shrubs are suitable for planting in front of the house under windows where taller plants would obstruct the view as well as light and air.

Plant Name	Maturity Height at	Color of Bloom	Time of Bloom	Comment
Blue Hydrangea (*Hydrangea macrophylla*)	3 ft.	Blue	June–Sept.	Color; low-growing, shrubby plant
Chaste Tree (*Vitex macrophylla*)	4–5 ft.	Lavender	July–Sept.	Dainty shrub
Coralberry (Indian Currant)	3 ft.	White	May–June	Coral-colored berries in fall
Deutzia Gracilis	2–3 ft.	White	May	Fine twiggy growth
Frosty Morn (*Philadelphus*)	40 in.	White	June–July	New dwarf mock orange
Globe Flower (*Kerria*)	4–5 ft.	Golden-Yellow	June–Sept.	Green branches
Green Leaf Barberry	3–5 ft.	Yellow	April	Red fall and winter berries
Honeysuckle (*Compacta Nana*)	4–5 ft.	Yellow	May	Red fall and winter berries
Honeysuckle, *Zabelii*	4–5 ft.	Pink	May–June	Blue-green leaves
Hydrangea, P. G.	4–5 ft.	White to Pink	July to Frost	Stately shrub
Hydrangea, Snowball	3–5 ft.	White	July to Frost	Good for shade
Potentilla, Gold Drop	3–4 ft.	Yellow	June to Frost	Mound of green and gold

Red Leaf Barberry	3–5 ft.	Yellow	April	Scarlet foliage
Snowberry	4–5 ft.	Pink	June	White autumn berries
Spirea, Anthony Waterer	2–3 ft.	Pink	June–Sept.	Fine dwarf shrub
Spreading *Cotoneaster divaricata*	4–6 ft.	Pink	June	Red autumn berries
Weigela, Eva Rathke	4–5 ft.	Red	May–June	Trumpet-shaped flowers
Weigela, Variegated	4–5 ft.	Pale Pink	June	Green and white foliage

Twig Dogwood (*C. stolonifera flaviramea*) with yellow stems, and *Kerria Japonica* with bright green stems.

SHRUBS FOR THE SEASHORE—Because the salty air near the seashore can damage new leaves of shrubs, the following varieties are recommended for cottages and homes in such locations.

Autumn Elaeagnus (*E. umbellata*)
Pfitzer's Juniper (*P. chinensis pfitzeriana*)
California Privet (*Ligustrum ovalifolium*)
Bayberry (*Myrica pennsylvanica*)
Beach Plum (*Prunus maritima*)
Rugosa Rose (*Rosa rugosa*)
Service-berry, Shad-bush (*Amelanchier*)
Chokecherry (*Aronia arbutifolia*)
Wintergreen barberry (*Berberis thunbergii*)
Summersweet (*Clethra alnifolia*)
Spreading cotoneaster (*Cotoneaster divaricata*)
Tatarian honeysuckle (*Lonicera tatarica*)
Swiss Mountain Pine (*Pinus mugo*)
Firethorn (*Pyracantha coccinea lalandii*)
Meadow rose (*Rosa blanda*)
Multiflora rose (*Rosa multiflora*)
Prairie rose (*Rosa setigera*)
Scotch broom (*Cytisus scoparius*)
Russian olive (*Elaeagnus angustifolia*)
Inkberry (*Ilex glabra*)
Regel Privet (*Ligustrum obtusifolium regelianum*)
Japanese Yew (*Taxus cuspidata*)
Withe-Rod (*Viburnum cassinoides*)
European cranberrybush (*Viburnum opulus*)

SHRUBS WITH AROMATIC FOLIAGE—*Aralia spinosa* (Hercules club); *Calycanthus floridus* (Strawberry shrub); *Caryopteris incana* (Blue Spirea); *Cotinus coggygyria* (*Rhus cotinus* or Smoke-bush); *Lindera benzoin* (*Benzoin aestivale,* or Spice-bush); *Myrica pennsylvanica* (*M. caroliniensis* or Bayberry); *Rhus aromatica* (Fragrant Sumac) and *Vitex.*

HEDGES—A hedge adds privacy to your lawn, garden and yard, acting as a fence to keep persons and animals off your property. The taller-growing hedges also act as a curtain in spring and summer when they have leaves, keeping strangers as well as your neighbors from looking at you—and you from seeing them.

In planting a hedge, be sure to dig a trench deep enough to hold the

SHRUBS FOR CORNERS

These taller-growing shrubs are suitable for planting at the corners of a house, garage or porch yard. For ranch houses, a single plant may be sufficient for the desired effect, but in houses more than a story high, several plants in each corner may be desirable for the "framing" effect given by these plants to the landscape.

Plant Name	Height at Maturity	Color of Bloom	Time of Bloom	Comment
Althaea (Rose of Sharon)	8 ft.	White, Pink, Purple, Red	August	Columnar growing
Forsythia, Spring Glory	6–8 ft.	Yellow	April–May	Brilliant new forsythia
Forsythia, Lynwood Gold	6–8 ft.	Yellow	April–May	Deep yellow blossoms
High Bush Cranberry	8 ft.	White	May–June	Scarlet fall and winter fruits
Lilac, French Hybrids	8–12 ft.	Assorted Colors	May	Double flowering
Lilac, Purple and White	12 ft.	Purple and White	May	Fragrant flowers
Philadelphus, Minnesota Snowflake	6–8 ft.	White	May–June	Large double flowers
Prunus Tomentosa, Nanking Cherry	4–5 ft.	White	April–May	Cherry-red fruit
Pyracantha, Firethorn	4–6 ft.	White	May	Orange-red berries
Snowball (*Viburnum*)	8 ft.	White	May–July	Pure white snowballs
Smoke Tree	12 ft.	Pink-Purple	May	Good accent plant
Sweet Honeysuckle	8–12 ft.	Pink	May	Red berries
Spirea van Houttei	6 ft.	White	May	Covered with blooms, graceful branching
Tamarix	8–12 ft.	Pink	May–June	Lacy effect
Variegated Leaf Dogwood	6–8 ft.	White	June	Silver and green foliage
Weigela Vanicekii, Cardinal shrubs	6 ft.	Red	Spring, Summer, Fall	Large trumpet-shaped flowers

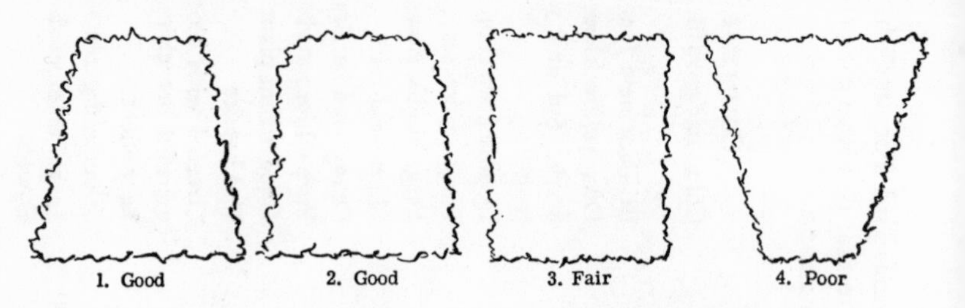

Hedges are trimmed in various shapes as shown here.

roots without crowding. After setting the plants into the trench, add soil to make a firm base for the plants. Water well, feed the soil once a year with a balanced plant food, pack sawdust or peat moss around the bottoms of the plants to keep weeds down. To achieve tighter-growing plants at the bottom part of the hedge—and thus add to your privacy—prune the plants severely to about 4 inches above the ground at planting time. Trim hedges as often as you like, but not later in the year than early September.

PLANTING TREES:

Planning in advance before planting a tree is even more important than when planting shrubs, because trees, once grown to any large extent, stand at their location as virtually a lifetime proposition. Moving them is difficult and, often, impossible. Cutting a tree down later involves considerable work or expense. Therefore selecting the right kind of tree, and planting it in the right way in the right location on your first attempt, is very important to you.

First of all decide why you want to plant a tree: Is it for shade? For decoration? To obtain the tree's fruits? Or maybe for all of these reasons. Or, perhaps, you would rather have a tree which gives you shade, but doesn't clutter up the grounds below it with falling fruits and flowers. If this last idea appeals to you, you need not give up planting certain fruit trees whose fruit production can be controlled and prevented by applying hormone sprays or chemical preparations available at your garden store. These hormone sprays contains naphthaleneacetic acid, which, if applied at blooming time, retards the fruit-producing capability of the trees. You can thus plant horse chestnut, crabapple, maple and numerous other trees without the annoyance of a lawn cluttered with falling fruits.

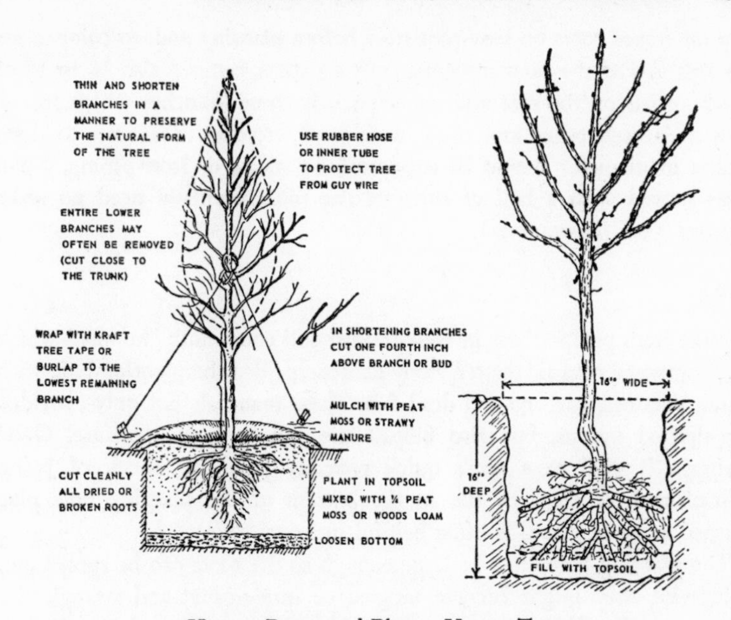

How to Prune and Plant a Young Tree.
In planting a young tree, prune it back at tops as shown above. Also make the hole large enough to accommodate the roots. Trim the tips of the roots back an inch or so, to remove frayed ends.

Avoid planting weak-wooded trees which break easily in storms and whose branches are brittle. These include catalpa, box elder, white and Carolina poplar, Chinese elm, silver maple, horse chestnut, tree of heaven, European white birch (susceptible to borers) and willow.

Keep sufficient space between trees. Consider the size of their roots and branches when fully grown. Crowded trees are likely to grow mis-shapen as their roots compete for food and moisture. Trees should never be closer than 15 feet from any building and should be kept a safe distance from sewer pipes, cesspools, sidewalks, driveways and curbs where their roots may cause damage or be injured or retarded.

All evergreen trees should be planted with their roots surrounded by a ball of soil. Non-evergreen trees whose trunk about a foot above ground level measures less than 3 inches in diameter can be planted "bare-root" without soil attached to their roots. But in that case the roots should be covered with moist burlap and should never be allowed to become dry.

Cut off frayed roots on bare-root trees before planting and, to compensate for this loss of the nourishment-supplying roots, remove also 1/3 to 1/2 of the branches on the side and top, especially those branches which rub or criss-cross each other and those with weak crotches. Trees up to three inches in diameter should be supported by stakes or iron piping. Small trees moved with a ball of earth at the roots normally need no stake support (see illustrations).

Soils:

Most trees prosper best in well-drained soil containing "humus," which is decomposed organic matter. Early gardeners filled the planting hole with rotten potatoes, garbage and dead fish. These materials not only provided the desired humus, but also helped the soil to hold moisture. Good drainage is vital to a tree's quick recovery from the shock of being transplanted. A piece of tile in the bottom of the planting hole plus crushed stone or gravel is often helpful in heavy soils.

The planting hole must be large enough so the roots can be spread out. Otherwise, they might become tangled or intercrossed and strangle the tree eventually. If the leaves on one side of an established tree in late fall have a lighter color and fall earlier than normal, chances are the roots are strangling it due to improper planting.

While trees may be planted in spring or fall, fall planting is occasionally unsuccessful because of dryness, rather than cold. Prolonged cold weather in winter can kill the newly planted trees, but more often trees planted in fall are killed by lack of moisture.

CARE OF TREES

Wrapping the Trunk:

Wrapping tends to prevent the bark from drying out; it also prevents sun scald and bark splitting. You can use burlap, sugar sacks, aluminum foil, or waterproof paper in strips 4 inches wide. Sew ends together and start at the ground, wrapping spirally with about a 2-inch overlap, then tie with twine to hold in place.

Feeding Trees:

Fall feeding is the best time because it stimulates soil bacteria which break down minerals into a form a tree can absorb. There are two common ways to feed trees: (1) Broadcasting, or scattering plant food on the ground and (2) punching holes in the ground and filling with either liquid or dry plant food. Either method is suitable, although most tree men prefer to punch holes into the soil. A crowbar makes a fine tool for making holes. Punch a series of openings 18 inches deep in concentric circles around the base of the tree. The first ring should be about 3 feet from the trunk, with holes spaced about 3 feet apart in the circle. Other circles should be placed three feet from each other until you reach the outside of the longest branch. Use about 1 pound of a balanced plant food for each inch of trunk circumference. We use 4 teaspoons of RA-PID-GRO in a gallon of water for each hole. Orchardists all over the country apply dry fertilizer on top of the ground, without drilling holes, and they get results.

PRUNING TREES:

This is best done in fall or winter when the trees are leafless and you can see weak crotches and poorly grown limbs. The cuts caused by pruning will heal fast in the early spring following winter pruning. Also, in winter the chances of tree diseases and insects is less likely because these enemies of trees are fewest then. Don't worry if a tree bleeds sap in winter. But summer pruning is necessary when limbs begin scraping buildings or have grown so low as to pose danger or inconvenience. Prune limbs flush to the trunk without leaving any stump. Pruning wounds under 3 inches will need no wound dressing. Larger wounds can be treated with asphalt base coating, spar varnish applied over shellac, or a paste of commercial bordeaux and raw linseed oil applied with a paint brush.

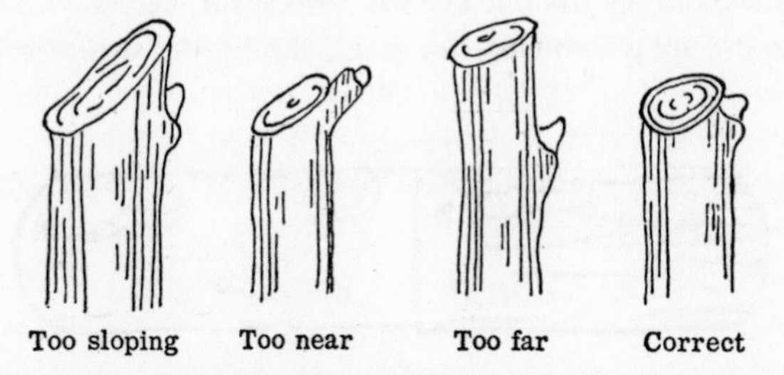

In trimming branches keep the location of buds in mind and the slope of the cut. Never leave a stub near the bud.

Courtesy Rochester Parks Dept.

Upper inset shows where old blossom head should be pruned to avoid losing next year's lilac crop. Lower circle shows where to cut broken branches.

TREATING DISEASES OF TREES AND SHRUBS

These ornamental plants fall heir to hundreds of insects and diseases not listed in this book. By using an all-purpose pesticide you can avoid having to diagnose the trouble. I've had wonderful success with the following all-purpose sprays, suitable for trees, shrubs and evergreens:

Old lilacs often get lilac borers. Squirt DDT or nicotine paste into the openings to check the pest.

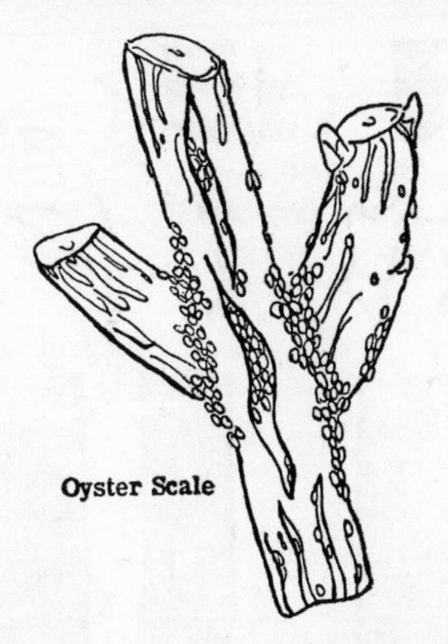

Oyster scale is a serious pest on lilacs and other shrubs. A dormant spray of lime-sulfur in early spring, followed by a summer spray of Malathion will check the pest.

Pest or Disease	Pesticide to Use	Amount per Gallon of Spray
Red spider, aphids	Malathion, 25% powder	4 tablespoons
Thrips, beetles, chewing insects	DDT 50% powder	2 tablespoons
Leaf spots, rusts	Zineb (or Parzate) 65% powder	1 tablespoon
Mildew	Karathane, 25% powder or Sulfur	½ teaspoon 1 tablespoon

Use slightly rounded tablespoons for the wettable powders. These are available at your garden store, mixed or separately. It's best to apply a pesticide before trouble begins. That means keeping a residue of spray on the foliage at all times by renewal doses every ten days. Applications are more effective when applied to dry foliage and allowed to dry on leaves in a short time. Do not spray flowers when in full bloom. If you use a dust, apply in the morning when dew is still on the foliage.

Some plants have a waxy leaf covering which causes sprays to run off or collect in droplets. Brand name detergents make a fine "wetting,"

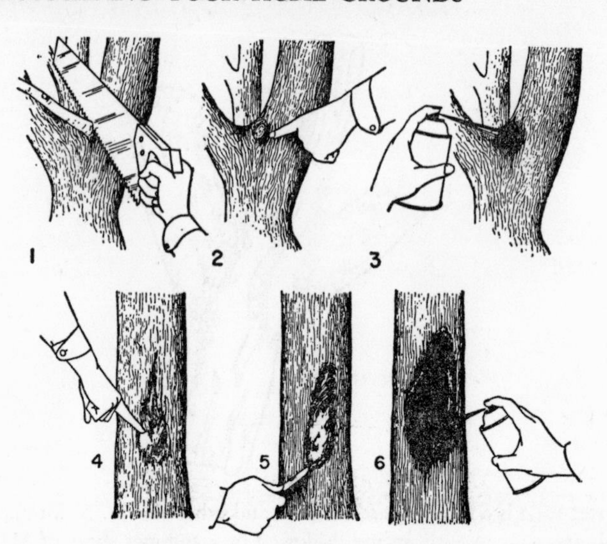

Courtesy Du Pont Co.

How to Prune and Treat Wounds: (A) Cut small branches off flush with trunk of the tree. (B) Open pruning wounds should be protected with a wound dressing as shown in No. 3. (C) Trunk injuries from power lawn mower collisions should be repaired, so tree can heal itself. (D) Cut away loose bark with sharp knife, leaving a channel at base to drain water away. (E) Spray tree wound dressing over the injured area.

"spreading" or "sticking" agent, if used with the pesticide at rate of ⅓ teaspoon per gallon of water.

Trees With Berries attract birds and add beauty to your landscape. Such trees include the mountain ash (the berries are suitable for making jam); the hawthorn (also known as Washington thorn), scarlet haw, English hawthorn, holly and bush honeysuckle.

Colored Foliage is produced by these shade trees: European beech and purple leaf plum give purple leaves; flowering dogwood, franklinia, Japanese maple, red maple, sugar maple, pin oak, scarlet oak, white oak, sourwood, shadblow, serviceberry and American sweetgum produce red autumn foliage. Cockspur hawthorn, American hornbeam, sugar maple, black oak, common sassafras and Tatarian maple produce orange autumn foliage. White oak, Kentucky coffee tree, gingko, common honey locust, American redbud, tulip tree and black walnut produce yellow autumn foliage.

For small size (20 to 35 ft. in height)

Ironwood	Amur maple	Tatarian maple	Flowering crab
Flowering cherry	Hawthorn	Althea	Flowering dogwood

Trees growing from 15 to 30 ft. high

Amur maple	Smoke tree	Japanese tree lilac
Shadblow	Hawthorn	Hedge maple
Yellowwood	Saucer magnolia	Mountain ash
Flowering dogwood	Flowering crab	Goldenrain tree
Red Japanese maple	Halesia	Kousa dogwood
Pink flowering dogwood	Sassafras	

Some large trees 40 ft. or more in height

Sugar maple	Schwedler's maple	Canoe or paper birch	Kentucky coffee bean tree
Thornless honey-locust	Shagbark hickory	American beech	European beech
Tulip tree	Cucumber tree	Tupelo (*nyssa*)	American plane
White oak	Scarlet oak	Pin oak	Red oak
Norway maple	Red maple	White ash	Black walnut

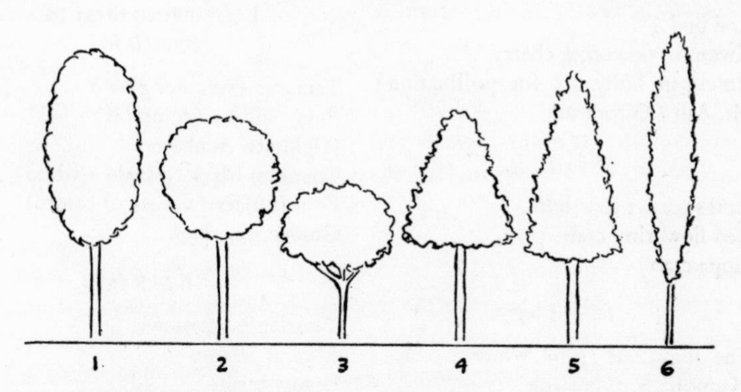

Trees have different shapes. (From left to right): (1) Oval Upright; (2) Round Head; (3) Globe; (4) Pyramidal wide base; (5) Pyramidal narrow base; (6) Columnar.

QUICK REFERENCE CHART SHOWING MANY TYPES OF SHRUBS AND TREES FOR LANDSCAPING THE HOME PROPERTY

Shade Trees

over 50 ft.

Moraine locust
Sunburst gold locust
Silver maple
Cut leaf weeping birch
Pin oak
Crimson king maple
Weeping willow
Norway maple
Rivers purple beech

25 to 50 ft.

Clump birch
Scholar tree (*sophora*)
Yellowwood (*cladrastis*)

Small Flowering Trees

25 to 30 ft.

Golden chain
White flowering crab (*dolgo*)

20 to 25 ft.

Red bud
Kwanzan flowering cherry
American holly (2 for pollination)
Mt. Ash (European)

15 to 20 ft.

Paul's scarlet hawthorn
Red flowering crab
Hopa crab

10 to 15 ft.

The dogwoods (pink, white)
Magnolia Soulangeana
Smoke tree
Purple leaf crab (*eleyi*)
Double flowering crab (bechtels)
Ruby tree (*Prunus* Newport)
Almey crab

6 to 10 ft.

Tree wisteria (purple)
Red Japanese maple
Tree hydrangea
Rose tree of China
Double red flowering peach
Tree roses

Fruits and Berries

Dwarf fruit trees
Howard miracle plum
Five fold apple tree (standard)
Five fold apple tree (dwarf)
Chinese chestnut
Black walnut (Thomas grafted)
English walnut
Butternut
Hybrid blueberries
Gooseberry
Currants

Flowering Shrubs

8 to 10 ft.

Tamarix (summer glow)
Pussy willow (common)
Highbush cranberry
Common lilacs (purple—white)
French lilacs (variety of colors)
Golden nine bark

6 to 8 ft.

Tatarian honeysuckle
Rose of Sharon
Beauty bush
Silver leaf variegated dogwood
Large flowering snowball
Lily of the valley shrub

5 to 7 ft.

Forsythia (Lynwood gold)
Forsythia (spring glory)
Cotoneaster divaricata
Spirea van houttei
Double mock orange
Amur river privet
Cardinal shrub

MEDIUM
4 to 5 ft.

Honeysuckle-*Zabelii*
Pyracantha lalandii
Ilex convexa
Hydrangea P. G.
Scarlet quince
Rosa hugonis
Euonymus alatus compactus
Calycanthus
Buddleia (var. of color)
Golden syringa
Viburnum carlesii
Winterberry
Variegated weigela

3 to 4 ft.

Dwarf honeysuckle
Blue hydrangea
Chartreuse shrub
Coralberry
Snowberry
Rhododendron (*maximum & catawbiense*)
Azalea mollis (red, orange, yellow)
Pink flowering almond
Hydrangea (hills of snow)
Nanking cherry bush
Double golden kerria

LOW
2 to 3 ft.

Deutzia gracilis (white)
Deutzia gracilis (pink)
Blue mist
Floribunda roses
Hybrid tea roses
Oregon grape holly
Red spirea
Hypericum hidcote
Red barberry
Green barberry

1 to 2 ft.

Dwarf red barberry
Evergreen bittersweet

EVERGREENS

Low—spreading Andorra juniper—
(purple spreading)
Pfitzer juniper
Taxus cuspidata
Globe arbor vitae
Mugo pine
Columnar upright—
Taxus hicksii
Pyramidal arbor vitae
Taxus capitata
Large clipped tree form—
Canadian hemlock
Norway spruce
Blue spruce (Colorado)

GROUND COVERS

Pachysandra terminalis
English ivy
Vinca minor
Hall's honeysuckle vine

VINES

Climbing *hydrangea petiolaris*
Climbing roses
Silver lace vine
Boston ivy
Clematis (in variety)
Evergreen bittersweet
Hall's honeysuckle
Gold flame honeysuckle
Trumpet vine
Bittersweet (*celastrus scandens*)

Purple wisteria
Dutchman's pipe

HEDGES

Althea (pink, purple, red, white)
Amur river privet
Red barberry
Green barberry
Dwarf honeysuckle
Spirea van houttei
Blue leaf hedge (Arctic willow)
Midget hedge (teucrium)
Chinese elm
Euonymus compactus
Lombardy poplar

GREEN THUMB TIPS

Good landscape planning pays! 90 per cent of home owners who do it themselves do it improperly.

Don't follow a hit-and-miss system of planting. Draw a plan first!

Invest in nursery-grown stock, at least for the foundation planting.

Steep banks can be licked by using ground covers such as Mytrle, Pachysandra, Euonymus or Hall's honeysuckle. Also, you can use shrubs, or build a dry stone wall, or a rock garden.

Keep your hedge trimmed regularly. Rounded tops tend to shed snow better than flat tops. The base should be wider than the tops.

Don't be afraid to use trellises, fences and gates to soften certain areas around your home. White is the best color to paint lattice or trellises.

Outdoor fireplaces are attractive and highly useful. Build them at least 50 feet from the nearest building.

Don't overlook the use of vines to enhance the value of your home. Avoid clinging vines on clapboards or shingle houses as they may rot them.

Poor soils mean poor growth. Use plenty of compost or peat moss if you are planting trees or shrubs, especially in foundation plantings.

Your shrubs or lawns won't look neat unless you keep the edges trimmed and the plants weeded or mulched.

Don't be afraid to spend as much money on the outside of your home as you would to decorate the interior. Remember, more folks see the outside than they do the inside.

A QUICK GREEN THUMB GUIDE FOR COMMON SHRUBS

SHRUBS	FEATURES	PRUNING	PROBLEMS	CONTROL
Althaea (Rose of Sharon) (*Hibiscus syriacus*)	White, purple, pink, red and blue flowers in late summer until frost. Grows in most well-drained soils. 6 to 12 ft.	Cut out winterkilled wood in spring or later. Annual trimming to two dormant buds keeps shrubs low and very floriferous.	Bud drop. May be due to hot, dry weather, lack of soil nutrients.	Water and feed plants well.
Buddleia (Butterfly bush)	Long spikes of white, purple, lavender flowers throughout late summer. 3 ft.	Cut back to ground in spring.	Winterkills.	Heavy pruning in spring.
Caryopteris (Blue mist)	Silvery green foliage, light blue flowers. 3 ft.	Cut back to ground in spring.	Winterkills.	Heavy pruning in spring.
Chaenomeles (Flowering quince) *Cydonia oblonga* is the quince grown for jellies and dwarfing rootstock for pears.	Called japonica or "burning bush." White, scarlet, salmon pink flowers. Produces flowers and fruit year after year. Fruit makes good jell.	Cut out dead twigs, those growing tall and leggy. Remove ⅓ growth each year. Early spring is best time.	Fireblight.	Remove dead wood.
Clethra (Pepper bush)	Compact, neat plant with finger-like clusters of small scented white or pink flowers. 4 to 5 ft.	In spring cut out excess branches.	None.	
Cornus (Dogwoods)	Colorful foliage, blossoms and neat habit of growth. 4 to 20 ft.	Need little pruning. Cut out dead wood.	Scale. Leaf curl.	Malathion dry weather.

A QUICK GREEN THUMB GUIDE FOR COMMON SHRUBS (*Continued*)

SHRUBS	FEATURES	PRUNING	PROBLEMS	CONTROL
Cotinus coggygria (Smoke tree)	A garden favorite for 2,000 yrs. Small yellowish flowers, plume-like threads produce interesting smoke effect. Center of attraction in lawn. 20 ft. high.	Prune out dead wood any time.	Wilt disease.	Prune and burn.
Cotoneaster (Pronounced Ko-to-nee-aster)	Highly polished dark green leaves. Red berries and foliage in fall. Likes drought, full sun. Up to 4 ft.	Trim new growth back to desired height in spring.	None serious.	
Deutzia gracilis (Dwarf deutzia)	Charming low growing foundation shrub, white and pink flowers. Likes full sun. 3 ft.	Trim little, if any, just after blooming.	None.	
	Deutzia Pride of Rochester, 5 ft.	Needs no pruning except for dead wood.	Tips may winterkill.	Trim off dead tips in spring.
Euonymous (Winged euonymous)	Has corky ridges on branches. Fall foliage a deep red. Brightly colored orange fruits.	Seldom needed. Snip out extra long shoots when needed.	None.	
Forsythias (Golden bells)	Handsome early-blooming shrub for boundary lines, banks and hedges.	Trim after blooming. Do not shear it into ball shape, as this is one shrub that likes to weep or grow gracefully.	Failure to bloom due to cold weather.	Do not prune heavily. Plant in protected spot.

A. G. *hydrangea* (Hills of snow)	Produces showy balls of white flowers. 4 ft.	Cut plants back to ground each spring or fall.	Powdery mildew, rust and botrytis blight.	Dust with sulfur.
Hydrangea (Pee gee hydrangea)	Coarse shrub with white flowers in August. Overused yet highly handsome. 10 ft.	Cut plant back each spring for shrub-like growth. If you want it tree-like, prune very little.	None.	
Lagerstroemia (Crape myrtle)	Fine lilac-like flowering plant blooming in late summer and early fall.	Prune back in fall.	Winterkills.	Give winter mulch and winter protection.
Malus (Crabapples)	See section under shade trees.			
Paeonia suffruticosa (Chinese tree peony)	A spectacular shrub, white, rose and purplish red blooms. Does well in semi-shady spots, well-drained soil, slightly on alkaline side.	Cut out dead wood in spring.	Leaf spot.	Dust with Captan.
Philadelphus (Mockorange)	Creamy flowers highly fragrant. Growth is coarse. 10 ft.	Prune after blossoming in spring. Overgrown plants should be shortened drastically in early spring. Thin out branches as they become crowded. Never shear mockorange.	Lack of blossoms due to cold; also pruning removes buds.	Do not prune tips.

A QUICK GREEN THUMB GUIDE FOR COMMON SHRUBS (*Continued*)

Shrubs	Features	Pruning	Problems	Control
Prunus (Flowering almonds)	Group includes shrubs 4 ft. to trees 30 ft. Early blooms in spring, usually before leaves come out.	Little pruning needed. Cut out sprouts from below point of graft, as wild stock may take over.	Nothing serious.	
Pyracantha (Firethorn)	Keeps shiny green foliage nearly all winter. Orange scarlet berries, thorny twigs. 4 to 6 ft.	Cut out wilted branches and burn.	Often bears every other year. Susceptible to fireblight.	Cut out and burn branches.
Salix (Dwarf willow)	Feathery plant ideal in wet or heavy soils. Foliage is neat blue-gray-green and can be clipped for formal effect or left natural. 4 ft.	Thin out old wood in spring.	None.	
Spiraea (Spireas)	An important group of landscape plants. S. van houteii (bridal wreath) grows 6 ft.	If neglected, cut it back to ground in fall.	Aphids.	Nicotine sulfate sprayed on as soon as noticed.
	S. anthony waterer (dwarf red spirea) and S. bumalda grow 4 ft., make good foundation plants.	Prune back to 6 in. of ground in spring before growth starts. If blooms are cut as soon as they start to fade, they'll continue until late fall.	None.	
Sweetscented viburnum (*V. carlesii*)	White fragrant flowers in spring, foliage bronzy in fall. 6 ft.	Needs little pruning. Thin out shoots after flowering.	None.	

Syringa (Lilac)	Shrubs having great nostalgic appeal. Flowers fragrant and profuse up to 20 ft.	Cut out most suckers in spring. You may or may not cut faded blooms. If you do prune, do so directly after blooming period. To rejuvenate old bush, cut ½ to ⅓ of old wood out in a 3 yr. period.	Leaf miner.	Lindane.
			Scale.	Lime sulfur in early spring.
			Borers.	Borer paste.
			Failure to bloom due to improper planting, too much shade, close planting, too many suckers at base, dry summers.	
			Powdery mildew (not serious).	Mildex.
			Bacterial blight: plants turn black and die.	None.
Tamarix (Tamarisk)	This handsome shrub has lacy pink flowers, slender feathery foliage. 10 ft. Do not confuse tamarix with tamarack (larix) or larch.	Prune after blooming period in spring.	Parts may winterkill.	Prune out dead limbs in spring.
Viburnums	This is a large and important group with showy spring flowers, green foliage in summer and vivid autumn coloration.			

A QUICK GREEN THUMB GUIDE FOR COMMON SHRUBS (*Continued*)

Shrubs	Features	Pruning	Problems	Control
Viburnum opulus European "snowball" or cranberry bush	Used for hiding unsightly spots, red berries in summer and fall. Leaves red in autumn. 15 ft.	Thin out plants in spring.	Aphids cause leaves to curl.	Nicotine sulfate or Malathion in early spring.
Weigela (Weigela)	Trumpet-shaped flowers. Variegated type has pale pink blooms and cream and green foliage. 5 ft.	Thin out badly neglected plants and cut back to proper size in fall or winter.		

GREEN THUMB FACTS ABOUT SOME COMMON FLOWERING TREES

Shade Trees	Uses, Habits and Features	Problems	Control
Aesculus (Horse chestnut)	Has showy flowers and large leaves. Grows 60 ft. Messy habit of littering lawn with nuts and scorched leaves.	Leaf scorch or drying of foliage.	Captan. Not practical for home gardener.
Acer palmatum (Japanese maple)	Fine specimen tree with bright red foliage. 15 ft.	Winterkills. Leaves turn olive green. Scorched leaves in summer.	None. Species are variable. Needs lots of water on hot days.
Other maples:			
Norway	Used for lawn plantings, street trees. 70 ft. tall.	Wilt disease.	Have gas company check. Cut out dead limbs.
Schwedler's Norway maple	Bright red spring foliage turning to bronzy green. A slow grower. 70 ft. tall.	Maple gall mite, causes tiny galls which disfigure leaves. Galls many shapes.	Lime-sulfur before leaves open.
Sugar maple	Grows 90 ft. Upkeep costs are low. Striking fall coloration.	Leaf-chewing pests. Midsummer leaf fall (due to wet spring or wilt).	DDT. None.
Silver maple	Weak-wooded, fast growing, 70 ft. tall.	Frost crack or winter injury. Causes long fissures on south or southwest side of tree, sometimes full length of tree. Bleeding of broken or pruned branches.	Scrape loose bark back. Trees on poorly drained soil are more subject. Nothing serious.

GREEN THUMB FACTS ABOUT SOME COMMON FLOWERING TREES (*Continued*)

Shade Trees	Uses, Habits and Features	Problems	Control
Silver maple (*Continued*)		Wetwood (sap oozing down trunk).	Insert drain tube.
		Woolly aphids on underside of leaves.	Malathion in early summer.
Ailanthus (Tree of heaven)	A tough tree, grows in worst soils.	Weak-wooded. Odor of male flowers obnoxious.	Avoid it if possible.
Albizzia (Mimosa)	A fast-grower, 20 ft. high. Foliage fern-like and attractive.	Winterkills.	Needs pruning each year to strengthen it.
		Hardy as far north as Washington, D.C. Weak-wooded.	
Betula Birch, gray and paper	Fine specimen trees. 50 ft. Canoe or paper birch is best.	Prone to borers, leafminer and die back disease.	Start spraying with lindane in May. Cut out dead branches.
Cercis (Redbud or Judas tree)	Fine specimen tree for small lawns. 15 to 20 ft. Pink blooms and heart-shaped leaves.	None serious.	
Cornus (Dogwood)	Prefers moving in spring. Ideal in small lawn. Resents deep planting. 20 ft.	Crown rot.	None.
		Anthracnose & leaf spot.	Spray with Captan during bloom period and during summer.
		Curling leaves (due to dry weather).	Keep watered and mulched.
Crataegus Hawthorn	Handsome small tree, 20 ft. Flowers bloom in clusters. Wood is spiny.	Leaf spot disease.	Captan sprayed weekly.

Hamamelis (Witch-hazel)	Interesting "offseason" trees. 20 ft., blooming in fall or winter when snow is on ground.	None.	None.
Larix (Tamarack, larch or hackmatack)	Valuable timber tree and ornamental conifer—a semi-evergreen losing its needles. 70 ft. tall.	Larch sawfly which strips foliage.	DDT in late May.
Magnolia (Magnolia)	Spectacular trees, ideal for specimen plantings. Not all hardy. 20–30 ft.	Scale and mealybugs cause black mold, suck sap.	Malathion, 2½ pints of 50% per 100 gals. of water in August.
Malus (Crabapple)	Smart colorful lawn trees, 10 to 20 ft. Fruit used for jelly. Hopa, dolgo and hyslop produce clouds of pink and white blooms in spring, red fruit in fall.	Susceptible to borers and other troubles of apples (see Apple).	Keep sprayed with DDT and Captan.
Platanus (Sycamore, London plane, buttonball)	Hardy tree ideal for landscaping under adverse conditions of soil, smoke, soot or smog. 70 ft.	Leaf scorch which is not serious.	None that's practical.
Populus (Poplar)	While a poor landscape tree, poplars are useful for soil erosion preventing, windbreaks, and along highways. 70 ft.	Female trees shed messy "cotton" flowers. Trees are weak-wooded and susceptible to cystospora or wilt.	No control.
Prunus (Flowering plums)	Includes flowering plums, cherries, almonds, and flowering peaches. All excellent for small yard. Up to 30 ft.	Same trouble fruit cherries have (see Cherries).	Keep trees sprayed with Captan and DDT.
Quercus (Oaks)	Among finest of trees, withstand storms, have fewer insects and diseases. Wonderful lawn trees. 70 ft.	Oak galls. Oak wilt fungus, a new threat to every species.	Lime sulfur dormant. Avoid injuring tree. Prune in late summer.

GREEN THUMB FACTS ABOUT SOME COMMON FLOWERING TREES (*Continued*)

SHADE TREES	USES, HABITS AND FEATURES	PROBLEMS	CONTROL
Salix (Willows)	Picturesque trees with graceful drooping branches, considered a "weed" by many. Tree is messy and sheds twigs, a natural habit. 70 ft.	Short-lived, has heavy root systems often troublesome.	Plant at least 40 ft. from sewer lines.
		Tar spot and black scab.	Wettable sulfur in spring.
		Willow beetles.	DDT in June.
Sorbus (Mountain ash)	Highly desirable lawn tree, 30 ft. Showy orange berries, ideal for jelly.	Lack of flowers or berries.	Age. Trees bear 5 to 7 yrs. May be due to poor weather at pollination time.
		Fireblight.	Prune out dead limbs.
Ulmus (Elms)	Stately trees, 70 ft. Graceful clean habits of growth. Tree may be doomed if Dutch elm disease cannot be checked.	Dutch elm disease.	None. Keep tree sprayed with DDT.
		Wetwood disease, sap flows down trunk.	Insert drain tube. If you can't grow American elm, grow Chinese elm, resistant to Dutch elm disease.
		Elm leaf drop due to fungus.	Don't worry about it. Rake and burn leaves in fall.
		Elm leaf beetle causes leaves to be riddled with holes.	Spray with 50% DDT about June 1st.

Green thumb note: Trees have many problems not listed above. Leaf-chewing insects, aphids, borers, countless diseases such as leafspot, twig blight, to name a few. (See all-purpose spray formula under shrubs.) Usually DDT, Captan or Ferbam will check most insect and disease pests. Dogs can burn a tree. In a city such as New York, about 45,000 trees are lost yearly, and the greatest part of this loss is blamed on dogs. A screen protects against this type of injury. Man too brings about many tree troubles, by burning leaves under a tree, or by hitting it with a lawn mower. Feed trees regularly to build up vigor and usually they'll live as long as you do, with proper selection of species.

10

Narrow-Leaved and Broad-Leaved Evergreens

Home owners have a choice between two excellent types of evergreen: the narrow-leaved or coniferous (cone-bearing) and the broad-leaved or flowering types. Both are useful for home plantings, although they require care of a different sort from that of the non-evergreen plants commonly used. They represent a greater first-cost investment, but over the years evergreens cost you no more for enhancing your home than does your lawn.

PART I

NARROW-LEAVED EVERGREENS (*Coniferous*)

Nine out of ten home owners prefer evergreens in a home planting, and there's no reason why you can't use them with non-evergreens to avoid monotony. The point to remember about evergreens is that they have definite shapes. Do not use large growing trees like spruce or pine near a home in a foundation planting unless you are prepared to clip them regularly. These tall-growing trees are better in a boundary planting.

If you want pyramidal forms, use the Pyramid Cedar (*arborvitae*), the Dundee Juniper, or clipped Japanese Yew. The arborvitae is used frequently, but be prepared to keep dogs away from it if you plant this shrub because it is very sensitive to "dogburn."

Round evergreens you can use are Mugo Pine or Globe Arborvitae. or you can trim the spreading yew into a round shape. Some spreading evergreen shrubs are the Savins, Andorra and Pfitzer's Junipers. The Japanese Yew is a fine evergreen, and is about the best for shady spots.

Evergreens are very good against a light background, but remember that they don't soften ugly lines as well as the loose-growing deciduous shrubs, and they won't grow where floods of water and snow fall from the roof.

PLANTING AND TRANSPLANTING EVERGREENS

Spring or fall are ideal times for setting out new evergreens. Always plant them as soon as you get the plants from the nursery where they are sold as "balled and burlapped" (called B&B). Never carry them by the tops, but rather by the entire ball of earth. If you cannot plant them immediately, keep the shrubs out of hot sun and drying winds, as these are fatal to balled evergreens, or any bare-rooted nursery stock. Wet sawdust around the roots keeps the plants happy until you're ready to plant.

Planting: There's no great trick to planting, although there are certain things to keep in mind if you want the trees to live. First, dig a hole larger and deeper than the ball of earth. Maintain a good loamy topsoil with plenty of peat or compost mixed in to fill around the ball. Don't cut the strings on the burlap as you plant ball and all. Even loosening the burlap at the top isn't necessary. Fill halfway with good soil and pack firmly with feet or settle by filling the hole with water. After that put in some soil, leaving a 2- or 3-inch depression around the plant to catch the rainwater or hose water. Never mound soil up around the base of the tree, as this sheds water. Never cover the hole completely, as you lose water that way. Water your evergreens twice a week, giving them a good soaking each time. On especially hot days you can syringe the foliage. Soak your evergreens at weekly intervals, since a sodden condition for any length of time may kill the tree. In November you can put a straw, peat, or cocoa bean shell mulch around the base. Anything you have available will work, but you should never let the evergreen go into the winter with a dry soil.

Feeding: Newly planted evergreens need a mulch and watering more than they need doses of plant food. Liquid feeding supplies both water and extra nutrients, but be careful about using chemical fertilizers. Once evergreens have become established, they will respond to occasional feedings. Water is more important for survival, and for that reason you must not count on rain or snow to fulfill this need. Keep evergreens at least 3 feet from the foundation wall because it acts like a blotter and draws moisture from the roots and soil.

Protect your investment: You've handled your balled evergreens like eggs. They've been carefully placed in the hole, watered heavily, and mulched with 2 or 3 inches of sawdust, peat moss, buckwheat hulls or what have you.

Next, if your evergreens are in a windy spot, your best bet is to build a screen of some sort to keep wind off for the first winter. Four posts driven into the ground, with burlap wrapped around the posts, does a fine job of protecting them from hot drying winds. Some gardeners wrap each evergreen individually, and this does the trick for new transplants. Actually, it's not necessary for established evergreens.

And as a final word, newly planted evergreens seldom need any pruning. After your tree is well established, you can do a little trimming each year, beginning before the plants have reached the full size desired. You can trim an evergreen just about any time "when the knife is sharp." In some nurseries, pruning or shearing is a year-around job, which indicates that the time you trim evergreens isn't too important. Following are some of the most common evergreens, with a few green thumb notes on caring for them.

ARBORVITAE (*Thuja occidentalis*)

Green Thumb Care: Arborvitae makes a fine windbreak, hedge or border planting. The Globe Arborvitae and the upright types are commonly used in landscape planning. The pyramidal arborvitae makes an ideal boundary-line hedge. All arborvitaes need full sun and lots of moisture in the soil. The golden arborvitae needs full sun to bring out its peculiar golden coloring. Both types stand shearing well and can be trained to almost any shape. They do best in a moist soil, but will thrive on any moderately fertile, well-drained soil. They do not like dry, dusty and smoky atmosphere or the dry soil conditions that generally prevail in cities.

Pruning: You can prune the upright or Globe Arborvitae any time of the year. Just take a pair of hedge shears and shear off the ends of the branches that extend beyond the normal outline of the plant. This makes the foliage nice and thick. Too frequent shearing may give the tree a sheared, unnatural look.

Neglecting the pruning job means you'll have to be drastic and remove a lot of growth, either all at once or over a period of three years. Heavy pruning may give that butchered look and it'll be quite a while before the tree can fill in again. An annual shearing of the ends of the twigs stimulates new side growth on the branches and makes the foliage thicker. That is why pruning is good for all plants. It improves the denseness.

Old plants that have been neglected can be "topped" (that is, the top cut back) any time to induce bushiness. If your pyramidal arborvitae is not already bushy, prune the top back and scatter plant food around the base.

Problems: Arborvitae "dogburns" badly and should be screened or fenced to keep these animals away. Various repellents are on the market. We've been highly pleased with results of using a repellent rope, treated with materials totally disagreeable to dogs. The rope is cut in pieces and placed around evergreens or in flower beds frequented by dogs.

Windburning is another problem of arborvitae and all other evergreens. This is due to hot dry winds and sunny days in late winter and early spring. Windburning is aggravated by dry soil, a good reason for soaking the soil in the fall.

CANADIAN HEMLOCK (*Tsuga canadensis*)

If you're looking for an unusually good evergreen which will grow in sun or shade, look to the graceful hemlock. The hemlocks are less formal in outline than the firs and spruces. Their limbs spread horizontally and they branch repeatedly into many small branchlets which generally droop most gracefully. With their fine feathery foliage they are attractive in youth, and attain great dignity in old age.

The hemlock will stand severe pruning, growing dense and velvety; thus they make excellent hedges. They grow best in an acid soil and like plenty of moisture.

Pruning: Although the Canadian hemlock will grow 60 feet tall, it still makes a good item in foundation planting. I have Canadian hemlocks in my own foundation planting and find that the best way to keep them down is to cut the tops out each spring or fall and to more or less shear the tips or end growth to keep the plants compact. A hemlock looks best if allowed to "weep" a little, and you get this effect from a plant growing in a limited area by shearing, and then allowing new growth to come out from the sheared branches.

Canadian hemlock, kept sheared, makes an ideal evergreen for the foundation planting. The more it's trimmed, the better it gets.

A 10-foot hemlock which needs to be reduced presents quite a problem.

I'd cut the top out as much as possible without leaving a gaping hole. Wait until spring and cut out one-half of the top. New growth will fill in, and in another year you might be able to cut the remaining top back.

Once you get it to the height you want, it should be trimmed to that distance each year. Constant trimming is the best way to keep evergreens down to the desired size. It's much easier to do this than to let them grow tall and reduce them later. Most evergreens do not bounce back or fill in as do non-evergreens.

Problems: Hemlock scale. If the tops of your hemlock plantings look denuded, blame it on the old-fashioned hemlock scale. The scale devitalizes hemlocks by sucking sap from twigs and injecting a poison into the sap streams. Injured hemlocks can be brought back to health by feeding the trees a complete plant food such as 5–10–5 in the fall and spraying early in March with a dormant lime-sulfur solution. Avoid getting lime sulfur on buildings, as it stains paint.

JUNIPERS (*Juniperus*)

Junipers are one of the most important groups of evergreens used in home landscaping. The most popular juniper is Pfitzer's (pronounced fits-her), a fast-grower which must be pruned regularly to keep it in bounds. Savin's is another spreader growing to the same height (4 feet to 5 feet).

Pruning: Young junipers, 2 or 3 years in the foundation planting, need little or no pruning. Limit it to cutting back the ends of branches. Let the shrub grow star-shaped, or zig-zag fashion. In other words, never prune it into a round shape, because Pfitzers do not grow that way naturally. Some pruning can be done every year or so. If carefully selected, long branches can be removed at the base of the plant. If these branches are beneath others, the upper branches will usually droop down to cover the scar made in removing the long branch, and will fill in the spot so that it won't be noticed.

Allow the end of one branch to stick out a bit farther than another so the shrub will be nice and graceful. Where Pfitzers have been neglected for some years there's not much you can do to rejuvenate the bush, without creating that "plucked chicken" look. Sometimes long branches can be cut off at the base of the plant. It's always nice to have a short branch directly above the long one that is cut, so that the gap will be filled more quickly. Always cut long branches off flush, to avoid stubs. Upright or columnar types are pruned by shearing in spring, summer or fall.

Problems: Scale insect. You can tell this trouble-maker by looking closely at the foliage. Look for small white objects. These multiply in great numbers, yet almost escape notice by gardeners. They suck the juice from the tissue, eventually causing the plants to brown and die. The pine needle scale is found on pines, spruce, hemlock, firs and junipers. These insects pass winter in the egg stage beneath the scale covering. Hatching starts in May and continues until the first of June or so.

Control: Use Malathion 50 per cent emulsifiable grade, at rate of 1½ quarts in 100 gallons of water, applied in late May. Or in April, use lime sulfur at rate of 1 quart to 9 quarts of water, applied any time before new growth starts. Lime sulfur should be used according to directions on the container. It does a fine job as a clean-up spray to control wintering forms of mites, scale, aphids, mealybugs and lace bug.

As we've said before, never use any dormant spray when the temperature is below 40 degrees or above 70 degrees. Above or below those temperatures, the oil may become separated and cause burning. Never use any of the so-called miscible ("mixable") oils on evergreens unless you follow instructions on the container. Evergreens are very sensitive to oil, and more tolerant to lime-sulfur sprays.

Red Spider Mite: If your junipers have a rather yellowish color on the foliage even though you fed and watered the plants be on the lookout for tiny red spider mites. They cause the foliage to grow more or less twisted and droopy, with a sickly yellowish cast. Too small to be seen with the naked eye, they often fool gardeners into thinking something is wrong with the soil. Another cause of yellowed foliage on Pfitzer, Savin, Irish and similar junipers is the juniper scale. Control for both: Mix a quart of 50 per cent wettable Malathion in 50 gallons of water and apply anytime in July, drenching the entire foliage.

Another effective mite killer is Kelthane, an item we've tested with good results. Kelthane is slower to kill than the phosphate miticides, but it does a good job. Some growers who have used it say that it isn't effective against mites, but this complaint is hardly justifiable.

Kelthane seems to kill red spider mites and then leave them in a lifelike condition for a few days. Consequently, if you do not make a close examination, you might conclude that mites weren't killed. You'll probably be hearing more about Kelthane later on, since it is quite new. Kelthane has no ovicidal (eggkilling) action, but due to its long residual action, the young mite larvae are killed as they are hatched.

Cedar-Apple Rust: If you see "sputnik-like" growth on your junipers, that's cedar-apple rust. Where apples and cedars grow together the cedars become infested with hundreds of galls an inch or more in diameter.

These galls form numerous long, yellow, tongue-like outgrowths (which some folks think are blossoms). Harmful spores are generated from these projections and are spread by the wind. These spores infect the leaves of apples, which often become so seriously infected that they drop prematurely. Damage to cedars is not too serious, although the ends of the branches bearing the galls usually die. Control: Spraying cedars with Elgetol when the "horns" begin to appear is helpful. Also, Ferbam does a good job.

PINES (*Pinus*)

Pines are increasing in popularity and they have the advantage of holding their needles well. In some areas, pines are now the most popular evergreen. Some may object to the Red Pine's tendency to be top-open and scraggly for a Christmas tree. Perhaps the Scotch Pine is preferable to the Red Pine because it is more compact. Its needles are shorter and stiffer.

Telling the principal pines apart is an easy matter, simply by counting the number of needles in each cluster. For example, the White Pine has 5 needles in a cluster, each cluster being 5 or 6 inches long, bluish green, and soft to the touch. Austrian Pine has 2 needles in a cluster, which is 6½ inches long, and stiff. Scotch Pine has 2 needles in a cluster; a cluster is 2 to 3 inches long and needles are twisted, as well as sharp at the tips. Red Pine has 2 needles in a cluster which is 6 inches long and rather glossy.

Pruning: In pruning pines, firs, and spruces, you follow a somewhat different method. Pruning should be confined to correcting defects and cutting back tips to make the tree more compact and dense. To achieve the effect of bushiness on firs and spruces shear off the soft new growth in spring and if necessary give them another pruning later on in the season. Try to cut at a point where there is a dormant bud, so that the little branch will be able to grow the following year from a new bud.

Most pines should be sheared or pruned between mid-June and mid-July, and all you do is trim back the leader (top) and laterals (side branches). The growth is soft then and limber, and there's enough of the growing season left for the tree to form a cluster of new buds at the end of the shortened leader and laterals.

Problems: Pine needle scale. A troublesome pest not only for pines, but of related conifers. This pest does its damage by sucking juice from the needles, causing them to turn brown and die.

The whitish pine-leaf scale yields readily to sprays of miscible oils. It's a good idea to give the trees a summer spray, and one again next May. To mix a gallon of spray, add 5¼ tablespoonfuls of miscible oil, or you can use the new scalecide, Malathion—four teaspoonfuls to a gallon of water. We like Malathion because it kills just about every kind of insect there is, including the toughies such as red spider and mealybug.

European pine shoot moth: The moth lays eggs which hatch into larvae that attack the ends of side shoots of most of our common varieties of pine. We've seen this happen to small and tall trees (up to 20 feet). The infected shoot will bend out of shape and usually continue to grow. Buds and shoots are often killed outright by the feeding of the tiny worm.

When this happens the secondary buds develop, resulting in bushy or broom-like tips. This type of injury slows down growth and causes the pines to be permanently crippled, losing their value as ornamentals or as Christmas trees.

The European pine shoot moth has caused considerable damage to Red Pine, Mugo Pine, Scotch Pine and the Austrian Pine.

Control: Cut out all infested branches, usually found at the tops of trees. Then burn them. Do this before May, because then the moths come out as dark brown worms, three-quarter inches long. Spraying early kills newly hatched worms as they feed on the needle bases before entering the buds. Use DDT as a dust or spray.

SPRUCE (*Picea*)

Spruces: The spruces have long been favorite Christmas trees because of their compact, bushy growth and conical shape. The Norway spruce, with its long dark, lustrous green needles, has the disadvantage of losing its foliage quickly, especially if the tree is jarred or brushed against. If the butt is immersed in water, the needles stay on longer. The white spruce (often called cat spruce, due to an alleged unpleasant odor given off by the needles when brought indoors) seems to lose its needles less quickly as a Christmas tree.

Colorado Blue Spruce (*Picea pungens*)—Few evergreens have had the popularity of the blue spruce. The seedling form known as the Colorado blue spruce is a magnificent tree. Sometimes one tree will develops more bluish color than others. Usually those of the most bluish color are found in deep gorges of high altitudes. When grown from seed, only a small portion of the trees develop the bright blue color. A great majority are of greenish cast with a slightly bluish tendency. The bluish color is due to a powdery substance on the outside of the needles. It is known as "bloom" or sheen. You see the same thing on a plum or grape. The color is pronounced during the late spring and summer but later, with rains and snows, most of the blue color disappears. For this reason, you cannot judge the color of the blue spruce except in the spring and summer. This popular evergreen has been adapted for ornamental planting all over because it grows well under a wide range of conditions. Everyone likes the narrow pyramidal crowns, "shingled" or layered effect of the branches and the deep bluish cast. It makes a fine specimen tree for the lawn, and can be used as a lighted Christmas tree. The Colorado blue spruce likes lots of sunlight, is sensitive to crowding from other trees. On sandy soils newly planted trees can be injured by dry weather. Therefore, they should be well watered during the first season, and it won't do a bit of harm to water them the second year after planting.

The blue spruce has been so striking it has been badly abused in indiscriminate foundation plantings. Some argue that a stiff blue spruce planted in front of the house is so conspicuous that it conflicts with the house as the center of interest. This is a matter of opinion.

Improving the Color: We are often asked if there's any way to enhance the colors of these trees. For an answer to this, I wrote D. Hill Nursery, Dundee, Illinois, one of the largest growers of evergreens in America.

These specialists tell us that blue spruces respond and improve their color where an acid condition prevails in the soil. In Minnesota and Iowa where the Colorado blue spruce takes on a very pronounced blue sheen, iron sulfate added to the soil is of great benefit. Gardeners may treat their Colorado blue spruces with iron sulfate for color improvement.

Pruning Spruces: Spruce can be pruned any time of the year. When pruning spruces (also pines and firs), keep in mind that the trees grow in whorls or layers. The pruning of this group of evergreens is confined to correcting defects and cutting back to make the tree more compact and dense in growth. To make the tree grow more dense, the pruning can usually be confined to removing part of the new growth. Make the cuts near a spot where there is a dormant bud, so that the little branch will be able to grow the following year. It should have an area of 20 feet or more in diameter to grow, but sometimes it becomes necessary to trim the sides or restrict the top growth. You can keep the spruce down artificially by shearing the soft tips in spring.

To do this you take a pair of hedge shears and snip off the tip ends of the furry growth only. Done annually, this will give you compact plants with that formal look, rather than the natural look. Plants so sheared regularly seldom develop into normal, natural-looking types. Do not attempt to bring a big spruce down to size by cutting into old wood. You can't be drastic with evergreens because they do not send out new growth like flowering shrubs.

If the top is taller than you like, it can be cut out and a new leader (top) will form to take its place. Sometimes the lower branches of a spruce die out; this is due to lack of sun or overcrowding. No type of pruning can help bring the dead branches back to life. Cut the dead branches flush to the trunk. No new growth will come to replace the dead limbs. You can prevent further loss of low branches by cutting out all nearby limbs that shut out light.

If your evergreen has the top broken, don't worry because you can grow another one on it. Select one of the side branches nearest the top of the tree, bind it vertically, tie it to a stake and it will train itself to start a new top. After a year or two the tree will have a brand new top and you can remove the stake.

Problems: Spruce gall aphids. They cause small pineapple-like growths on the branches. Aphids remain in the cone-shaped galls until August when the unsightly growth cracks open and allows the winged aphids to escape.

Ordinarily, you can spray in early spring while the trees are dormant, using lime sulfur or miscible oil. Spray trees with Malathion in mid-April, or sooner; also, concentrate on catching the adults in August, using Malathion, one teaspoon to four quarts of water. This will kill the aphids as they are released from the cones.

Spruce mite. The spruce mite may be troublesome on spruce, arborvitae, hemlock and many other evergreens. It can be checked by spraying or dusting with a rotenone-sulfur combination, four tablespoons of wettable sulfur plus four tablespoons of 4 per cent rotenone in each gallon of water or use Malathion, 1 teaspoon to 2 quarts of water.

It will take two to three treatments at seven to ten day intervals to do the job. Even a stiff syringing with plain water from the garden hose, if repeated every few days for a month will greatly reduce this spider infestation.

Twig canker disease. If bottom limbs die off and you see pitch oozing near the affected parts, look for twig canker. Oozing pitch near the point of infection is common, and usually the branches near the ground become infected and die first. Dead needles persist for a while, then shed in early summer. Control: Cut out and burn dead and dying branches. Spraying the trees with Ferbam at 4 ounches in 12 gallons of water will help prevent the spread of the trouble—if two doses are made 14 days apart. Put the first dose on when new growth starts to appear in spring.

JAPANESE YEW (*Taxus*)

One of the most outstanding evergreens on the landscape today is without doubt the *Taxus,* commonly known as Yew. People like the Yew because of the dark evergreen needles, its attractive red fruit, its freedom from many insects and diseases and its adaptability to most soils. Another factor accounting for the yew popularity is its high degree of tolerance to shade. When the Japanese Yew is grown from seed it is an upright tree, 30 feet or more in height; if it is reproduced by cuttings, it forms a wide-spreading, slow-growing shrub as found in the nurseries. This shrub may be more expensive to buy than common evergreens; the reason is that it takes years for them to be sheared and grown into shapely plants in the nursery.

The University of Michigan has been studying Yews for years and has selected what it feels are the most outstanding.

Here they are: *Taxus media hicksii* known as Hicks Yew, this Yew is upright, compact, and has ascending branches that are ideal for accent plants on corners, in sun or in shade. *Taxus media hatfieldii* is somewhat more vase-shaped and maintains its foliage better than *hicksii.* It may winter burn in windy spots. *T. media hicksii columnaris* is a very compact, columnar plant, free of objectionable horizontal side branches.

T. cuspidata capitata (Upright Japanese Yew) is the only true upright or pyramidal Yew, growing naturally with a 2-to-1 height-spread ratio. In Michigan this variety is losing favor in some areas due to center die-out "disease" (cause unknown). This pyramidal form can be used to soften corners. Nurserymen sometimes grow this Yew from cuttings, selecting the tips of the upper branches for growing into upright trees, and using the tips of the side branches for growing the spreading types. In fact, the term *capitata* is not a valid name and all "*capitatas*" are the wild tree types of Japanese Yew.

T. baccata repandens, a good, dark green, low spreading shrub has drooping branches. *T. cuspidata nana* is a slow growing, irregular shrub that's spreading and dwarf. *T. media densiformis,* a low compact type grows twice as wide as it is high, and is a dwarf spreader. *T. cuspidata thayeri* is the outstanding large spreading type of Yew—vase shaped, flat topped, compact and with good dark green color.

Both *T. cuspidata nigra* and *T. media brownii* are also good; they are moderately compact shrubs that spread as far as they are tall. No doubt there are other Yews just as good as these mentioned in the Michigan studies.

Ground "hemlock" is not a hemlock but *Taxus canadensis,* a native American sprawling evergreen often found in woods. It grows 1 to 2 feet tall, has scarlet berries. We use the greens in our greenhouse work, but I doubt if you can move it from the shade of forest trees since it is not too well suited to open windswept spots.

Feeding: Bear in mind that all yews are heavy feeders and respond to feedings of manure or fertilizers. Yews also like a cool, moist soil for best development, so give them a mulch of peat moss or sawdust.

Mulching: Since the plant is relatively shallow-rooted, it should never be cultivated. A peat moss or sawdust mulch keeps the roots moist and cool in hot summers. This handsome evergreen needs yearly pruning to develop compact, well shaped plants.

Problems: The taxus weevil. If your Japanese Yew (*taxus*) is wilting, or the foliage is turning yellowish and the plant is dying, look to the soil for the trouble. The taxus weevil is becoming so serious a pest that nurserymen are searching for suitable substitutes to replace this wonderful evergreen plant. If our Yews are ruined, then the queen of all evergreens is lost.

Look under the sod around your plants for the presence of black adult beetles. If they're present, apply some Chlordane or Dieldrin spray (or dust); be sure to coat the branches close to the ground heavily. Also, treat the soil surface. By doing this, you give a soil deposit protection against newly emerging adult beetles the following season.

We understand that soil treatments will not kill the taxus weevil grubs, but it doesn't do a bit of harm to give the soil a thorough soaking. Cornell recommends these spray mixes: Two pounds of 25 per cent Dieldrin wettable powder per 100 gallons, or five pounds of 40 per cent chlordane wettable powder. Rate: 500 gallons per acre, which is approximately 1 gallon to a 10-by-10-foot area, or one large six-foot plant—also, spray the foliage.

June is the time to fight the pest. Incidentally, the taxus weevil, or black vine weevil is troublesome on many other evergreens, but particularly on taxus and hemlock.

One of my friends coped with this pest by using five pounds of arsenate of lead, five pounds of 50 per cent wettable DDT, and 25 pounds of 5–10–5 fertilizer. Mix all three together and put two handfuls around the base of each taxus bush. Do this in June, July and August. This treatment is sure death to the taxus weevil and the strawberry beetle, he reports.

Mealybugs. Another pest, mealybugs appear as white masses on the tips of the branches and along the trunk. Spray with Malathion—1 tablespoon to 2 quarts of water. Lecanium scale also may infect the yew. Malathion sprayed early in summer checks this.

PART II

EVERGREENS (*Broad-leaved*)

Andromeda: (*Pieris floribunda*) If you want a good evergreen shrub with clusters of lily of the valley-like flowers that bloom in March, April or May, try planting the andromedas. The native mountain andromeda (*Pieris floribunda*) is hardy in this region, grows to six feet. The Japanese andromeda (*P. japonica*) is perhaps a handsomer shrub, but it is not as hardy. In our region the mountain andromeda bears clusters of tiny, cream-colored, waxy bells in May. Andromedas like a moist, peaty soil, and partial shade.

Rhododendrons: Why aren't many good rhododendrons used for a supreme landscape effect? Perhaps the reason is that, while some species are hardy, others are finicky. That's why it is so important to check with your local nurseryman on the hardiness of various species before planting them in your yard. There's a 25 year old Rhododendron Catawbiense in our cemetery, bearing flowers year after year, and withstanding temperatures sometimes as low as 29 degrees below zero.

My advice to gardeners who want hardy rhododendrons is—stick to two native flowering types: (1) *R. maximum* (Rosebay), a broad-leaved, high-growing (6 feet) type familiar to visitors in the Alleghenies. It blooms in June with lavish colors of pink to white. (2) *R. catawbiense,* which blooms rose-pink in color in May, is orchid to rose pink in color and grows 3 feet to 5 feet tall. Its leaves are smaller than *R. maximum.*

The *Rhododendron maximum* is hardiest of all, while *R. catawbiense* is one of the showiest, its chief drawback is its lilac-magenta color.

We've been observing the varieties that are hardy in Highland Park (Rochester, N.Y.) and we would like to mention a few hybrids that you might try: Album elegans, Boule de Neige, Caractacus, Charles Dickens, Lee's Dark Purple, Mrs. Charles Sargent and Roseum elegans. The small-leaved *Rhododendron carolinianum* is inclined to bear heavily and is also perfectly hardy.

Location: Most rhododendrons prefer partial shade, although a number of varieties will grow in full sun. A general rule to follow is that the larger the leaf surface, the more shade is required. This doesn't always hold true since we have seen large-leaved rhododendrons growing in full sun in a cemetery at North Cohocton, New York. Very large-leaved varieties should be planted in shade or their leaves will assume a wilted appearance and the entire plant suffers.

Acid Soils

(1) Azaleas, rhododendrons and heaths actually like acid soil. In a limestone region such as central New York, it is imperative to make the soil acid before planting these ornamentals. This may be done by digging a pit about 2 feet deep and filling it with soil which has had large quantities of organic matter added—as much as one fourth to one half by volume may be organic matter. The remainder can be ordinary garden soil. Peat moss, rotted manure or pine needles are useful for his purpose. Now add a small amount of finely powdered sulfur and work it into the soil. Sulfur is good at the rate of one pound per 100 square feet. Never add lime to acid-loving plants. (See section on "Soils.")

An ideal soil for rhododendrons should contain humus, mostly peat moss to keep roots cool in hot weather. They do not like a heavy soil that's poorly drained.

Oak leaf mold or peat moss should comprise about 50 per cent of the soil, as this takes care of acidity, aeration and drainage. A mulch of peat moss alone is ideal. Decaying oak leaves, pine needles, any rotted vegetable material is used for rhododendrons by many nurserymen.

Poor drainage due to clay soils is often responsible for mottled gray coloring of foliage. If your soil is poorly drained about the only thing that can be done is to install drainage tile.

Rhododendron Problems

Wind and Sunburn: This causes the leaves to turn brown in summer or winter. The new so-called "anti-wilt" sprays of plastic or wax emulsions do slow down the rate of water loss from leaves and can protect both narrow and broad leaved evergreens from heat and drought. In addition, you should plan on watering your plants. Keep in mind that rhododendrons are shallow rooted, therefore should never be cultivated but rather mulched and left undisturbed.

Rhododendrons get leaf spot (fungus) disease, which can usually be checked by dusting with Ferbam. Also, these broad-leaved plants are attacked by a die-back blight caused by the same fungus which is responsible for lilac blight. If you see a general infection advancing rapidly down the twigs, followed by wilting or death of parts above, that's die-back.

Control: Prune diseased areas below the brown parts, also avoid pruning rhododendrons near diseased or old lilacs. The lace bug is a serious problem. It punctures the leaf tissue, sucks out sap, causes light spotting and eventually dries the leaves. Spraying with DDT, Isotox or any of the newer insecticides checks this.

There's also a stem borer which causes trouble. Keeping your plants sprayed with DDT will protect them against this pest, as well as the midge, white fly and other pests.

Another fungus disease, bud and twig blight, has been rampant; it causes flowers to blast or to rot on rhododendrons and azaleas. Prune all blasted buds and dead twigs. Spraying with Bordeaux mixture, Captan, or Parzate, after the flowering period is over, protects new buds and kills the fungus, plus spores.

HOLLY

Interest is zooming in hollies, especially the hardy, native, American Holly (*Ilex opaca*). Many gardeners have shied away from this tough plant because it was believed that it wasn't hardy enough for our rugged winters. This is a fallacy. I know of an American Holly plantation near us which survived the 30 degrees below zero weather last winter, proof that these plants can take it. But all hollies are extremely sensitive to early freezing of poorly ripened wood.

Holly likes good drainage; swampy ground will not do. If you can dig a hole in which water will stand for 2 or 3 weeks at a time, that means drainage is too poor for holly growth. Also, hollies do not like extremely windy situations. Plant them where a building or a stone wall will shunt the wind, or you can make use of a natural evergreen windbreak. Holly does well only in a drained soil and one that's acid. Oak leaf mold added each year will keep the soil acid.

Hollies like sun, but will bear in shade. Too much shade causes plants to be scraggly and they seldom bear as heavily in shade as in sun. At any rate, if you want a good specimen tree, allow plenty of room for growth. You can buy hollies with a neat ball of earth ready for transplanting in March, April or May, also during the fall. With good care, such a tree grows from 6 to 12 inches a year. Top branches grow faster than side branches.

Professor Ray R. Hirt of the College of Forestry, Syracuse University, has been working with American Hollies and his selections have survived the 24 degrees below zero of one winter, with little damage. The American Hollies set their flower buds in the spring, consequently they are not subject to winter killing if the blooming wood survives. His hollies are never wrapped nor covered in any way for winter. The American selections (*Ilex opaca*) that have withstood our winters are: Old Heavy Berry, Cardinal, Stann, Bountiful, Merry Christmas, Old Leatherleaf (male), Christmas Hedge, Freeman, Arden, Delia Bradley, Son of Delia Bradley (male) and several unnamed specimens. You might try some of these.

Professor Hirt has many exotic hollies that give evidence of considerable hardiness. The English Hollies set their flower buds in the autumn. Although the wood and foliage are winter hardy, the flower buds survive only the mildest of winters. He has Japanese Hollies that are drifted over with snow each winter and also, they have survived winters with practically no snow. The Japanese Red Berry Holly (*Ilex cornuta burfordii*) makes a nice pot plant indoors in a basement for winter. It blooms in March with a sweet fragrance and will set fruit without pollination. However, it cannot stand our winter temperature out-of-doors.

Pruning: Pruning the American Holly is a simple job because they don't seem to mind where you cut them. Just make sure your clippers are sharp. If you want them to grow to tall columns or pyramids, trim the sides. You can cut off the tops to make broad bushes. Pruning is important because it improves the holly—makes it more bushy. It doesn't do a bit of harm to prune at Christmas time for indoor bouquets. Young trees should be pruned at the tops to help them branch out early and after the fourth year or so, shaping is needed to get the outline you like.

GREEN THUMB TIPS FOR EVERGREENS

Evergreens are ideal for "specimen" plantings. That means they are useful as an individual specimen tree in a lawn.

Plant a specimen evergreen in memory of someone, and use it for a livin Christmas tree outdoors.

If you plan to landscape your home, first make a sketch, then go to yo local nursery and see what the balled evergreens look like before buy them.

Always water evergreens (especially newly planted ones) during dry summers, and in the fall.

Evergreens do not winterkill from freezing. They are affected by t winds and the sunshine of the fall, winter and spring months.

Be prepared to trim evergreens regularly. If you don't, they'll gr a jungle and hide your home. It takes less time to trim them does for you to wash your car.

Keep your foundation planting of evergreens neatly trimmed; it off your plants better. Plant annuals such as alyssum, marigold among your evergreens in summer, tulips and daffodils in fall blooms.

Don't plant a lot of tree-like evergreens in front of your ho spreaders under windows, taller types at the corners; allo feet between each plant.

Water newly planted evergreens two, three or four times a week, keep them mulched with sawdust, peat moss, buckwheat hulls or anything else you have.

Be prepared to replace old evergreens with new ones every fifteen to twenty years. Evergreens, like wallpaper, drapes and rugs, outlive their usefulness, and should be replaced.

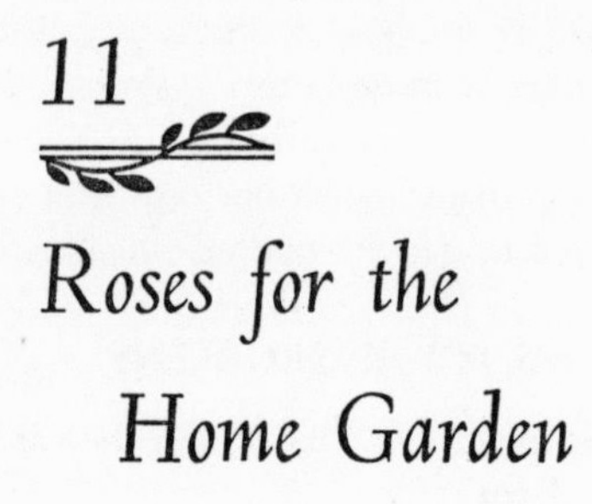

11

Roses for the Home Garden

By almost any count roses continue to be the favorite flower of our countrymen. This is not a new development and for this reason rose literature abounds. Over the years and in many lands roses have had the attention of the best gardeners and as a result one can trace fashions in roses. Several groups have arisen, flourished, and then declined as interest passed to another group. Today we have a renewal of interest in some of the types of roses grown long ago. Classifications, both old and new, as represented in catalogs today are presented in the accompanying charts with brief helpful data for each.

Hybrid teas are the most important of all roses. Most of the roses grown for cut flowers in greenhouses are hybrid teas. As a rule, the buds are long and pointed. Your catalog will give you detailed description of this rose. If you are interested in the Moss or "Cabbage" roses, you'll be heartened to know these old-fashioned favorites are still available.

Hybrid polyanthas or floribundas are terms you commonly find in catalogs. These terms are practically synonymous, although floribunda is the more recent term. With this variety, flowers are borne in clusters. Plants are attractive alone in beds or borders, or along with herbaceous perennials, flowering shrubs, or evergreens.

I feel that the floribunda group of small-flowered roses are fast becoming the rose of today. They don't grow too tall, have clean foliage to the ground and give a constant show of blooms over a long season. Floribundas have greater resistance to disease and insects and can be used in landscape plans readily. Beds of floribundas are always bright and showy. You can use them to line a driveway, an entrance walk, to ring a pool or a birdbath, or lawn lamp. They give a splash of color to foundation plantings, and can even be used for a gay blooming hedge, one that stays within bounds. They are well adapted for use around contemporary homes.

You just can't beat floribunda roses, especially if you're a busy gardener who doesn't want to spend a lot of time fussing with susceptible roses. Give your floribundas a light pruning of the dead roses and you'll encourage the plants to put all their strength into new blooms instead of stems and foliage.

The newest class of roses, the grandifloras, have an exciting future cut out for them in the home landscaping. This new class has large-growing, everblooming plants, and big flowers. They are more vigorous growers and need less care than many rose types. Quality grandifloras will produce colorful accents when placed among the other plants on your property. They can be planted in the rose garden with the usual hybrid tea roses, but should be planted a little farther apart and to the back because of their size. They will grow as tall or taller than the largest hybrid teas and will produce more flowers. As specimen plants, the grandifloras are excellent, producing bright flowers throughout the season, with heavy blooming periods in late spring and fall. The grandifloras are often used with the floribundas for landscape effects. Since there are more floribunda varieties, the colors extend over a greater range and offer fascinating color contrasts to the grandiflora colors.

Rosa Multiflora Hedge: Where should you use the "multiflora rose"? As a living fence for the farm, it deserves all the publicity it has received, but it should be remembered that the average city property doesn't have the space for this plant. The variety used for fencing grows rampant, is very thorny and bears white flowers that are not particularly showy when compared with garden ramblers.

Bright red fruits (rose hips) are produced in the fall. Three to four years or more may be needed before the fence is high and thick enough to act as a barrier against animals. Before planting all your property lines, you should study the characteristics of this thorny rose to make sure you'll be satisfied with it once it's established.

PLANTING ROSES

Which is better for planting bare-root roses—fall or spring? Nurserymen are still arguing and debating this subject although most nurserymen we've talked to favor spring planting. Their reason: fewer complaints

QUICK CHART FOR ROSE CLASSIFICATION (WITH GROWING TIPS)

(From small to large)

Class	Description	Uses	How to Prune
MINIATURES	Grow less than 1 ft., with blooms less than 1 in. Example: Pixie	Pots, miniature arrangements, ideal indoors or outdoors.	Trim back in spring same as hybrid teas.
POLYANTHA	Replaced by floribunda, height 2 ft. Example: Margo Koster	Used for Mother's Day as potted rose from florists.	Potted plant can be set outdoors. Prune to live wood in spring.
FLORIBUNDA	Smaller flowers than hybrid teas, but many more of them borne in clusters. Low growing, height 2 ft. Example: Fashion	Ideal for beds, borders, mass plantings. Good with evergreens in foundation plantings. Good for hedges and potted plants.	Prune in spring. Cut out dead or frozen wood.
HYBRID PERPETUAL	Grows up to 6 ft. or more. Foliage is large, thick and leathery. Blooms brilliantly in early summer, with some flowers throughout summer and fall. Example: Paul Neyron	Good in rose gardens. Individual specimens also for background plants.	Prune back to live wood in spring.
HYBRID TEAS	Grow 2 to 6 ft. tall. Have large individual blossoms borne on single stems, or attractive clusters of three to five flowers. Example: Tiffany	Ideal for rose gardens, individual specimens, cut flowers.	Prune back to live wood in spring.

GRANDIFLORA	New, big, vigorous, tall growing, 6 ft. Bloom profusely in clusters, flowers large with individual stems long enough for cutting. Example: Queen Elizabeth	Serve well for backgrounds, tall hedges and screens.	Prune much like the hybrid teas in spring.
PILLAR	A bush rose with extra long canes. Grow 8 ft. high or more. Unlike the climber, does not need much support, nor does it grow as tall. Example: Spectacular	A colorful accent plant.	Keep in bounds by training against pillar, or post, lamp post, or rural mail box.
CLIMBERS	Bright splashes of color that need support such as trellis, fence or wall. Height 10 ft. or more. Example: Blaze	Ideal against porches, garages, clothesline poles.	Prune in July after blooming is over. Shorten canes in fall to prevent whipping.
SHRUB ROSES	A hardy group of wild species, hybrids and varieties. Usually bear single blossoms, have bright attractive fall fruits, glossy, colorful foliage. Example: Rosa Hugonis, Yellow	Some are good for screens, hedges, mix plantings and as specimens.	Require little pruning except to keep them in bounds. Prune when needed.

from their customers. It is practically impossible to get thoroughly dormant bareroot stock early in the fall, especially in areas where there's been a wet summer and prolonged growth due to favorable weather. If

To plant roses, dig a large hole and spread out roots

Add some soil to hole, tamp and mound with 6-8" of soil

The way you plant a rose may make or break the plant. Follow steps in the illustrations and you should have good luck.

we had our choice we'd prefer to plant roses in the spring. In a wet fall season the canes may not be hardened enough and as a result there's some likelihood of severe winterkilling. If you plant in the fall the ideal stage is after a freeze has killed the foliage, leaving the top dormant. The roots remain quite active; this makes fall an ideal time for planting.

Location: If you are planning to grow roses, make sure they are in a spot where they will get about six hours of direct sunlight each day. Light shade in the afternoon is an advantage. Never place roses close to trees with matted surface roots, such as some of the maples, elms and poplars. Although roses should not be planted in a dead air pocket with no air circulation, some protection from high winds is desirable.

Spacing: Roses need plenty of room for full growth. Hybrid teas should be from 1½ to 2 feet apart in the best part of your garden. The floribundas are somewhat bushier in growth habits and produce flowers in heavy clusters of brilliant color. Most roses of this class need about the same amount of space as the hybrid tea, or a little more.

Plant roses in good, well-fertilized soil and trim the roots before planting. Make large holes so that roots can be spread out and the plant placed so that the "bud mark" is at least two inches below ground level.

This practice is questioned by some rosarians. Plant the roses 15 to 18 inches apart. The tops should be cut back when planted and each spring thereafter, about 6 to 8 inches above the ground.

If it is not possible to set plants out as soon as they arrive, unpack and "heel" in the ground to prevent drying out. Never let bare roots be exposed to drying winds or sunlight. Heeling is simply covering roots with soil temporarily until you can plant them.

If planted in the fall, the soil should be drawn up around the stems, in the manner of "hilling up" potatoes. Straw, evergreen branches, or similar material may be used to cover the entire bed. This treatment applies to all types of roses when fall-planted in cold sections.

Plants brought from reputable nurseries are packed so that they will stand a week or more, from time of shipment, in the package without serious damage if kept cool (40 to 50 degrees F.).

Soils: A lot has been said about soils for roses. Actually these plants aren't too fussy. A belief persists that roses cannot be grown successfully unless the soil is of a clay-like character. Experience shows roses will grow in almost any soil. Roses tolerate clay to a remarkable degree, but they do not prefer it to a loose soil. If your soil is heavy, it can be lightened by adding rotted manure to it. If it's loose and sandy, the same treatment makes it hold retentive moisture better.

The main thing is to give roses a soil that's well drained. Oddly enough, they grow well in a clay soil, although you often see roses dying in such soils due to inadequate drainage. Well rotted manure, peat moss, or compost makes a good conditioner for a sandy or clay soil. Gypsum makes a good conditioner for a clay soil since it tends to aggregate the soil into a crumbly structure. Peat dilutes the soil, holds moisture in a sandy soil, and creates air spaces in a clay type. Use a bushel of peat to three bushels of soil.

How to Prepare the Soil: If you are preparing a new bed, dig the soil to a depth of 18 to 20 inches, and incorporate about three pounds of superphosphate or five pounds of 5–10–5 plant food for each 100 square feet of soil, before setting out the plants. Peat moss and manure can be used together at the rate of one bushel of manure, two bushels of peat, to ten bushels of soil. Never use fresh manure. Horse manure, if well rotted, is good as cow manure, and even hen manure is usable at the rate of one bushel for each 100 square feet.

Feeding Roses: Everyone has his own method of feeding roses. Fertilize old established plants with 5–10–5 at the rate of five pounds per 100 square feet each spring. If soil is sandy or porous, larger amounts are needed. If the soil is very acid, one to two pounds of lime per 100 square feet will correct the condition. If it becomes too alkaline, one pound of sulfur per 100 square feet will be beneficial.

A friend of mine who has good roses feeds one rounded teaspoonful to a square foot (equivalent to 4 pounds a 100 square feet) and he feeds at the same rate every three weeks up to the middle of August. For first-year plants, he uses one level tablespoon a square foot (three pounds a 100 square feet) where roses are grown in beds. When grown in rows, he applies one pound for each 25 feet of row, putting half on each side of the row.

We feed our roses RA-PID-GRO (23% N–21% P–17% K) as a liquid plant food applied with a Hozon applicator. They are fed about every three or four weeks. If you foliage feed, do so in early morning (so the sun can dry the leaves before night) and include fungicides and insecticides in your fertilizer solution.

Drought can do considerable damage to roses. Many are so weakened they are apt to winterkill easily. By maintaining the fertility of the rose bed, you can do much to toughen up the plants. Far more roses starve than are overfed. This does not mean you should overfeed your plants, since it may cause them to grow too much and retard proper ripening of the wood in the fall.

Watering: Roses like plenty of water. Flood the beds once every week or ten days so that water may reach the roots. Avoid wetting the foliage in the evening, for this encourages blackspot and spreads mildew diseases. Give your roses a good mulching (see "Mulches") and they'll have all the moisture they need when hot weather comes.

Propagating Roses: Roses are started by seed, budding, grafting, layering, and cuttings. One of the easiest ways to start new roses is by taking a "slip" or a "greenwood" cutting, or you can use mature wood ("hardwood"). In summer you take a cutting about 4 inches long and insert it in soil or sand, and cover with a fruit jar, after watering. This glass jar acts like a small greenhouse and maintains proper humidity. Leave the cutting in there all winter, and in the spring you can remove the glass and plant the rooted cutting.

Plants are easily started from "slips," the home gardener's method for starting roses and other shrubs. Leave the cuttings under the glass "greenhouse" (fruit jars) all winter, remove in spring.

Pruning: I'm going to try to eliminate much of the mystery in pruning and tell you how we prune our roses. They may not jibe with those of dyed-in-the-wool rosarians, or with rules set down in many rose books, at least, they work for us. Until recently it was believed that roses should be pruned severely to the right height above the ground. Now, many think roses should not be pruned heavily.

Climbers and Pillars: The climbing and the pillar roses are pruned in midsummer just after the blooms have faded. At that time the old canes which have just produced flowers are cut close to the roots of the plants. New canes for next year's bloom will be several feet long. Care should be taken not to break or bruise these in the pruning process. This kind of pruning is practiced on such varieties as Dorothy Perkins, Paul Scarlet and American Pillar. Such semi-climbing varieties as Dr. Van Fleet, Dr. J. H. Nicolas and others should have older flowering wood removed only.

What should be done with the long rambler canes in fall? If they windwhip or have grown longer than their space allows, it's best to break a few rules and shorten the canes to prevent rubbing on the house. The only time climbers are cut back completely is when they have been neglected to the point that it's almost impossible to cut out the old wood.

Hybrid Teas: Prune in spring after all danger of winter injury has passed. Hybrid tea roses can be pruned once the winter protection has been removed. Any wood that has blackened can be cut off to the nearest live bud and at the same time, trim out any weak branches. It is also advisable to cut out weak and spindly growth which is smaller than a lead pencil in diameter, provided there are left two or three more vigorous canes. The vigorous living canes should be cut back to 6 or 8 inches. This is usually necessary because of winterkilling. It may be too severe in milder climates. If the plants are exceptionally vigorous and there is available live wood, it may be left to 10 inches or a foot above the soil. You can prune monthly roses by: (1) Cutting all dead and injured wood. (2) Removing weak shoots. (3) Cutting back the largest canes to 9 to 12 inches above the ground. Make cuts slanting and about one-quarter inch above a bud that points outward.

Suckering Roses: Be sure to remove suckers or sprouts which arise from the base of grafted or budded roses. These may overtake and crowd out the parent plant. Remove the sucker at the point from where it emerges, by giving it a quick sharp *pull!* Cutting them off at ground level is only a temporary measure.

Winterizing Roses: If you live in cold regions, mounding or hilling tea roses with extra soil, 8 to 12 inches high, is protection from changing temperatures. Do not take earth from between the bushes, as it may expose the roots. A covering of straw over the mounds is added protection. Even so, you may lose some roses due to winter cold. Tree roses must be covered or they will succumb. Simply remove soil away from one side of the plant, gently bend it over into a narrow trench, peg it down and completely cover it with soil. Climbing roses can be pegged to the ground, although many gardeners (including myself) do not take the time. In spring we merely cut the long canes back to live tissue and get bushels of blooms, without winter protection. (See illustrations.)

DISEASES AND INSECTS OF ROSES

The best way to check most diseases and insects of roses is to hit them before they get started. Don't wait until they attack your plants. You can buy all-purpose rose dusts or sprays or you can make your own.

Here's a home-made spray I've used with success: Ferbam or Captan, 3 level tablespoons; wettable sulfur, 2 level tablespoons; DDT, 50 per cent wettable powder (or Malathion), 3 level tablespoons. These are mixed in a gallon of water to which has been added a level teaspoon of a detergent. Another one used commonly consists of 1 tablespoon of Dithane (or 2 tablespoons of Parzate); ¾ tablespoon of Karathane; 2 tablespoons of wettable 50 per cent DDT (or 3 tablespoons of 50 per cent

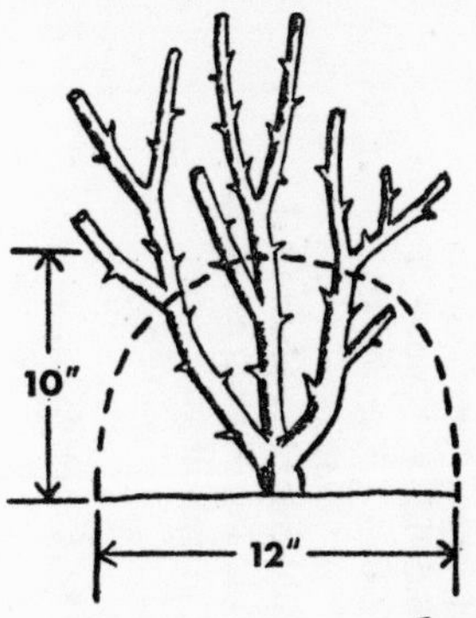

Courtesy Jackson & Perkins Co.

How to Winterize Roses:
If you live in a region where winters are rugged, your roses have a better chance of coming through if protected against winter winds, sun, frost and cold. Bring in extra soil and mound it around the base of your rose plant, to a height of 10 inches. Do not gather soil from between your plants, as it may expose the roots to winter cold. As added protection, place straw or marsh hay over the mounds. Climbing roses as a rule need no protection. If you want to protect them, untie the canes, lay them on the ground and cover with 5 or 6 inches of soil.

methoxychlor), and 2 tablespoons of 25 per cent Malathion to a gallon of water. Dust or spray every week!

Probably blackspot is the most serious disease of roses, but it can be licked using the above combinations. If neither formula works then use Zineb or Maneb at the rate of 1 ounce to 4 gallons of water, starting just before the buds break, and spraying once every 10 days. You can also get good control of blackspot with a combination of sulfur and Captan if you prefer.

The following chart offers a quick key to rose troubles. Once you determine what's bothering your roses, it should be an easy matter to get a cure.

A QUICK KEY TO ROSE TROUBLES—*Symptoms, Common Causes and Cure*

(Prepared with assistance of Dr. R. C. Allen, noted rosarian)

Leaf Symptoms:	Some Common Causes	Control
Prominent black spots	Black-spot disease	Captan, Maneb, sulfur, Ferbam, Phaltan, cleanliness (see black spot section)
Tips turned brown	Spray or dust burn	Avoid heavy doses
Margins brown	Spray burn or potash deficiency	Avoid heavy doses, feed regularly
Leaves skeletonized	Rose slugs	Malathion, DDT, or Methoxychlor
Strong yellow mottling of leaves	Soil too alkaline	Have soil tested, add sulfur
Faint yellow stippling of foliage	Red spider mites or leafhoppers	Malathion, Aramite, Tedion
White moldy patches on leaves, stems	Mildew	Mildex (Karathane) sulfur, Fixed copper fungicide
Pale green or yellow appearance	Nitrogen deficiency	Add complete plant food
Wilting of foliage	Drouth or borers in stems	Add water; keep canes sprayed
Shedding of foliage—red spider	Drought and black spot	Cut out infected canes
	Other causes of foliage shedding include nutrient deficiencies, also spray and dust injury	Check each for cause

Stem Symptoms:	Some Common Causes	Control
Brown patches in spring	Brown canker	Dormant spray lime sulfur (in April)
Dark brown patches on stems	Common canker	Dormant spray lime sulfur (in April)
Entire stem dark brown in spring	Winter injury	Prune out black canes
Holes in cut end after pruning	Rose slugs and small Carpenter Bees	DDT or Malathion
Failure to elongate, remains stubby	Rose midge	DDT or Malathion
Grayish white, moldy patches on young growth	Mildew	See Mildew (above)
White dots in summer	Brown canker	Dormant spray (in April)
Green, pink or red lice on tops or tips	Aphids or plant lice	Nicotine sulfate (1 tsp. to 2 qts. water)

Flower and Bud Symptoms:	Some Common Causes	Control
Buds covered with grayish mold	Mildew	See Mildew
Tiny buds turn brown	Rose midge	Methoxychlor, DDT
Holes in buds	Chewing insects	Methoxychlor, DDT
Large buds fail to open	Thrips, wet weather	DDT, Dieldrin or Malathion
Petals riddled	Chewing insects	DDT, Dieldrin or Malathion

12

Plant Propagation

One of the greatest joys to come from home gardening is plant propagation, the science of increasing plants from existing ones. Plant propagation falls into two main groups: (1) Those raised from seed. Such plants involve sexual union, and the process is referred to as sexual propagation. (2) Those raised "vegetatively" or without benefit of sexual union. This method is known as asexual propagation, or vegetative reproduction. It includes division, cuttings, grafting and budding which are described later. Sexual propagation by seed gives rise to many new strains of value to horticulture. Without it we would not get most of our new varieties. Asexual increasing does not produce new strains, but is of importance to the home gardener because it maintains the identical characteristics of the parent plant. For example, a white rose started by cuttings (described below) will produce plants with white flowers. However, seed from a white rose may not produce white flowered plants.

ASEXUAL OR VEGETATIVE PROPAGATION OF PLANTS

Division: The simplest form of increasing plants asexually is known as division. All you do is take an axe or a large knife or a spade, and cut the clump or rootstock into convenient sizes for planting. The other vegetative means for multiplying plants are by cuttings, layering, budding and grafting.

Cuttings: Softwood cuttings should be taken from shrubs during the summer months. Select only the tips (3 to 8 inches in length). Cut the stem at a node, and insert in sharp coarse sand. About half the leaves should be removed from the lower end and the cutting then planted firmly in sand to a depth equal to about one-half its length. You can propagate roses, hydrangeas, dogwood, and others this way. In fact, most of our common shrubs can be propagated from cuttings. Some root best from hardwood cuttings, others respond to the softwood cutting, while some can be started by both methods.

We want to mention the "semi-hardwood" cutting method. This is similar to "softwood" cuttings (such as you use in starting geraniums, mums, begonias, to name a few), except that the wood is somewhat hardened.

Most semi-hardwood cuttings are made between June 1 and the middle of July, from shrubs growing outdoors. These include roses, blueberries, boxwood, oleander, weigela, dogwood, forsythia, privet, viburnum and deutzia.

Take 4- to 6-inch cuttings from the end or side shoots that are still growing or that have only recently stopped growing. These are stuck in clean moist sand, and kept shaded for several days. After that, give them stronger light, and keep the humidity high. Always protect them from strong sun and drying out. An inverted glass jar makes a fine miniature greenhouse for starting these.

Perennial flowers may also be started by cuttings. Take cuttings in early spring when young shoots are about 3 inches above ground. Cuttings should be planted in semi-shade and covered with an inverted fruit jar.

HARDWOOD CUTTINGS

A common method of making new plants of fruits such as blueberries and a wide variety of woody ornamental plants such as spiraea, barberry, butterfly bush, lilac, rose, and others consists of using "hardwood" cuttings.

You simply start these by gathering cuttings in the fall (anytime after frosts have matured the wood) or anytime during winter dormancy. The cuttings can be from 6 to 10 inches long. With most plants it's best to cut about ½ inch below the lowest bud and ½ inch or more above the uppermost bud. Tie the cuttings in a bundle (anywhere from 10 to 25, if you wish), with the basal ends (butt end) all in the same direction. Bury them horizontally in moist sand or sawdust in the cellar.

In the spring, set the cuttings in rows about 18 inches apart, with the cuttings 2 to 4 inches from each other. The top bud should be about even with or slightly above the ground level. Make sure the earth is packed firmly about the lower end so the cuttings will not dry out. On hot summer days, water the cuttings to hasten rooting. Some cuttings which are hard to root in sand often will do better in a mixture of sand and granulated peat, equal parts by volume. Usually at the beginning of the second year, the cuttings should be transplanted and at the end of the second year they can be moved to a permanent position in a garden.

Rooting Powders

Gardeners who want to use plant hormone powders to stimulate rooting can do so, but you don't gain anything on cuttings easy to root. The best way to apply the plant hormones is in a powder form.

You can buy small packets or pound cans, but for the home garden a packet is plenty since a pound can will treat over 40,000 cuttings. Just dip the base end in the powder before inserting it in the rooting material. In the spring, these cuttings have a callus on the lower end and that's the time to dip them in plant hormone powder.

Stem Cuttings

You don't need a greenhouse to root plants from stem cuttings. Simply fill a 6-inch clay pot with coarse sand and let stand in a tray of water. This makes a neat propagating "bench" for starting geraniums, ivy, and other subjects. You will be surprised to see how quickly these take root in sand. The sand should be free from dirt and trash. There are very few cuttings that will not start in sand.

Leaf Cuttings

Any plant in which the leaves or leaf stalks (*petioles*) are more or less fleshy can be propagated by leaf cuttings. This is commonly used with begonias, lifeplant (*Bryophyllum*), African violets, gloxinia, peperomia and others. You need coarse sand, perlite or vermiculite (some have good luck with plain water but we prefer sand).

Cut the stem short and insert it and small portion of the leaf base in the sand. With begonia, all of the leaf may be used or it may be cut into wedge-shape pieces, each having a large vein through the center. Several new plants may be obtained from a single leaf of begonia laid flat on the sand, and pinned in with a hairpin. Puncture each main vein and cover lightly with moist sand. A new plant will form at each point of injury.

Rooting Materials

For years sand has been the standard rooting medium for starting new plants, and so has peat moss. These materials are still very good. However, recently new materials used for insulating homes have been found satisfactory, and one of these is vermiculite, which has caused considerable interest among gardeners. Vermiculite is mica ore that has been treated to high heat until it pops. This results in layers of mica being separated to make the material spongy, water retentive and free from disease, making it ideal for rooting cuttings. Root hairs penetrate the particles, and enable cuttings to root fast. We mix it with peat, and some use it with sand. Vermiculite is sold under many trade names and can be purchased in any hardware store. Perlite, a volcanic-ash material, also is ideal for rooting. It can be used alone or with sand and peat.

Layering

Most woody ornamentals may be propagated by "layering," a system used by nurserymen and gardeners alike for increasing favored varieties of trees, vines, evergreens or shrubs. Plants that are increased by layerage always "come true," that is, have the same flower, fruit, and leaf characteristics of the parent plant.

There are several forms of layering: (1) Simple layering. This is done by making a trench 8 inches deep near the plant to be increased. Then you slit and bend a stem in order to place the wounded area 3 or 4

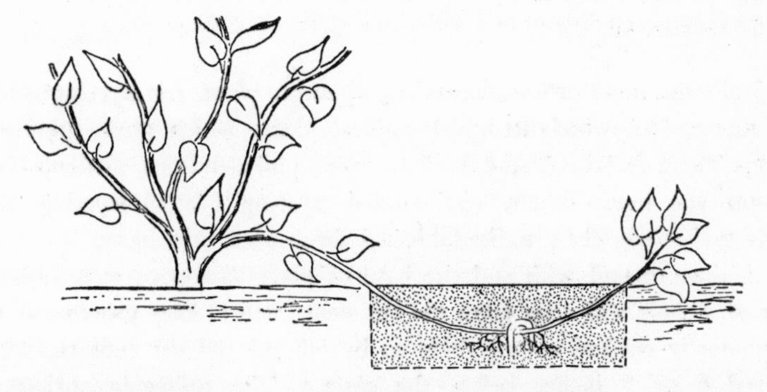

In simple layering a branch is buried in a depression and pegged down with a piece of wire. Roots will form within 1 to 6 months. Rooting is faster with some plants than with others.

inches deep in the prepared trench. The tip of the stem, with foliage intact, is left to protrude above ground. Then you firm the soil around the stem and hold it in place by means of a rock (see illustration). Roots form in the slit area in from 1 to 6 months. (2) Air layering. To air layer you slit the stem as you do with simple layering. Pack 3 or 4 handfuls of moist sphagnum moss around the wound and wrap the entire ball with plastic bag, tied tightly at each end. Rooting takes place

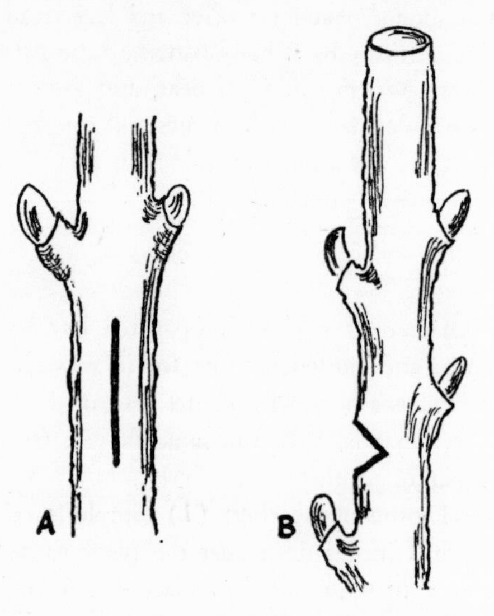

(A) Shows how a stem is first slit before it is layered. (B) Notching the stem near a node or bud will give you the same effect.

in 3 months, more or less, depending upon the plant. Air layering is used to shorten tall woody-stemmed tropical plants which grow spindly or leggy. These include dracaenas, ficus, some philodendrons, dieffenbachias, croton, and many others. (3) Mound layering ("Stool layering"). In early spring you cut a well-established shrub back to 6 inches above soil level, then mound with soil the base of plant so top of stub ends are buried. Shoots will arise from the cut stems, and as they grow taller soil is gradually worked among them so by fall the old cut ends should be buried 4 or 5 inches below the surface. The following spring the mound of soil is gently forked away, rooted stems are cut off and set out as young plants.

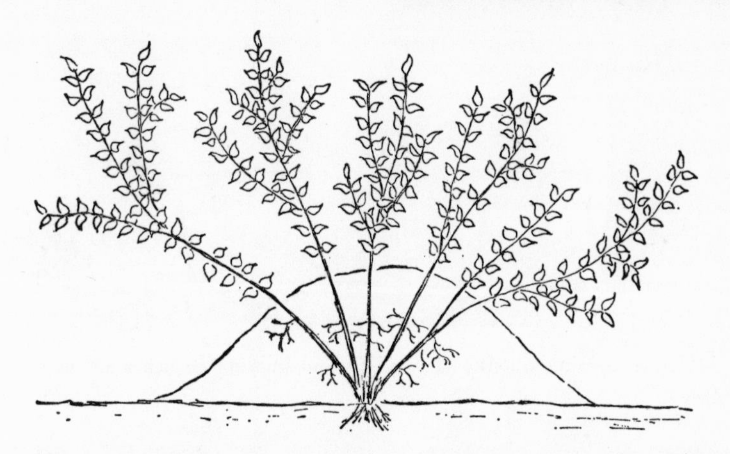

Mound layering is another simple way to increase plants. Mound soil over the base of the plant, after you scar or slit the bark. Roots form in the wounded area and the newly rooted plants are severed and set out.

Care of Rooted Plants

When the young layered stems have rooted sufficiently they are cut away from the parent plant in early spring and planted in the garden. Water well during dry spells, especially during the first growing season. Watering and feeding each season will stimulate growth and produce stronger plants.

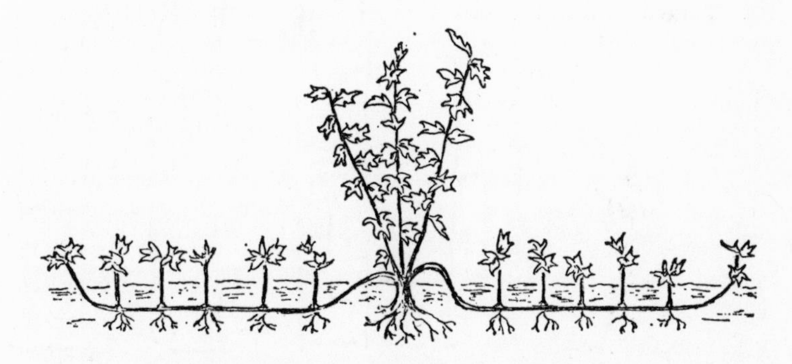

Another trick, "branch layering" produces several plants from a single branch. Lay long branches in a trench, cover with soil and new roots will form at various intervals (wherever you scarred the stems).

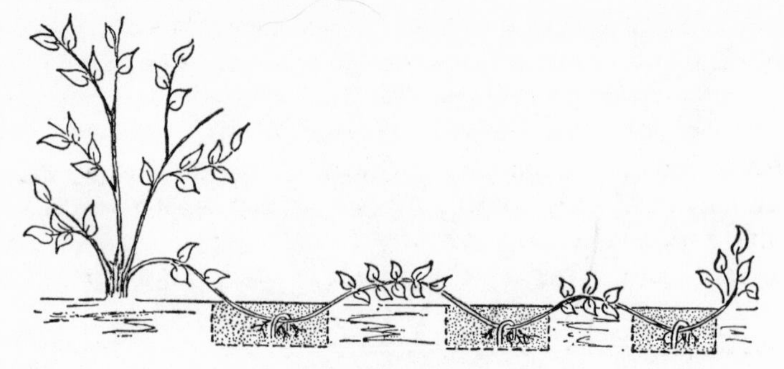

Multiple layering consists of bending and burying branches in several places.

BUDDING

Budding, practiced in most nurseries, is another simple form of grafting used for increasing your supply of plants.

You can do the job of budding in August and right up until September. The sap is running in August or September and that's the time when the bark lifts easily from the wood. If you haven't tried your hand at budding, then sharpen your knife, go out to a good fruit tree and look for some nice fat buds on this year's growth. You'll find the buds in the axils of the leaves, the place where leaves are joined to the branch. Buds

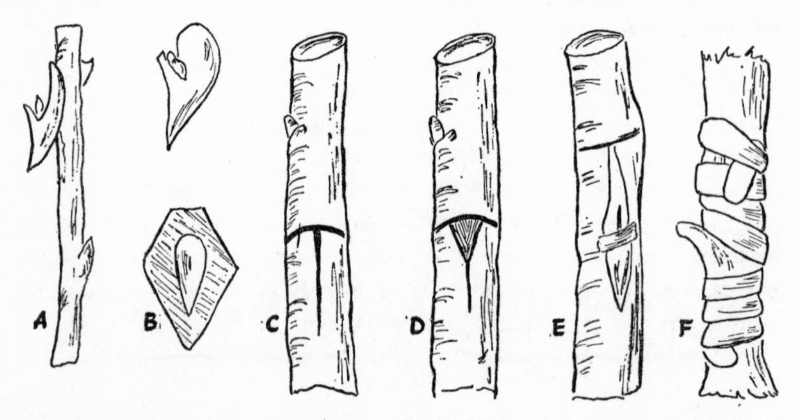

Steps in budding: (A) Bud Stick; (B) Buds cut off; (C) T-shaped slot; (D) T-slot ready to receive the bud; (E) Bud in place; (F) Bud wrapped with rubber band.

taken from the central two-thirds of the growth are better, in our estimation, than buds taken from the tip or bottom ends of the growth. The bud is cut off, with the leaf, then the leaf stem is removed, leaving about a half inch as a handle when inserting the bud.

Make a slit in the young, green wood of this season's growth, and insert the bud. Then, you take a strip of rubber band and wrap the bud in the T-shaped slit you make in the twig. Keep in mind that buds will "take" quicker and better if inserted in young, tender growth. The thicker the bark, the less likely the buds are to succeed.

Budding is a lot of fun, and it's not as complicated as it seems. It's a lot simpler than grafting, which many nurserymen no longer do. You don't have to wax the buds, as you do when you graft. You can tell within a couple of weeks if your bud has "taken." Just be sure that you bud the right types on the trees. For example, you cannot select a bud from a stone fruit (such as peach) and bud it on to a seeded fruit (such as apple). The fruits have to be closely related. You can bud varieties of the same species, for example, a Cortland apple can be budded on to a Northern Spy, or apricot on peach.

Grafting

Grafting is nothing more than transferring a piece of twig (called scion) to a limb (called stock) in such a way as to join the narrow cambium layer of growing cells of each at some point so that a union is secured. The scion continues to grow and produce the top of the plant with such characteristics of flower or fruit or leaf as are desired while the stock remains as the base of the plant.

Often the scion is inserted inside of the stock plant. First the end of the scion is sliced to a slender wedge shape to fit a slit made in the stem of the stock. Usually it is held in place by a thin rubber band or grafting wax may be used. Temperature and humidity are important factors in inducing union of the two areas. Formerly most grafting was done in greenhouses, but now polyethelene enclosures provide sufficient control so that successful grafting can be done outdoors in the spring.

Bridge-grafting is an emergency measure used for saving the life of a shrub or tree girdled by rodents or other causes. Immediately after the injury small twigs of the same species or from the tree itself can be inserted so that the cambium layers (just below the bark) are joined at both ends. Use plenty of twigs and wax in place. (See Green Thumb Tips at end of chapter.) Water and food will then be transported through the twigs and enable scar tissue to heal the wound.

SEED OR SEXUAL PROPAGATION OF PLANTS

It's fun to start your own plants from seed, but *start with good seed!* Seed is cheap. Buy the best from a good seedhouse so you can be sure of good germination and trueness to name. If you wish to save your own seed, save it only from non-hybrid plants. Select the seed from your best

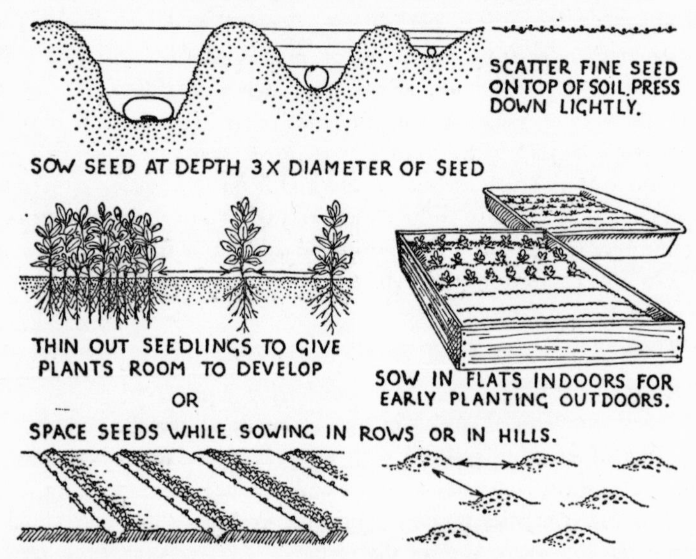

Starting plants from seed is the simplest and most common form of plant propagation. Start out with good seed, use a good soil mix (see text) and you'll have all the plants you and your friends can use.

plants, those showing outstanding growth or yield. For seed purposes, make sure the plant and fruit are free from disease. The plant should be husky, well shaped and have a good growing habit. When the fruits are fully ripened, pick and remove the seeds, then spread them out to dry. Be sure they are thoroughly dry before storing them.

INDOOR SOWING

Soil Mixture for Indoor Sowing: Seeds do not need rich soil. The main thing is to have a loose, well-drained mixture. A good formula is 2 parts loam, 1 part peat moss and 1 part coarse sand. Heavy soil just won't do. Fill your seed box half full of this mixture and the balance with screened and moistened leafmold, fine grade peat moss or sphagnum. Level it off with a stick (don't pack it down), and sow the seed in rows or "broadcast."

Sterilizing Your Soil: Many seed-starting materials contain harmful organisms which must be killed before you sow seed. There are several ways to treat your soil. Formaldehyde: You can use ordinary commerical formalin (40 per cent formaldehyde) at 2½ tablespoonfuls per bushel or 1 tablespoon to a 20 x 14 x 3 inch flat. Dilute with 5 parts water and sprinkle on the soil. Allow to stand 24 hours before sowing.

Baking: Get the soil mixture fairly moist, and fill a baking pan or roaster 3 or 4 inches deep. Level it off and cover the pan with heavy aluminum foil, sealing down the edges. Punch a small hole through the middle of the foil and insert the bulb of a meat thermometer into the center of the mixture. Bake at 200 degrees F. for 30 to 40 minutes. Avoid higher oven temperatures since they destroy organic matter and soil structure.

Hot Water: Insert a cooking thermometer into a box of soil and pour boiling water onto the soil until the temperature reaches 180 degrees F. Let soil dry a day before sowing seed.

Pressure Cooking: Place soil in pressure cooker and cook for 15 minutes at 15 pounds pressure.

Commercial Disinfectants: Patented products are available from garden-supply stores. Follow directions of the manufacturers.

Sowing Seed: Sow thinly and do not cover, especially fine seed, such as petunias. Simply press the seed in lightly, then dust with Ferbam or Captan.

The next step is most important. *Do not* water from the top, since this favors "damping off" disease, the villain that mows tiny seedlings down in swaths. Set the container in a pan of water so that water seeps up from below.

Light and Temperature: Place a glass pane or plastic sheet over the container to prevent drying out and to hasten germination. Be sure to remove as soon as you see the seeds bursting open or they'll grow crooked in later life. The best temperature is between 60 and 70 degrees. Seed does not need sunlight for germination.

A room temperature of 70 degrees is suitable until seedlings appear, then give full light in a sunny window or they will grow tall and spindly. If possible, move to a room with temperature of 55 to 60 degrees for sturdy growth. Never allow temperature to run over 70 degrees.

All seed will germinate more quickly if the box is placed on a radiator for bottom heat. After it has sprouted, move immediately to a sunny window as described above.

After the seedlings are an inch or so tall and have 2 sets of true leaves, transplant to pots or flats and move to a well-lighted spot. Here they need lots of air and a fairly rich soil, but they won't be ready for plant food until later, and don't give them too much water. Seed may be started and seedlings grown under fluorescent lights in the basement. (See Poor Man's Greenhouse.)

Watering: Try making a self-watering seed box. All you need it a Fiberglas wick and a box. Drill a hole in the bottom of the box and draw a wick 8 inches long through it. Fray the top of the wick and imbed it in the soil; the bottom of the wick drops into the pan below. Just fill the pan once a week; the soil will keep moist and the seedlings will prosper.

Transplanting: Seedlings large enough to handle should be moved to other boxes, flats or pots. The new peat pots are excellent containers. A plant needs all the roots and leaves possible and will recover faster from transplanting if you leave them intact. Avoid breaking any roots in the transplanting process.

Put the potted seedlings in a hotbed if you have one or in a coldframe after danger of cold weather has completely passed, usually not before the first week in May.

SOWING SEED OUTDOORS

Sowing Seed Thinly: Sow exactly where plants are to remain, sowing 3 to 5 seeds in each place to insure against failure of some seedlings from the diseases and accidents which beset young plants. If several survive to the stage of vigorous growth, the extras may be moved to other locations.

Don't Cover Too Deeply: Press fine seeds into the soil. Heavier seed can be lightly covered with peat or mulch so that it's just out of sight. Cover the soil with burlap or vermiculite to maintain moisture but remove as soon as the seeds start to sprout.

Don't Crowd: Thin the seedlings so that each plant has room to develop properly. Even with high-germinating seeds, you should sow more than will have room to mature, because accidents are likely to destroy some plants, and vacancies may be difficult to fill.

When seedlings show their second set of true leaves, pull the extra plants so that the remaining ones are spaced 12 to 20 inches apart. Those you pull may be replanted if you wish.

With all flower seeds, the depth to which they are covered and the light porous character of the soil that covers them are most important. The covering soil is more important than the soil below them. If your soil has much clay and you have a limited amount of humus, the best place for the humus is over the seeds. The main point is to prevent a crust from forming and it will pay in many cases to prepare a special soil for covering.

GREEN THUMB TIPS

When starting plants from seed, do as florists do: Use a sterile substitute such as sand, vermiculite, perlite or a sand-peat mix. Avoid soil, unless you sterilize or dilute it.

Soil mixtures may be sterilized by baking them in an oven 200 degrees F. for ½ hour, or by pressure-cooking them at 15 pounds pressure for 10 or 15 minutes.

Seed may be started outdoors safely, at the time when maples are coming into leaf. Or, they may be started earlier indoors in a coldframe or hotbed.

Some flowering annuals often self-sow and may be planted directly in the garden in the fall.

Wrapping your graft with plastic laundry bags helps insure greater success. These plastic covers are also ideal for covering a box of seed.

Plant breeding can produce a new and interesting flower for you. Try transferring pollen from one plant to another (make sure they're in the same family) and see what you get.

Nature sometimes produces a new variety on an old plant. This sudden change is called "mutation" or "sport." Keep your eye open for mutations.

An apple grower received $6,000 for one branch of red apples growing on his green-apple tree.

A good grafting wax may be made by mixing 1 pound of rosin, 3 ounces of linseed oil and 5 pounds of paraffin together. This may be applied with a brush. Wrapping a graft with plastic bag achieves the same effect.

If you have a "wild" apple tree, or a poor variety, put it to work by grafting or budding a cultivated variety to it.

13

Insect and Animal Control

Getting rid of insects (and keeping them away) seems, at first sight, as impossible as reaching for the stars. Fortunately, you don't have to be a "bug" specialist to fight them.

Here are a few common insects which might startle or annoy you.

INSECT	WHAT IT IS AND DOES	CONTROL
ANTS:	Lives in mulches, on peony buds, in lawns, and foundations of homes.	Spray or dust with Dieldrin or Chlordane. Pour solution into ant hills.
CLOVER MITE:	Hordes of tiny mites, found on foundations, clapboards, in lawns. Harmless to humans.	Control is not simple. Try dust or spray of Malathion, 50 to 80% liquid or 25% powder; or Aramite, or Kelthane, 2 teaspoons in a gal. of water.
COCKROACHES:	Found in cupboards, along baseboards.	Spray baseboards with chlordane or DDT.
EARWIGS:	Fast moving pest 1″ long, with pair of forceps at rear of body. Found in flowers, under any object in the back yard. Harmless to humans, devastating to plants.	DDT or Dieldrin around trees. Bantam chickens are wonderful earwig-killers.

Insect	What It Is and Does	Control
FLIES AND GNATS:	"Bunch" or "Cluster" flies invade homes in fall, to become a nuisance on warm days. Regular House flies are different.	Use aerosol push-button spray cans. Also vacuum sweeper sucks them up by the hundreds. Sanitation around the home.
MOSQUITOES:	Pesky in dry or wet weather, mosquitoes hide under porches, shrubs during day.	Spray shrubs with 5% DDT, also under porches.
SLUGS & SNAILS:	Slugs are "naked" snails. Both are night marauders, hiding under trash, stones, and boards during day. Equipped with 8,500 teeth each can do serious damage!	Scatter metaldehyde baits in areas where these pests work. Place shingle in garden during day to attract snails. Scrape off and destroy them.
HOUSE SPIDERS:	Make unsightly dust-catching webs to catch insects. "Black widow" has red "hourglass" marking, but is rarely deadly.	Spray area with 4 oz. of 25% Lindane in gallon of water.
TERMITES:	Wood-eating worker termites can be troublesome. Flying forms mean there is a colony nearby.	Treat area with chlordane of Dieldrin, same materials used for powder post beetle.
WASPS & HORNETS:	These are beneficial but unwelcome because of nests built in attics or on porches.	Spray area at nighttime when all have returned. Use DDT. Remove nest at night and burn.

BIRD AND ANIMAL CONTROL

BIRDS:	Bats, pigeons, and sparrows can be messy on porches or in attics.	Spray with "Roost-no-More" repellent. For keeping birds out of fruit, use open mesh paper netting, Caw-Caw firecracker ropes, scarecrows, plastic sheets over blueberry bushes.
CATS & DOGS:	Cats like to sharpen claws on trees, dogs frequent evergreens and dig up tulip bulbs in search of bones.	Use a fence, scatter moth balls in among the beds, and spray shrubs with nicotine sulfate. Bonemeal attracts dogs. Use superphosphate 18% grade instead. Dip cotton in ammonia and hang on evergreens twice a week or use rope repellent.
MOLES:	While they burrow for food, they eat very little plant life. 95% of diet consists of insects. They do dislodge plant roots and bulbs. Mice use mole runways and do the real damage.	Mole traps. Treat lawns with chlordane, DDT, Dieldrin or lead arsenate. Materials effective from 2 to 5 years, in killing grubs which moles are after.
MICE & RATS:	Very destructive around fruit trees, tulip beds and pantries. Rats destroy or contaminate foods during a period of a year.	Use snapback mice traps. Bait and set traps in runways or areas where mice are. Rats are also trapped or killed by baits. Pour lye down a rat hole.
RABBITS:	Biggest injury comes from girdling fruit trees and shrubs, in winter when snow is heavy. Eats tips of tulips.	Wrap stems with aluminum foil, mesh, or spray with rosin-alcohol mixture. Dissolve 7 lbs. of rosin in 1 gal. of denatured alcohol and paint tree trunks. In garden, spray vegetables with aluminum sulfate solution 1 oz. in gal. of water to which is added 1 cup of hydrated lime. Wash vegetables before eating. Moth balls in tulip beds.
SNAKES:	Most snakes are harmless, yet they aren't pleasant in the lawn or garden.	Remove boards, rocks and trash piles where they hide. Clubbing or killing with .22 rifle best means to reduce snake population.

BIRD AND ANIMAL CONTROL (*Continued*)

SQUIRRELS & CHIPMUNKS:	Sometimes these occupy attics, and double walls. Also they eat tips of spruce trees, tulips.	Rat traps. Squirrels are protected by game laws in some states. If property is damaged, get permission from game officer to take action.
SKUNKS:	These animals work at night, digging up lawns in search of grubs.	Grubproof your lawn and skunks will go elsewhere. Trapping is effective.
WOODCHUCKS:	Young woodchucks are born in April or May. They eat vegetables, dig holes in hedgerows and fields.	Gassing with woodchuck bombs, or exhaust from automobile. Fence off your garden to keep them out. .22 rifle effective.

14

Greenhouse Gardening

PART I

THE HOME GREENHOUSE

Time was when a small greenhouse in the backyard was for the rich only, but today there are greenhouses one can put up by himself right in his own backyard. The cost will fit the pocketbook and be an excellent investment for health, fun and profit.

Many greenhouse construction companies have hobby-type greenhouses that are relatively inexpensive. They can be purchased in kit form to construct, or can be erected by the company. Before building or buying it is best to contact a greenhouse construction company. They can furnish plans and materials for the most satisfactory structure, and can outline the best arrangement of benches and walks.

Gardeners who are handy with a hammer and saw can build themselves a small lean-to type of greenhouse attached to their home. This makes a true winter garden and you can step from a warm house into a warm greenhouse without sloshing through snow or mud. Besides this, electricity, water and drains are usually handy for connecting to the greenhouse. If you heat with hot water, the house heating plant can be extended for heating the greenhouse. The best location of the greenhouse is on the south or east side of your home so the plants will receive as much sun as possible. It should be located away from trees and buildings so that light from the south, west or east is not blocked off. It is recommended to buy or build the largest greenhouse you can afford because you'll find your family of growing plants will increase rapidly.

PLASTIC GREENHOUSES

When greenhouse construction is considered, the use of plastic as a substitute for glass should be investigated.

By and large, many of the commerical growers who have them find the plastic houses quite satisfactory and practical. Many home gardeners are completely satisfied with plastic houses. Plastic is not as durable as glass, but a plastic house can be built for a third the cost of a glass house.

Flexible sheet plastics are used for covering the frame of the greenhouse. The cheapest plastic on the market is polyethylene, costing from 2 cents to 18 cents per square foot. The estimated life of polyethylene is three months during the summer and nine months during the winter. The breakdown of polyethylene and many other plastics is caused by the ultraviolet rays of the sun. The more expensive the plastic, the longer it lasts. Sheet plastics may be obtained in any thickness and width. The thickness normally used for covering greenhouses varies from 2 mils (.002 inches) to 15 mils (.015 inches). The thicker the plastic, the more expensive per square foot. The width of a plastic sheet varies from 2 feet to 40 feet. Plastics may also be obtained in comparatively thick (1/16 to 1/8 inch) rigid panels. The cost per square foot of this material is greater than for flexible sheet plastic, but the rigid panels last much longer. Rigid plastic panels are not as transparent as sheet plastic. This would not be a problem in the summer, but when the light intensity is naturally low in the winter months only those plants that require low light intensity, such as African violets, orchids and some foliage plants can be grown successfully. Because promising and new plastics are coming on the market every day, it is best to check with your county agricultural agent about the type best suited for your needs.

A large number of plastic houses have been designed. Three major types are conventional, sash and quonset.

The conventional plastic greenhouse is built with the same general design as the rectangular shape glass greenhouse. Sheet plastic is rolled on and stapled to the roof and sash bars. When the plastic has been applied, wood lath is tacked over the bars. If the plastic house is to be used during the winter months and a snow load is expected, roof bars should be no farther than 20 inches apart.

Ventilation of the conventional plastic house is similar to a glass house except the vent mechanism is simpler. Exhaust fans can be substituted for ventilators, but must be large enough to remove all the air in the house once each minute in summer, and once every ten minutes during the winter.

The sash greenhouse is the same shape as the conventional type except for the roof, which is made up of panels or sashes. The panels may range in size up to 4 x 15 feet and are constructed to slide in channels on the roof. The panels are covered with sheet plastics and thus easy to handle. Ventilation is achieved by sliding the panels up and down. The important and outstanding advantages of this house is that the panels can be removed and stored in a dark room when the greenhouse is not in use. This greatly increases the life of the plastic.

Quonset greenhouses are patterned after the quonset huts of World War II and designed for plastics. The half-circle frames are made of either wood or metal (aluminum). They are covered with one piece of plastic. This type of house is constructed up to 20 feet wide. The greatest advantage is the ease of erection and covering with plastic. Ventilation is only by exhaust fans at the ends of the house.

The details of framing need not be elaborate but must be sufficient. Simple design using 2 x 4's and 2 x 2's can be erected without highly skilled labor.

Two layers of plastic are better than one, since the dead air spaces give insulation value which cuts down on heat loss. This also reduces condensation of moisture on the inside of the plastic.

Soils and Soil Treatment: A soil mixture for the small greenhouse may consist of one part garden soil, one part peat moss and one part sand or perlite. Perlite holds large quantities of air and moisture, and is usually better adapted to heavy soils than sands. Twenty per cent superphosphate should be added to the soil mixture at the rate of 4 ounces to the bushel. The above mixture is also recommended for starting seeds.

In a small greenhouse, the soil should be changed every two years unless there is equipment to steam-sterilize. Every three weeks apply a liquid plant food (23%–21%–17%) to potted and benched crops at the rate of 1 teaspoon in 2 quarts of water, after the crop has started. Liquid feeding is easy because the food is applied with a hose attachment as the plants are watered.

The most discouraging part of growing plants in the small greenhouse is getting seeds to germinate and grow. When seedlings die after germination before they are transplanted, the cause is "damping off" disease. There are several methods to avoid "damping off" and these include soil sterilization, starting seeds in sterile media such as perlite, vermiculite or a sand-peat mixture and using liquid soil drenches. (See Starting Seeds under "Plant Propagation.")

Treating Soils for Hotbeds and Greenhouses: While commercial growers steam-treat their soils, it's hardly practical for the small greenhouse operator. A recommended treatment by the use of formaldehyde to control soil fungi is still preferred. The disadvantages are that the soil cannot be planted for 10 to 14 days after treatment and that the soil must be diluted with large volumes of water. It does not control nematodes or insects.

The treatment is as follows:

1. In the bench or the ground of hotbed the soil is worked up thoroughly to a depth of 6 inches.

2. A solution is made of 1 part commercial formalin to 50 parts of water.

3. The solution is applied with a watering can at the rate of 2 quarts to 1 square foot of bed.

4. The bed is covered with moist sacks, canvas or several layers of newspaper. It is kept moist for 2 to 3 days.

5. It is uncovered at the end of 3 days and must be aired for 10–14 days or until no odor exists.

Seed flats or pots of soil are treated in the same manner. Treating the soil and flat together prevents contamination from putting sterilized soil in dirty fungus infected flats or pots.

Heat sterilization of soil mixtures is very satisfactory and easily accomplished when only small quantities are needed. Heating the soil to 180 degrees F. for 30 minutes is required.

The author has had good luck using a drench known as Pano-drench for treating seed flats. Two teaspoons to three gallons of water applied at the rate of 1½ to 2 pints per square foot of soil is recommended. When soil is treated in the seed flat before sowing the seed, a couple of days are allowed for soil to dry out for easier planting. Pano-drench will not harm plants when used as recommended. The solution can also be applied as a post-emergence drench. The seedling stems should be wet one-half inch above the soil level. If "damping off" has started, the infected area should be well saturated by the drench.

Pano-drench is useful for treatment of cuttings. The cuttings are dipped deep enough in the solution so one-half inch of the treated stem will be above soil level after sticking in the soil.

Another good drench can be made by mixing 2 ounces each of Captan, Terraclor and Ferbam in 12 gallons of water. Pour this on bare bench soil to help eliminate fungi, prior to planting.

Watering: It should be remembered that plants vary in their ability to tolerate either a dry or wet soil. Kalanchoes and other succulents do best in relatively dry soils, while hydrangeas, gardenias, geraniums, etc., do best with a constant supply of soil moisture. Most plants are not harmed by wetting the foliage, but there are some exceptions. Mum plants may develop mildew or black spots on the foliage if moisture is left on overnight. Plants such as African violet, calceolaria, gloxinia and others with thick, hairy foliage are injured if water is splashed on the foliage. On African violets, cold water (water lower than room temperature) will cause white or yellowish spots or rings.

In the greenhouse or home, morning or early afternoon are the best times to water the plants, since foliage has a chance to dry before evening, thus reducing the dangers of disease.

When a plant is repotted the soil should be watered immediately. Water should not be withheld for several days following repotting because water is needed to encourage root formation. Plants in small pots dry out faster than those in larger pots due to a smaller volume of soil, so they may need watering a second time during the day.

Insect and Disease Control: Most greenhouse pests can be licked using smoke generator bombs, effective against the spider mite, aphids and white flies. Malathion sprays will banish scale and mealybugs. Sanitation is the best way to keep diseases from flaring up among your plants.

Gardeners interested in greenhouse gardening should subscribe to *Under Glass* magazine, published bi-monthly by the Lord and Burnham Company, Irvington, New York, or *Grower Talks* by George J. Ball Company, West Chicago, Illinois. These firms will tell the best ways to keep insects and diseases at a minimum in your little greenhouse.

GREEN THUMB TIPS ON GREENHOUSE GARDENING

A small greenhouse is within the reach of nearly all gardeners.

One of the best crops you can grow in a small greenhouse is geraniums. Start plants from cuttings in fall for Memorial Day blooms.

During hot summer days, apply a shading compound to your glass roof to keep the sun out. Most garden supply houses handle shading compounds.

A low night temperature (45 to 50 degrees) is ideal for most plants. During the day a temperature range of 65 to 80 degrees is suitable.

Good ventilation is important in a greenhouse or coldframe.

Raise your own bedding plants. It's an easy way to get your money back on your investment. Raise enough to sell to your neighbors.

Liquid feeding is simple, effective and a timesaver for the man who owns a small greenhouse. Feeding can be done with a "Hozon" attachment while watering.

Window boxes add cheer and gaiety to a home. Build yourself a small box and grow your own plants for it.

Don't be afraid to change your greenhouse bench soil, or use new soil in porch or window boxes. Disease organisms tend to build up on used soils, unless you can sterilize them.

Pay a visit to a successful commercial greenhouse operator and learn tricks from him. He's in business to make money, and his experience can help you get more mileage from your greenhouse efforts.

Don't hesitate to study literature offered by commercial suppliers of greenhouses, seeds and related topics. There's a wealth of information available free for the asking.

PART II

A POOR MAN'S GREENHOUSE

Every home owner has an ambition to own a small indoor greenhouse. One doesn't need a lot of glass to grow and experiment with flower and vegetable plants. An empty corner in the basement, a few dollars worth of wood, a couple of used fluorescent fixtures and one can build an indoor greenhouse.

Here are the details:

Bench: A 30-inch-high bench can be erected with a frame of 1 inch by 6 inch boards to form the sides for the table top or bed. Redwood lumber or pine treated with cuprinol will be adequate. The frame should be made of 2 x 4 lumber for stability. The table or bottom of the bench can be made from ¼-inch tempered masonite or better still "transite," which is an asbestos and cement board commonly used for greenhouse benches. The bottom should be cross-braced every 16 inches with 2 x 4 lumber. For pot culture a 3 to 4 inch layer of sand is placed on the bottom for drainage.

The lights: It would be advisable to start growing plants by use of a 4-foot, 2 or 3 tube, 40-watt industrial fixture with a reflector. For convenience and efficiency a poultry-type clock switch should be placed in the circuit. If the temperature is abnormally low, i.e., lower than 50 degrees at times, provision should also be made for a heating cable to provide bottom heat. Probably a separate circuit will have to be provided for the heating cable. Follow the instructions given for installation of heating cable under hot beds.

Daylight or cool white fluorescent tubes are preferred for plant growth. Intensity is another factor to be considered because each plant has its own requirements. To provide maximum flexibility, the fixture should be hung on pulley arrangements. Raising the fixtures lowers the light intensity at plant level, while lowering the fixture increases the intensity. For starting seeds of vegetable and flower plants, it's advisable to lower the fixture to within 6 inches of the seedling plants. Spring bulbs are forced at low intensities thus calling for a smaller fixture perhaps.

The chart shows appropriate temperatures, daily light periods and location of fluorescent fixtures above the plants. These recommendations are general and may have to be adjusted from experience to suit conditions.

Since the amount of light required by a plant is based on the duration of that light it may be necessary to give a longer light period to compensate for too low an intensity. Twenty-four hour lighting of plants is not harmful except where the length of day affects short-day plants for flowering.

Watering: Plants will require more watering because of the low humidity in the basement. A 4-inch layer of sand kept moist will help maintain the humidity. If high humidity happens to be a problem, an electric fan located nearby will keep the air in motion and help prevent disease.

Soils: The same type of soils and mixtures as suggested under greenhouse gardening can be used for the poor man's greenhouse. Sterilization of these soils is important and can be accomplished by the heat method or by use of formaldehyde. However, perlite, perlite-and-peat-moss mixture, sphagnum moss or vermiculite can be used without sterilization.

Disease and insects should be no problem provided good sanitation and culture is practiced. If trouble occurs, however, treat as in a greenhouse.

LIGHTS AND TEMPERATURE CHART

Plant	Duration	Temperature	Height above Plants
African Violets	12–18 hours	60–65 degrees	10–12 inches
Begonias	12 hours	60–65 degrees	8–10 inches
Cineraria	15 hours	40–50 degrees	6–8 inches
Cyclamen	15 hours	50–60 degrees	6–8 inches
Geraniums	15 hours	55–60 degrees	6–8 inches
Gloxinia	15 hours	55–60 degrees	10–12 inches
House Plants	12–18 hours	60–65 degrees	12–24 inches
Tulips	12 hours	50–60 degrees	18–24 inches
CUTTINGS AND SEEDLINGS			
Alyssum	15 hours	65–70 degrees	6–8 inches
Chrysanthemums	15 hours	55–65 degrees	6–8 inches
Dahlia	15 hours	60–70 degrees	6–8 inches
Marigold	15 hours	60–70 degrees	6–8 inches
Petunia	15 hours	60–70 degrees	6–8 inches
Stock	15 hours	55–65 degrees	6–8 inches
Tomatoes	15 hours	65–76 degrees	6–8 inches
Zinnia	15 hours	65–70 degrees	6–8 inches

University of Wisconsin

PART III

HOW TO MAKE COLDFRAMES AND HOTBEDS

Coldframes and hotbeds are similar in construction with the principle difference in heat and insulation.

A coldframe utilizes the sun's heat, with no artificial heat supplied. The soil is heated during the day and gives off the heat at night to keep the plants warm. The frame may be banked with insulating material like straw, sawdust or leaves to insulate it from the cold outside air. Mats of straw, paper or cloth may be placed over the sash at night to conserve the heat.

Coldframes are used to "harden" plants which have been started in the

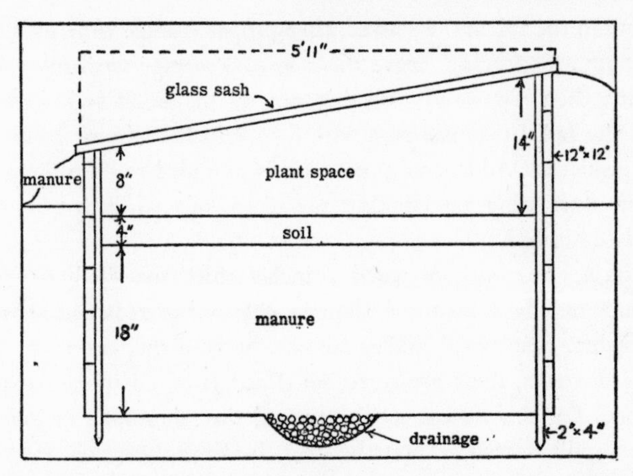

Cross section of a homemade hotbed, heated by manure is an old-fashioned method still in use by many who have access to barnyard manure. Electrically heated hotbeds are easy to rig up, inexpensive to operate.

greenhouse or hotbed before transplanting to the garden. The process of hardening matures succulent tissues. This reduces injury from sudden temperature drop and from conditions which favor rapid drying after transplanting.

Early lettuce and radishes as well as bulbs and perennials are forced in a coldframe a few weeks before normal season. Coldframes are also used for azaleas, heather, hydrangeas and other tender plants. These plants may be set directly in the soil of a coldframe or in pots or flats. Chrysanthemum stock plants and biennials are also placed in a coldframe for winter protection. Cyclamen, azaleas and some house plants may be grown in a coldframe during the summer. Partial shade should be given to these plants in the summer by using lath sash or roll of snow fence in place of the glass sash.

Since coldframes are movable, they can be erected or set over beds of pansies, violets, primroses, etc., in very early spring to bring these plants into bloom ahead of normal season. Just set the frame over the plants which are to be forced and bank the outside with leaves or straw to keep out the cold. Rhubarb can also be forced a couple of weeks earlier, in the same manner.

Spring flowering bulbs planted in flats or pots of soil are placed in the cold frame in the fall and removed after proper storage time to the house or greenhouse for forcing. Leave them in cold storage until the first week in January, then remove. To do this, pot up the bulbs and place in the frame in the fall. Cover the pots with 6 to 8 inches of peat moss or sawdust for insulation. Additional protection is provided to keep the temperature from fluctuating by banking the sides and covering the glass as previously described.

Cold frames are built of wood 2 inches thick for rigidity, but wood 1-inch thick may be substituted. Cypress, chestnut or redwood are the best now available. Heartwood grades are best because they are most resistant to decay. However, there are corrosive effects from compounds contained in redwood. For this reason, it is suggested that aluminum or hot dipped galvanized nails, screws or bolts be used to fasten the wood.

Wood preserving materials containing zinc or copper are best for treating wood to be used in frame construction. Wood that has been treated for decay resistance with pentachlorophenol, mercury or creosote compounds must not be used in plant growing structures. Toxic fumes from these compounds will injure or kill plants.

Materials needed for construction of a two-sash coldframe are:

1 piece of wood 2″ x 8″ x 6′
1 piece of wood 2″ x 14″ x 6′
1 piece of wood 2″ x 2″ x 6′
2 pieces of wood 2″ x 6″ x 5′ 11″
2 pieces of wood 1″ x 3″ x 5′ 11″
2 pieces of wood 2″ x 2″ x (8″ tapered to 2″) x 5′ 11″
(This may be made from one 2″ x 10″ x 5′)
2 L-irons 2″ x 2″ x 6″
2 L-irons 2″ x 2″ x 12″
24 round-headed bolts ⅜″ x 3″ with washers
30 number 8 nails

Hotbeds or heated frames are similar in construction to coldframes except for the addition of an 8-inch board below ground. The walls are sometimes insulated and are usually higher than those of coldframes to permit tall-growing plants to be placed in them.

Artificial heat is supplied by electricity, i.e. light bulbs or electric cable, steam or hot water.

Heated frames or hot beds are used for bulbs, azaleas, hydrangeas and chrysanthemums. They are ideal for starting vegetable and annual flower-

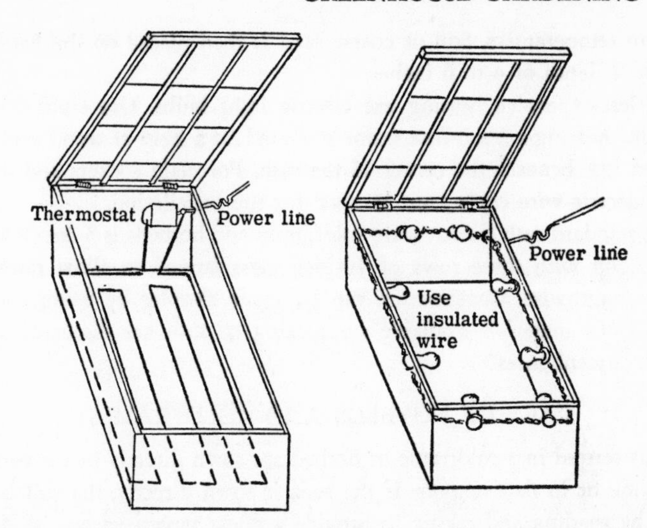

A small, electrically heated hotbed may be made from scrap material about your home. You can buy a heating cable from any greenhouse specialty company. Left illustration shows hotbed heated by cable. On the right, light bulbs are used to generate heat.

ing plants from seed. Summer propagation of cuttings from woody plants and ground cover like pachysandra is also accomplished in a hotbed.

An electric lead covered cable is the most often used method for heating hotbeds. The lead covering is necessary to resist soil corrosion. This heating cable is operated by a thermostat which controls the hotbed automatically, saves electricity and assures constant temperature.

Heating cable is purchased in lengths of 60 to 120 feet with 60-foot length being used on a 110-volt power supply and the 120 feet of cable on a 220-volt power supply. Each 60-foot length of cable will heat 36 feet of frame space.

Both heating cable and thermostats can be purchased from garden supply houses.

To install the cable in a frame put a 12-inch layer of fine gravel or cinders below the hotbed to provide both insulation and drainage. Next, add a 1-inch layer of sand or soil which acts as a bed for laying out the electric cable. Loop the cable back and forth across the bed, 3 inches from the sides and with the lines 6 inches apart. On top of the cable place hardware cloth, ¼-inch mesh to act as a heat conductor and for keeping uniform temperatures. Soil or coarse sand is then placed on the hardware cloth to a depth of 4 to 6 inches.

For less-expensive heating use electric light bulbs. Use eight 25-watt bulbs for heating a 3 x 6-foot frame mounted on a strip of wood spanning the bed just beneath the center of the sash. Porcelain sockets and waterproof electric wire cable must be used for the installation.

The standard sash for covering coldframes and hotbeds is 3 feet wide by 6 feet long with three rows of 10-inch glass lapped to allow rainwater to run lengthwise. Construction can be made simpler by using plastics. The various materials available for glazing of sash are discussed under "Plastic Greenhouses."

CARE OF HOTBEDS AND COLDFRAMES

Seeds started in a coldframe or hotbed are sown directly in the earth of the frame or in flats or pots. If the seed is sown directly, the soil is prepared by spading and raking to provide a finely puverized bed. A 4-inch layer of fine peat moss added before spading is beneficial.

For sowing in pots or flats, 3 to 4 inches of the soil is removed and replaced with cinders. This provides drainage for the bed and prevents earthworms from entering the pots or flats.

Cuttings may be started in the frames during the summer months by substituting the soil for sand, sand and peat or perlite instead of sand.

Ventilation of the coldframes during the spring months is important. The temperature inside the frames should not rise above 70 degrees during periods of sunshine. Wooden blocks are used to raise or lower the sash on the side opposite the direction of the wind. The sashes are closed before sundown to conserve heat. If the night temperature is expected to fall below 40 degrees F., insulating mats are used to cover the sash.

Watering must be done in the morning so that the plants will dry off before closing the frame for the night. Care must be taken to avoid getting the soil too wet during periods of low temperature and cloudy days. Such conditions favor "damping off" fungus, which quickly kills young seedlings.

PART IV

WINDOW BOXES

A porch or window box brings the glory of the garden right up to your door. Window boxes help to soften a home's architectural features, and make it gay and cheery.

Plants like coleus, fuchsia, begonia, vinca and tradescantia can be brought inside before frost and planted indoors in boxes, planters or hanging baskets for use in the home or office. The only care plants in window boxes need is regular watering and a little plant food.

How to Make a Porch or Window Box: Window or porch boxes are made of metal or wood. They should be 8 inches deep (inside measurement) and the length depending on space available. If made of wood, brass or galvanized screws are used to resist rusting. To prevent decay the inside is painted with Cuprinol. Metal containers are usually provided with false drainage bottoms. Otherwise broken pieces of pots or pebbles are placed in the bottom layer for drainage. A hole every 6 inches is needed for drainage in a wooden box. For a standard single window, a box 3½ feet long, 8 inches deep and 10 inches wide is a good size. Measure your window and make the boxes to fit.

Window boxes usually take a lot of water, sometimes requiring daily watering. A self-watering window box can be made using simple carpenter tools. The length of the box is determined by the width of the window for which it is to be used. One inch by eight inch boards are used. The width at the top of the box should be 8 inches and the bottom tapered to 6 inches wide. The end pieces and the sides and the bottom are cut and fastened together with galvanized or brass screws. The false bottom board located 2 inches from the bottom of the box is held in place with small wooden cleats. It should fit tightly to prevent soil from seeping into the reservoir. The bottom edge of the side boards are planed to provide a flat surface to which a bottom board is fastened with screws. Before assembling, all joints except those of the false bottom should be caulked with a strip of caulking compound. When completely assembled the inner surfaces of the box are painted with horticultural asphalt paint to preserve the wood and make it waterproof. Horticultural asphalt is safe to use because it does not contain creosote, which is toxic to plants.

Holes ⅜ to ½ inch in diameter are drilled every 8 inches along a center line of the false bottom to receive the wicks. A larger hole ¾ inch in diameter is drilled to receive an 8 inch long, ¾ inch size galvanized iron pipe through which water is poured to fill the reservoir.

Wick material should be cut into 4- or 5-inch lengths and inserted through the holes to the bottom of the reservoir. Glass wicks can be purchased from a garden store or florist. Twisted lengths of burlap may also be used for the same purpose but are not as permanent as glass wicks.

Boxes can be fastened to the house by means of metal or wooden brackets. The color of the box should be a subdued, dull color like dark green rather than a bright color. The color of the flowers, foliage and vines should harmonize with the color of the house.

PLANTS SUGGESTED FOR PLANTER USE

(Outdoor annuals not hardy for year 'round use)

The following plant combinations have been chosen for pleasing combinations of color, growth habits and leaf texture.

Taller plants are listed first, which you can use for the center or back of planters, window boxes, tubs or cemetery urns. Others are low growing, which you may group around the center plants.

For Full Sun:

1. French marigolds and *Ageratum* (blue bedder)
2. Scarlet sage (*Salvia splendens*) "St. Johns Fire" and dwarf snapdragon (*Antirrhinum*)
3. Zinnia (scarlet); French marigold (*Tagetes*—yellow); creeping zinnia (*Sanvitallia procumbens flore-pleno*—yellow)
4. Bedding-type snapdragon (*Antirrhinum*); dwarf celosia (*Plumosa*); verbena (scarlet) with variegated periwinkle (*Vinca major variegata*)
5. Annual phlox (red, pink, and white); ageratum (blue); sweet alyssum (white)
6. Geranium (white); balcony petunias (dark purple)
7. Petunia (pink); balcony petunias white and crimson (pink)
8. Heliotrope (blue); French marigold (*Tagetes*—yellow with maroon); dwarf nasturtium (*Tropaeolum*—scarlet flowers)
9. *Lantana camara* (orange); verbena (purple); variegated periwinkle (*Vinca major variegata*)
10. Geranium (salmon pink); balcony petunia (deep blue)
11. French marigold (yellow); African marigold (deep orange); ageratum (blue)

12. Scarlet sage (*Salvia splendens*) red; dwarf celosia plumosa gold; Portulaca (golden yellow and scarlet)

13. Petunia "Comanche" (scarlet); verbena (dark purple); verbena (blue or white)

14. Rainbow pink (*Dianthus chinensis heddewiggii*) (dark scarlet); marigold (*Tagetes tenuifolia, T. signata*) (orange); ageratum (blue)

15. Petunia (white, striped red); dwarf morning glory (*Convolvulus tricolor*) deep blue with white throat; variegated- (ivy) leaved geranium (*Pelargonium peltatum*)

For Light Shade:

1. *Begonia semperflorens* (red, pink and white); hanging lobelia (*Lobelia*) (blue with white eye)

2. Geranium (dark scarlet); Geranium (salmon); geranium variegated foliage with variegated periwinkle

3. *Torenia fournieri compacta* (deep blue with white); cup flower (*Nierembergia*); "Purple Robe" (purple); sweet alyssum (white)

4. Geranium (leaves variegated); dwarf geraniums

For Northern Exposure:

1. Fuchsia (red and blue) or "Tom Thumb"; hanging basket fuchsias such as "Trailing Queen" or "Cascade"

2. *Coleus blumei* "Golden Bedder" (foliage golden yellow) *Begonia semperflorens* (red foliage, scarlet flowers)

3. *Coleus blumei* (dark red foliage, margined orange); coleus "Trailing Queen" (small-leaved—green and red variegated)

4. Tuberous begonias (red, white, salmon and yellow); hanging tuberous begonias (scarlet); small-leaved periwinkle (vinca minor)

5. Coleus; *Impatiens sultanii* (scarlet)

Soil Mixture: A common mistake is to make soil too rich for porch boxes, and as a result get all "bush" and no blooms. A good mixture is one-half garden loam, ¼ peat moss, or finely sifted humus, and ¼ sand. To this add an ounce of high grade plant food like 5–10–5 in each bushel. Soil should be changed once a year for best growth. This soil mixture can be conveniently sterilized before use by the formaldehyde method as outlined under greenhouse soils. To fill the box, a ½ to ¾ inch layer of sand is placed over the false bottom and the wicks are spread out. The soil mixture is next added to within 1 to 2 inches of the top.

Location: Most porch boxes are exposed to a relentless midsummer sun, hence need plants which will tolerate sun. Select plants according to exposure from the list "Plants Suggested for Planter Use."

Planting: Plants should not be crowded. If the box has a surface area of 4 square feet for instance, the right proportion would be five erect plants, such as geraniums, and three vines, as vincas, or tradescantia. The wider the box, the more plants can be grown. The more soil there is, the less liable are the plants to become dry in hot summer weather. Plants can be set directly into the soil or be allowed to remain as potted in the box.

Watering and Feeding: Window and porch boxes are exposed to sun and wind, and thus should be looked at for water every day. If weather is rainy and cool, water is applied less frequently. If plants such as petunias, etc., are allowed to go dry, they quickly turn brown, go to seed and the box becomes unsightly. Water is the most important item in maintaining a porch box. When plants have been sufficiently established, one or two applications of RA-PID-GRO, a water soluble fertilizer, a month apart should be sufficient to carry them through the summer months.

Summer Care: The growing tips of the plants should be nipped off now and then to keep them from becoming too tall. This makes them bushy and more attractive. Faded blossoms should be removed before they go to seed. Seed pods are a drain on the plants and make them unsightly.

As a final word, be on the lookout for red spider, the most offensive pest for window boxes. Frequent syringing with a garden hose will help control this pest, or they can be sprayed with Aramite, an effective mite killer. Malathion is a good all-'round insecticide to use for both mites and leaf-chewing pests.

Winter Care: In winter, porch or window boxes need not be bare. Instead of storing them they can be filled with evergreen trimmings. The kind of greens used makes little difference, although some kinds are better than others.

Norway spruce is showy for a little while, but the needles drop or become yellowish. Colorado blue spruce is good, but balsam is one of the best for color and persistence of needles.

Australian pine, red pine, Swiss mountain pine (Mugo pine) are all good candidates for the window box outdoors. It's better to use one kind rather than branches of 2 or 3 different varieties. In arrangements, have the taller branches in the center with the lower ones in front and on the ends. (Soak the soil in the window box.) Sharpen the ends of the branches to a point and insert them into the soil. Water them and the earth will freeze the soil, holding the branches in place all winter. We like to string Christmas tree lights on ours, and they're showy when the snow falls on them.

As an added feature cones (both natural and colored) can be wired to the branches. A few branches of red ruscus from your florist makes attractive and decorative material. Also the foliage of evergreens (or laurel branches) can be spray-painted for color effect.

Window boxes can be used for tulips, hyacinths and other bulbs in spring before the regular season of bedding plants arrives. Bulbs planted in the fall in the boxes, stored in cool cellar or coldframe and brought into a warm window in the spring will bloom indoors or may be moved outdoors.

Cemetery Urns: A common mistake in fixing urns and pots is to put stones in the bottom for drainage. Instead of encouraging water to drain away organic material like peat moss, sphagnum or even a layer of perlite is placed in the bottom to absorb and hold the moisture. Water is usually at a premium especially during the hot, dry months. Sometimes in wet periods water may accumulate in the pots or urns, but, can be drained off by tipping the pot on its side.

When the plants don't do well it's usually because of a lack of water.

The same soil mixture and its preparation as recommended for window boxes is satisfactory for urns and tubs. For plants used in urns and tubs refer to the list of plants suggested for planter use.

Don't crowd too many plants in a cemetery urn. These plants need room for expansion, so leave space between the plants.

Tub Gardening: Growing plants in movable plant boxes or tubs is a new way to concentrate color where you want it. These movable tubs can be rearranged just as you would shift furniture in your living room. The wooden tubs can be made, or purchased from a florist. Some gardeners grow decorative plants in 5-gallon paint cans or even in nail kegs. These containers are ideal for tuberous begonias, fancy-leaved caladiums, geraniums, fuchsias and many vines to decorate the porch or terrace. Shade is no problem with these items. Even sun-loving plants can be used on the shady terrace by rotating them every week.

If you're handy with a saw, you can make your own plant tubs. There's no trick to it, and you'll be surprised to see what effect the tubs can create.

15

Chart of Conversions for the Home Gardener

Few things are more exasperating to a gardener than to read a pesticide recommendation calling for "100 gallons per acre" or a "1 to 1,000 dilution." Since most gardeners have only a few house plants or a small patch in the backyard, they are not interested in gallons per acre. With this in mind, I've prepared these tables which help get the amounts down to usable size. These tables will be helpful if you spray fruits and vegetables or grow corn.

(For more Conversion charts, see Index.)

TABLE A:

FOR DRY INSECTICIDES

For 100 gallons of water	For 50 gallons of water	For 25 gallons of water	For 6¼ gallons of water	For 3⅛ gallons of water
1 pound	8 ounces	4 ounces	1 ounce	1 T.
2 pounds	1 pound	8 ounces	2 ounces	2 T.
4 pounds	2 pounds	1 pound	4 ounces	4 T.

If manufacturer's instructions call for 1 pint of liquid (abbreviated EC for Emulsion Concentrate) per 100 gallons of water, then use Table B to reduce the proportions to a workable amount.

TABLE B:

For Liquid Insecticides

For 100 gallons of water	For 50 gallons of water	For 25 gallons of water	For 6¼ gallons of water	For 3⅛ gallons of water
½ pint	¼ pint (4 fl. oz.)	4 T. (2 fl. oz.)	1 T. (½ fl. oz.)	½ T. (¼ fl. oz.)
1 pint	½ pint (8 fl. oz.)	¼ pint (4 fl. oz.)	2 T. (1 fl. oz.)	1 T. (½ fl. oz.)
1 quart	1 pint (16 fl. oz.)	½ pint (8 fl. oz.)	4 T. (2 fl. oz.)	2 T. (1 fl. oz.)

T = 1 level tablespoon

WORKABLE CONVERSIONS FOR SOIL AREAS

1 oz. per sq. ft. equals 2,722.5 lbs. per acre.
1 oz. per sq. yard equals 302.5 lbs. per acre.
1 oz. per 100 sq. ft. equals 27.2 lbs. per acre.
1 lb. per 100 sq. ft. equals 435.6 lbs. per acre.
1 lb. per 1,000 sq. ft. equals 43.6 lbs. per acre.
1 lb. per acre equals ⅓ oz. per 1,000 sq. ft.
5 gals. per acre equals 1 pint per 1,000 sq. ft.
100 gals. per acre equals 2.5 gals. per 1,000 sq. ft.
100 gals. per acre equals 1 quart per 100 sq. ft.
100 gals. per acre equals 2.5 lbs. per 1,000 sq. ft.

AMERICAN DRY MEASURES

3 level teaspoons equal 1 tablespoon.
16 level teaspoons equal 1 cup.
2 cups equal 1 pint.
2 pints equal 1 quart.
8 quarts equal 1 peck.
4 pecks equal 1 bushel.

(Note: A liquid pint is 28.875 cubic inches; a dry pint is 33.6 cubic inches but for all practical purposes in measuring fertilizers, don't worry about the difference.)

AMERICAN FLUID MEASURES

80 drops equal 1 teaspoon (tsp.).
3 teaspoons equal 1 tablespoon (tbs.).
2 tablespoons equal 1 fluid ounce (fl. oz.).
8 fluid ounces equal 1 cup.

2 cups equal 1 pint (pt.).
2 pints equal 1 quart (qt.).
4 quarts equal 1 gallon (gal.).
1 gal. equals 4 qts., or 8 pts., or 128 fl. oz., or 256 tbs., or 768 tsp., or 61,440 drops.
1 quart equals 2 pts., or 32 fl. oz., or 64 tbs., or 192 tsp., or 15,360 drops.
1 pint equals 16 fl. oz., or 32 tbs., or 96 tsp., or 7,680 drops.
1 tbs. equals 3 tsp. or 240 drops.

(Note: The apothecaries' measures have 60 drops, or 1 fluid dram (medicine teaspoon); 4 fluid drams equal 1 tablespoon; 2 tablespoons equal 1 fluid ounce. The standard teaspoon is ⅓ larger than the fluid dram or medicine teaspoon.

MISCELLANEOUS MEASURES

1 acre equals 43,560 sq. ft. or 4,840 sq. yds., or 160 sq. rods.
1 tablespoon equals 3 teaspoons.
1 fluid ounce equals 2 tablespoons.
1 cup equals 8 fl. oz. or 16 tablespoons.
1 pint equals 2 cups or 16 fluid ounces.
1 U.S. gal. equals 231 cu. in. or 8.34 lbs. of water.
1 Imperial gal. equals 277.4 cu. in or 10 lbs. of water.

EMULSIONS OR WETTABLE POWDERS

Emulsions may be substituted for wettable powders and they leave less visible residue.
2 lbs. of 50% DDT wettable powders equal 2 qts. of 25% DDT emulsifiable solution.
4 lbs. of 50% Malathion wettable powder equal 3 pints of 50% Malathion emulsifiable solution.
1 lb. 25% Lindane wettable powder equals 1 pint 25% Lindane emulsifiable solution.
2 lbs. 50% Ovotran wettable powder equal 2½ qts. 20% Ovotran emulsifiable solution.
2 lbs. 15% Aramite wettable powder equal ½ pint 50% Aramite emulsifiable solution.
1 lb. 15% Parathion wettable powder equals ½ pint 25% Parathion emulsifiable solution.

DILUTION TABLE

Here's a helpful table in mixing items that come in liquid form:
1 to 1,000. . ¼ tablespoon per gal. water.
1 to 750. . ⅓ tablespoon per gal. water.
1 to 500. . ½ tablespoon per gal. water.
1 to 250. . 1 tablespoon per gal. water.

1 to 200. . 1¼ tablespoons per gal. water.
1 to 150. . 1⅔ tablespoons per gal. water.
1 to 100 (about 1%) 2½ tablespoons per gal. water.
1 to 50 (about 2%) 5 tablespoons per gal. water.
1 to 33 (about 3%) 7½ tablespoons per gal. water.
1 to 25 (about 4%) 10 tablespoons per gal. water.
1 to 20 (about 5%) 12½ tablespoons or ¾ cupfuls per gal.
1 to 10 (about 10%) 25 tablespoons or 1½ cupfuls per gal.

CLAY POTS ARE HANDY FOR MEASURING

2 in. clay pot equals ⅓ cup.
2½ in. clay pot equals ⅔ cup.
3 in. clay pot equals 1 cup.
4 in. clay pot equals 2½ cups.
5 in. clay pot equals 4½ cups.
6 in. clay pot equals 8 cups or 2 qts.

MEASURE FOR FERTILIZER

Superphosphate (20%) 1 to 2 tablespoons to an 8-qt. pail.
Wood ashes (4% potash) 1 cup to 8-qt. pail.
Dried blood (12% nitrogen) 3 tablespoons to 8-qt. pail.
Bone meal (20% phosphorus) 2 tablespoons to 8-qt. pail.
Complete fertilizer (such as 5–10–5) 4 tablespoons to 8-qt. pail.
Ground limestone 4 tablespoons to 8-qt. pail.
Muriate of potash (50–60% potash) 1 teaspoon to 8-qt. pail.
Nitrate of soda 1 tablespoon to a gallon.

CONVERTING LIQUID MEASURES

Here are some figures you might want to use to convert liquid measures:
1 gal. equals 4 qts. or 8 pints or 16 cups or 128 oz., or 256 tablespoons or 768 teaspoons or 3840 grams. 30 grams equal 1 oz. or 6 teaspoons; 1 teaspoon equals 5 grams.

From any of these equivalents we can find out the "parts per million" (PPM) usually recommended by manufacturer—for instance:
10 ppm—4 grams per 100 gals. or ⅘ tsp. per 100 gals. water.
20 ppm—8 grams per 100 gals. or 1⅗ tsp. per 100 gals. water.
40 ppm—16 grams per 100 gals. or 3⅕ tsp. per 100 gals. water.
40 ppm also equals ¼ tsp. per 8 gals. water.
60 ppm—24 grams per 100 gals. or 5 tsp. per 100 gals. or ½ tsp. per 10 gals.
80 ppm—32 grams per 100 gals. or 6 tsp. per 100 gals. or ⅗ tsp. per 10 gals.
100 ppm—40 grams per 100 gals. or 8 tsp. per 100 gals. or ⅘ tsp. per 10 gals.
200 ppm—80 grams per 100 gals. or 16 tsp. per 100 gals. or 1.6 tsp. per 10 gals.

Index